The Psychoanalytic Study of the Child

VOLUME FORTY-SEVEN

Kindly submit seven copies of new manuscripts to

Albert J. Solnit, M.D.
Yale Child Study Center
P.O. Box 3333
New Haven, CT 06510

The
Psychoanalytic
Study
of the Child

VOLUME FORTY-SEVEN

New Haven and London
Yale University Press
1992

Designed by Sally Harris
and set in Baskerville type.
Printed in the United States of America by
Vail-Ballou Press, Inc., Binghamton, N.Y.

Library of Congress catalog card number: 45-11304
International standard book number: 0-300-05249-9
A catalogue record for this book is available from the British Library.

The paper in this book meets the guidelines for
permanence and durability of the Committee on
Production Guidelines for Book Longevity of the
Council on Library Resources.

2   4   6   8   10   9   7   5   3   1

Contents

v

The Moses of Freud and the Moses of Schoenberg

On Words, Idolatry, and Psychoanalysis

YOSEF HAYIM YERUSHALMI

Two debators were standing before Hadrian. One was extolling the virtues of speech; the other, those of silence. Said the first: "My lord, there is nothing better than speech, for without it how could the praises of the bride be sung, how could there be commerce in the world, how could ships embark on the sea?"

Hadrian turned to the second: "What have you to say in favor of silence?"

Salo Wittmayer Baron Professor of Jewish History, Culture and Society at Columbia University, New York.

I publish this Freud Anniversary Lecture exactly as it was delivered at the New York Academy of Medicine on April 16, 1991. Except for the addition of the superscription, not a word of the text has been altered, nor have I seen fit to encumber what I said with an apparatus of footnotes. All English quotations from Freud's work are taken from James Strachey's *Standard Edition*, with the exception of some passages from *Moses and Monotheism*, where I have favored the 1939 translation by Katherine Jones, or offered my own rendering. Fully aware that the complex issues raised could easily be elaborated further, I have deliberately chosen to convey to the reader only what was heard by the original audience. I take this opportunity to thank the New York Psychoanalytic Institute for the high privilege accorded to me; Dr. Edward D. Joseph, former president of the Institute, who first sent me the invitation; Dr. Aaron Esman, its current president, and Dr. Leon Balter, both of whom did their best to make me feel at ease on the platform. Dr. Peter Neubauer, who introduced me so graciously, is a very dear friend, as is Dr. Albert Solnit. That my lecture should now appear in the distinguished annual with which they are so intimately and creatively associated is for me a particular pleasure.

As he was about to reply, the first reached over and
slapped him on the mouth.
    The king said: "Why did you slap him?"
    "Because, my lord, I use speech in favor of speech.
But he wants to put my cause to work for his!"
                                    Yalkut, Ba-midbar, 12

With a comparison of Freud's Moses and Monotheism *and Arnold
Schoenberg's opera* Moses und Aron *as its point of departure, this
lecture emphasizes Freud's faith in the power of "words" and explores the
challenge and importance of language for the future of psychoanalysis.*

SURPRISED, GRATIFIED, WORRIED BY YOUR INVITATION TO SPEAK (WHO
but the New York Psychoanalytic Institute could ever have intimidated
me into renting a tuxedo in order to give a lecture?), anxiously sifting
my competences from my more numerous incapacities, I thought
originally to address you on the psychoanalysis of Judaism prior to
Freud's *Moses and Monotheism.* If I have come to you with a different
topic, not a chapter in the history of applied psychoanalysis but, as my
title suggests, a more precarious comparative meditation, it is because a
fortuitous circumstance propelled (perhaps I should say compelled)
me beyond the shores of caution.

Last fall my wife Ophra and I attended the City Opera's courageous
if long overdue New York premiere of Arnold Schoenberg's master-
piece *Moses und Aron.* Although, unlike Ophra, I am not a musician but
a music-lover, as a historian I have also long been interested in Schoenberg as a particularly fascinating exemplar of the convolutions of Jewish modernity. Yet even my cursory prior acquaintance with the text
and music of the opera did not prepare me for the piercing, revelatory
experience that night of the fully staged production of this unique
creation. What intensified and perhaps complicated my reaction was
the fact that just about that time I was putting the final touches to the
manuscript of a book which I have entitled, perversely but accurately:
Freud's Moses: Judaism Terminable and Interminable. And so the Moses of
Freud and the Moses of Schoenberg inevitably engaged one another in
my imagination. In retrospect, I think that by the time I came home I
had more or less decided my theme for this evening.

But is there any basis for the juxtaposition other than my quirky
coincidence? Do Freud and Schoenberg have enough in common to
warrant any comparison of differences?

Both are among the great modern innovators; Schoenberg's revolution in music was as Copernican as was Freud's in psychology. Both

were Viennese Jews (Freud arrived at age four), sons of immigrant fathers from the East, both grew up in the Leopoldstadt, the crowded Jewish district of Vienna. Both loved and detested the city, admired Karl Kraus (that self-hating Jew but intrepid guardian of the chastity of language), and both avidly read his magazine *Die Fackel* where, occasionally, Kraus savagely lampooned psychoanalysis but never attacked Freud. While we have no evidence that Freud was aware of Schoenberg, Schoenberg was certainly aware of Freud. In passing let me add that the uncanny, almost "psychoanalytic" text of *Erwartung,* Schoenberg's opera or "monodrama" for a solitary woman singer and orchestra composed in 1909, was written by a young Viennese medical student, Marie Pappenheim, a relative of Bertha Pappenheim, Freud and Breuer's "Anna O." The relationship is emblematic of the web of fruitfully incestuous intellectual and spiritual ties within the metaphoric family that was once Central European, especially Viennese, Jewry.

Freud and Schoenberg each lived their lives driven by an idea and a cause that required both sacrifice and ruthlessness in the face of what Freud, borrowing from Ibsen, called the "compact majority." As with all prophets, Moses included, much of their lives was lived in deferment, Schoenberg's perhaps even more than Freud's. But you can see it clearly in Freud's *On the History of the Psychoanalytic Movement* and in his letters. Even as late as 1938, agonizing in Vienna over the perils of publishing Part III of his *Moses,* Freud writes:

> . . . malice and sensationalism will counterbalance any lack of recognition of me in the contemporary world's judgment. . . . But that need not prevent my writing it. . . . It may then be preserved in concealment till some day the time arrives when it may venture without danger into the light, or till someone who has reached the same conclusions and opinions can be told: 'there was someone in darker times who thought the same as you!'

And Schoenberg in an essay written a year before on "How One Becomes Lonely" (a title that could have been Freud's):

> I knew I had to fulfill a task: I had to express what was necessary to be expressed and I knew I had the duty of developing my ideas for the sake of progress in music . . . but I also had to realize that the great majority of the public did not like it . . . and yet . . . there might come the promise of a new day of sunlight in music such as I would like to offer to the world.

Both were always acutely sensitive to anti-Semitism, suffered from it, reacted to it with aggressive pride, and ended up in exile because of it, Freud in England, Schoenberg in California. Significantly, both were repeatedly accused, even before the rise of Nazism, of invading the sacred spiritual precincts of the *Volk* with an alien and arid "Jewish" intellectualism, Freud thereby debasing the Aryan soul, Schoenberg corrupting German music.

Both had an array of problems with the meaning of their Jewish identity. Freud rejected the religious praxis of Judaism with a ferocity whose roots have yet to be fully uncovered and explained. Schoenberg at age eighteen actually converted to Protestantism. Yet both felt almost mystically Jewish at their innermost core, and each came to a passionate affirmation of his essential Jewish identity. For Freud there is copious evidence which I have quoted elsewhere, his declaration to the Vienna B'nai Brith and his preface to the Hebrew translation of *Totem and Taboo* being only the best-known. Schoenberg writes to his disciple Alban Berg in 1933: "As you have surely observed, my return to the Jewish faith took place long ago . . . most especially in my drama *Der biblische Weg* [The Biblical Way]." That play, whose full German text remains unpublished, was conceived in 1922 and written in 1926–27 while Schoenberg was still nominally a Christian. Its hero, the journalist Max Aruns (the name already evokes both Moses *and* Aron) attempts to found a Jewish state but tragically fails. For the record one must add that in their Jewishness the major difference was that while Freud was an atheist, Schoenberg was, by his very nature, a religious man, though not in a dogmatic sense.

In 1933 Hitler came to power. As Freud's correspondence with Arnold Zweig demonstrates, this event was the immediate catalyst for the writing of *Moses and Monotheism*: "Faced with the new persecutions, one asks oneself again how the Jews have come to be what they are and why they have attracted this undying hatred." The manuscript draft was completed in August, 1934. On a related, but far more personal level, the book was to answer the question that had haunted Freud most of his life—why, "Godless Jew" [*Gottloser Jude*] that he was, he was still so profoundly Jewish.

In 1933, ejected from the Prussian Academy of the Arts, Schoenberg fled Berlin for Paris. In one of his first acts, not required by Jewish law but obviously a psychological imperative, he went to a Liberal rabbi on the rue Copernic, formally declared his return to Judaism, and received an official document to that effect signed by two witnesses, one of them Marc Chagall. Schoenberg was then in the midst of the opera *Moses und Aron,* having begun the libretto in 1928 and the music in 1930. He would never finish the work, a point to which I shall yet return.

What is so striking is the fact that Freud, the *homo atheisticus,* and

Schoenberg, the *homo religiosus,* should both turn to the Bible in grappling with their most acute spiritual problems and that both should focus on the figure of Moses: Freud—to discover what has made the Jews Jewish; Schoenberg—to ask how the God of Israel, the Absolute, can possibly be expressed in words or, should you prefer a more secularly intimate layer of interpretation (the two are not in conflict), how can the artist possibly express and communicate the plenitude of his own vision? Both become, in a deep sense, radical biblical interpreters and each, in his own fashion, creates a powerful modern Midrash, Freud as a historian (for he was convinced he was recovering a historical truth), Schoenberg as an artist who is here also a philosopher-theologian.

I

The bare plot (though not the full drama) of Freud's *Moses and Monotheism* is well-known, especially among this audience. I have dealt extensively with the drama in my book. For our present purposes it will suffice briefly to recall the plot. Thus:

Monotheism is not of Hebrew origin but an Egyptian discovery. The pharaoh Amenhotep IV established it as his state religion in the form of an exclusive worship of the sun-power, or Aton, thereafter calling himself Ikhnaton. The Aton religion, according to Freud, was characterized by the exclusive belief in one God, rejection of anthropomorphism, magic, and sorcery, and the denial of an afterlife. Upon Ikhnaton's death, however, his great heresy was rapidly undone, and the Egyptians reverted to their old gods. Moses was not a Hebrew but an Egyptian priest or noble, and a fervent monotheist. In order to save the Aton religion from extinction he placed himself at the head of some oppressed Semitic tribes then living in Egypt, brought them forth from bondage, and created a new nation. He gave them an even more spiritualized, *imageless* form of monotheistic religion. But the crude mass of former slaves could not bear the rigors of the new faith. In a mob revolt Moses was killed and the memory of the murder repressed. The Israelites went on to forge an alliance of compromise with kindred tribes in Midian whose fierce volcanic god, named Yahweh, now became their national god. As a result, the god of Moses was fused with Yahweh and the deeds of Moses ascribed to a Midianite priest also called Moses. However, after a period of latency lasting some centuries, the submerged tradition of the true faith and its founder resurfaced and emerged victorious. Yahweh was henceforth endowed with the universal and spiritual qualities of Moses's God, though the memory of Moses's murder remained repressed among the Jews, reemerging, albeit only in a very disguised form, with the rise of Pauline Christianity. Otherwise, for Freud, Christianity after Paul is barely distinguishable from paganism.

Although Schoenberg's *Moses und Aron* has a huge cast and several crowd scenes, the entire plot revolves around the tension and conflict between the two brothers (Freud, incidentally, had doubts that Aron ever existed).

Out of the Burning Bush in the desert Moses hears God's command to free his people. Moses pleads that he is too old, that no one will believe him, above all that his tongue is clumsy, unsupple (*ungelenk*; the original biblical phrase is *kevad peh*—"heavy-mouthed"), that he can think but not speak (*Ich kann denken, aber nicht reden*). God promises that He will enlighten Aron so that "he shall be your mouth (*er soll dein Mund sein*)! From him will your own voice speak, as from you comes My voice." However, that seemingly simple chain of articulation is not to be. Moses meets Aron, who is elated by the mission, but the conflict between prophet and priest is inevitable. Moses is obsessed with the pure Idea of God, who can hardly be conceived, let alone visualized or expressed. Aron, realist that he is, knows that a God who cannot be communicated will not be accepted by the people. And so, constantly compromising the purity of Moses's Idea, Aron is always prepared to offer them at least a verbal notion of God, to demonstrate the divine power through miracles, to win their favor through earthly promises, all of which Moses finds abominable and idolatrous but, despite his protests, cannot prevent.

The pivot of the opera, then, is the paradox that Moses, the servant of the Absolute, is inarticulate; Aron, who cannot really share his brother's vision, is the man of words, overflowing with eloquence. But how, in an opera, can the hero be silent? Here, in a stroke of genius, Schoenberg came up with a wonderful artifice. In the opera, Moses, a basso, only speaks; Aron, a lyric tenor, sings. The ultimate irony in *Moses und Aron* is that speech is the symbolic equivalent of inarticulateness.

The rest of the plot can be quickly summarized. Dazzled by miracles, enthused at being elected by God, the Israelites overcome their skepticism and, at the end of Act I, follow Moses and Aron out of Egypt. Act II finds them in the desert waiting for Moses to descend from Mount Sinai where he has been gone for forty days. Restlessness and despair at his apparent disappearance give way to rage. They threaten to kill Aron and the other priests. They demand their old, visible gods. Aron relents and makes the Golden Calf. The people are wild with joy. An orgy of drunkenness, sacrifice, and sex ensues. Suddenly from afar someone sees Moses descending the mountain. He arrives with the Tablets of the Law and immediately the golden idol vanishes. Moses and Aron are left alone to have their final reckoning. Moses chastises Aron for the betrayal. Aron defends his actions. What he has done was also for the sake of the Idea and out of love for his people, ordinary men and women who cannot grasp Moses's abstractions. "No folk can grasp more than just a partial image, the perceivable part of the whole idea." Moses is unrelenting, but to no avail. When he shows Aron the Tablets engraved with the words of the Law, the latter responds cunningly: "They are images also, just part of the whole Idea." Whereupon Moses smashes the Tablets. In the background the people are seen following first a pillar of fire and then a pillar of cloud. "Idolatrous images!" Moses exclaims. "God's signal," Aron retorts. "Therein the Infinite shows not Himself but the way to Him and the way to the Promised Land." The people and Aron depart. Alone on the stage, Moses utters his heartrending cry:

> Inconceivable God!
> Inexpressible, many-sided Idea,
> Will you let it be so explained?
> Shall Aron, my mouth, fashion this image?
> Then I have fashioned an image too, false,
> as an image can only be.
> Thus am I defeated!
> Thus all was but madness
> that I believed before,
> and can and must not be uttered!
> O word, thou word, that I lack!
> [*O Wort, du Wort, das mir fehlt!*]

With this the opera ends. Act III, for which there is a libretto but for which, significantly, Schoenberg could never write the music, would have been an anticlimax. *O Wort, du Wort, das mir fehlt* is both the close and the quintessence of the entire work. Nor is the earlier breaking of the tablets by Moses due, as may be supposed, to his realization that the stone tablets are a material object. The sudden awareness is far deeper and infinitely more devastating—that the very words on the tablets, not because they are on stone but precisely because they are *words,* are ultimately no more than images, icons, idols.

Now it would be an intriguing exercise to anatomize both *Moses and Monotheism* and *Moses und Aron* in relation to the biblical text, to see in detail what was appropriated, what was omitted, what was transformed, and why. That seductive task, however, must be left to another occasion. In what follows I want to confine myself to a comparison of Freud and Schoenberg at two interrelated nodal points: abstraction and idolatry, language and reality. Both sets of problems, I believe, are relevant to Freud and to psychoanalysis.

II

Common to both *Moses and Monotheism* and *Moses und Aron* is the firm conviction of the ultimate superiority of abstraction over sense experience. We have already seen it clearly in Schoenberg. Here is Freud in Part III, the section entitled "The Progress in Spirituality" (*Der Fortschritt in der Geistigkeit*):

> Among the precepts of the Mosaic religion there is one that has more significance than is at first obvious. It is the prohibition against making an image of God. . . . the compulsion to worship a God whom one cannot see. . . . [It] was bound to exercise a profound influence. For it meant subordinating sense perception to what may be called an abstract idea, a triumph of spirituality over the senses [*einen Triumph der Geistigkeit über die Sinnlichkeit*], or, more precisely, an instinctual renunciation with all its necessary psychological consequences.

Both Freud and Schoenberg seem convinced that the very essence of Judaism and of Jewish survival is the pure monotheistic Idea. In the opera Moses proclaims: "[The people] must comprehend the idea; they live only for its sake!" While at a crucial juncture in his book Freud declares:

> Moses, as we know, conveyed to the Jews an exalted sense of being a chosen people. Through the dematerialization of God a new, valuable contribution was brought to the secret treasure of the people. The Jews preserved their inclination toward spiritual interests. The political misfortune of the nation taught them to appreciate the only possession they had retained, their Scripture, at its true value. Immediately after the destruction of the Temple in Jerusalem by Titus, Rabbi Yochanan ben Zakkai asked for permission to open at Yabneh the first school for the study of the Torah. From then on it was the Holy Scripture and the intellectual effort invested in it that held the scattered people together.

Finally, in their common conviction that Moses was the bearer of an idea of God so pure as to be untainted by any hint of anthropomorphism, magic, or the miraculous, Freud and Schoenberg did not hesitate to blithely violate the plain sense of the biblical narrative. Freud shifted all the qualities he found repugnant in the biblical God of Israel onto the hypothetical Midianite Yahweh and his Midianite Moses, Schoenberg shunted it all away from Moses to Aron. For example, in the opera it is Aron alone, not Moses, who turns the staff into a serpent and, after making Moses's hand leprous, cures it.

Ironically, however, the problem of abstraction is not at all biblical except in a limited sense. Among the decisive revolutions that constituted biblical monotheism, too complex to be discussed here, the attack against idolatry meant a rejection of all pagan beliefs which situated the divinity within nature and, as a partial consequence, the prohibition of "idolatry," of worshiping a material representation of god. But while the Bible is plastically iconoclastic, it is verbally anthropomorphic, indeed exuberantly so (the Lord delivered the Israelites "with a mighty hand and an outstretched arm"), and this is true of the Talmud as well. In *words,* God is described unselfconsciously through vivid metaphors drawn from the sphere of Nature and by analogy to the human, and these verbal images were never equated with idolatry. *Dibrah Torah bi-leshon beney 'adam,* the sages had occasion to observe, "the Torah spoke the language of human beings" (shades of Schoenberg's Aron!), and it is in the quality of human speech to be metaphoric, analogic, concrete. Though the Hebrew Bible is aware of the possibilities of silence ("To Thee silence is praise," the Psalmist states at one point), on the whole the Bible is an affirmation of speech and the potency of the word.

If, as can be argued, the problem of abstraction is already implicit in biblical monotheism, the fact is that this was not recognized as such until the Middle Ages.

The demand for true and total abstraction, the onslaught against even verbal anthropomorphism, came to the Jews out of the medieval encounter between Judaism and Greek philosophy in Arabic garb, and in this battle the great warrior was another Moses—Moses Maimonides, for whom any attempt to describe God's attributes in positive verbal terms, along with any literal reading of biblical metaphor concerning God, was tantamount to idolatry. How, then, can one at all speak of Him? *Guide of the Perplexed,* Part I, chap. 58:

> Know that the description of God . . . by means of negations is the correct description—a description that is not affected by an indulgence in facile language and does not imply any deficiency with respect to God. . . . On the other hand if one describes him by means of affirmations, one implies . . . that He [God] is associated with that which is not He and implies a deficiency in Him.

And at the end of the chapter:

> Glory then to Him who is such that when the intellects contemplate His
> essence, their apprehension turns into incapacity . . . and when the
> tongues aspire to magnify Him by means of attributive qualifications, all
> eloquence turns to weariness and incapacity!

Shades of Schoenberg's Moses. . . .

But what of Freud's Moses? In *Moses and Monotheism* Freud seems
never to doubt Moses's ability to communicate his idea and its corol-
laries through speech. Moses "created the Jews" all by himself. "He
enhanced their self-confidence by *assuring* them that they were the
chosen people of God; he *declared* them to be holy and laid on them the
duty to keep apart from others." How did he assure them, if not in
words? What did he declare, if not words? Did they understand? In
Freud's scenario they apparently understood enough of his teaching to
find it unendurable and to kill him for it. And what of Moses's heav-
iness of speech? Freud shrugs it off in passing by suggesting that either
he really had a speech impediment, which would be biographically
interesting, or it may mean that he spoke Egyptian and needed a
translator, thus a veiled confirmation of his alleged Egyptian origin.

The problem of communication in *Moses and Monotheism* is not one of
words or speech per se, but that of the formation and transmission of a
religious tradition and its power to grip its adherants through the
generations, over vast stretches of historical time, which is a very different matter. In *Moses und Aron* the problem is intrinsic to language itself
which, in relation to that Reality which is most important to express, is
found to be impotent.

On a certain level Freud would seem to agree. In *An Outline of Psychoanalysis* he writes categorically that "Reality will always remain un-
knowable." The reality with which Freud is here concerned is the
Unconscious, which, like Schoenberg's God, cannot be known in itself.
But, lo and behold, there is no Schoenbergian despair, no shattering of
tablets, no cry of "thus am I defeated." If we cannot know this *Ding an
sich* directly, we can know it obliquely, through other means. In his
essay on "The Unconscious," Freud inquires:

> How are we to arrive at a knowledge of the unconscious? It is of course
> only as something conscious that we know it, after it has undergone
> transformation or translation into something conscious. Psycho-analytic
> work shows us every day that translation of this kind is possible.

In the *Outline* he observes:

> . . . we infer a number of processes which are in themselves 'unknowa-
> ble' and interpolate them in those that are conscious to us. And if, for
> instance, we say: 'At this point an unconscious memory intervened',

what that means is: 'At this point something occurred of which we are totally unable to form a conception, but which, if it had entered our consciousness, could only have been described in such and such a way'.

The key words in the two passages are "translation" and "described," both essentially verbal activities.

Thus, by a somewhat circuitous route, we have stumbled upon a fundamental crux of difference between Freud and Schoenberg whose implications far transcend the two works that were our point of departure. Provisionally, I shall formulate the difference as follows: Freud, I propose, was a verbal optimist, though hardly in a naïve sense; Schoenberg, a verbal pessimist, though not a consistent one. Since I am addressing the New York Psychoanalytic Institute and not the Juilliard School, it is Freud who will engage us now.

III

Although Freud, to my knowledge, never offered a comprehensive theory or even a systematic discussion of language, he retained throughout his life a primal belief in the potency of words, whether as a vehicle for his conscious thoughts and teachings or as a means of access to the unconscious. For all the advances in his own understanding of what takes place in the psychoanalytic situation, he never lost faith that words lie at the very heart of it. The texts I shall cite run from 1905 to the eve of his death. Though you have obviously read them more than once, I shall quote some of them aloud, so that the silently read be refreshed with the greater vitality of the spoken.

Thus, in the 1905 essay on "Psychical Treatment":

> Foremost among such measures is the use of words; and words are the essential tool of mental treatment. A layman will no doubt find it hard to understand how pathological disorders of the body and mind can be eliminated by 'mere' words. He will feel he is being asked to believe in magic. And he will not be so very wrong, for the words which we use in our everyday speech are nothing but watered-down magic. But we shall have to follow a roundabout path in order to explain how science sets about restoring to words a part at least of their former power.

In 1913 comes the famous, lapidary formulation of the "Fundamental Rule": "Say whatever goes through your mind" (*Sagen Sie alles was Ihnen durch den Sinn geht*), and the *Introductory Lectures* (1916–17) contain what almost amounts to a little rhapsody in praise of words:

> Words were originally magic and to this day words have retained much of their ancient magical power. By words one person can make another

blissfully happy or drive him to despair, by words the teacher conveys knowledge to his pupils. . . . Words provoke affects and are in general the means of mutual influence among men. Thus we shall not underestimate the use of words in psychotherapy. . . .

By the time we reach *The Question of Lay Analysis* we realize that the "magic of words" has become a *leitmotiv* in Freud's work. When the hypothetical "Impartial Person" says contemptuously, "Nothing more than that? Words, words, words as Prince Hamlet says. . . . So it is a kind of magic . . . you talk and blow away his ailments," Freud replies:

> Quite true. It *would* be magic if it worked somewhat quicker. . . . But analytic treatments take months and even years: magic that is so slow loses its magical character. And incidentally do not let us despise the *word*. It is, after all, a mighty instrument (*ein mächtiges Instrument*). . . . No doubt, 'in the beginning was the deed'; and the word came later. . . . But originally the word was magic—a magical act; and it has retained much of its ancient power.

In *Moses and Monotheism* unconscious thought processes or "whatever may be analogous to them in the id" become conscious "along the path of the function of speech." The universal capacity for linguistic symbolism is marshalled as proof of the "archaic heritage" of transmitted acquired characteristics. And, in discussing the "omnipotence of thoughts":

> All the magic of words, too, has its place here, and the conviction of the power which is bound up with the knowledge and pronouncing of a name. The 'omnipotence of thoughts' was, we suppose, an expression of the pride of mankind in the development of speech. . . . The new realm of intellectuality was opened up, in which ideas, memories and inferences became decisive. . . . This was unquestionably one of the most important stages on the path to becoming human.

And in the final, posthumously published *Outline of Psychoanalysis:*

> Conscious processes on the periphery of the ego and everything else in the ego unconscious—such would be the simplest state of affairs. . . . But in humans there is an added complication through which internal processes in the ego may also acquire the quality of consciousness. This is the work of the function of speech, which brings material in the ego into a firm connection with mnemic residues of visual, but more particularly of auditory, perceptions.

Freud's belief in the "magic" of words and, by extension, in the "slow" magic of psychoanalysis, is all the more remarkable in light of his profound recognition of the potential and actual treacheries of language. His faith lay in believing that even these could be detected and so interpreted as to yield truth. Nor need Freud be posthumously told that patients (the euphemistic "analysands" sticks to my palate) communicate with more than words. For his awareness of the semiotics of gesture we need only conjure Dora on the couch as Freud keenly watches her toying with her reticule (his particular interpretation is not at issue here). That, although we may often not mean what we say, Freud believed that we can say what we mean, is attested by his own lifelong effort to communicate his ideas in speech and in writing. Indeed, within the terms I discussed earlier I will hazard the following: In relation to language Schoenberg is Maimonidean; Freud is biblical. Only twice, to my knowledge, does his confidence in verbal expression falter, both times in trying to define the nature of his Jewishness (see the address to the B'nai Brith and the preface to the Hebrew translation of *Totem and Taboo*). He did not rest, however, until he *had* found the words. The result was *Moses and Monotheism.*

IV

Freud's verbal optimism must seem especially strange today. In a recent little book entitled *La force d'attraction* the eminent French analyst J. B. Pontalis cites Freud's statement, "I believe that I did everything possible to render accessible to the others that which I knew and had experienced," and observes: "One declaration, among so many others, that testifies to an extraordinary confidence in the resources of language. Extraordinary for us, who have lost this confidence."

And so we have. We seem closer, in this respect, to Schoenberg than to Freud. If Schoenberg's Moses cries out, "O Wort, du Wort das mir fehlt," we, lesser beings, readily empathize with him. Surrounded and inundated by words as never before, we find them increasingly drained of real meaning, inert, false, idols. The crisis of speech, language, text, reading, communication, has become endemic to our daily lives, our society, our culture. For some time now it has not only created turbulence in linguistics but has reverberated in modernist literature, literary criticism, philosophy, and other disciplines. By now, given the pervasive influence of so-called logical positivism in Anglo-Saxon philosophy, of structural anthropology, of literary deconstruction in both its Gallic and native varieties, it is spilling over into psychoanalysis itself. At the heart of the general discomfort is a creeping and sometimes strident loss of confidence in the ability of words to convey reality, however that reality be defined, be it in the external world or in the unconscious, but then—definition is itself, by definition, a matter of words, and so an initial linguistic despair desperately circles back upon itself in endless spirals.

Yet in many ways the problems inherent in language and speech are very old and have a long history. The ancients were far from credulous innocents in such matters. Greek philosophy debated whether words are natural or conventional, speculated on their relation to truth and reality, distinguished between types of words that it labeled "equivocal," "amphibolous," "univocal," and such phenomena as metonymy, metaphor, analogy, allegory (see, just for starters, Plato's *Phaedrus, Cratylus, Theaetetus, Sophist,* Aristotle's *Poetics* and *On Interpretation*). The Hebrew Bible recognizes the problematics of speech within its own more concrete contexts, in the ubiquitous figure of the prophet (not only Moses!) who initially balks at his mission to speak until, as in Isaiah, his lips are purified with a glowing ember, or Ezekiel, who must first swallow a written scroll and physically incorporate the words, and above all in the problem of distinguishing between true and false prophecy (see Jeremiah 23). I will not detain you with the protracted battles between Nominalists and Realists in the Middle Ages, nor with the more arcane sophistications of Indian and Arabic linguistic theories. Despite all the many and various perceptions of the pitfalls of language there remained, on the whole, a fundamental trust that, properly used or interpreted, language can convey, if not an ultimate Platonic reality, then at least a genuine if partial knowledge.

If the problematics of language are old, the crisis of language as we experience it is a modern phenomenon. Here it is no longer only a question of the ontological or epistemological status of words, of truth or falsehood in the Socratic or biblical sense (though, to be sure, such lingering issues remain part of it), but of the very capacity of language to express anything beyond itself.

This terminal point of linguistic skepticism was not reached overnight. It is but the final stage in a crisis that reaches back to the nineteenth century. Its causes are complex, "overdetermined," subject to debate. Some have simplistically blamed Freud himself, for was it not he who made us peer into the abyss of ambiguity and contradiction out of which words emerge and over which language hangs suspended?

In fact, however, it seems to me that far from undermining the meaning of language, Freud expanded and amplified it. It was he who showed that speech, however fragmented or distorted, is never meaningless, that often the word that initially seems the most casual and banal, the most impoverished, is the most significant, the richest. It was he who extended the metaphor of language to somatic symptoms and to dreams. And if dreams, themselves a language, are the "royal road to the unconscious," words are vehicles which, when they do not break down or run out of fuel along the way, bring back to us their strange but vital cargos.

The crisis of language emerged before psychoanalysis, developed alongside it, and, by and large, independently of it. It is already manifest in Nietzsche, in the *Sprachkritik* of Freud's contemporary Fritz Mauthner, in the much misunderstood Wittgenstein. It is equally evident in literature. In his *After Babel* George Steiner writes:

> From the beginnings of Western literature until Rimbaud and Mallarmé poetry and prose were in organic accord with language. . . . A classic literacy is defined by this 'housedness' in language, by the assumption that, used with requisite penetration and suppleness, available words and grammar will do the job. There is nothing in the Garden or, indeed, in himself, that Adam cannot name. . . . So far as the Western tradition goes . . . a pact negotiated between word and world lasts until the second half of the nineteenth century. There it breaks down abruptly. Goethe and Victor Hugo were probably the last major poets to find that language was sufficient to their needs.

We may quibble with Steiner about the precise point of breakdown, but it doesn't matter for us, who have already experienced Beckett and Ionesco. Let me not be misunderstood. I happen to admire both playwrights, as well as Nietzsche and Wittgenstein. Far from creating the crisis of language, they recognized that it was there and tried to respond to it. The point about Freud is that he seems to have remained singularly untouched by the general agitation. Among the great figures of modernism Freud's faith in language remains almost anomalous. This, I think, is no longer quite the case with current psychoanalysis.

V

The radical mistrust of the word impinges upon psychoanalysis at four crucial junctures: the speech of the patient; the speech of the analyst; construction (or reconstruction) of the patient's life history; the written case history.

What is at issue at all four points is what has been commonly termed—I am not merely referring here to the title of a recent book—"narrative truth and historical truth." Thus: How can one ever be certain that the patient's words really convey the dream; that the memories triggered by verbal associations and then verbalized by the patient recapture the past; that the collaborative grammar forged by analyst and patient which links words into meaning is not an artifice; that the case history is a true report of the analytic process and not a distortion or, worse, a fiction?

You will not, I trust, expect me to unravel these knots within the space of a lecture, nor do I have the temerity to tell you your clinical business. What I have to say is merely suggestive and schematic.

Historians have grappled far longer with similar problems than have psychoanalysts. How to recover and evoke the past, what, if any, are the causal links between events and between past and present, are problems that lie at the very heart of their older vocation. Yet although they have been far from immune to the corrosive skepticisms I have mentioned, by and large historians have not succumbed to the kind of malaise that shadows and, in my opinion, potentially threatens the very essence of the psychoanalytic enterprise more than do competing therapies, the strictures of philosophers of science (to which you render yourselves unnecessarily vulnerable by continuing to literalize Freud's scientific claims), or, for that matter, the utopias now offered by psychopharmacology. Concerning the latter it all depends on how one conceives the psychoanalytic mission. If merely as a therapy for the removal or alleviation of symptoms, then indeed medication has opened unexpected new vistas. But pills alone cannot achieve that other mandate which is surely embedded in the Freudian legacy, the ancient admonition to *know* ourselves.

The analyst, the patient, the historian, seek truth; but what is truth, especially historical truth? Leopold von Ranke, one of the founding fathers of modern historiography, went directly into the archives and was convinced that the past could be recovered *wie es eigentlich gewesen*—"as it really was." That is no longer the goal, for it was an illusory goal to begin with. Even H. G. Wells's time-machine could not bring us back to the past "as it really was" because, once arrived at our destination, it is still we, with our twentieth-century knowledge and sensibilities, who would be experiencing what was there.

In truth, however, the past as such does not exist as something lying about, waiting to be found. Only traces of the past, whether verbal or material, are available, and it is they who have traveled through time. The document in the archive is not the past, nor does a collection of documents amount to history. The archaeological artifact is, in itself, just that—an artificial fact. Documents, artifacts, literary texts, and oral traditions, all these do not become historical facts until the living historian scrutinizes them critically and contextually. And even then, as the British philosopher R. G. Collingwood reminded us all, a sequential recital of historical "facts" is at best only chronography. History is concerned with *events,* and facts do not become events until, filtered through the mind and imagination of the historian, they are *interpreted* and articulated. Granted, then, that there cannot be one, final interpretation. But that does not mean that interpretation need be anarchic or arbitrary or that what is recaptured and reconstructed laboriously and critically is not "true" in a historical sense.

I have sporadically encountered analysts who have envied me my archives and my artifacts; I could equally envy their possibility of interrogating the living subject. There is nothing, of course, to envy on either side, both being impossible professions. Rather, there are affinities—I do not say identities—between the analyst's work and that of the historian which each could profitably recognize. The major difference, I think, is that many analysts still cling or aspire to a scientific model forged by nineteenth-century positivism, while most historians have given it up without surrendering the quest for a differently conceived historical truth. The real analogy between psychoanalysis and historiography is that both deal with fragmentary messages out of the past that are themselves, in the broad sense, parts of a language that must be deciphered, translated, and that become historical through a continuously self-refining process of interpretation. The event is not the Napoleonic invasion of Russia but how this was experienced by the French and the Russians, how it affected subsequent events, how it has been remembered. The most vital historical documents were already interpretations to begin with, and most often the historian is an interpreter of interpretations.

But what, again, of the treachery of words? What hope for reality with words interpreting words? Would it be impolite if I propose that here both historians and psychoanalysts have something to learn from theology? For you don't have to be a believer to recognize that it is theology, especially biblical exegesis, which represents the longest and most formidable tradition of close reading and of grappling with the interpretation of words in the Western heritage. Freud himself recognized this when, in *The Interpretation of Dreams* he remarked that he had treated dreams "like a sacred text" (*wie einen heiligen Text*).

Thus in 1925 Martin Buber and Franz Rosenzweig exchanged letters on whether biblical revelation included the Law, that is—whether the Law is not merely a human interpretation. Rosenzweig who, unlike Buber, affirmed the binding character of the Law upon himself, wrote:

> Revelation is certainly not Law-giving. It is only this: Revelation. The primary content of revelation is revelation itself. "He [God] came down"—this already concludes the revelation; "He spoke" is the beginning of interpretation, and certainly "I am."

A psychoanalytic paraphrase might run:

> "I had a dream last night"—this already concludes the revelation.
> "I dreamed that . . . "—is the beginning of interpretation.

Please do not search for any Jungian overtones here equating God and the Unconscious. The point is strictly a hermeneutic one. What is important is how Rosenzweig continues:

> But where does this interpretation stop being legitimate? I would never dare state this in a general sentence; here commences the right of experience to give testimony, positive and negative.

The narrative interpretations forged in the course of analytic work pose the same question and must evoke a similar response. No a priori boundary can be drawn between what is legitimate and what is not, only an unfolding coherence and the experience of both analyst and patient can testify. For psychoanalysis as for history "narrative truth" and "historical truth" posit a false dichotomy, and this is true of the case history as well. There is no communicable historical truth apart from its narrative, though the narrative strategies may vary. True, not words but the taste of a madeleine dipped in a cup of tea is the trigger that first summons up Proust's lost past in *A la recherche du temps perdu*—literally, "In Search of the Lost Time." But this past does not fully become Proust's history until, in the epiphany of the final volume, *Le temps retrouvé*—"Time Retrieved"—he decides at last to verbalize it in his oceanic narrative.

VI

In the end we are left with words. Books extolling silence are written in words. Philosophers must use words to describe the limitations of words. Literary deconstructionists write texts full of words to convince us that the text as such no longer exists, that it is the perpetual creation of the reader, not the author, but I observe that they make certain to sign their books with their own names. Maimonides and Schoenberg assure us, in words, that no words can describe God. But even the awesome and austere tradition of verbal negation must rely on words. In *Moses und Aron* Moses is, negatively to be sure, as verbal about God as can be, stringing beads of glistening adjectives: *unvorstellbar* ("unimaginable"); *unsichtbar* ("unseeable"); *unüberblickbar* ("ungraspable"); *unendlich* ("unending"); *unaussprechlicher* ("unutterable"); but also *ewig* ("eternal"); *allgegenwärtig* ("ever-present"); *allmächtig* (all-powerful). And how many musical compositions of Schoenberg are set to words,

and what of the texts he himself wrote to convey his thoughts, including the massive *Theory of Harmony* (*Harmonielehre*)? For Schoenberg was
both Moses *and* Aron, as I dare say Freud was too, and the rest of us as
well.

It all has something of the quality of Zeno's Paradox. Theoretically
we should never be able to cross the threshold, yet we walk across and
do it. I stand before you speaking words. How often, in preparing this
lecture, have I thought—*O Wort, du Wort das mir fehlt*. No doubt I
accepted this invitation partly to indulge my narcissism and who knows
what else. Still, I would like to think that I am not only communicating
with myself.

My defense of the primacy of the word is certainly not an invitation
to verbal complacency. On the contrary, words require constant and
utmost vigilance. Otherwise they *can* become idols, not in the Maimonidean sense of daring to express the ineffable but, much worse, because
having once expressed a living reality, they have been mechanically,
idolatrously repeated and reduced to clichés. That this has occurred
within the vocabulary and discourse of psychoanalysis is, I think, demonstrable, but I would prefer to leave such a critique to you. "Sometimes," Wittgenstein wrote, "an expression has to be withdrawn from
language and sent for cleaning—then it can be put back into circula-
tion." Where better, if you will forgive the homely simile, than in the
laundries of your consultation rooms?

As psychoanalysts it is you, I submit, who should be among the
primary custodians and explorers of language. It is for psychoanalysis
not merely to reflect the crisis of language, but to inquire how much of
it is really a progress in knowledge and awareness, and how much an
absorption of cultural fashion. Do not be beguiled by the latest critical
calisthenics, for cultural fashions change. There are quarters where
structuralism and deconstruction are already outmoded. Linguistic
skepticism and minimalism are not the whole of modernist literature.
Joyce exuberantly exploited all the resources of language, his own and
several others. Nabokov cavorted euphoriously in Russian and English, translated Pushkin's *Evgeny Onegin* in its entirety, and entitled his
autobiography: *Speak Memory*. (Indeed!) What is currently termed
"psycholinguistics" is essentially behaviorist and has little or nothing to
do with psychoanalysis. Where is the *psychoanalytic* linguistics that you
should be forging? It is you, as heirs (not idolators), of Freud, who must
keep faith with the magic of words and help us to understand the
nature of this power.

For ever since Freud you have been privileged to hear speech as it
has never been heard before, not by the Delphic oracle, nor by priests,

rabbis, gurus, lovers, not even in the solitary intimacy of mirrors. It is a unique burden and an astonishing opportunity. Your patients are poets for whom August is the cruelest month, and you are privy to the verbal odyssies of real Molly Blooms, though there may be days on end when the word is not forthcoming ("Say whatever comes into your mind"—"O Word, thou Word that I lack!").

I leave you with fragments of two poems. One, by the great modern Greek poet Constantine Cavafy:

> Let us speak, let us speak—silence does not suit us
> since we have been created in the image of the Word.
> Let us speak, let us speak—since within us speaks
> divine thought, the soul's unbodied speech.

And Eliot, in *Four Quartets*:

> So here I am in the middle way. . . .
> Trying to learn to use words, and every attempt
> Is a wholly new start, and a different kind of failure. . . .
> . . . And so each venture
> Is a new beginning, a raid on the inarticulate. . . .

In relation to psychoanalysis that last phrase, it occurs to me, says it all.

DEVELOPMENT

The Development of a Capacity for Imagination in Early Childhood

LINDA C. MAYES, M.D. and
DONALD J. COHEN, M.D.

> There are no days in life so memorable as those which
> vibrated to some stroke of the imagination.
> EMERSON, *The Conduct of Life* (1860)

Imagination as a mental capacity is part of a line of development that begins in the earliest symbiotic interactions between mother and infant, takes further shape as the child moves from dyadic to triadic relations, and culminates in a fully mature capacity to reflect upon in thought one's wishes and feelings vis-à-vis multiple others. Particularly for the 3- to 5-year-old child, imagination represents a special mode of mental functioning which allows him to expand his internal object world, motivates him toward increasingly complex relationships with others, and is a central precondition for the creation of the self-defining fantasies characteristic of the oedipal phase. The central neurocognitive precondition for an imaginative capacity is the ability to distinguish thought from action and understand that others as well as oneself are motivated to act because of mental states such as feelings, beliefs, and fantasies. In this paper, we present a view of imagination that integrates observations from psychoanalytically informed studies of the emergence of fantasy

---

Dr. Mayes is the Arnold Gesell Associate Professor of Child Development in the Yale Child Study Center and a research candidate in the Western New England Institute for Psychoanalysis. Dr. Cohen is the Irving B. Harris Professor of Child Psychiatry, Pediatrics, and Psychology and director of the Yale Child Study Center, Yale University School of Medicine.

23

play in the oedipal phase with findings from recent work on how children acquire an understanding of their own and others' mental processes.

POPULARLY CONCEIVED, IMAGINATION IS THE PROVINCE OF PLAY, ART, and scientific genius and properly belongs to children, artists, and the gifted few who are able to see old problems in a new light. These individuals are given a license to imagine for the rest of the world to respect and simultaneously contain lest such license carry its holder beyond the limits of accepted creative ambiguity. While imagination is seen as the opposite of reality and is as free and unlimited as logical thought is methodical and rule bound, there are limits to what we intuitively accept as imaginative and what we do not. We praise the creative imagination of the artist or young child but are suspicious of the inventions of the conspirator and eccentric. We admire imagination in the service of resourcefulness and solutions to difficult dilemmas but may scorn the individual who rarely has a product or settlement to show for his musings, however "imaginative" or novel they may be. We delight in the playfulness of a good storyteller, child or adult, but become uneasy when the fantasy becomes too fantastic or violates too many veridical conventions.

Whenever a term with so many layers of meaning and implications is absorbed into a general psychology of mental functioning, its technical applications may be confounded and interwoven with its popular usage. Within psychoanalysis, imagination is broadly used as both verb and noun, as process and product. It is the process of creating mental images in the service of wish fulfillment or defense but is evident in the products of dreams, symptoms, children's play, parapraxes, and transferential phenomena, each of which represents the data of the psychoanalytic process. It is seen as ubiquitous to all mental life and at the same time special to the creative act (Lee, 1949). Imagination is often used synonymously with unconscious fantasies, primary process, mental representation, or free association. As in the popular usage, there is an assumed optimal balance between the actions of too much and too little imagination in the services of reality testing, the regulation of tension, and ego organization. Too much imagination impairs the individual's capacity to judge reality and to use thought as trial action, while too little imagination grounds that person in a stale, rarely novel, affectively impoverished world.

Imagination then in the psychoanalytic frame of reference broadly encompasses a number of interrelated functions and concepts (Beres, 1960a, 1960b; Rosen, 1960), including the capacity to create a fantasy, the ability to use such a fantasy in the service of affect regulation and/or defense, the synthesis of memories and percepts into a mental image of a person or thing which is not present, and the inner world of mental representations as opposed to the external world of sensory perceptions. From the psychoanalytic point of view, imagination involves the creation of an inner world of subjectivity against which one judges (consciously and unconsciously) the objective, veridical world and in which there is the freedom to perceive and remodel others as one wishes or needs them to be. Implied, but not directly highlighted, by this broad application of the term is how the capacity to imagine the other in multiple ways is a central precondition for the creation of the self-defining fantasies characteristic of the oedipal phase.

For example, in the following brief fragment of play, a 5-year-old girl uses her imagination to try on multiple roles for herself and her relationships with others. As she quietly arranges furniture in a dollhouse, she introduces a family including a little girl, the father, a baby brother, and a mother. She arranges and rearranges the dolls, first placing the two children together between the parents, then the baby brother with the mother, the little girl with the father, then the father and mother together with both children off to the side. She sings and whispers to herself as she places her characters in their assigned beds. Abruptly, the little girl takes her baby brother, and they leave to go on a very long trip to a magic place. They take few supplies, but the little girl is very resourceful. She knows where to look for food and how to take care of everyone including her baby brother who feels quite lonely and hungry. The little girl reassures her brother that she can do everything just like their mother. The parents are very worried and do not know quite what to do. The mother tries several times to find her children but stops her search when it gets dark. Only the father is able to make it through the cold snow, dense forest, and other continuously appearing tests of endurance to find his two lost children. He praises the little girl for her resourcefulness and for how grown-up she is and promises her that he will protect her always even from her mother's anger at her for going away.

The capacity to tolerate multiple, often conflicting views of the object world is made possible by a capacity to imagine; and the ability to represent wishes and desires vis-à-vis multiple others characterizes the fantasy play of the oedipal-aged child (Cohen et al., 1987; Marans et al., 1991). These fantasies move development forward, for it is through them that the child develops a view of himself in relation to others and is able to try on and act out the consequences he anticipates from the imaginary relationships he creates. In turn, the capacity to imagine the other requires the integration of a number of specific neurocognitive functions that also mature between the third and sixth year of life, e.g., distinguishing thought from action and understanding that others as well as oneself are motivated to act because of mental states such as feelings, beliefs, and fantasies (Wellman, 1988, 1990).

In this paper, we offer an integration of observations from psychoanalytically informed studies of the emergence of fantasy play in the oedipal phase with findings from recent work on how children acquire an understanding of their own and others' mental processes (reviewed in Astington et al., 1988). Based on observations from our ongoing studies of the play of oedipal-aged children (Cohen et al., 1987; Marans et al., 1992), we mark out the preconditions for *one* aspect of imagination, that which is involved in the creation of an internal object world. Imagination as a mental capacity is part of a line of development that begins in the earliest symbiotic interactions between mother and infant, takes further shape as the child moves from dyadic to triadic relations, and culminates in a fully mature capacity to reflect upon in thought one's wishes and feelings vis-à-vis multiple others. We suggest that particularly for the 3- to 5-year-old child, imagination represents a special mode of mental functioning which allows him not only to demarcate the physical (or perceivable) and the mental (or fantasied) world but more importantly expands his internal object world and motivates him toward increasingly complex relationships with others.

With a capacity for imagination, relationships with others are colored both by the child's previous experiences and by his imagined wishes and beliefs. The capacity for sustained imaginary play emerges in parallel with the child's acquisition of an understanding of how the actions and words of others reflect and are motivated by their feelings, beliefs, wishes, and memories, each actions of mind. Such an understanding allows the child to imbue the persons in his imaginary play with complex feelings and desires toward others, and to create the stories, or an inner world, by which he defines himself and through which he will continue to view and define his external world.

THE PREVERBAL ROOTS OF THE MENTAL CAPACITY FOR IMAGINATION

The verb imagine and its related derivatives imagination and imaginary have their origin in two related words, the Latin verb *imaginari* and the noun *imago*. The combination of these two root words gives a fundamentally object-related quality to the process of imagining for *imago*, especially in the plural, referred to portraits of ancestors which were placed in the atria of Roman homes or carried in family funeral processions (Glare, 1982). As a verb, *imaginari* implied the act of picturing to oneself. Later usages of *imago* by poets such as Vergil and Ovid conveyed the notion of a mental image, an idea, or pretence, most often of another person. With time, the word imagine came to mean the creation of a mental image of something never before wholly or similarly perceived in reality by the imaginer or the capacity to form concepts beyond those derived from external objects (*Oxford English Dictionary*, 1989).

Freud never discussed imagination as a process per se but did use the term generally to imply the creation of mental images and the use of fantasy in the service of wish fulfillment and the mastery of anxiety. In *Beyond the Pleasure Principle* (1920), he described his observations of an 18-month-old child who responded to a parent's absence by playing a disappearing game with an object on a string. The child actively and pleasurably made the object vanish and then reappear by pulling on the string. By so doing, he turned his passive experience of anxiety and sadness at the disappearance of important objects into active pleasure at being able to make the toy disappear and reappear at will. As Rosen (1960) also points out, such play in action is analogous to the difference between passively perceiving an object when present and actively evoking the memory, or later imagining the scene, when the object is absent. In her concept of developmental lines, Anna Freud (1965, 1973) did not specifically discuss imagination or the process of being able to create actively a fantasy in the service of anxiety regulation. She did, however, outline the line of development that proceeds from the physical to the mental world, which includes the progression from play with body to play with fantasy and from direct somatic expression of wishes and conflicts to the capacity to express the same in thoughts and language. While this particular progression captures some of the manifest qualities of the development of an imaginative capacity, it does not expand upon how the capacity for imagination develops out of a social matrix and how, in early development, imagination is essential for the child's appreciation of an increasingly complex social world.

Stated simply, the *need* for an imaginative capacity comes into being as the child wants or desires those individuals whom he does not or cannot have at that moment. The fantasies of the oedipal-aged child express, and in some ways gratify, these desires, but there are a number of functional preconditions for the characteristic oedipal phase fantasies. In the first three years of life for normally developing children, several perceptual, neurological, and cognitive functions mature in such a way as to allow the child increasing separateness from the parent. These functions involve minimally the capacity to evoke a mental image of the other, to remember previous experiences with that other, and the ability to modulate one's own states of anxiety in the other's absence. Evoking a mental image of the other is part of the ability to know that the other is absent and to look for that person. For example, Piaget (1937) outlined how the child's understanding of objects in their absence progresses from the 3-month-old's visual tracking the path of a disappearing object without further searching after the object is out of sight to the active searching of an 8- to 10-month-old along the path of displacement. By the beginning of the second year, the child takes into account sequential displacements of an object and will search for it where he last saw it. Finally, by the latter half of the second year, children are able to deal with invisible displacements, that is, they are able to search for something without perceptual reinforcements. Presumably, at this age, the child has a mental representation of the object that exists apart from immediate perception, and is capable of true evocative memory with few to no perceptual cues.

The coming together of these various perceptual and early neuro-cognitive functions into a capacity first to remember the other in his or her absence (and later to imagine the other in whatever ways the child wishes) fosters the child's increasing independence and moves toward separation and allows him to tolerate the frustration, fear, and sadness engendered by such separation. The infant's move toward a definition of other as distinct from self and the development of a capacity for imagination are tandem processes. Each depends upon the other, and each depends upon the integration of maturing perceptual and neu-rocognitive abilities to perceive persons as distinct and to remember.

A central contribution of the psychoanalytic theory of early development has been the conceptualization of the related processes of self-other differentiation, individuation, and internalization, each firmly rooted in the earliest interactions between infant and mother (Loewald, 1977; Mahler, 1968, 1971, 1974; Mahler et al., 1975; Ritvo and Solnit, 1958; Weil, 1970). In brief summary, the elements of that early mother-infant matrix essential for a developing imaginative capacity involve the connections between the affective experience of the infant and the creation of a representational world (Loewald, 1977). At the beginning of psychological life, from the infant's point of view, the outside world consists mainly of mother, or perhaps of mother not as person but as the source of food and warmth. At this stage, mother represents the world that acts contingently on the infant's needs, but she exists intrapsychically only inasmuch as the infant needs physically. Such a stage cannot exist for long since the infant soon experiences the frustration engendered by the mother's inevitable absences and delays. Frustration and the ensuing discomfort represent a first break in the sensation of immediate gratification and the first experience of the infant with the separateness between states of physical need and satisfaction of such needs. Through such inevitably repeated experiences and the beginning feelings of separateness, desire for another takes shape for it is that other who can alleviate discomfort.

The contingency of a mother's nurturing acts on the infant's discomforts and the association between her absence and the infant's sense of frustration establish referencing links between the mother's behavior and the affective outcome for the infant. These links in turn contribute to the beginning of a representational world. Through these repeated experiences, both frustrating and gratifying, in the presence of another, memories laden with affective traces are created, and the other of the inner, representational world gradually takes shape (Loewald, 1977; Mahler, 1968). In the psychoanalytic frame of reference, we say the infant has begun to internalize a sense of the other through the collective memories, now beginning representations, of repeatedly satisfying (or frustrating) experiences. In the neurocognitive frame of reference, we say the infant has developed a set of schemas based on previous experiences with another person, and such schemas are the basis of his expectations that the other will reappear and behave toward him in certain predictable ways (Lewis and Goldberg, 1969).

Internalizing a sense of the other (or developing experiential schemas) is the essential precursor for developing a capacity to imagine the other since rudimentary fantasies about the specific (and general) other are created from these early experiential representations. With time, the infant is able to draw on these beginning representations in moments of discomfort or frustration and evoke memories of previously gratifying moments with mother (Loewald, 1972). Consider, for example, how the crying, hungry infant is temporarily soothed by the sound of his mother's voice calling out from another room, or at times even by the familiar sounds of mother preparing the bottle. We presume with the facilitation of perceptual cues, the infant is "remembering" previous feeding experiences, and these memories are briefly as comforting as the actual experience itself. The capacity to evoke memories of the other is a precursor for the capacity to imagine the other inasmuch as the memories serve to organize the infant and regulate states of tension. Further, in evoking a memory of the other, the infant "uses" a mental activity to re-create the other in mind and to regulate a heightened state of arousal.[1]

---

1. The ability to store perceptions in memory and to evoke those memories with appropriate stimuli is a central prerequisite not only in a developmental line for imagination but also in our psychoanalytic models of the self-other differentiation. How

Beginning to create a sense of the other as separate from self with the attendant emergence of a representational world requires the integration of a number of basic perceptual and neuroregulatory functions. In the first 6 months, these include the capacities to quiet oneself and to maintain a sustained alert state, to attend to selected elements of the environment, and to make the auditory, visual, and tactile discriminations that are critical for interactions in the animate world (Mayes and Cohen, 1993). For example, within the first 3 months infants are able to discriminate visual patterns of increasing complexity and contour density (Banks and Salapatek, 1983) and to discriminate changes in the pitch of a speech sequence (Kessen et al., 1979), both essential abilities for social interaction. Similarly, between 1 and 3 months, infants evidence the ability to distinguish among different facial affective expressions (Nelson, 1987) and show visual scanning patterns that permit definition of the external boundaries of a face as well as selective scanning of internal features such as eyes or mouth (Haith et al., 1977). Capacities such as these make it possible for the infant to "metabolize" the input from the social world and to begin to form early representations (or schemas) of experiences. Further, these early perceptual experiences with others are necessary not only for the creation of mental representations of others but also for the later ability to use percepts of people in novel ways in the activity of imagining. For example, the young child's pleasure in playing with incongruently matching types of voices to characters is built upon an early perceptual capacity to match congruently voice and facial expression (Walker, 1982). If the saliency of social cues is not reinforced experientially or is diminished because of constitutional impairments (e.g., congenital blindness or deafness), early disturbances in self-other differentiation result (Fraiberg and Adelson, 1973) with the attendant impairments in later imaginative activity.

In the latter half of the first year and beginning of the second,

---

early is it apparently possible for the infant to "remember" a previously experienced condition or person? In the studies of contingent learning, 8- to 12-week-old infants evidence recognition memory for certain situations, particularly if those situations were pleasurable (Rovee-Collier and Fagan, 1981; Rovee-Collier et al., 1980). Within the first month of life, recognition memory tasks demonstrate that infants remember nonfamiliar speech sounds for up to two days (Ungerer et al., 1978), and within the first 6 months, infants require both less exposure time to encode the information and evidence longer retention (Rovee-Collier, 1987). Whether or not young children have a similar capacity for evocative memory is a more difficult empirical question (Nachman and Stern, 1984). It is important to note that while we assume clinically that young children do have the capacity to evoke a memory of the other long before they can describe a memory in words, the empirical evidence for this is unclear.

infants respond with a greater specificity and directedness to their social world, a circumstance that speaks to the increasing fidelity of their mental representations of others and a developing sense of self as agent. The infant becomes the active initiator of more and more communicative exchanges, which also become more specific and differentiated (Bullowa, 1979). The infant draws his mother's attention to a situation—e.g., "joint attention" (Bruner, 1975)—and she in turn provides the contextual meaning for the situation and for the infant's actions. Through their joint efforts, the infant learns to use his feelings and actions to engage others (Shotter and Gregory, 1976) not just for comfort and care but now for play and shared communications. During this time, infants delightedly respond to and sometimes seek out disappearing games such as peek-a-boo that enact with shared pretense the brief comings and goings of the other. The ability to tolerate such games and even to seek them out with pleasure precedes (and is a necessary precondition for) the capacity to create similar situations in thought, that is, to *imagine* the comings and goings of another. Also, the infant's pleasure with such games contrasted to his distress with actual separations during this period (see below) suggests that there is a rudimentary sense of pretense, that he "knows" mother is really there and both parties "know" the external reality. Being able to engage another in a playful context, or more accurately, to pretend to alter the external conditions is another precondition for imagination in which reality is playfully altered in thought.

Another transition in the infant's concept of self and other evident in the latter half of the second year is the infant's looking to parents for affective guidance in situations of uncertainty or novelty (e.g., social referencing; see Sorce et al., 1985). Parents' affective responses to such bids do alter the infant's exploratory behaviors. When their mothers intentionally display negative affective expressions, 12-month-old infants are less friendly to strangers (Feinman and Lewis, 1983), and inhibit playing with specific, novel toys (Hornik et al., 1987). Conversely, positive affective signals from the parent facilitate and encourage exploration of novel objects, people, or situations (Feinman and Lewis, 1983; Gunnar and Stone, 1984; Hornik et al., 1987).

Social referencing suggests minimally that the infant has developed a sense that information from the parent has meaning for him vis-à-vis his own activities or feelings in the face of novel situations and persons. The infant's social referencing activities engage the parent in a shared experience based on both parties' assumption that one understands at least in part the other's request. Assuming that the feelings of others have meaning vis-à-vis one's own behaviors is a step toward differentiation of self and other and is essential for later imaginative activity in which the child imagines how others might respond to him. Later stages in neurocognitive maturation enhance the child's ability to conceptualize others' feelings and beliefs (see below), but social referencing is the first evidence that the child actively seeks the different affective responses of others to regulate his own actions.

The differentiated meaning of the parent to the child also is seen during this period by the child's reaction to both a parent's absence and a stranger's presence. The child's dysphoric change in state (crying or angry protests) on anticipated separation and excited pleasure on reunion is evidence that the child is beginning to make at least rudimentary connections between his own feelings in relation to his parents and their actions and to understand that others are available to appreciate and care about the child's distressed states.

Situations such as the response to separation and the child's social referencing in response to novelty or uncertainty are paradigmatic for the increasing differentiation of self as agent and for the increasing need for an imaginative capacity. Not only is the child able to draw on the stored representations of early experiences with the other but now encounters himself as an active agent in engaging the other. At this point, wishes, desires, and expectations for the other are not only possible but also the beginning understanding that one possesses an inner subjective world. The self-object world has begun to fill out and move beyond the bounds of pleasurable or unpleasurable experiences or of simply regulating tension states. It has acquired the dimensions of causality and intentionality, of agency, and the infant's appreciation that other individuals have differentiated feelings is more evident. From the psychoanalytic point of view, these shifts or maturation in the definition of self are manifest in an increasingly elaborate inner world of differentiated wishes toward another. Others increasingly populate the child's internal world, and he draws on them, remembers them, and experiences differentiated feelings in response to his memories. In part, the infant's more active efforts to engage the other also are motivated by the wish to share experience with that other, whether the experience of the infant's uncertainty or his pleasure in discovery. It is the earliest form of sharing with another one's inner experiences or fantasies in the form of affects. Later with the emergence of a capacity for imagination, the child will engage others not just with affects but with the more elaborate fantasies and wishes which his capacity for imagination makes possible.

In summary, these developments in the first 18 months of life are the underlying substrate for, and beginnings of, a capacity for imagination. Once the very young child has acquired the capacity to use memory in the service of self-other differentiation, that is, to be able to evoke the memory of satisfactory past times in the other's absence, the next step is to imagine the scene as one might wish it. Imagination draws upon, but is not equivalent with, evocative memory or the creation of mental images of others. Between 24 and 36 months of age, a number of maturing neurocognitive capacities are necessary for the full integration of an imaginative capacity and for this next step to occur. At the very least, imagination requires that the child grasp the difference between the physical and the mental world and understand that thinking about something or someone is an action of mind which is different from being physically with that person or possessing the toy. To imagine is to recognize a difference between the subjective and objective worlds and to appreciate that mind, mental activities, or thoughts define a world different at least in part from sensory perception. Further, in the act of imagining another, the child not only demarcates an inner world of subjectivity that is understood to be different from the objective, veridical world, but he also creates a world in which people behave toward him because of certain feelings which he imagines them to have. In short, he not only looks to others for their affective reactions as he did in the first two years, but he now attributes beliefs and feelings to the others of his inner world. He imbues them with mental states that guide their actions toward him, and ultimately his actions toward them.

Consider the following scene. A 4-year-old boy waits for his mother to pick him up after nursery school. Though he is playing outside with several of his friends, he closely watches the sidewalk beside the playground where his mother will be walking. Maybe she will be late, who else might she be with, perhaps she is with his father, what might they be doing? He begins to imagine a story in which he sees in his mind her rushing out of the house to the car. He imagines her humming to herself in the car as she drives to the playground, he thinks about her smiling as she comes down the sidewalk and hugging him when she gets close. He thinks how good she will smell, how she will laugh and ask him about his day, maybe even race him to the car, and then they will have a very special ride home, just the two of them. Suddenly he looks up and she is there smiling just as he had imagined, and it is as if he had not been waiting even for those few minutes.

Several features of this story reflect aspects of the integration of neurocognitive and psychic processes that emerge between 24 and 48 months and are a part of the maturing capacity for imagining. For one, the story is a combination of remembered and created elements. Like the infant's evocative memory activity at moments of frustration, the boy's imagination has been brought into the service of easing his loneliness and the anxiety of his waiting. But unlike the infant, the boy does not rely solely on his memory of when his mother has come before. He adds to the story and creates images of what his mother must do in order to come for him. He is engaged in a higher order of mental activity. He brings his mother there in his mind, he holds her mentally even before he holds her physically, but he uses his imagination to delay his need for action and for physical contact with her. Second, he creates a context for his scene that is not necessarily exactly as it will happen. He imagines his mother running to the car or walking down the sidewalk. He holds a belief (e.g., a mental state) about what she will do and imagines it accordingly. Third, he imagines that his mother *wants* to come for him, to have a special time with him. She is not there at that moment, but her love and desire for her son, which he imagines, will bring her to him. He attributes to her the mental state of loving him which motivates her actions toward him. And fourth, he imagines that she leaves others with whom she also wants to be to come to him, that there are other persons in her life toward whom she also has feelings and wishes. He understands her separateness from him and fills in that separateness through the act of imagination.

The separation between the mental and physical world and the relation between action and mental states for both mother and boy are the neurocognitive underpinnings of his imaginative activity and are necessary for the creation of a full inner fantasy life that can be used for affect regulation. Only when the child has acquired a concept of mind can he "understand" that he is imagining that which he does not have. Acquiring a concept of mind is both a subtle and a crucial step in providing children the mental tools for understanding that imagination demarcates a subjective, pretend world. It is the step that heralds the beginning of the fantasy play of the oedipal-aged child (Cohen et al., 1987; Solnit, 1987) and is a necessary precondition for the child's entry into full and complex loving relationships with others through the deepening of a capacity for imagination.

UNDERSTANDING THE CONCEPT OF THE MENTAL WORLD AND MENTAL STATES

Normally functioning adults are able to distinguish between imagining a person or an action and actually being with that individual or doing the act. They understand basic mental entities such as dreams, ideas, fantasies, or mental images. When we use terms such as remembering, thinking, dreaming, feeling, wanting, believing, or imagining, we are describing mental states and concepts. Understanding that people have mental states, or more broadly, understanding the notion of mind is basic to appreciating the fundamental nature of social relatedness, i.e., people behave toward each other in ways that are interpretable on the basis of mental states such as desires, feelings, and beliefs. Such understanding eventually allows children and adults to distinguish between wishes and reality, truth and deception, intention and accident (Estes et al., 1989), and between imagining and actually experiencing.

Until recently, it was generally claimed that young children did not distinguish between the tangible, physical world and the mental world or between doing something and thinking about or imagining doing it (Broughton, 1978; Keil, 1979; Wellman and Estes, 1986). In his 1927 work on the *Child's Conception of the World,* Piaget wrote that children are unable to separate the mental from the physical and that they attribute physical properties to mental phenomena. For example, the young child places his dreams in the external world as observable entities or pictures that he sees (p. 94) and believes that thinking is equivalent to talking or enacting. The consequences of failing to distinguish the mental from the physical are minimally that the thought and that which is thought about are confused. As Piaget states, "there is confusion between the sign and the thing thought of. From this point of view, the child cannot distinguish a real house, for example, from the concept of a mental image or name of the house" (p. 55).

Imagination requires that there be a distinction between the mental and the physical; that the child create in his mental world that which is not immediately, if ever, present in his external world. If, as was claimed in classic cognitive theory, children are unable to do so until age 6 or 7, then imagination in the young child serves primarily an evocative function. Young children conjure up thoughts which serve as temporary substitutes in their play for the real entities they have at some point experienced, but they do not "know" that such thoughts are a part of the mental activity of imagining.

However, it now seems clear that between 3 and 4 years of age, children are able to distinguish the mental and physical worlds (e.g., Estes et al., 1989; Flavell et al., 1990; Wellman and Estes, 1986). They understand that there is a distinction between mental entities and the corresponding real objects and do not attribute real properties (e.g., sensory qualities or behaviors) to mental phenomena (Wellman and Estes, 1986). Young children between the ages of 3 and 4 are also able to distinguish between a real state (e.g., a boy who has a new bicycle) and a mental state (e.g., a boy who is thinking about a new bicycle). In the first case, the bicycle, whether actually physically present or not, is a physical entity in the boy's possession, whereas in the second, it is in the boy's "imagination" (remembered or fantasied) (Wellman and Estes, 1986; Estes et al., 1989). And 3- to 4-year-old children understand that while one may be able to visualize one's own thoughts, others cannot (Estes et al., 1989; Flavell et al., 1990). Mental states do exist apart from the external world.

The second level of mental operations which underlies imagination is the understanding that mental states, either one's own or those of others, guide actions. At the very least, creating a story about someone involves the mental state of desire, of wanting to interact in some way with that person—either aggressively or lovingly. From the beginning of toddlerhood onward, normal children are aware of a number of different mental states such as desires, thoughts, promises, and beliefs (Harris, 1988). Beginning around age 3 years, children also indicate that they understand the difference between mental entities such as dreams and other phenomena such as smoke, shadows, sounds that possess some of the qualities of mental states (e.g., intangibility or temporal unpredictability) (Estes et al., 1989; Wellman and Estes, 1986). The understanding that people act on their desires and wishes is apparent even before the understanding of what particular beliefs or presumed knowledge may have guided the action. For example, in explaining actions, 3-year-olds consistently cite the individual's wish (e.g., He wants the apple) even if they are unable to understand the belief behind the person's action to obtain the apple (e.g., He thinks the apple is in the red basket; thus, he looked there first) (Moses and Flavell, 1990). It may well be that the earliest evidences of a cognitive appreciation of the link between mental states and actions is the even 2-year-old's understanding that because people desire or want something, they try to get it and react differentially when their desires are not met (Wellman, 1990; Wellman and Wooley, 1990). They are either happy because of their success or disappointed and sad with their failure.

The third level of mental operations that an imaginative act involves is the understanding that beliefs as well as desires guide actions, that individuals do something because they hold to a particular belief or they think a given condition is true. For example, in the terms of an inner fantasy life, a 4-year-old child acts toward his parents in a certain way because he holds to certain beliefs (as well as desires) about how his parents will behave toward him. Conversely, he "understands," or at least feels that he understands, that his parents' actions toward him give him information about the beliefs which they hold to be true, especially those beliefs which pertain to him. He uses his appreciation of the link between actions and mental states to measure the depth of his parents' love or disapproval, their pride or disappointment.

To add yet another level of complexity, as social relationships become more sophisticated, not only must the child be able to conceive of others' mental states, but also at some point be able to judge the "correctness" of such states relative to the world as he both perceives it and believes it to be. Beliefs can be true or false, and the state of verity may be relative in time and situation or consistently true or false across all situations. The understanding of deception and intent rests in part on the ability to judge verity, and such an ability is inherently a part of the imaginative process. For example, children may imagine a situation intentionally different from the way they perceive it in order to experiment in thought with how a situation might change others' beliefs or feelings.

In their original study of children's capacity to understand the mental states of others, Wimmer and Perner (1983) argued that a child's understanding of a false belief was the most stringent test of the capacity to attribute meaning to others' action. In the case of a false belief, children must distinguish between their own (or true) belief and their awareness of another's different (false) belief and demonstrate the understanding that the other person is acting on his false belief. A series of procedures have been developed to test for such a capacity, and each involves either a displacement of an object or change in a perceivable situation. For example, the child being tested watches a marble being moved to a second basket from a basket where it was originally placed by a second child who has now left the room. When the second child returns, he or she does not know of the displacement and must believe the marble is still in its original location. The question for the child being tested is where does the second child look for the marble, i.e., where does he believe the marble is? Between 3 and 5 years of age, normal children begin to demonstrate the capacity to understand the connection between false beliefs and actions (Bartsch and Wellman, 1989; Moses and Flavell, 1990; Wimmer and Perner, 1983), that is, the second child will incorrectly look for the marble in the first basket because that is where he believes it to be. Further, they evidence the ability to take the perspective of the other, to understand, or in a sense to imagine, his state of mind even when it contradicts that which they directly perceive.

The achievement of an understanding and representational capacity that allows the young child to attribute psychic processes to others and to understand that such psychic states guide actions is a significant advance in the organization of experience and in the capacity to imagine how others are thinking and believing. Before the achievement of an appreciation of the mental states of others, the child's understanding of the motives of others toward him is not differentiated. As the child begins to understand mental states and the broader notion of mind, he is able to explain the other's emotions and attitudes and to act or feel accordingly. Similarly, an understanding of the other's mind allows the child to imagine the other's feelings toward him and to imagine how things might be were such feelings and beliefs different. At that point imagination emerges as an ego function which serves a number of psychic organizational functions for the child.

The development of an understanding of the concept of mind and mental states, and thus, of imagination, opens the way for sharing experiences with another, for talking about feeling states toward the other, and for experiencing and understanding feelings reciprocally. Understanding mental states also provides the neurocognitive substrate for fantasy play, since with a notion of the mind of the other it is possible to try on through various enactments what happens when different characters act on their desires and beliefs. Consider, for example, the 3- to 4-year-old child's imaginary companion (Lax, 1990; Nagera, 1969). The imaginary friend serves a number of functions, including providing a sense of mastery and agency (Bach, 1971), but minimally the ability to create such a companion requires both an understanding of the fundamental difference between the possessions of one's mind and physical world as well as the capacity to "play" with imagined mental states in others. Through the imaginary friend, children may also preserve some sense of that state of total satisfaction or power when through their desires, others acted as quickly and unconditionally as their imagined companion (Sperling, 1954). The imaginary friend is, in a sense, an intermediary stage in the capacity to represent the products of one's imagination. In the imagined companion, the child talks to "someone" who is separate from himself but still a part of his own mind—an intermediate step toward the capacity to live with several different views of oneself and others within one's own mind.

One further point is important to underscore about how the emergence of a capacity for imagination represents a developmental line which integrates the neurocognitive functions necessary for developing an understanding of the subjective world with the process of self-other differentiation that occurs in the first 2 years of life. The collective empirical evidence presented above suggests that the various capacities that contribute to a fully developed understanding of the mind of the other begin to appear around the second year of age. But the cognitive capacity for understanding the mind and mental states of another—or at the most rudimentary level grasping the concept of the difference between the mental and the physical world—does not abruptly turn on at age 18 to 24 months as these empirical accounts suggest (Leslie, 1987). The capacity to observe, appreciate, and react to the one's own and others' mental states, and thus to imagine, is intertwined with the emerging understanding of other persons as separate and distinct (McGinn, 1982) and in the early interactions between parent and infant (Hobson, 1991).

All interactions between parent and infant are contextualized by the mental states of the parent. These early interactions set the stage both for how the young child will use his imagination and for his recognition that the act of imagining, of creating a fantasy or even of remembering a situation as one would have liked it to be, can be inherently pleasurable and anxiety reducing. The child's ability to think about mental states is facilitated and supported by his interactions with others who respond predictably and contingently to his needs. In these early interactions, a child is surrounded by others acting on their own feelings toward him, and how he makes sense of these moments influences how he sees himself as separate from others and how he will understand mental states when he has more sophisticated neurocognitive capacities available to him.

The recognition of the importance of the other to one's own comfort and the feelings of longing for that comfort are powerful factors in the maturation of the capacity to attribute meaning to others and to imagine the other. Such is the nature of the mental state of desire and of the infant's emerging capacity to experience that desire especially for his parents. Investigators of children's understanding of mental states suggest that the understanding of the state of desire precedes understanding of all other mental states (Wellman, 1990; Wellman and Wooley, 1990). If phenomenologically true, it is likely due to the fact that desire for others defines the affective context in which the infant develops, that is, in the context of the parents' desire for him, his capacity to desire others emerges. This is another of the complementary contributions of psychoanalysis to the more cognitive concepts of the capacity to understand the nature of the mental, subjective world and to attribute meaning to others. Desire, attributing meaning to others, self-definition, and imagination are parallel, mutually dependent processes—one does occur without the others, but it is the desire for another and the capacity to experience that desire that define the motivation for imagination as well as for the development of a differentiated understanding of other minds.

A DEVELOPMENTAL LINE FOR AN IMAGINATIVE CAPACITY

A developmental line for imagination proceeds from the infant's earliest efforts to hold onto an image of mother in her absence to the 5-year-old's fantasy play that reflects his own subjective world and his understanding of the concepts of mental states and mind. When placed in this context, we may understand what are the necessary neuroperceptual and neurocognitive precursors in infancy and early childhood for an imaginative capacity to develop and how early impairments in the development of stable mental representations of others are associated with subsequent impairments in the capacity for imagining.

For example, studies of individuals with the early pervasive developmental disorders that are characterized by an impairment in relatedness and in the sense of self provide evidence for the interrelatedness of imagination, the understanding of the mental states of others, and self-other differentiation. Children who do not develop a capacity for differentiated relatedness to others similarly do not have an ability to imagine the other or to use such an imaginative process for affect regulation. For more than four decades, many clinicians including psychoanalysts have been interested in children suffering from early, severe, and persistent disturbances in the processes involved in becoming an autonomous, social individual (Kanner, 1943; Putnam et al., 1948; Rank and Macnaughton, 1950; Ritvo and Provence, 1953). The best defined group has been those children whose disturbances in social relations and communication are captured by the categorical diagnosis of autism. In addition to autistic children, however, there are many other children with severe developmental difficulties emerging during the first years of life whose symptoms and natural histories resemble those with autism but seem distinctive from autistic children in a variety of ways. Rather than the impoverished social relations shown by autistic individuals, these children show atypical social relations and have been given a variety of diagnostic labels including borderline, atypical development, or, most recently, multiplex developmental disorder (Cohen et al., 1986, 1992; Dahl et al., 1986).

Clinically, children with early disorders of social relatedness seem unable to "metabolize" the affective and caring input of others. Ordinary events are perplexing because these children do not understand what they are feeling or how their own behaviors make others feel.

There is a profound failure in the use of imagination for anxiety regulation and for developing relationships with others, and their inner worlds appear fragmented by anxiety and a pervasive sense of tension. While the thought content, which those individuals with the capacity for language may describe, often has many of the characteristics of a fantasy creation, the products of their imagination are frequently as terrifying as they are richly complex. For example, they may wonder if their dreams had actually taken place or imagine violent stories of bodily harm which they suddenly fear have really occurred (Cohen et al., 1992). It is not only the blurring of the distinction between pretend and real but also the failure to imagine others' feelings, beliefs, and wishes that marks these disorders as examples of the failure to develop an imaginative capacity that supports ongoing social differentiation. For these children, the sustained imaginary play characteristic of the oedipal phase rarely develops. Their inner worlds remain more fragmented and far less integrated around fantasies and wishes about others. Further, the concepts of mind which we outlined above that are clearly in place by age 3 or 4 years remain perplexing for children with early impairments in social relatedness. Evidence from studies of autistic individuals is suggestive of a deficit in how children with disorders of early social development conceptualize other minds (Baron-Cohen, 1989, 1991a, 1991b; Baron-Cohen et al., 1985; Perner et al., 1989).

These disorders are relevant to child psychoanalysis inasmuch as they highlight what must be in place for a child's imagination to come into the service of psychic structure building and revision. In order for a child's play to represent his thoughts, feelings, and fantasies about others in his world, there must first be the capacity to appreciate and understand that those others have differentiated feelings and beliefs toward him. Fantasy or imagination without a sense of, and desire for, the other as a being also with desires and beliefs may serve only to blur the distinctions between the subjective and objective world and, at the very least, does not facilitate development toward more mature levels of social relatedness or toward the ability to share experiences with others.

The relation between an integrated capacity for imagination and adaptive development is particularly evident in those children who are able to create rich and complex inner worlds despite their external experiences. Children from socially impoverished or disorganized environments or those experiencing early traumatic events who are nevertheless able to build up a richly sustaining world of internal objects show how a capacity to imagine takes as substrate the child's wishes and desires even in the absence of external gratification to create the idealized objects of inner world. For children whose early experiences do not necessarily provide them the experiential, external raw material for creating through imagination an enduring inner world, the capacity to understand the mental states of oneself and others is critical. When the external world is impoverished, the beliefs and feelings of the others of the inner world become sustaining. The idealized mother, the family romance, even the wishful daydream come out of the capacity to imagine others' feelings and beliefs which, once possible, relies only partially on memories and percepts and is fueled by instinctual life. Once in place, an imaginative capacity allows the child (and adult) to populate his or her own mind with objects who then influence conscious life and perception and permits him to be in the company of others even when externally alone. In this way, imagination is developmentally adaptive, growth promoting, and allows children and adults to be alone without being incapacitated by loneliness. Conversely, it is exactly this ability to create through imagination an inner world populated by others that permits the child to be separate and alone even in the company of others, for through his imaginary inner world he is never really alone and can thus remain a separate individual (Winnicott, 1958).

Recognizing that an understanding of mind and of mental states is fundamental to the imaginative process and to the ability to use imagination adaptively also helps us understand what is functionally required for the child involved in the analytic process and raises a number of empirical issues. There is an implied, but necessary, understanding between child and analyst that the play in which they are jointly engaged through its imaginative activity conveys the child's desires and beliefs about his own world. Such understanding makes interpretive activity possible. Indeed, it is often when fantasy is not produced by an integrated imaginative capacity that it seems least communicative and most cut off from the child's world of relationships. In the child's acceptance of imagination as a communicative process, he understands that the analyst also "knows" that what the child is presenting is a product of mind. And just to be sure the lines are clear to all participants, young children commonly begin their play with context-demarcating statements such as "let's pretend" or "not really." How, or if, imagination contributes to observable psychic change in an analysis and how the imaginative process becomes involved in self-awareness and self-reflection are serious questions for clinical analytic study. But at the very least the capacity for imagination becomes linked to reflecting upon one's own wishes and beliefs since the child is in the company of another who reflects back to him in the language of mind and mental states what the child says in his imaginative play.

SUMMARY

The capacity for imagination represents a synthetic ego function that emerges through the integration of several neurocognitive capacities into one mental activity which results in a psychic product (e.g., fantasy) that serves a psychological function (e.g., affect regulation). The capacity for imagination develops in tandem with the child's increasing differentiation and separation from others and provides a way for the child to be a separate individual while at the same time creating an inner world filled with others. The process of imagination is distinctly different from memory inasmuch as imagination creates the object world as one wishes it to be. Albeit part of the imagined situation or person is based on previous experience, but the imaginative process extends and revises that experience. The imaginative process is given full shape and depth with the ability to understand the nature of the subjective world and the nature of other's and one's own mental states. With the achievement of an understanding of mental states, of the relation between mind and action, and, hence, the emergence of an imaginative capacity, the child has opened to him a vastly enlarged world not only for fantasy but also for deepened relationships with others.

BIBLIOGRAPHY

ASTINGTON, J. W., HARRIS, P. L., & OLSON, D. R. (1988). *Developing Theories of Mind.* Cambridge: Cambridge Univ. Press.

BACH, S. (1971). Notes on some imaginary companions. *Psychoanal. Study Child,* 25:159–171.

BANKS, M. S. & SALAPATEK, P. (1983). Infant visual perception. In *Infancy and Developmental Psychobiology,* ed. M. M. Haith & J. J. Campos. New York: Wiley, pp. 435–572.

BARON-COHEN, S. (1989). The autistic child's theory of mind. *J. Child Psychol. Psychiat.,* 30:285–298.

——— (1991a). Precursors to a theory of mind. In *Natural Theories of Mind,* ed. A. Whiten. Oxford: Basil Blackwell.

——— (1991b). Do people with autism understand what causes emotion? *Child Develpm.,* 62:385–395.

——— LESLIE, A. M., & FRITH, U. (1985). Does the autistic child have a "theory of mind"? *Cognition,* 21:37–46.

BARTSCH, K. & WELLMAN, H. (1989). Young children's attribution of action to beliefs and desires. *Child Develpm.*, 60:946–964.

BERES, D. (1960a). The psychoanalytic psychology of imagination. *J. Amer. Psychoanal. Assn.*, 8:252–269.

—— (1960b). Imagination and reality. *Int. J. Psychoanal.*, 41:327–334.

BROUGHTON, J. (1978). Development of concepts of self, mind, reality, and knowledge. In *New Directions for Child Development*, ed. W. Damon. San Francisco: Jossey-Bass, pp. 75–100.

BRUNER, J. (1975). The ontogenesis of speech acts. *J. Child Language*, 2:1–19.

BULLOWA, M., ed. (1979). *Before Speech*. Cambridge: Cambridge Univ. Press.

COHEN, D. J., MARANS, S., DAHL, K., MARANS, W., & LEWIS, M. (1987). Analytic discussions with oedipal children. *Psychoanal. Study Child*, 42:59–84.

—— PAUL, R., & VOLKMAR, F. R. (1986). Issues in the classification of pervasive developmental disorders. In *Handbook of Autism and Pervasive Developmental Disorders*, ed. D. J. Cohen & A. Donnellan. New York: Wiley, pp. 20–40.

—— TOWBIN, K., MAYES, L. C., & VOLKMAR, F. V. (1992). Precursors, emergence, and continuity of the self. In *Developmental Follow-up*, ed. S. L. Friedman & H. C. Haywood (in press).

DAHL, E. K., COHEN, D. J., & PROVENCE, S. (1986). Clinical and multivariate approaches to nosology of pervasive developmental disorders. *J. Amer. Acad. Child Psychiat.*, 25:170–180.

ESTES, D., WELLMAN, H. M., & WOOLEY, J. D. (1989). Children's understanding of mental phenomena. In *Advances in Child Development and Behavior*, ed. H. Reese. New York: Academic Press, vol. 22, pp. 41–87.

FEINMAN, S. & LEWIS, M. (1983). Social referencing at ten months. *Child Develpm.*, 54:878–887.

FLAVEL, J. H., FLAVEL, E. R., FREEN, F. L., & MOSES, L. J. (1990). Young children's understanding of fact beliefs versus value beliefs. *Child Develpm.*, 61:915–928.

FRAIBERG, S. & ADELSON, E. (1973). Self-representation in language play. *Psychoanal. Q.*, 42:539–562.

FREUD, A. (1965). *Normality and Pathology in Childhood*. New York: Int. Univ. Press.

—— (1973). A psychoanalytic view of developmental psychopathology. *Writings*, 8:57–74.

FREUD, S. (1920). Beyond the pleasure principle. *S.E.*, 18:3–64.

GLARE, P. G. W., ed. (1982). *Oxford Latin Dictionary*. Oxford: Clarendon Press, p. 831.

GUNNAR, M. R. & STONE, C. (1984). The effects of positive maternal affect on infant responses to pleasant, ambiguous, and fear-provoking toys. *Child Develpm.*, 55:1231–1236.

HAITH, M., BERGMAN, T., & MOORE, M. J. (1977). Eye contact and face scanning in early infancy. *Science*, 198:853–855.

HARRIS, P. (1988). *Children and Emotion*. Oxford: Basil Blackwell.

HOBSON, R. P. (1991). Against the theory of 'Theory of Mind.' *Brit. J. Develpm. Psychol.*, 9:33–51.

HORNIK, R., RISENHOOVER, N., & GUNNAR, M. (1987). The effects of maternal positive, neutral, and negative affective communications on infant responses to new toys. *Child Develpm.*, 58:937–944.

KANNER, L. (1943). Autistic disturbances of affective contact. *Nerv. Child*, 2:217–250.

KEIL, F. C. (1979). *Semantic and Conceptual Development.* Cambridge, Mass.: Harvard Univ. Press.

KESSEN, W., LEVINE, J., & WENDRICH, A. (1979). The imitation of pitch in infants. *Infant Behav. Develpm.*, 2:93–100.

LAX, R. F. (1990). An imaginary brother. *Psychoanal. Study Child*, 45:257–272.

LEE, H. B. (1949). Creative imagination. *Psychoanal. Q.*, 18:351–360.

LESLIE, A. M. (1987). Pretense and representation. *Psychol. Rev.*, 94:412–426.

LEWIS, M. & GOLDBERG, S. (1969). Perceptual-cognitive development in infancy. *Merrill-Palmer Q.*, 15:81–100.

LOEWALD, H. W. (1972). Perspectives on memory. In *Papers on Psychoanalysis*, New Haven: Yale Univ. Press, pp. 148–173.

———— (1977). Instinct theory, object relations, and psychic structure formation. Ibid., pp. 207–218.

McGINN, C. (1982). *The Character of Mind.* Oxford: Oxford Univ. Press.

MAHLER, M. S. (1968). *On Human Symbiosis and the Vicissitudes of Individuation.* New York: Int. Univ. Press.

———— (1971). A study of the separation-individuation process. *Psychoanal. Study Child*, 26:403–424.

———— (1974). Symbiosis and individuation. *Psychoanal. Study Child*, 29:89–106.

———— PINE, F., & BERGMAN, A. (1975). *The Psychological Birth of the Human Infant.* New York: Basic Books.

MARANS, S., MAYES, L. C., CICCHETTI, D., DAHL, K., et al. (1991). The child psychoanalytic play interview. *J. Amer. Psychoanal. Assn.*, 39:1015–1036.

MAYES, L. C. & COHEN, D. J. (1993). The role of constitution in psychoanalysis. In *Concepts in Psychoanalysis*, ed. B. E. Moore. New Haven: Yale Univ. Press (in press).

MOSES, L. J. & FLAVELL, J. H. (1990). Inferring false beliefs from actions and reactions. *Child Develpm.*, 61:929–945.

NACHMAN, P. A. & STERN, D. A. (1984). Affect retrieval. In *Frontiers in Infant Psychiatry*, ed. J. D. Call, E. Galenson, & R. Tyson. New York: Basic Books, vol. 2, pp. 95–100.

NAGERA, H. (1969). The imaginary companion. *Psychoanal. Study Child*, 24:165–196.

NELSON, C. A. (1987). The recognition of facial expressions in the first two years of life. *Child Develpm.*, 58:889–909.

Oxford English Dictionary (1989). Oxford: Clarendon Press.

PERNER, J., FRITH, U., LESLIE, A. M., & LEEKAM, S. (1989). Exploration of the autistic child's theory of mind, knowledge, belief, and communication. *Child Develpm.*, 60:689–700.

PIAGET, J. (1927). *The Child's Conception of the World.* New York: Harcourt Brace, 1929.

—— (1937). *The Construction of Reality in the Child.* New York: Basic Books, 1954.

PUTNAM, M. G., RANK, B., PAVENSTEDT, E., ANDERSON, I. N., & RAWSON, I. (1948). Roundtable 1947: Case study of an atypical two and a half year old. *Amer. J. Orthopsychiat.*, 18:1–30.

RANK, B. & MACNAUGHTON, D. (1950). A clinical contribution to early ego development. *Psychoanal. Study Child*, 5:53–65.

RITVO, S. & PROVENCE, S. (1953). Form perception and imitation in some autistic children. *Psychoanal. Study Child*, 8:155–161.

—— & SOLNIT, A. J. (1958). Influences of early mother-child interaction on identification processes. *Psychoanal. Study Child*, 13:64–85.

ROSEN, V. H. (1960). Imagination in the analytic process. *J. Amer. Psychoanal. Assn.*, 8:229–251.

ROVEE-COLLIER, C. K. (1987). Learning and memory in infancy. In *Handbook of Infant Development*, ed. J. D. Osofsky. New York: Wiley, pp. 98–148.

—— & FAGAN, J. W. (1981). The retrieval of memory in early infancy. In *Advances in Infancy Research*, ed. L. P. Lipsitt. Norwood, N.J.: Ablex, vol. 1, pp. 226–254.

—— SULLIVAN, M. W., ENRIGHT, M., et al. (1980). Reactivation of infant memory. *Science*, 208:1159–1161.

SHOTTER, J. & GREGORY, S. (1976). On first gaining the idea of oneself as a person. In *Life Sentences*, ed. R. Harre. New York: Wiley.

SOLNIT, A. J. (1987). A psychoanalytic view of play. *Psychoanal. Study Child*, 42:205–219.

SORCE, J., EMDE, R. N., CAMPOS, J., & KLINNERT, M. (1985). Maternal emotional signaling. *Develpm. Psychol.*, 21:195–200.

SPERLING, O. E. (1954). An imaginary companion, representing a prestage of the superego. *Psychoanal. Study Child*, 9:252–258.

UNGERER, J., BRODY, I., ZELAZO, P. (1978). Long-term memory for speech in 2- to 4-week old infants. *Infant Behav. Develpm.*, 1:177–186.

WALKER, A. S. (1982). Intermodal perception of expressive behaviors by human infants. *J. Exp. Child Psychol.*, 33:514–535.

WEIL, A. P. (1970). The basic core. *Psychoanal. Study Child*, 25:442–460.

WELLMAN, H. M. (1988). First steps in the child's theorizing about the mind. In *Developing Theories of Mind*, ed. J. Astington, P. Harris, & D. Olson. Cambridge: Cambridge Univ. Press, pp. 64–92.

—— (1990). *The Child's Theory of Mind.* Cambridge, Mass.: MIT Press.

—— & ESTES, D. (1986). Early understanding of mental entities. *Child Develpm.*, 57:910–923.

——— & Wooley, J. D. (1990). From simple desires to ordinary beliefs. *Cognition*, 35:245–275.

Wimmer, H. & Perner, J. (1983). Beliefs about beliefs. *Cognition*, 13:103–128.

Winnicott, D. W. (1958). The capacity to be alone. *Int. J. Psychoanal.*, 39:416–420.

Dreams

A Developmental and Longitudinal Perspective

EUGENE J. MAHON, M.D.

In young children's dreams the infantile wish appears almost un-disguised. Freud used this prototypical expression and representation of the infantile wish in a child's dream to bolster his conviction that the infantile wish was at the genetic root of adults' dreams as well. As development proceeds, a child's dream grows in disguise and complexity. This study of one analysand's dreams at age 5, 13, and 20 addresses the complexity from a longitudinal point of view and attempts to track the infantile wish through all of its developmental vicissitudes and disguises.

WHAT CAN A 5-YEAR-OLD'S DREAM, A 13-YEAR-OLD'S DREAM, AND A 20-year-old's dream tell us about developmental aspects of mental life if the dreamer in all three instances is the same person? This question came to mind recently when an old patient who had been a child analysand from age 5 to 10 returned at 13 and 20 for brief consultations about academic and other matters.

If a dream is the disguised fulfillment of an infantile wish, would dreams from different developmental phases give us an evolutionary perspective of desire and disguise that would deepen our understanding of the adult dreaming process? Such questions, easier to pose than to address, will nevertheless provide a focus as I examine the many currents of analytic data involved in any longitudinal investigation. I will begin by presenting the anamnesis and the three dreams and will

Faculty (child analysis and adult analysis) at Columbia University Psychoanalytic Center for Training and Research; assistant clinical professor of psychiatry, College of Physicians and Surgeons, Columbia University, New York.

then try to describe the analytic and postanalytic contexts that the three dreams emerged from.

THE THREE DREAMS

The three dreams, manifest content only, are presented first with anamnestic, psychoanalytic, and developmental contexts to follow.

The First Dream (age 5)
There was an octopus. As big as the Empire State building. I had a stick. It [the octopus] swallowed me. I was fighting it. It spat me out.

The Second Dream (age 13)
I am running in the woods. Snakes appear. They come close to my face. I run and run. There are other children younger than me playing nearby. I try to make the snakes go in their direction.

The Third Dream (age 20)
I am in a Batmobile. Batman is driving. I'm in the back seat. The Batmobile is not all it's cracked up to be. We are trying to chase some bad guys. We are slow to pull out of the garage in pursuit because we have to make several broken "U" turns just to get out of the driveway. Finally we get going. I take the wheel. Eventually we catch up with the bad guys. We follow them over a desert and give chase round and round an oval.

CLINICAL MATERIAL

THE ANAMNESIS

Alexander's[1] parents sought help for their 4 ½-year-old for a variety of symptoms, some of which they had noticed, some brought to their attention by the nursery school. The parents were alarmed by his boastfulness, boisterousness, lying, provocativeness; the school was alarmed by his unruliness and hyperactivity: he seemed to wear his castration anxiety on his sleeve, grabbing at the penises of other children as if to acquire more of what he feared to lose. At nap time while others slept or at least rested, he needed to be on the go, activity his only resource it seemed against the pressure of anxiety.

In the playroom for the initial consultations, his words, deeds, drawings, and play began to reveal the seething unconscious energies that lay behind all of his symptomatic acts. He could be provocative scatologically one minute, presenting his anus in mock submission to

---

1. The fictitious name Alexander comes to mind because the wish to be "great" made for caricature rather than character as personality and development proceeded.

the "baboon" who was "interviewing" him; another minute he could be telling a story and illustrating it coherently and cooperatively. If there was a desire to shock and provoke, there was also a clear wish to communicate which made the prospects of induction into analysis slightly less daunting. His initial stories and illustrations describe small animals who leave home and have lots of adventures with huge adversaries. They usually have two psychological escape routes—the oral or the phallic. They eat up the universe or they try to become as big as it. Poignantly the ant hero will make his way to the top of the Empire State building, a preposterous King Kong mask bravely covering the terror of the little endangered face.

Here is a story edited slightly which prefigures much of his analysis and gives a good sense of the 4 ½-year-old, his terrors and his defenses, his hopes and desperations.

> Once upon a time there was a bunny. He always wanted to go away from his father and mother. He had to go to the hospital because he was a bad bunny and a gorilla ate his tail off. A great bull came running by his house and he, the little bunny, wanted to teach the bull how to hop on two feet and act like a rabbit. He ate orange carrots and turned orange. Then he discovered if he ate clear carrots, he would turn purple. Then the little bunny played hide and seek with a dinosaur. Then he jumped from the top of a tree after eating a whole bunch of leaves. He discovered he could fly instead of hopping. The very next day he discovered he could never ever ever land from his flying. And then he discovered that there was a boat down in the sea and he flew over to the ship and they pulled him down, but he flew up again and then he stopped flying with his wings and then he dropped down into the ship. So the next day he discovered that the word Alex was spelled 200 years ago Fred and the very very very next day in 1966 he discovered Alex was spelled Alex. Then the very next day he wanted to eat all the bucktooth rabbits that were smaller than his mother and father and him. He wanted to eat every single thing in the whole country of New York, so that day he wanted to eat every word that wouldn't make sense, so he got so impressed at talking that he did not want to talk anymore. So he never ever ever came back home to his family.

The story is rich in dynamic meanings, so much so that the subsequent 5 years of analysis could be thought of as a series of associations to the profound themes raised in a seemingly light-hearted manner behind the masks of fiction. Obviously a full exploration of all the psychodynamic threads that informed this story and weaved their way into the psychoanalysis would go beyond the limits of the current inquiry which aims at outlining the anamnestic setting that leads to the first of the three dreams under scrutiny. The story is "convenient"

from an anamnestic point of view since it paints such a vivid picture of a
young mind's struggles with size, castration, impulses (flying), control
(the ship), identity (Alex, Fred), identification (could the bunny learn
to run like the bull, could the bull learn to hop like the bunny?), etc. As
an opening statement about the analytic situation and whether it is safe
to bring words and play and dreams to it, the child's ambivalence seems
palpable. One interpretation of the text could be constructed or de-
constructed as follows: "If I leave home, I may never return. If I eat,
there may be consequences. If I fly, I may not be able to return to earth,
but I do hope the ship will be able to ground me. If I lose my name
[Alex, Fred], I hope the regression is not permanent. I know I can
learn something from the bull, but maybe a bull can learn something
from me, too. Identification is not intimidation after all. There's love
and reciprocity in it too, or else it's propaganda and indoctrination. If
words don't make sense, I want to be able to eat them. Intellect that
ignores appetite makes no sense to children."

THE FIRST DREAM

The first dream was reported in the seventh analytic session. In the
preceding sessions Alex had talked and played, presenting himself
basically as brash and defensive on the one hand and open and communicative on the other. Digging to the bottom of the sandbox, he
commented, "I want to get to the bottom of things." He also hoped that
the analyst would give him "the greatest memory in the world." All the
meanings of this request would slowly emerge later in the analysis. He
would build tall structures out of blocks of wood, reveling in the spatial
majesty and in the destructive glee of toppling and dismantling. He
would write his name on the blackboard and chalk in the number of
times he had seen me, a somewhat arrogant "pupil" seizing as much
control as possible from the "teacher" analyst.

I will present session seven in its entirety so that the dream and its
context are fully exposed.

Alex entered the playroom, noticed that the block design from the
previous session was not exactly as he had left it, and complained,
"Why didn't you leave them up?"

ANALYST: You're angry that things are not exactly as you left them?
[Pause] Could we make it again?

ALEX: No.

ANALYST: Oh?

ALEX: I can't remember. The mouse who takes things from the back
of my head to the front . . . I can't get him to work now.

ANALYST: He's angry, too! He'd like things to stay in their place forever.

ALEX: Not forever. For one day!

ANALYST: [Touché—not voiced.]

ALEX: I'll make a bed. Pee Pee Doo Doo Wee Wee.

ANALYST: That's the way you talked when you were . . . how old?

ALEX: Three. I did peepee in bed last night.

ANALYST: Oh? How come?

ALEX: I wanted to.

ANALYST: Oh?

ALEX: To get Mommy to clean the sheet.

ANALYST: Oh, you get back at Mom that way?

ALEX: Yeah.

ANALYST: How did she get to you?

ALEX: She spanked me.

Alex suddenly climbed on the block shelves. I moved instinctively to protect him should he fall (the shelves were "tall" given the size of the child).

ALEX: Why did you move?

ANALYST: To make sure you were safely up.

ALEX: [Independently] I'm up now.

From his perch on the shelf he erased his name and the number of sessions he had seen me from the blackboard, saying good-bye Alex to his name as it disappeared and began to draw. "I want to draw a dog," he said, but instead he drew a dinosaur, a brontosaurus, and the bird dinosaur, saying, "The bird can eat the brontosaurus but not the tyrannosaur." Then he drew a lady snake and snake eggs and then a star, saying a star was a part of the night, "I don't like night."

ANALYST: Why not? Is it the dreams?

ALEX: Yes.

ANALYST: Last night?

ALEX: Yes.

ANALYST: What about?

Alex tells the following dream:

There was an octopus. As big as the Empire State building. I had a stick. It swallowed me. I was fighting it. It spat me out.

ANALYST: It sounds scary.

ALEX: I had another dream about an octopus in a spook house.

ANALYST: What's a spook house?

ALEX: I don't know.

ANALYST: Sounds scary, too. Was it?

ALEX: Yeah.

ANALYST: Where do you think those dreams came from? Were you worried about something maybe?

ALEX: Yeah, an accident.

ANALYST: Oh?

ALEX: Grandfather died. [This turns out to be a lie, but I am unaware of this at the time.]

ANALYST: Oh, I'm sorry to hear that. You miss him?

ALEX: Yeah and my uncle Abe.

Alex went to a drawer, extracted a hammer, and started to make a plane, cars, and a motorbike tinkering away like a mechanic.

ANALYST: It feels good and strong to make things, especially when talking about scary dreams.

ALEX: [Went to the sandbox.] Let's bury grandfather.

He spilled a lot of sand in the process and I asked him to try not to, even if he was showing his feelings that way.

ALEX: I like to spill the sand.

ANALYST: Yes, you told me you like to mess and have someone else clean it up. Like a baby, I guess?

ALEX: I'd like to be a baby.

ANALYST: Oh? How come?

ALEX: I wouldn't have to eat roast beef and squash.

ANALYST: Oh? What would you prefer?

ALEX: "Sol."

ANALYST: What's that?

ALEX: Soft baby food. I still like it.

[It's time to stop.]

ANALYST: Let's stop here.

ALEX: Oh, I'll take the airplane.

ANALYST: Can you leave it so we can use it again when we need to?

ALEX: Oh, but I want to paint it. [And he runs off with it.]

I shall postpone commentary on the first dream at this point and attempt instead to give a synopsis of the subsequent psychoanalysis and developmental progressions so that the second and third dreams also will have a context.

A SYNOPSIS OF THE PSYCHOANALYSIS

The analysis brings to mind Ernest Jones's conviction that pathology of the phallic phase of development is intimately related to earlier disappointments at the breast. In other words, a phallus that "protests too much about its captivating seductiveness" is really a mouth in disguise, a mouth that did not possess the nipple adequately and, feeling dispossessed in one erotogenic zone, tries to make up for it in another. Too much phallic pride, in other words, is a sign of oral incompetence. What has just been stated in a libidinal, zonal language could be restated in structural or object relational terminology, but shorthand in a synopsis is permissible, if not mandatory.

Using the first dream as a guide to the initial transference communications, I believe Alex implied that his needs were urgent and even octopoid and that the little stick of his defenses might not be up to the task of taming so primitive an instinctual source unless an ally could be found in the analytic situation. There were many other "meanings" of the first dream, one could argue, but this particular transferential meaning highlighted the opening phase of analytic work and was being accentuated for that reason.

Two themes from the first year of analytic work seemed to grow like offshoots not only of the first dream but also of the story outlined in the anamnesis above. One theme developed into a play sequence where the analyst was Dr. Doolittle, the block-shelf which had wheels and could therefore "voyage" around the playroom becoming a ship for Alexander and Dr. Doolittle to explore wild territories and "tame" all the wild animals. The other "theme" was closely related to this analytic investigation of Alexander's instincts and his struggles with control and compromise, adaptive expression, and symptomatic action. In this theme the ship was actually compared to the analytic situation itself in a remarkable piece of insight for such a young child. When a ship was lost at sea and buffeted by storms but still managed to make it home safely to port, Alex interrupted the play for a moment and compared the work of analysis and the relationship he had with me to a voyage and a return trip to the safety and security of the analytic "port," so to speak. If Alex wished to fly and spit and swallow, he also hoped that there was a "vessel" somewhere that could contain him, hold him. In the final analysis, an analysand learned that the vessel was, of course, nothing other than one's own mind and its structures and instincts operating in that ironic harmony called conflict and compromise. In the course of the analytic journey one did not always feel that the mind was one's own as it leaned so desperately and so dependently into the deep paradox of transference that regressed it the better to strengthen it. At times the vessel seemed hopelessly lost at sea, and contact with another "human" vessel was mandatory if safe harbor was ever to be reached.

These two images of "taming" and "vessel" are not the only generative metaphors of a lengthy analysis, but they have an organizational focus that can be exploited in the interest of making a long analytic story short.

If Alex was frightened as well as exhilarated by forces that could dispatch analytic grandfathers—not to mention extra-analytic ones even closer to home—his skills at taming and vessel building were beginning to give him the confidence needed to pursue his analytic voyages no matter where they led to. In child analysis, vessel building is not merely a metaphoric image: Alex actually carved boats out of wood, their meanings as variable as their contexts. For instance, a boat that he carved early in the analysis had quite a different meaning from the boat he carved at the end of the analysis. The first boat was carved in a context of exploration which was complex and painful. The termination boat was more of a statement about journey's end than an exploration of any new unconscious territories. The first boat was called "The Catch Up" and the termination boat could have been called "The Letting Go" but was, as will be disclosed later, given a more personal hieroglyphic code name as befits latency and all its developmental intrigue. "The Catch Up" was carved while Alexander was reviewing some complicated affects about a substitute caretaker Rosa, who left abruptly when Alexander was 3, promising to return but never keeping the promise. In a poignant moment when Alexander's phallic shield was lowered a little, he admitted that he took her at her word and counted the days to no avail. The loss of Rosa was made more traumatic by the even earlier emotional loss of mother (the mother had confided in me that it was not in her nature to be close to Alex at bedtime, an emotional legacy that she inherited via the constricted affects of her own mother). If the little bunny left home never to return, it was emotional retaliation, not first strike, it seemed in Alexander's Talionic morality. But "The Catch Up" seemed to be an attempt to go beyond repetition compulsion and heal developmental wounds, not just rub them. Alex was trying to break a vicious cycle of neurosis in the mutative process of analysis: he was trying to replace neurotic convictions that warned (a) that loss of the object and its love would always cramp his phallic style; (b) that phallic disguise could always hide a broken heart (c) with the new conviction that would assure him that his libidinal expressiveness need not lead to such tragic consequences.

This new conviction was the offspring of several years of psychoanalytic working through. Highlights of this process will give the gist if not the bulk of the analytic work over a few years. The latency years of the analysis were conducted in the typical climate of schoolboy psychology and defensiveness: an obsession with sports and other games hid the unconscious life of the mind with a developmental expertise that

was impressive and at times impenetrable. However, in "scientific experiments" that were conducted by mixing "detergents" and other
objects from every "primal" crevice of my office, affects were discussed
and compared and contrasted according to their "properties" of speed
or density. Anger, for instance, was an extremely "fast" affect, whereas
sadness was extremely "slow." Out of this alchemy of affects came the
admission that the grief in the wake of Rosa's rejection was "slow" to
leave him, the sadness lasting many months as he counted the days.
Even the "baseball" resistance would occasionally surrender an unconscious meaning or two. Once in the middle of a baseball game with me,
Alex complained that he had to interrupt the game to go to the
bathroom, a deprivation that would not be necessary if the bathroom
and the playroom were all one room instead of being separated. When
I commented how much Alex hated "separations" and "interruptions," Alex said, "When the doodie goes out, the poopie goes up."
Analysis of this cryptic comment in the ensuing months and years
made it clear that what was said casually had quite deep levels of unconscious meaning. Since doodie was Alex's infantile word for feces and
poopie his word for penis, his comment was a variation on Freud's
penis = feces equation. In Alex's psychological calculus, when the
doodie goes out the poopie goes up meant: when you are faced with
loss, you can cover your ass with an erect penis. The phallic boast
attempts to hide the anal loss or the more deeply repressed oral loss.
Penis = feces = breast, to complete Freud's equation.

As Alex began to make remarkable progress on all fronts (social,
academic, domestic, athletic) and as termination began to make an
impression on the clinical process, the baseball resistance reluctantly
yielded a few important insights. When I interpreted the flurry of
baseball resistances with a question, "Why so much baseball now that
we're thinking of bringing our work to an end?" Alex replied, "Every
baseball game has to end," proving that resistance is often an analyst's
word for his own ignorance and that the analysand was in fact working
on the termination phase in his play.

One of the final "symbols" of the analysis was the aforementioned
boat which might have been called "The Letting Go" but which was
actually given a more phase-appropriate title by an industrious 10-
year-old. Alex combined his own initials, my initials, and the numbers
of our houses and street addresses into an impressive code name. At
journey's end the boats were left behind in the playroom to be retrieved perhaps in some future nostalgic catch-up or letting go. In the
meantime, they remain among the treasured possessions of the
nostalgic analyst.

This "Letting Go" boat was carved out of wood, while many termination themes were being analyzed. Alex attempted to draw "a portrait of the analyst with a broken arm" in which his aggression toward the abandoning object could not be concealed. His anger at Rosa, his parents, his sister, and his analyst were worked over for many weeks. His fear in the face of all this aggression was that his hatred would destroy the object totally or at least the object's love for him. If he met Rosa in the street now, would he recognize her? Could he have a photograph of me to assure himself that his aggression had not destroyed all hope of ever seeing me again? Concerns such as these had to be broken into their genetic components (he felt like killing Rosa and his mother and father and feared that they would attack him or stop loving him or abandon him) before Alex could begin to realize that the past could be kept "in its place" and that the present could hold the promise of a future uncontaminated by the past.

THE SECOND DREAM

At age 13 Alex returned for a consultation about the boarding school he would be attending soon. Boarding school was at least the manifest content of a visit that had obvious latent agendas as well which could be addressed when he recounted a dream and began to work on it as if the analysis had not ended at all! (This immediacy of transference availability years after an analysis has terminated is well documented elsewhere, particularly in regard to adult analyses.) The Dream:

> *I am running in the woods. Snakes appear. They come close to my face. I run and run. There are other children younger than me playing nearby. I try to make the snakes go in their direction.*

Alex's associations were of the superficial variety at first: he had watched a TV program on snakes, which explained their presence in the dream. The younger children referred to all the children that would be left in his school after he went off to boarding school. Then Alex went a little deeper: "close to his face" meant there was something dangerous he had to face—leaving home. Perhaps he was imagining the worst about boarding school. Was he seeing it as dangerous? Was he viewing it as punishment, being sent away? Was his "badness" catching up with him? Alex seemed relieved by airing some of these worries, affects, and distortions, but the dream seemed to be "crying out" for deeper exploration. Alex was now 13 years old, had grown a lot since I had seen him three years earlier. The transformations of puberty seemed to be waging a psychological civil war with the conservative forces of latency, and a developmental nudge in the form of an interpretation seemed appropriate. "What if the snakes represent your

penis which must have grown a lot like the rest of you?" I asked somewhat humorously. "Why do you suppose you'd be sending them away
in the direction of younger children?"

Alex had no trouble getting the point. His immediate response was a
confirmation of the interpretation in the form of a complaint: "My
sister [2 years older] didn't get her period until she was 13. I've had wet
dreams and erections since 11. It's not fair." Soon the irony of his own
statement began to dawn on him. Here was the most "phallic" of boys
suddenly renouncing his penis now that he was old enough to put it to
use! This classical dilemma of the 13-year-old who finds progression
and regression equally problematic was certainly not unique to Alex,
but with five years of analysis behind him, it was easier for him to put
words to his plight and recognize the deeply ambivalent psychological
currents of his dream. Could he *face* the transformations of puberty,
could he acknowledge that his penis (snake) with its wet dreams and
erections belonged to him and need not be delegated to others? Or
would he invoke the personal myth of the deprived child whose older
sibling had it easier. Even biology was kinder to her than to him,
granting her a longer childhood while he was expelled prematurely
from the innocence of Eden by his hyperactive, precocious hormones!
As Alex began to "play" with these associations, laughing at himself a
good deal in the process, it became clear that his conflicts about sexuality, boarding school, and growing up were the "average expectables"
of developmental life and not insurmountable obstacles that were
about to derail him.

THE THIRD DREAM

Seven years passed before Alex consulted me again. By chance he had
seen me on the street and recognized me, giving lie to one of his
termination fears (his anger would destroy the relationship; I would
become unrecognizable). He was home from college working as a cam-
eraman's assistant on a movie being made not far from my office when
the chance encounter occurred (actually I was unaware of the encounter).

The manifest reason for his visit was to discuss academic performance in college which was reflecting his conflicts rather than his
potential. But several more "latent" communications quickly came to
the fore: (a) He had learned recently that Rosa's whole family had been
killed in an auto accident. He was not sure whether Rosa herself had
been killed or not. (b) A two-year relationship with a girlfriend had
ended six months earlier: new relationships seemed ambivalent, tentative. (c) It was depressing to come home. His old room was now "a

storage room." Mother still seemed obsessed with herself and domestic details rather than with the emotional nuances of his development and conflicts.

We ran out of time on the first visit. We agreed to meet again, at which time Alex began the session with the following dream.

I am in a Batmobile. Batman is driving. I'm in the back seat. The Batmobile is not all it's cracked up to be. We are trying to chase some bad guys. We are slow to pull out of the garage in pursuit because we have to make several broken "U" turns just to get out of the driveway. Finally we get going. I take the wheel. Eventually we catch up with the bad guys. We follow them over a desert and give chase round and round an oval.

Alex had a wealth of associations to this dream. He had come into my office carrying a bicycle wheel, the rest of the bicycle locked to a tree outside for safekeeping. The bicycle wheel symbolized his return home to relative dependency (in college he had a beat-up used car and much more freedom). He jokingly referred to this bicycle wheel as the "Batmobile," making it clear that vehicular symbolism was on his mind. He had a lot of fun with the idea that the Batmobile in the dream was not the magical vehicle from the recent movie but a much more down-to-earth version. The "broken U's" were emblematic of his recent academic progress which had been anything but "linear" in direction. Alex had developed a capacity for laughing at himself, quite a contrast to the sensitivity and defensive bluster of his latency years. Alex's most emotionally laden associations were reserved for comparisons between the new "catch up" vehicle (the Batmobile) and the old "catch up" of yesteryear. It was in such a nostalgic moment that Alex referred to the automobile accident that claimed the lives of Rosa's family and maybe even Rosa herself. Alex's uncertainty about the fate of Rosa seemed highly significant. While she had not been "a presence" in his life for 17 years, she had become symbolic of love, treachery, object constancy, transience—all the contrary motions of outer experience and inner psychology that left him confused at best, neurotic at worst. Rosa was no longer a disappointing object out of the past: she had become a symbol of the internalized loving objects at the core of his self-esteem—one of the lynch pins that would determine the stability of his adolescent consolidations. In this context it was very clear to Alex that the Batmobile represented himself at the crossroads of his life. Batman was a reference to the idealized mother and father (Rosa too perhaps) who had to be diminished psychologically speaking if he was to assume the responsibility for the wheel of his own life. (At this point in the hour the bicycle wheel leaning on the radiator beside Alex's chair assumed its full tragicomic significance!) "Chasing the bad guys round an oval" led to several associations: the oval referred to the shape of the baseball field, "a field of dreams" he wished to return to and abdicate all adult ambition and conflict. In fact, in another dream fragment that Alex reported, he "surrenders" an old girlfriend to a rival while he in oedipal defeat becomes preoccupied with baseball. The pursuit of the bad guys leads to the most important association of all: Alex's realization that the "bad guys" are no longer "out there" as it seemed in latency times but "within." Alex reflected on the fact that his academic progress was a very precise barometer of the state of his object relations. On reflection he could "see" that the breakup of a two-year relationship with his girlfriend had affected him academically and emotionally more than he had been willing to admit prior to the consultation.

DISCUSSION

In discussing three dreams that straddle 15 years of development, I must avoid the temptation toward synthetic zeal, lest a process that could be compared to "secondary revision" smoothes out all the rough edges and tries to portray a polished anagogic theme that covers up all the dynamic unrest and even chaos underneath. It is the beauty of the associative process that prevents the clinician from such simplemindedness and keeps a wild analyst honest. As Alex learned how to free associate, the latent meanings of the second and third dreams could be deciphered. The first dream was another matter. Associations were sparse and the kinetic mind of the child was unable to see any value in the passivities of sleep. I had to be alert to every nuance that preceded the dream and pursue it to capture the elusive meanings of it. The following is a microanalysis of the hour "frame by frame" in an attempt to interpret without the benefit of a mature free-associative process.

If a dream is also "a part of the night," this will be an attempt to light a semiotic candle in the darkness. Every noun and verb in the sketch that language tries to preserve from amnesia could be viewed as a wish. "I wish I were an octopus with eight long extensions not merely one endangered protrusion." Even the numerical advantage does not satisfy: a size dimension has to be introduced. The octopus has to be as big as the Empire State building! If this is wish fulfillment, why is the next image necessary, the poignant image of the dreamer in the reported "I had a stick." One can assume that the numerical, spatial greed that casts him in a grandiose fearless limelight one moment casts him in a consequential fearful retaliatory light an unconscious moment later. If repression claimed the latter moment, the next frame in the unconscious sequence is not censored: "I had a stick" is let stand as a defensive posture that gives the dreamer some solace even if it seems poignant to the countertransferential eyes of the much taller analyst. Images of swallowing, fighting, spitting ensue in rapid succession, the assignment of action to octopus or dreamer depending on wish and retaliation and the self-deception that octopus and dreamer are other than the 5-year-old unconscious Fellini responsible for the whole nocturnal cinematography in the first place.

My appeal for day residues of rationality that might connect the fantastic and the pedestrian, a piece of day with a piece of the night so to speak, met with further flights into the fantastic: the lie about grandfather's death, "an accident" as he calls it. Mendacity and accident are of course "associations" that attempt to remove the dreamer, now fully awake and reporting all to his analytic grandfather from the scene of the crime. "Not guilty," he seems to be proclaiming, a state of innocence belied by his subsequent play in which he attempts to "bury grandfather." The aesthetics of play seem unable to contain all the affects homicide has generated in the transference—regressions are called for in the spilling of the sand and the open admission of a desire for babyhood and the final piece of acting out, the "theft" of the airplane.

The clinical events that precede the telling of the dream can be viewed as a string of associations: the hour begins with anger at me who did not preserve the decor of the playroom as it had been at the end of the previous session. An appeal to reason (couldn't we make the same block design again?) is dismissed. He can't remember the design since "the mouse who takes things from the back of his head to the front of his head cannot be asked to work right now." One can see rudimentary psychological theory in statu nascendi in such pronouncements. The theme of the angry "mouse" is taken up again immediately in play about wetting the bed (pee pee doo doo wee wee) and taking revenge on mother in this manner. He shifts from play to drawing, saying goodbye to himself as he erases his name which he had chalked on the blackboard in the previous session. (It is alright for him *actively* to remove things from the playroom as opposed to being passively subjected to my arbitrary actions.) The drawings elaborate the theme even further. He wants to draw a dog but draws a dinosaur, a brontosaur, and the bird saurus, commenting that the bird can eat the brontosaurus but not the tyrannosaurus. He then draws eggs, snake eggs, a lady snake, then a star, saying, "A star is part of the night. I don't like night." Sensing that the analytic material is moving toward the oneiric,

I ask, "Why not? Is it the dreams?" The octopus dream follows immediately.

His commentary on his own drawings suggests that the "mouse" has graduated and is trying on the "bird" for size and contemplating his rivals: he can dispatch brontosaurus, but what about tyrannosaurus? And what about the egg-making lady snake? If the mouse roars, will an octopus swallow him? Can his small solitary stick match a rival with numerical and spatial advantage?

This microanalysis, while not devoid of some interpretive imaginings, is not replete with speculative "wildness" either. The description of the subsequent analysis tries to show how this endangered immature psyche with its octopoid instincts and stick-like ego weathered the developmental elements, not merely surviving but prevailing.

The second and third dreams stand at the entrance and exit of adolescence like sentinels of progress. Now the dreamer is equipped with a maturing free-associative process, and dream analysis becomes a joint enterprise rather than a labor of the analyst alone. In fact, if one were to highlight the differences rather than the similarities between the first dream and the later ones, two issues seem obvious but crucial: (a) the rapidly expanding free-associative abilities of the developing mind make analysis interpretive rather than wild; (b) the developmental context becomes part of the therapeutic process.

Addressing (b) first, since (a) has been alluded to already, I believe that Alex at ages 13 and 20 is keenly aware of the developmental context that informs his dreams. In fact, if one were told these three dreams without their developmental context, one would be hard pressed to guess the age of the dreamer. As the developmental context triggers the associations in the second and third dreams, it becomes clear that the transformations of puberty (Freud, 1905) and the consolidations of adolescence (Blos, 1979) are the conflictual triggers beneath the manifest architecture of these dreams. This is not to say that the infantile wish does not comprise the deepest layer of meaning in any dream but simply to add that the infantile has developmental dimensions that give a dream from each developmental phase different shapes and contours as the infantile wish weaves its way through developmental pathways. In less poetic language, in Alex's second dream the infantile wish to use his snake-penis in an oedipal context is disguised not only in the service of defense but also in the service of development. In sleep Alex appeals for a developmental respite from the inexorable transformations of puberty to give his ego a chance to catch up with his id. By displacing the sexual in the direction of the younger children, Alex's economic strategy seems to imply that as a young "imaginative" boy he can get away with murder and incest, but a young "physical" adolescent with a "transformed" pubertal body could actually commit the oedipal crime and deserve actual punishment. The infantile wish may be the same for the 5-year-old or the 13-year-old, but the transformations of puberty provide an existential context that is perhaps even more terrifying than the original prelatency context. Similarly, the Batmobile dream could be interpreted as an expression of the infantile wish to have a most impressive penis, to take the wheel from Batman, and to pursue the "incestuous" bad guys, a thinly disguised depiction of his own forbidden wishes. But it is the developmental context that brings specificity to these theoretical speculations. The oedipal wish of a 20-year-old is processed by an ego that has integrated or failed to integrate the transformations of puberty into its development. Blos (1979) has described this "adolescent passage" of the mind in great detail as id, ego, superego, and ego ideal clear a space for all the libidinal realignments and structural rearrangements that object removal calls for. It is a dramatic developmental story that can only be referred to rather than described at this juncture. For an additional insight to augment the dynamic understanding of the dream a developmental point of view is mandatory: Alex is not merely taking the wheel-penis from Batman to castrate father and make off with mother, he is contemplating a future free of parental influence, free of infantile dependence in a nonincestuous setting in which he will act out his oedipal and preoedipal ambitions and longings in a new home of his own as good if not better than his parents'. This is the oedipus complex in a new developmental key. Its implications are as rewarding and exciting and terrifying as the prelatency version of the conflict. The infantile wish has grown up, so to speak, and Alex's dreams reflect not only the source of the wish but all of its transformations.

SUMMARY

Three dreams were presented from the same dreamer covering a developmental span from prelatency to postadolescence. A child analysis of 5 years' duration separated the first dream from the two later ones. From a therapeutic point of view the most striking differential between the early dream and the later ones was the development of a more and more sophisticated free-associative process which allowed the older dreamer to be a more inquisitive ally in the psychoanalytic dialogue (Leavy, 1980). From a theoretical point of view (not meaning to imply in any way that the therapeutic and the theoretical are mutually exclusive), emphasis was placed on the idea that the infantile wish goes through profound transformations as development proceeds, making the oedipal wish of a 5-year-old, a 13-year-old, and a 20-year-old *the same* and yet profoundly different. Dream interpretation in adolescence is almost unthinkable without such developmental perspectives, lest one see only the adult sexuality in the Doras of this world and neglect the emotional sturm and drang of "object removal" (Katan, 1937). In Alex's case, three dreams from different developmental periods show how a stick, a snake, and a Batmobile reflected an original phallic preoccupation, infantile wish informing the symbolic content in each dream. However, as development transformed the infantile wish, the later dreams reflected this complexity, and dream interpretation that does not address such complexity is reductionistic in the extreme. A dream is undoubtedly the fulfillment of an infantile wish, but the infantile has developmental extensions that cannot be ignored. Such "developmental complexities" may exist throughout the life cycle passing through the prism of dream unnoticed. Longitudinal and developmental perspectives may help us not to ignore them.

BIBLIOGRAPHY

BLOS, P. (1979). *The Adolescent Passage.* New York: Int. Univ. Press.

FREUD, S. (1900). *The Interpretation of Dreams. S.E.,* 4 & 5.

———— (1905). Three essays on the theory of sexuality. *S.E.,* 7:125–243.

JONES, E. (1933). The phallic phase. *Papers on Psychoanalysis.* Boston: Beacon Press, 1961, pp. 438–457.

KATAN, A. (1937). The role of displacement in agoraphobia. *Int. J. Psychoanal.,* 32:41–50, 1951.

LEAVY, S. A. (1980). *The Psychoanalytic Dialogue.* New Haven: Yale Univ. Press.

On Feeling and Being Felt with

ERNA FURMAN

The development of feelings in early childhood is traced, with special emphasis on the mother's role during the toddler phase when she facilitates her child's transition from sensorimotoric discharge to the mental experience, ownership, and use of modulated affects. Many child analytic patients use defenses to ward off feelings, many have not even reached the developmental level of experiencing feelings. How this difficulty manifests itself, the reasons for the developmental lag, and the analytic means of helping such patients are discussed and illustrated.

WELL OVER 40 YEARS AGO, WHEN I PRESENTED THE INITIAL ANALYTIC work with my first case at Anna Freud's seminar, she focused her discussion on the contrast between the earlier need for an introductory phase and the interpretation of defenses against affects—then a recent technique—as a way of helping a child to engage in the analytic process. She attributed this helpful innovative change to the work of Bornstein. This sparked my interest in Bornstein's work and led to my lifelong appreciation of her ability to feel with her patients' most warded-off feelings, to assist them in getting in touch with them, and to use this approach, not only as an introductory device, but as the ongoing basis for the child analytic work. Her feel for Frankie's helpless littleness behind his fantasy of occupying the omnipotent throne (Bornstein, 1949), or for the obsessional Sherry's love of her father, hidden under ostensible fear and anger at him (Bornstein, 1953), are classics we are all familiar with. Yet, although we all value and use Bornstein's emphasis on feelings, the understanding of their development and role has been a bit of a child analytic stepchild. Thus, A.

From the Cleveland Center for Research in Child Development, the Hanna Perkins School, and the department of psychiatry, Case Western Reserve University School of Medicine.

The Marianne Kris Memorial Lecture, Association for Child Psychoanalysis, St. Louis.

Freud's (1962, 1963, 1965) and Nagera's (1963) diagnostic profile
work contains no section on affects. Likewise, analytic observational
studies of toddlers have not focused on the development of feelings.
Even Greenspan's (1989) recent work on early communication does
not include this aspect.

There have been some notable exceptions. Two of these have been
especially helpful to me. The first is A. Katan's (1961) deceptively brief
"Some Thoughts about the Role of Verbalization in Early Childhood,"
a classic in its own right. A. Katan stresses the importance of a mother
helping her toddler to name feelings and express them in words. She
points out that this developmental step not only channels motoric into
verbal discharge and hence behavioral control, but has a pronounced
effect on the developing functions of thinking, reality testing, and
integration. A. Katan discussed emotionally disturbed youngsters who,
unlike Bornstein's patients, whose feelings were defensively banished
from consciousness, had missed out on the developmental step of
learning to put their feelings into words. She described how, at the
Hanna Perkins Nursery School, their parents and teachers often could
belatedly help them with this step more quickly through daily educational interaction than an analyst could in individual therapy. Since
many children enter preschool without having fully accomplished this
developmental task, it is frequently a main focus of our treatment via
the parent (R. A. Furman and A. Katan, 1969; E. Furman, 1957, 1969).

R. A. Furman addressed this topic in greater detail in 1978. This is
the second of the two contributions I referred to. He used two cases to
illustrate his points. In the first case, mother and child neither verbalized affects nor could they feel in themselves or with each other.
Here the teachers started by feeling for the child, encouraging his
feelings and responding to his feeling needs, such as comforting when
they noted sadness. Gradually, "words were offered in the context of a
caring and protecting environment that wanted to meet his needs and
help him acquire mastery and control" (p. 193). In this environment
the mother, by being included, could take the steps with her child.
Having and communicating feelings became a tool for understanding
a situation and knowing what to do about it. The second case was a
treatment via the parent which, over several years, traced the later
steps of the role of the mother in helping her child to make this function an integral part of his personality. This boy already experienced
feelings, and putting them into words was a first and relatively easy
step. But he found it hard to endure intense feelings and to resign
himself to the fact that they could not always be relieved through
action, even when communicated. His mother, in turn, found it hard to

recognize that her son had feelings of his own. Even after she could acknowledge this, she still found it difficult to help him own and use them. Instead, as with a much younger child, she made it her own job, either to relieve them through helpful action or to struggle with the frustration of there being no relieving action. The boy was in kindergarten when mother and child finally succeeded in his owning and using feelings and her appreciating his doing so.

For both boys, verbalization of feelings was an important accomplishment, but only one step in a complex developmental process. In the one instance, it was first necessary to create an emotional milieu in which the caring adults appreciated feelings and responded to them with relieving actions. In the second instance, verbalization of feelings had to be followed by helping the child to endure and use them as his own, and even to forego relieving action, including verbalization, whenever this would be the appropriate way of coping, e.g., in elementary school, where being angry at a teacher is often thought but not said. In tracing the successive steps and the mother's changing role in them, R. A. Furman rightly suggested that the developmental unfolding of every ego function undergoes a similar process.

In this paper, I shall focus on what I consider the first and most crucial step in the development of feelings, namely, the sense of being felt with. I shall trace some of its beginnings in toddlerhood, then apply it to the analytic work with patients, and discuss some of its effects on personality functioning and the analytic relationship.

Honoring Marianne Kris on this occasion, I hope that this paper would have pleased her. She is well known and respected for her teaching in the area of its topic.

THE DEVELOPMENT OF FEELINGS AND THE MOTHER'S ROLE DURING THE TODDLER PHASE[1]

Whereas initially the infant responds to distress with bodily forms of discharge, in time he experiences his discomforts mentally, i.e., he feels uncomfortable. This first real feeling is always related to recognizing bodily discomfort or pain, and the baby uses it to protest, to seek and accept comfort. This major achievement is usually accomplished by the latter half of the first year and is linked to the related achievement of feeling good (Hoffer, 1950). In "On Fusion, Integration, and Feeling Good" (1985) I described the mother's role in helping her child to

---

1. This section is adapted from *Toddlers and Their Mothers* by Erna Furman, copyright Erna Furman, 1992. Reprinted by permission of International Universities Press.

experience both of these basic feelings. For the purposes of this discussion, and assuming a relatively normally endowed child, I wish to underline two of the prerequisites on the part of the mother: (1) her own ability to feel bodily good and bad; and to know, bear, and contain these feelings sufficiently so that she can use them to initiate appropriate responses; (2) the mother's ongoing libidinal investment of her infant (E. Furman, 1969). This investment has to contain sufficient narcissistic elements (the child as a part of herself) so that she is able to feel and do for him what she can feel and do for herself, i.e., recognize and gather up his diverse sensations and motoric discharges and give them affective mental form and content with a name: "That feels good," "That feels bad." At the same time, mother's investment has to contain sufficient object-libidinal elements (the child loved as a separate person) so that she can recognize and appreciate his feelings when they are different from hers and can value and support his knowing, bearing, and using his feelings (not make them her own). When all aspects of these two prerequisites are available to a "good enough" extent, the mother can feel with her child or, as we tend to say, she is "in tune." She is in a good position to embark on the intricate gradual steps of transferring to him her own appreciation and know-how of having and using feelings and of supporting his increasing ability to do so, while remaining in feeling touch, usually.even after he has made this an integral part of his personality, independent of her.

Even though feeling bodily pain is the first feeling acquisition, it remains vulnerable. It is easily lost during the early years when mother is absent or emotionally unavailable, e.g., toddlers in daycare often fail to experience and protest pain and recover their ability to do so only on reuniting with mother, or even not at all (E. Furman, 1984). It also tends to be the last feeling to be used independently to initiate appropriate action, long after this has been achieved with many later affects. Thus it is the rule, rather than exception, for college-aged young men and women to call home first when they are ill, and only then to contact their local physician. In spite of this prolonged developmental process, the early achievements of feeling and protesting pain and seeking and accepting mother's comfort not only are crucial to survival but are the basis for the mother-child work on other feelings. In our Hanna Perkins Mother-Toddler Group (E. Furman, 1989, 1990, 1992) we have therefore learned to pay close attention to our toddlers' and mothers' attitudes to bodily pain, try to understand just which aspects facilitate or impede mastery, and to help educationally and therapeutically.

Chris, a healthy infant, had suffered much discomfort from teething. At 18 months, and with the help of his mother, they related that morning's experience: Chris had called his Mom, looked teary and unhappy, pointing with his finger inside and to the back left of his mouth, and reached out to her. She picked him up for a hug, told him she understood he had a toothache and was so sorry it hurt. He then took her to the refrigerator where he pointed out the bottle with a local analgesic they kept for relieving teething pain and took part in applying it. They could both feel the bump. The medicine helped, but throughout the day Chris remained aware of his discomfort and alerted Mom to it. She offered him a Tylenol she had brought along and at one point he took it. Mom sympathized and praised his choice of cold soft foods to eat. She also told him how good it was that he knew it did not feel good, that the hurt was coming from a new tooth, that he could tell her and find the right things to do for it. Although Chris was subdued, he maintained his usual good functioning.

Kent, also a healthy and loved infant, had suffered several strep throat infections. When he was over 2 years old, I noticed one day that he was listless, irritable, poking his hand into the back of his mouth, yawning. I shared my observations with his mother. She was aware of them, added that he had not eaten well and woken during the night. She thought a tooth might be bothering him, but she had not talked with him about it, nor was she solicitous of his evident discomfort. I told her I thought Kent was not feeling well and had a sore throat. She disagreed, then suddenly and matter-of-factly asked him, "Does your throat hurt?" He resented the intrusion and pushed her away with an angry "No." The next day Kent's functioning had deteriorated. He fell twice, screamed and kicked with the least frustration, messed with his snack. When Kent at one point coughed as if choking and grabbed at his neck, his mother phoned the doctor at once and rushed him off to be examined. Had I not interfered, she would not have stopped to explain all this to her boy and to prepare him. Kent had a very sore strep throat and was put on antibiotics, which she administered conscientiously. When she complained that he spat out his medicine and pushed away the squirter she used to insert it, I sympathized with mother and child how hard it was not to feel good and not to be able to make it feel good and, since both of them wanted to make the throat better, perhaps Kent would like to suck the medicine off a spoon himself, and she might have a candy ready afterward to alleviate the bad taste. This helped with the medicine and with the hard feelings between them. The mother's deep distress and hurt at having failed to diagnose the illness prompted her to work on this in the treatment via the parent which led her to a beginning appreciation of her child's feelings as well.

Let us now look at a less drastic case to illustrate how the mother-child attitudes to bodily pain are carried over to the development of other feelings.

After an earlier history of either not protesting pain at all or, help-lessly overwhelmed, burying herself in mother's lap and arms, Barbara showed a similar all-or-none response with embarrassment and anger. At 2 ½ years, she appeared quite unconcerned over wetting and soil-ing, which mother attributed to her "not being ready." But when Bar-bara spilled a little juice while pouring it from the pitcher into her cup, she felt mortified, cried helplessly, climbed into Mom's lap, and buried herself in mother's enveloping arms, as the mother kindly reassured her. When angry at Mom, Barbara at times disintegrated into a temper tantrum, again pushing into mother who contained her in her arms, often telling Barbara and us that the child was just tired or had a bit of a cold. But for the most part, Barbara did not show anger at all. When peers took her toys, she did not protest; and when they intruded on her play, she let them. Initially the mother was pleased that Barbara "shared so well" and was "kind to others," but she came to appreciate our concern with Barbara's lack of self-defense. She related it to her own trouble with saying "no," taking on tasks that overburdened her, and ending up in uncontrollable situations with much mutual anger. Not wanting to pass on her difficulty to her child made her want to work on this. She acknowledged to Barbara her own trouble with anger and promised to help her so Barbara could do better. And Barbara soon did. She began to stand up for herself and even took the lead with mother. One day, when the mother disapproved of Barbara's good painting of angry monsters, Barbara said, "But, Mommy, it's only a picture." Another day, when the mother again suggested that Barba-ra's angry defiance of a request was due to fatigue, the child yelled, "No, I'm not tired, I am angry." Mother agreed. With mother's sup-port, despite her trouble, Barbara learned to have and use her own anger.

Embarrassment was harder for Barbara. Here the mother had to help in a different way. She told Barbara that feeling ashamed for making a mess was hard for everyone, but that Barbara would feel better if she took care of the feeling and mess herself, instead of Mommy doing it for her. With the next spill, Barbara crawled under the table. The mother pointed out that hiding only made others notice it more. She would feel better if she cleaned up and were more careful next time. Barbara did so with downcast eyes. In time she mastered not only pouring juice but using the toilet.

It may seem that Chris, Kent, and Barbara had simply taken over their mothers' feeling or lack of feelings and that this is how children develop feelings. It is not. Feeling what mother feels bypasses the development of the child's own feelings and results in a lasting inner confusion and uncertainty, covered by the adaptational use of other people's ways of showing feelings, but never enabling the child to use his feelings as a guide to action.

In an extreme example of this, a 9-year-old analytic patient told me a joke. I told her it did not sound funny to me. She repeated it, lest I had not understood. I still did not think it funny. She protested, "But at school everyone laughed at it." "Maybe they thought it funny, but I don't. Do you?" A bewildered look crossed her face and she quickly replied, "Of course. I laughed because they all laughed." Then she added very quietly, "How else would you know whether it is funny?" Although she could be helped in time to find her own feelings, she never dared to voice hers, being sure of them only when she found someone who could validate them.

When the toddler takes his cue about what to feel from his mother, she has actually failed to feel with him, has assumed that he would only feel what she feels. Truly feeling implies assisting the child in crystallizing his own feelings and coming to know them with the help of her validation and appreciation of them as his. He can then identify with her means of containing, differentiating, and using them, and verbalization is among those means. When A. Freud and D. Burlingham (1942) noted that during the London blitz youngsters panicked or remained calm, depending on their mothers' frame of mind, the implication was not that they took over their mothers' fear or lack of fear, but responded to their mothers' means of coping with fear.

For these reasons I question the experiments used by some developmental psychologists to investigate the role of affects in early mother-child interaction. In one of Emde and Sorce's (1983) experiments, 12-month-olds approach a "visual cliff" and look at mother's face to gauge her expression. She sits in the room, but at a distance. "At this point our experimental design calls for trained mothers to pose either a happy or fearful facial expression" (p. 26), and the child responds accordingly. In another of their key experiments, the mother places her young toddler in the center of a room with toys. A strange woman reading a newspaper sits on one side. Mother sits down on the opposite side, says, "Now Mommy's going to read," and then reads her newspaper without paying attention to her child. After 6 minutes there is a knock, mother and stranger exchange seats, without a word, and continue reading. Next the stranger looks interestedly at the child and then "a remote control robot toy came out from under a table and moved toward the infant" (p. 27) for 3 minutes. Then another knock alerts mother to stop reading and become emotionally available while still seated at a distance. The results indicate that the children then seem happier and more active, but showed neither fear nor distress before. An "in tune" mother would not expose her child to a potentially disorienting experience, would not distance herself bodily or emotionally, would not impose false affect. No child would experience feelings when decathected and shown "trained" as opposed to spontaneous affect. It seems to me that the experiments preclude normal mother-child communication to such an extent as to raise serious questions about the validity of the results.

When toddlers have not been helped to make affective mental sense of their sensations and motoric discharges to know and value their own feelings, they may persist with bodily manifestations or may adopt mother's feeling responses, but they may also use a variety of primitive defensive maneuvers, described by Fraiberg (1982), or a developmental continuation of them.

Two-year-old Alan fought the world. His screaming could be heard from the hall; when he entered our room, he barged around from toy to toy, handling them roughly, snatching things from others, angrily denying every request, often hitting out or teasily running off and throwing things. He was unable to sit for his snacks and tried to grab all the food; at circle time on the rug he tried to poke into mother or at others and disrupted our songs with his noise and aggressive hyperactivity. His mother's constant verbal directions went unheeded and, as often as he could, he wrenched away from her bodily hold on him. Everyone felt intimidated, and this provided the first clue: I assured Alan this was a safe place and that neither he nor others could be hurt. And I enforced this, calmly but firmly. Although he had no understandable speech, he began to make eye contact with me and relaxed somewhat. I then noticed that, just before his sudden bouts of hollering and acting up, there would be a moment when he looked scared. I verbalized this sympathetically and encouraged him to show us what was scary. Finally one day he pointed to the ceiling. With effort, I could make out the slight noise of a toilet flushing on the second floor. He was much relieved that I understood, explained, and declared it safe. When I had initially shared my observation with his mother, she could not believe that her tough boy was ever scared, but she became more receptive and supporting of Alan as, day by day, we learned of more fears—noises, changes, visitors, fears of being sent away, of being stupid, helpless, and incompetent. Being felt with, he could increasingly feel his fears and use his feeling to help himself, sometimes to seek explanation, sometimes to learn to master an activity, or to modify his behavior. He also became softer, could experience pleasure, and show loving feelings. He became a person.

Developmentally, Alan's fighting mechanism had been at the transition point between motoric discharge and identification with the aggressor. Unlike Alan, however, many even younger toddlers are well able to experience a variety of feelings, but they cannot trust and accept them and cannot feel they themselves are acceptable, when mother does not feel with them. Early defense mechanisms then come into play; above all, we observe poor bodily and mental self-regard, lack of trust in themselves and the world around them, and increased dependence on mother.

Two-year-old Carole clung to her mother and was standoffish with the teachers. She chose very easy activities to do privately with her mother, but never seemed pleased with her accomplishments. When a teacher approached or asked to look at her work, she crossly refused and hid it away. Yet she herself keenly observed everyone and tried to attract admiration by wearing bows and jewelry. The mother was surprised when we pointed out Carole's evident loyalty conflict, but she considered this and assured Carole that it was alright to like the teachers and that there would still be lots of love left between Mommy and Carole. This helped the relationships but not Carole's liking of herself.

The father had left the family several months earlier after protracted severe marital discord and some abusive outbursts at the mother and Carole's older brother. Visits with the father were more or less weekly, but Carole never mentioned him, nor did the mother. When other fathers visited the toddler group, Carole was subdued and reacted with pained side-long glances at the fathers and increased closeness to her mother. We alerted the mother to this so that she could support us when, at the next opportunity, I quietly told Carole and Mom, "A girl might miss her own Daddy and wish he could be with her too, like the other Daddy. That's hard, but a Dad can still like his girl and be a very nice Dad, even if he can't come to visit." Carole's eyes filled with tears and the mother hugged her. On their way home, the dam broke. Carole was furious at Mom, blaming her for "kicking out" Daddy, whom she loved, who was so nice, and with whom she wanted to live. In her rage she even threw out her own beloved teddy which the mother retrieved. Having been prepared by the therapist and teachers, the mother could begin to feel with Carole, apologize for not having understood, and help her. The mother confessed that she had not believed us because she simply could not imagine that Carole's feelings about the father were so different from her own. Mother's new empathy and appreciation of Carole's feelings led to much improvement in her daughter's strides in bodily self-care, zest, and pleasure in activities as well as kindness with mother, teachers, and peers. She even happily showed off gifts from her Dad.

FEELING WITH CHILDREN IN ANALYSIS

Most of our child analytic patients are not in touch with their feelings, not because they failed to develop the ability to feel, but because their feelings arouse so much unpleasure or anxiety that they defend against them. As we all know, interpretation of these defenses produces unpleasure or anxiety. It does not usually bring back the warded-off feeling, much less the ability to tolerate and use it; often enough, the mere threat of the feeling intensifies the defense or leads to instituting another defense. Without access to his feeling, the patient cannot be helped to link it meaningfully to its appropriate ideational content, nor can he use it to explore further the relevant connections in his past experiences. We are therefore faced with the task of helping the child to value, bear, and contain his feeling, and we achieve this by feeling with him, whatever route we take or words we use.

Jennifer, a smart and pretty 8-year-old, had great difficulty owning and tolerating any feelings. She used a variety of rigid defenses, and we had worked on this for a couple of years. At one point she was busy planning her birthday party, and her parents had agreed to make it quite elaborate and special, but she could not write the invitations, in spite of her happy anticipation. First she put off the task, then wrote in the wrong date, then mislaid them. My attempts to engage her in observing that something was getting in her way met with cross rebuffs. I found myself helpless, as I put it to myself, "to find a way in." This was my first feeling signal. Then came a session in which she totally ignored me. She brushed off my inquiry, saying she was concentrating on the pretty leaf patterns of the tree outside our window. I said she was giving me a very hard feeling, the feeling of being left alone and unwanted, because she was so busy with something that she liked better than me. It was a feeling I knew well because I, like everyone, sometimes had it. She turned on me brusquely, "That's just silly, I don't know what on earth you are talking about." I replied that this made the feeling even harder, because it made it seem that I was all alone in having it and that I was silly and strange to feel it. But, I added, I still thought it was an important feeling, even though it was so hard, important because it was part of me and because it could help me. Jennifer turned away and buried her head in the couch cushion. After a while I said I was using my left-out and unloved feeling to help me understand how one would have trouble inviting people to a wonderful party. Maybe one would worry that they might say, "No, I am busy with better and more important things," and then one would feel left out, hurt, and unwanted. "Not at all, I already know three that will come." "How nice, but it would be nicer yet if one could be sure of all of them." She relaxed, her facial expression and body posture conveyed softness, and she was especially nice to me on leaving. I learned the next day that she had phoned each guest the previous night and one had refused. I said I was sorry and she replied quietly, "It's that feeling you talked about." The girl who had refused because she was doing something else was a girl Jennifer especially wanted as a friend, but she had increasingly withdrawn from Jennifer. As she could now bear her unwanted feeling with me, I could tell her how brave she was to bear it and how it helped her to be kind, instead of having to be so scared of this feeling that she had to make others feel it, and then worry they would not like her because she was unkind.

Without helping her to bear her underlying feeling, she would have had to reject my interpretation of her widespread habitual defense of passive into active, or even of its secondary effect on her relationships and self-esteem. I knew from past material that many specific situations, including the parents' relationship and ability to make babies, had been experienced as rejections, but she could not link her defense to these contents as long as she could not own her feeling about them. I also knew that these past contents had been so unbearably painful because they were embedded in the context of the parents' inability to feel with her, the rejection she so harshly identified with in calling my feeling silly, strange, and ununderstandable. But any interpretation of this identification and of the parents' difficulty would also have been felt as a rejection of herself and of the parents. Only when she was able to feel rejected would she be able to integrate this with empathy for the parents, instead of again defensively rejecting the parents, myself, and others. She was not yet ready for this work, but there had been a beginning. Of course, I did not think through any of this until afterward. During the sessions, feeling with the patient is one's main and surest guide to interpretation.

Many of our patients have not even reached the developmental level at which feelings are warded off. Like some of our toddlers, they are arrested at earlier stages of experiencing bodily sensations or discharges which have not yet crystallized into mentally experienced feelings and need the analyst's help to achieve this.

Martha was a healthy, intelligent 10-year-old with a debilitating learning disturbance. It soon became clear that she could neither know things nor feel. Vaguely distressed, she would curl up in the corner of the couch, twirling her hair and half hiding her thumb sucking, complaining of being cold or of one or another part of her body hurting. Her mother, feeling at a loss, would sometimes take solicitous care and keep her home from school, sometimes declare Martha was making up excuses and send her off without sympathy. I always sympathized how hard it was not to feel good, but also suggested that, by feeling cold and hurting, her body was, in its own way, saying that there were uncomfortable feelings about other things. Feeling with Martha enabled us gradually to be a bit more specific—feeling unhappy or lonely or "everyone is mean to me" or "I feel mean." As bodily symptoms subsided, the nonverbally communicated feelings became more intense and conveyed primitive terror, pain, and rage. Martha constantly tested my ability to feel, articulate, and contain these feelings with her. So, when she took to getting under the couch and signaling to me only with hand gestures, I thought it yet another test. After weeks of this, however, we were able to reconstruct an early experience of being in pain, confined in a crib, and trying to reach someone to be with her bodily and mentally. I finally wondered about a hospitalization and, much to our shared surprise, the parents confirmed what they had until then forgotten and omitted from the history: at 11 months, there was an emergency operation. Martha was hospitalized for a week and the parents complied with doctor's orders not to visit her to avoid upset. Unbeknownst to Martha, they had observed her for short periods at a distance and found her quietly sitting, sucking her thumb, and twirling her hair. On her return, she seemed alright, began to crawl, and say words, and the parents never referred to the experience again. The mother recalled missing the nursing which had stopped at the time and missing taking care of Martha, but she was unaware that she had lost being in feeling touch.

Helping Patients with Uncontrolled Behavior

It is even harder to feel with our patients and to gauge the developmental level at which they feel, when their expressions are in the form of motoric discharge, assaulting our senses and bodies, and endangering themselves or the office and materials. Such activity may be defensive (e.g., representing an identification with the aggressor or abuser, or an externalization of a harsh superego introject, or warding off helpless or even loving feelings), or it may be related to primitively unfused aggression with insufficiently available libido to tame it, or it may show early states of being overwhelmed, with or without the use of defensive maneuvers of "fighting," as was the case with our scared toddler Alan. In each instance, it is mainly the analyst's ability to feel with the child which helps him determine what may be going on.

Some years ago, the father of a Hanna Perkins child introduced their new housekeeper to our school during the mother's hospitalization. He explained that this was a special school where kids were first helped to get in touch with their feelings and then they could be expected to be responsible for their behavior. This summed up better than I could the teachers' educational approach and the goal we help the parents pursue. It also applies to aspects of the analyst's work, but whereas the parents' and teachers' task is to help the child know his feeling in a current situation and to use the adult, and parts of himself, to gain mastery, the analyst has to help the child to use his or her feeling to explore its history and role within the total personality. Feeling with the child's anger or angry defenses and allowing the relevant affects and contents to emerge gradually can take a long time and involve a lot of uncontrolled behavior. How can we best assure safety as well as analytic process?

Analysts vary greatly in how much physical aggression and destruction they can tolerate and contain, be it having one's space invaded by screams, pushes, and kicks, or paper airplanes; be it wasting of paper, spilling of water, or turning over of furniture; or be it unsafety of the patient himself. In 1967, R. A. Furman described the rule he made with little Billy that all messes had to be cleaned up before the end of the session, and they set aside part of each session to do so. He explained that they would work on understanding the causes of Billy's messing, and then he would not have to mess, but until then he would feel better if he left the office cleaned up. A. Freud, on reading R. A. Furman's paper, agreed completely. She said she was perhaps so definite about this because she was a teacher and regretted that many of her co-workers took a different view, fearing that such educational control would interfere with the unfolding of the analytic process. I also am a teacher, but I do not think this fact, or my personal touchiness about messes and hurts, is my main reason for taking very early and definite steps to ensure my basic analytic rule with my patients: "You, I, and everything here has to be very safe." This rule derives from learning over the years that children who are physically aggressive to the analyst, destructive with material things, or unsafe with themselves are the very ones who are most frightened by these impulses and by the least evidence of damage they cause. Their terror, often of an unconscious nature, stems from aspects of the etiology of their behavior, regardless of whether it is defensive in its current form. They are either youngsters who have been the victims of aggressive-destructive behavior (whether intentional or merely perceived as such) and/or they function at very early levels in terms of feelings. In the latter case, they have not been helped with channeling sensations and motoric discharge into feelings and often had not even developed the basic protest and comfort-seeking use of bodily pain. They therefore live in a state of inner turmoil and fear of being overwhelmed. In either case, they cannot trust a differentiation between inner and outer reality, cannot trust that a contained feeling will serve as a barrier between impulse and action or serve to tame and control the action, in themselves or in others. Feeling with this anxiety helps us to appreciate how extremely vulnerable they are. Their underlying fear, often a fear of annihilation, overshadows all else to such an extent that they cannot effectively work on and integrate other psychic contents, even if they produce them as analytic material. The question is not how much anger and destruction can the analyst contain, but how much can the patient contain. With the uncontrolled child, the answer is none. The analyst's task therefore is to provide utmost safety in order to create a productive analytic milieu, one in which these basic fears can be explored and understood.

Some practical measures may help to illustrate this, but they have to be adapted and timed to serve the individual patient. The children's implied question about safety usually arises at the very start, perhaps as they carry scissors across the room, harshly bang the door shut, or take their magic marker activity to the upholstered couch instead of the table. I pick up on the first clue I notice, articulate the question, provide my overall rule reply, and usually ask them to figure out the reasons for its particular application, e.g., why would it not be safe to use the couch for work with magic markers? They tend to come up with more reasons than I would have thought of, although they may deride them at the same time and contrast them with their different home rules. As soon as possible, I point out that there is a part of them that wants everything to be safe—like the part that is so good at figuring out all the reasons for using magic markers at the table—and I want to help that part of them. It is the part that feels good when it can keep things safe, and it is also the part that can do the best work on troubles. Like R. A. Furman with Billy, we have a clean-up and fixing-things time, during or at the end of the session. I relate it not only to helping them to feel good and in control, but to their own expectation of finding everything in good repair and in its place. If I let them leave things in a mess or damaged, how could they trust that I would not allow others to do so? If putting things right is so interfered with that it extends beyond the end of the session, we may need to arrange to take the extra minutes off their next session. Again, taking away another's time without making up would lead them to expect that I would let others infringe on their time. And if cleaning up is impossible for them—and of course I always point out that such troubles will be understood in time and will not always have to leave them feeling badly—then the materials left in a mess or disrepair will be off limits. We then gauge together when the sensible part is strong enough to be better in control of using them. This applies also to items which are aggressively misused.

Seven-year-old Jane suddenly threw the scissors at me. Sudden brutal attacks were among her symptoms. She usually denied them or minimized their effect on others, and we had already done much work on safety. We decided to put the scissors away for now, in an accessible box, which she accepted. When we later agreed she was ready to give them a new try, her controls were still labile, so I said she would need to ask me each time she wanted them and I would sit next to her at the table while she used them. In spite of some protests, she was greatly relieved. Eventually she could safely use scissors independently and even graduated from a rounded to a pointed pair. But in the process of this progression, many of the issues related to her attacks could be worked on in regard to minor incidents. One day she tested me, surreptitiously trying to take the scissors out of the box. I was aware of it, which enabled her to put them back, and we could then wonder what had made *her* feel unsafe. At a neighborhood party the previous evening, the children had been left unsupervised and a notoriously aggressive boy had pushed her off the swing, all in the midst of excited and aggressive interplays. She felt hurt and guilty and had not reported the incident for fear of being blamed. This allowed us to help her understand that her self-blame as well as the uncontrolled behavior preceding the accident (a masturbatory derivative) had served to ward off her helpless unsafe feeling when her mother disregarded her and failed to protect her at the party from inner and outer dangers.

When Jane tried to mistreat me, even if only by aggressively getting too close, I would state my dislike of it in words and take measures to protect myself. As I discussed in greater detail in "Aggressively Abused Children" (1986), I have found this especially important in tuning into these children's difficulty with effective self-defense, "If I don't stand up for myself and protect myself, how could you believe that I could help you to stand up for yourself?" With Jane, too, this proved helpful. Although she could attack viciously and even fight back, she could not fend for herself with her unprotective parents and alert them to her needs, which often included their disregard of bodily pain and illness.

I am always amazed that the initially most uncontrolled patients later reveal themselves to be the most astutely aware of the most minor damages.

One early latency boy had to be held off bodily at times and, to avoid the stimulation of bodily contact, needed to spend times in my rather spacious and well-lit closet, where he could give himself a better chance to feel safe and to regain control of himself, while remaining in reassuring verbal touch with me. At later points in our work, he would draw my attention to such minor transgressions as using two Kleenex instead of one, which he called "wasting and spoiling" my property. It turned out to represent his helpless oral rage and fear of being overwhelmed, which he had first experienced as an unattended hungry infant and which later dogged him at every developmental level. Without the safety of our office, these terror-filled experiences could not have been tolerated, understood, or mastered.

Feeling with the child patient's earliest anxieties about safety and protecting him as well as helping him to protect himself support the analytic work. They do not interfere with it.

ROLE OF FEELINGS IN EGO GROWTH AND IN THE ANALYTIC RELATIONSHIP

Developmentally, a child is helped to know, own, and use his feelings when the parents feel with him in a contained manner and assist him with it, step by step. This achievement has wide-ranging effects on all ego functions, especially on his organizing ability, i.e., integration and differentiation. A. Katan (1961) and R. A. Furman (1978) referred to this role, and it has been implicit in this paper. Tracing these mutual ego influences in detail deserves separate discussion. At this time, I merely wish to underline an aspect I discussed in a different context (1988), namely, that an individual's independent reliable testing of outer reality grows out of knowing and trusting his inner reality, his sensations and feelings. In analysis, when we help a patient to develop, or regain, his ability to feel, this progress also needs to be assessed and compared in the other areas of ego functioning. Improvements may be limited, especially when there are developmental deficits.

Feeling and being felt with also play a special role in the patient-analyst relationship and working alliance. Some years ago, when our informal workshop discussion at the Association meetings focused on children's motivation for analysis, we agreed that children do not primarily seek insight, and I doubt that this is the main aim with many adults. H. Kennedy (1982) at that time said that children want to be understood. I agree, but I would go a step further. I think that "being understood" means being felt with and helped to master. This is the most difficult aspect of our work but also the most gratifying. As child analysts, we self-select ourselves for this task. To an extent that rarely faces the analyst of adults, we bear the ego strain of tapping into our earliest, most primitive feelings in empathy and, like parents, assist our patients to bear, own, and use their feelings at the same time. It is the real gift the child analyst gives, and gives generously and unconditionally. Yet it is a gift our patients reciprocate, because feeling with them provides a deep rich satisfaction and helps us to learn more about analysis and ourselves.

BIBLIOGRAPHY

BORNSTEIN, B. (1949). The analysis of a phobic child. *Psychoanal. Study Child*, 3/4:181–226.

——— (1953). Fragment of an analysis of an obsessional child. *Psychoanal. Study Child*, 8:313–332.

EMDE, R. N. & SORCE, J. F. (1983). The rewards of infancy. In *Frontiers of Infant Psychiatry*, ed. J. D. Call, E. Galenson, & R L. Tyson. New York: Basic Books, pp. 17–30.

FRAIBERG, S. (1982). Pathological defenses in infancy. *Psychoanal. Q.*, 5:621–635.

FREUD, A. (1962). Assessment of childhood disturbances. *Psychoanal. Study Child*, 17:149–158.

——— (1963). The concept of developmental lines. *Psychoanal. Study Child*, 18:245–265.

——— (1965). *Normality and Pathology in Childhood*. New York: Int. Univ. Press.

——— & BURLINGHAM, D. (1942). *Young Children in War-Time*. London: Allen & Unwin.

FURMAN, E. (1957). Treatment of under-fives by way of their parents. *Psychoanal. Study Child*, 12:250–262.

——— (1969). Treatment via the mother. In *The Therapeutic Nursery School*, ed. R. A. Furman & A. Katan. New York: Int. Univ. Press, pp. 64–123.

——— (1974). *A Child's Parent Dies*. New Haven: Yale Univ. Press.

——— (1984). Mothers, toddlers and care. Pamphlet series of the Cleveland Center for Research in Child Development, Cleveland, OH. Also in *The Course of Life*, vol. 2, ed. S. I. Greenspan & G. H. Pollock. Madison, Ct.: Int. Univ. Press, 1989, pp. 61–82.

——— (1985). On fusion, integration and feeling good. *Psychoanal. Study Child*, 40:81–110.

——— (1985). The seduction hypothesis. In Panel on The Seduction Hypothesis, A. E. Marans, reporter. *J. Amer. Psychoanal. Assn.*, 36:759–771.

——— (1986). Aggressively abused children. *J. Child Psychother.*, 12:47–59.

——— (1989). Toddlers and mothers. Read at the Association for Child Psychoanalysis, Philadelphia.

——— (1990). The toddler phase. Read at the Association for Child Psychoanalysis, Sante Fe, N.M.

——— (1992). *Toddlers and Their Mothers*. Madison, Ct.: Int. Univ. Press.

FURMAN, R. A. (1967). A technical problem. In *The Child Analyst at Work,* ed. E. R. Geleerd. New York: Int. Univ. Press, pp. 59–84.

——— (1978). Some developmental aspects of the verbalization of affects. *Psychoanal. Study Child*, 33:187–211.

——— & KATAN, A. (1969). *The Therapeutic Nursery School*. New York: Int. Univ. Press.

GREENSPAN, S. I. (1989). *The Development of the Ego*. Madison, Ct.: Int. Univ. Press.

HOFFER, W. (1950). The development of the body ego. *Psychoanal. Study Child,* 5:18–23.

KATAN, A. (1961). Some thoughts about the role of verbalization in early childhood. *Psychoanal. Study Child,* 16:184–188.

KENNEDY, H. (1982). Personal communication.

NAGERA, H. (1963). The developmental profile. *Psychoanal. Study Child,* 18:511–540.

Latency Development in Children of Primary Nurturing Fathers

Eight-Year Follow-up

KYLE D. PRUETT, M.D. and
BRIAN LITZENBERGER, B.A.

This paper is an 8-year follow-up of 17 families in which fathers began as primary caretakers early in the lives of their children. The emphasis is on the developmental consequences for the children, now in the latency period, as well as their psychological experience of the father's increased significance.

THE DECADE JUST CLOSED WAS THE FIRST TO WITNESS SIGNIFICANT SCHOLarly contributions to the understanding of the effect of direct, ongoing paternal involvement on child development (Pruett, 1983, 1985, 1989; Chused, 1986; Radin and Goldsmith, 1985; Russell, 1982). A historical shift has brought increasing numbers of men into increased contact with their children, whether or not they choose to be there. It is incumbent upon researchers of the psychoanalytic developmental persuasion to continue to examine, observe, and follow this phenomenon carefully as it does not appear to be a fad. Until very recently, intimate father-child interaction in the early years has enjoyed a status of dubious merit. Early evidence from some studies, however, suggests that this nurturing arrangement, even when the father is the child's primary caregiver, may be quite adequate for the task of providing goodenough care.

Kyle D. Pruett is clinical professor, Yale University Child Study Center and Department of Psychiatry. Mr. Litzenberger is a Ph.D. candidate in clinical psychology at the University of Michigan.

A version of this paper was originally presented at the American Psychoanalytic Association Fall Meeting, New York City, December 16, 1989.

In the service of addressing the question of whether or not intimate paternal care was good for children developmentally, I began a small longitudinal study of intact families in which fathers served as primary caretaker of the family's children (Pruett, 1983). The study addressed the development of infants from 2 to 22 months (the ages of the children who presented for study), the psychological characteristics of the fathers and the mothers, the father's nurturing patterns, and the marital relationship patterns.

The 17 families recruited ranged across the socioeconomic spectrum from those on welfare to blue- and white-collar workers and professionals. Eight fathers were unemployed, but the rest were graduate students, blue-collar workers, sales representatives, artists, computer programmers, real estate brokers, lawyers, writers, or small businessmen. If employed, their incomes ranged from $7,000 to $125,000 a year. The mothers were nurses, teachers, secretaries, lawyers, taxi drivers, sales representatives, real estate brokers, blue-collar workers, or welfare recipients. If employed, their incomes ranged from $8,000 to $75,000 per year.

Of the 17 children, 8 were male and 9 were female. The parents ranged in age from 19 to 36 with a mean age of 24 for fathers and 25 for mothers. Surprisingly, 16 of the 17 children were firstborn, although this was not part of the research design.

The average age at marriage had been 23 for men and 24 for women. Of the 34 adults, 2 had been married previously, both women. One 30-year-old had been married for 3 years when her first husband died. The other was 22; her marriage had lasted less than a year and had ended in an uncontested, mutually agreed-upon divorce.

Some subtle subgrouping emerged with regard to *when* during the conception and pregnancy the families decided that the fathers would "mother." Asked *when* the families decided on this arrangement of child care, they all shared only one decision characteristic. *None* of the families considered this a permanent situation at its inception.

At the outset, the families' "decision phase" could be grouped roughly into thirds: the first third (6 families) decided that the father would be the primary caregiver prior to the pregnancy; the second third (another 6 families), during the pregnancy; and the final third (5 families), during the neonatal period.

The early-deciding group of men tended to be professionals, graduate students, or upper socioeconomic people. A typical example was the father who decided to "take some time off from his career" (education) while the wife pursued hers (retail sales) and care for the baby because it seemed either "fair or interesting or both to do for awhile."

The attempt to time conception carefully was a hallmark of this group. They tried to plan everything ahead of time.

The middle third was similar in reasoning but typically was influenced by some change in the mother's feeling about staying home with a baby after she had begun carrying it. Or it had become increasingly clear that the mother's job or career would be jeopardized seriously by extended maternity leave. Meanwhile, the father's economic status was changing anyway, or his established career could withstand better a prolonged leave of absence.

The late-deciding third was in some ways the most interesting. These families often had the decision "forced" upon them at the last moment, usually for economic reasons; for example, when the father lost his job while the mother retained hers. Not surprisingly, this group contained the highest number of initially reluctant, uncertain fathers.

The mothers came from families just as culturally and socioeconomically diverse as their husbands. Three of the men had been only children, whereas 2 of the women were without siblings. The number of siblings was slightly higher for the men than it was for the women, average father's family being 5.2 members, and the mother's averaged 4.3.

As a group, the women were no more or less homogeneous than the men. One life choice did separate out one subgroup from the rest, i.e., those who chose to leave or suspend work and stay home full time to care for the children after the birth of a second child. These women had mothers who were somewhat similar. When I looked back at the early histories they gave at the first interview, I (K. D. P.) discovered that, as a group, they had tended to describe their own mothers as being "unhappy, cold, unavailable." One of the group said the only time she ever heard her mother laugh was when she watched the "Honeymooners" on TV. This group of women seemed to feel identified more strongly with their fathers, whom they generally regarded as more nurturing and "supportive," "more available" to them emotionally than their mothers. Such women also reported feeling less competitive with their spouses, and tended to identify positively with their husband's nurturing of the first baby.

These children raised primarily by men were active, vigorous, robust, and thriving infants. They also were competent. The majority of study infants functioned somewhat above the expected norms on several of the standardized tests of development. The youngest group of infants (2 to 12 months) performed certain problem-solving tasks on the same level as babies who often were 2 to 4 months their senior; personal and social skills also were ahead of schedule. The older babies in the group (12 to 22 months) performed as well.

Second, apart from the quantitative scored aspects of these babies' performance, qualitative or stylistic characteristics emerged quite frequently; for example, these infants seemed to be especially comfortable with and attracted to stimulation from the external environment.

A third finding, hard to quantify, looked something like this: many of the babies seemed to expect that their curiosity, persistence, or challenging behavior would be tolerated, even appreciated by the adults in their environment, whether they were parents, examiners, or observers. The expectation that play would be rich, exciting, and reciprocated, or that block designs or puzzles eventually would succumb to sheer determination, was widespread in this group of babies. One of the older children, 22-month-old Helen (of whom we will speak later), knocked over her tower of 10 small, red cubes (which she had so carefully and proudly constructed a moment before) with a broad sweep of her closed fist. She sat forward quickly on the edge of her baby chair and, with a broad, open-mouthed smile, fixed her eyes with excited anticipation on the face of the examiner as if to ask expectantly, "Well?"

The babies were doing well. The fathers, meanwhile, demonstrated the capacity to nurture another being adequately to insure his survival and to assure his humanity. They "read" and understood their babies well enough to feed, change, comfort, pick them up and put them down on time. These responses reasonably conformed to the baby's most complex needs.

Although as a group they achieved the relationship at different rates, all the fathers had formed the deep, reciprocal, nurturing attachment so critical to the early development of the thriving human baby. The depth and rapidity of the attachment amazed even them. *How* it happened varied, of course, from man to man and baby to baby.

Unique caregiving styles emerged as the men gradually began to think of themselves as parents in their own right. Most of the men kept this feeling to themselves, as though they could not quite believe it or trust it, or maybe should not even have it.

The changes in the families over the next 2 years were far-reaching. Second children had been born into 7 families. Fathers had continued to serve as the primary caregiving parent in 8 families, including 4 in which there now were 2 siblings. Mothers had become the primary parent in 3 families, all of whom had second children. Fathers had returned to work or school in 6 families (3 with second children) and had ceased to function as the primary parent. There had been one parental separation in which the father had retained custody.

At the 4-year follow-up, if these children were not troubled, were they different in some way? The answer is both yes and no. When one looks at the level and range of emotional maturation, quality of the human relationships, and the ability to handle the stress of everyday life, there were no gross personality characteristics to differentiate reliably these children from their more traditionally mother-raised peers. Comfortable dependency, zest for life, assertiveness, a vigorous drive for mastery, and the usual childhood worries all were clearly present in both boys and girls.

There also seemed to be no significant lack of emotional flexibility in any of these children. Nor could one call them as a group inhibited or constricted. If anything, there were rudimentary signs that these children might be, in fact, developing a resilience and flexibility in certain personality domains, particularly in the ease with which they moved back and forth between feminine and masculine behavioral roles—not identities, but roles.

If there is anything unique about their internal images of themselves or their parents, it may be the prevalence in their play of father as a nurturing force. Over the entire study there was empirical evidence to strengthen the initial speculation that having a father as a primary nurturing figure stimulates more curiosity and interest in father as procreator than is found in most traditionally reared children. The children in this study saw father as a *maker* of human beings along with mother, who makes and births them.

Fifteen families were still available for study after 8 years. The children now ranged in age from 8 to 10 years. Seven female and 8 male children and their families were interviewed. Of the 15 families, 11 still had fathers in major nurturing roles, either sharing equally or providing the majority of child care responsibilities, joys, and sorrows. Ten of the 15 families had had siblings born into them. A second divorce is pending.

Interestingly, both marriages that foundered were from the group that chose earliest to have the father serve as the primary caretaker, even before the conception of the firstborn child. Both seemed enamored of the plan intellectually from the beginning and gave it a "good try." Both mothers felt that that child care decision had had a role in the marital dissolution. As one mother said, "It seemed like such a good idea at the time, but it sure turned sour."

This follow-up focused on the child both in his or her *family* and *world* more than it had previously. There no longer seemed to be any question regarding the developmental competence of these children. Furthermore, with the postoedipal latency hegemony of the ego in full sway, it seemed that the diagnostic play interview was less likely to reveal important aspects of psychic function. Coupled with the desire to broaden the focus to include the developmental tasks of *all* family members, and not just those of the index children, and the fact that any child's familial and social adaptations are the hallmarks of latency functioning, anyway, a decision was made to conduct extended, child-centered family diagnostic interviews at home with all family members of the household present and the television turned off. The interviews were at least two hours in length and recorded by one interviewer and one observer, whenever possible. They were semistructured in nature, shaped roughly around these open-ended prompts: (1) Take us through your day from who gets up in the morning first to who goes to bed last at night. (2) As you reflect upon what one or another has said about this day in your life as a family, what have you heard that has struck you? (3) Are there some things you would like to say about your life together as a family that we have not yet had a chance to hear?

This approach provided myriad opportunities to observe play, dialogue, dyadic and triadic relationships, both intra- and intergenerational, nonverbal communication, family-wide standards and values of conduct, problem-solving behavior, displays of affect, patterns of limit setting (or lack thereof), humor, etc. We shall discuss our initial findings after reviewing a few common observations and summarizing what we already know of the traditional father's role in this developmental epoch.

From the perspective of latency, all of the children seen are able to reflect upon the experience, which was in no way unusual for them at the time, of being raised primarily by their fathers in their early years. They are now all quite conscious that this is a relatively unusual profile for an early nurturing domain, as they see through their experience with other families and other social institutions, such as school and after-school care settings.

In summary, their gender identities remain stable, oedipal resolutions seem to have been relatively successful, and the flexibility of gender role performance reported previously has continued to manifest itself, though in a more age-appropriate complexity. The families themselves have undergone a variety of configurational changes, several mothers having served as the primary caregivers to siblings born subsequently. Sibling relationships, themselves, often seem influenced by the circumstance of one child having been raised by one parent, with subsequent children being raised primarily by another. The impact of this arrangement upon sibling rivalry, and the importance of siblings as love objects for this particular group of children, will also be explored.

It seems helpful to review briefly, first, the metapsychological and developmental agenda of latency and the role of the traditional father in this epoch. Benson and Harrison (1980) have referred euphemistically to this stage as the "eye of the hurricane"; others, as the "golden age of childhood" because of its characteristic stability, flexibility, and relative calm. Theoretically, this period of calm stands, psychosexually, between the sturm of the oedipal phase and the drang of adolescence. The ego is given a brief respite from the bombardment of instinctual demands, and the self increasingly enjoys fair winds and following seas.

Erna Furman (1980) summarized the characteristic requirements and transitions of early latency. First, there is the onset of infantile amnesia, highlighted by the often palpable sense of loss to the child of large segments of his past life and history. Second, there is the clinical phenomenon of children's awareness of the new voice of conscience and superego formation; they often experience difficulty defining its origin or identity as either clearly external or internal. Third, she notes that object relationships, though secure, often are buffeted about by the narcissistic injury of the child's rejection, especially for boys, inherent in the oedipal solution leading to a momentary downgrading of parental images. Instead of being part of the oedipal child's vigorous, libidinized interaction with the external world, latency parents find themselves drifting toward the cheap seats. This often coincides with increasingly narcissistic object choices of peers, chosen carefully for particular characteristics often desired, and sometimes feared, by the child himself. Fourth, ego function begins to accelerate in the face of the relative easing of instinctual demands, permitting the independent maintenance of certain functions which previously rested in the parent, such as the capacities to neutralize instinctual energy, to mediate structural conflicts, to establish the secondary autonomy of function and activities, and to effect more advanced forms of identification. This is particularly true of the capacity to identify with the aggressor, with its special combination, according to Anna Freud (1936), of introjection, projection, and turning the passive into active to avoid guilt. These functions are idiosyncratic of early latency as defined by Bornstein (1951), who originally suggested the subdivision of latency into two periods, the years 5 ½ to 8, and 9 to pubescence.

One typically sees in latency a number of intensive defense operations designed to prevent breakthroughs of oedipal libidinal wishes between children and the parents of the opposite sex. Girls may present a swaggering tomboyishness or an omnipotent, imperious attitude toward boys. Boys may become especially provocative and manipulative of adult women and sarcastic, devaluing, and abusive with girls their own age. In fact, Anna Freud (1965) points out that intense relationships with peers who share the same attitudes are based more on identifications than on object love.

As for the *parental* response to latency, mothers and fathers frequently remember rather fondly their own latency period, because of the sense of mastery of experience and the amount of energy available for adventure and exploration. It often is a time which the parents remember as the beginning of "friendships" with *their* parents, characterized by Erna Furman (1980, p. 28) as "a time when the child can be an easy friend and congenial companion for adults and peers without the heart-rending heights and depths of emotion which tend to accompany the earlier infantile, and later adolescent, relationships."

Schechter and Combrinck-Graham (1980, p. 106) further describe the opportunity for mastery inherent in latency, "This period is one of exciting growth in self-esteem, a capacity to separate from family and interact with peers and other adults, a shift from primary process to secondary process, a greater joy in bodily control, a further development of sexual identity, a control of primitive impulses leading to sublimated pleasures and a gratification in learning, a sense of humor, and a sense of mastery and competence."

It is important to remember that, in the early latency period, the ego still finds itself under more instinctual pressure than it will later on. It also is under close scrutiny from the superego as well. Regression is still used frequently to defend against certain primitive impulses. Identification with the aggressor is particularly helpful during this period, as it permits an alliance between the parental superego and the child's newly forming conscience to keep such impulses at bay.

It is abundantly clear to contemporary clinicians that sexual *interest* persists during latency in a variety of vigorous forms. Nevertheless, sexual *impulse* life is expressed less directly during this phase than in the period immediately preceding it. Sarnoff (1976), in particular, has championed the point of view that drive pressure continues unchanged during this period.

In the latter half of the latency period, we see the child acquiring significant amounts of information regarding the real world and his own interrelationship to society as blessed by the family. The traditional father, because of the pressures of the functional and pragmatic imperatives he faces in the day-to-day process of working and living, often tends to highlight the functional and practical in dealing with his own children. Logical thought processes and problem-solving are highly prized. Ambivalence and ambiguity are both tolerated more generously at home, whereas more rigid expectations enter the life of the latency-age child through school and club activities. The traditional father also helps the child distinguish between the tolerance for ambiguity at home, and the intolerance for it that can lead to problems in the world of work or school. As Sarnoff (1982) states, "The classic father brings to the [child's] *approach* [to the world] new experiences, and a background of overall intolerance to ambiguity. The child who identifies with such a father has a strengthened approach to fresh and new problems" (p. 258).

Using this summary for orientation, I would like to articulate a number of preliminary conclusions from our observations of the 8-year follow-up. First, we encountered a style of communication rich in affect, both verbal and nonverbal, which is both discursive and interactive. It was as though one is expected to be active and useful in the sharing of each other's experience. When we arrived at now 10 ½-year-old Helen's house, she greeted us at the door with a warm handshake and a "look 'em right in the eye" welcome. As we milled about the living room trying to decide where to sit, she comfortably and preemptively took the largest chair in the middle of the room. Throughout the evening Helen served as participant and facilitator of the discussion. The considerable comfort she expressed with our presence in her home was palpable, though not indiscriminate. She was eager to respond to our questions, anticipating the fun of the next one, and was articulate when she responded. She was animated physically and vocally when she spoke, easily holding our attention.

Helen made it clear that she was conscious of her audience. Early during the interview, she tapped her younger, 6-year-old, sister on the head and called her over "to talk." Helen proceeded to lecture her on her behavior and to make it clear to her that she should be on her best behavior for the guests. Her sister complied happily and gave us the family's special "everything is fine" hand signal (interpreted by Helen as such) and got up to fetch a Barbie doll, smiling at all of us as she left.

There were other moments when Helen demonstrated her ability to monitor and control the conversation in more subtle ways. She often picked up on the topic of conversation and offered her opinion or an anecdote from her life to elaborate, occasionally stepping on the heels of her parents' narration. At such moments it seemed she was *demanding* attention, although it was never to the detriment of the content or feeling of the conversation. It was more the exhibition of a familiar mode of communication. This mode was marked by frequent shifts of speaker and ease with which they could all interrupt each other. Helen had mastered these special rules of communication within her family and was busy teaching them and modeling them for her younger sister. Interestingly, the ease with which Helen interrupted her parents in conversation seemed to parallel the ease with which she was able to interrupt them in other circumstances. Helen described to us the common weekend morning experience of jumping into bed with her mother to "get Mommy's head out of her book." This active style, seen in many of the other families, stopped short of rudeness in the eye of the observers, because it stayed playful and was not so much aggressive or intrusive as it was assertive.

Helen was quite involved in many of the decisions that her family made. When the family discussed some of the behavior problems her sister was having, Helen voiced her opinion right next to those of her parents. This was indicative of a commitment to, and valuation of, the two girls' participation in family decisions.

We began to notice in the majority of these families a certain "up front" style of communication. The message seemed to be that "We all know each other well; we find each other interesting; we find this way of knowing each other useful, fun, and it is not pursued at another's expense. I can speak directly about my needs." When Helen's younger sister was feeling somewhat excluded, she got up, walked into the middle of the room, leaned up against her father, and said, "I feel left out; talk to me." Another example was the ease with which 8-year-old Katelin could interrupt a long narrative with a sudden, intrusive thought and pass it onto her father unobtrusively, "Oh, Dad, I need a note for school," without worrying about not being heard. What's more, these children seem to be saying I don't need to just have a relationship with my father through my mother, or with my mother through my father because our relationship is based on our common experience.

As a group, all the children seen so far are now quite aware that their earlier experience with their fathers and their mothers was not the average, expectable configuration of the nurturing domain. Not only is their experience unique, but they seem to feel a bit unique as a consequence. Dressed in her Brownie uniform and squeezed comfortably between her mother and father on the small couch in their living room, 8-year-old Katelin reflected at length. "I thought *everyone* had a dad for a mom. I was regular. I realize my Dad was going to be there for the rest of my life. And that my Mom was going to be at work for the rest of my life. I'm used to this. I really like my father. I feel 'specialier.' I'm a little bit different. I feel lucky. He's great, and he's willing to stay home and take care of me.

"I learned from the beginning, kind of from visiting other families, like I was a little different, you know like the song Kermit sings, 'It Isn't Easy Being Green'?

"When I was little and I started growing up—I mean *who cares* when you're a baby—they both stayed home and looked after me at the beginning. But I was about 2 and I started to notice whenever I went to a friend's house that, every time I went, the dad was not there. I would ask them, 'Why isn't your Dad here?'

"It's not that different having a dad home for a parent instead of a mom. But I felt kind of weird once when my dad had to come to nursery school, and he was the only man who was there dancing around with the other mothers playing with this chiffon thing. I know he felt weird, and he sure looked weird! To tell you the truth, it's not such a big deal now. Some of my friends teased me when I was in kindergarten, 'Your mother has a mustache,' and that really hurt my feelings." When asked how she got her friends to stop teasing her, she said, "I told them that it was really fun sometimes having a dad for a mom, and I enjoy being a little bit different from you. You'd really have a good time with your father, anyway. Dads are neat!"

On hearing this last statement, the research assistant later reported, "It set off every paternal nerve ending I had!"

Katelin's vigorous exploration of this phenomenon in her life is continually fueled by pressing latency paradigms. This is a period of peak interaction with peers and their families through school, sporting events, social groups, and religious affiliations. The energy available for friendships, competition, learning, social mastery, and adaptation is never again quite so unadulterated by conflict or the complexities of intimacy.

Katelin is an eloquent spokesperson for her cadre of fellow explorers. She was right—they all feel to some extent "specialier."

Given the comfort in *belonging* during latency, I had expected at least a bit of anxiety about "being specialier," with its tinge of public narcissistic gratification. But Allen, now 9 years old (a child who, like Helen, has been discussed previously), explained, "It's not weird for my *Dad* to be home or Mom to make money. They like their jobs." The freedom from anxiety seems to be rooted in a positive identification with father and mother, both of whom were comfortably "specialier" *and* grown up. What's more, it did not seem to do their parents any harm. Our observations to date have also led us to conclude preliminarily that increased flexibility in gender roles expressed by the parental nurturing coalition may be finding its way to some extent into the expression of gender role and (to a lesser extent) identity in these children. Although that flexibility exists, it is not yet expressed as a risk. The girls are all comfortably feminine, the boys, masculine.

The girls' feminine identifications with their mothers seems quite secure. These daughters admire their mothers' jobs and their power and authority at home. They copy their mothers' tastes in clothes, skills. They tease a lot about having new babies (10-year-old Sarah, "Mommy's got the best oven in the family because she cooks the best babies—me and Tim," her younger brother). Feminine identification in these families seems powerful and worthy of support. Biller and Weiss (1970) note that the father, by dint of his essential differentness (including sexual identity) from the mother and the daughter, helps to differentiate masculine from feminine roles for his daughter. These daughters are learning a great deal about their femininity by contrasting themselves with their masculine, nurturing fathers. This also allows the daughter to identify selectively with aspects of the father without having to adapt a wholesale masculine identification. Katelin elaborated her father's "fascination with small living things" in a unique way during her phallic oedipal years. "I used to *love* worms. Maybe I wasn't the only girl who did. Maybe other girls liked worms too, but they were too shy to admit it. [A note of exhibitionism here.] I've always been interested in worms since I was little. I had these weird questions like: Why don't they seem dirty when you pull them *out* of the dirt? How could anything stay clean when it lived in the dirt? Do they have a left and right side? How do you tell the front from the back?" She went after her fascination in a style reminiscent of her professor mother's thoroughness in the exploration of ideas and research questions.

Nurturing and generativity are highly valued aspects of these latency children's gender identities and are probably rooted more broadly in their identities as a whole. The nurturing behavior most commonly observed during the study was that directed toward siblings. Not that sibships were devoid of rivalry, competition, and envy, but the nurturing behavior seemed innately satisfying and strongly fueled by positive identification with nurturing mothers *and* fathers. Susanne seemed to take particular pride in her competence and maturation in dealing with her 4-year-old sister Amy. During a home visit, Amy disappeared into the bathroom and yelled for help with her overalls. Susanne jumped up and yelled back, "What do you want, you little . . ." as she ran to the bathroom with mock irritation to help before a parent could respond. Later, Susanne was sitting on the floor playing a subtraction game with blocks. Amy wanted to play with the blocks as well, and continued to reach over to grab at them. Amy said, "You make it, and I'll wreck it, okay?" To this, Susanne, trying to modulate her sister's impulsivity, replied, "Yeah, but I'll tell you *when*." This did not deter Amy, and she continued to grab at the blocks. Finally, Susanne playfully tackled Amy and wrestled her to the floor, giggling all the while. She repeatedly said, "You've got to let me do my homework; it says so on my report card," as she tried to push her little sister away. Her father ultimately mediated the dispute by giving Amy a smothering hug while talking to her about other options. While he was getting her another set of blocks, Amy continued to make small adjustments to Susanne's blocks. As she did this, Susanne said, "Amy, that's a great help, but can't you help me *later*?" This seemed very reminiscent to us of the modulating interventions which the father seemed to use throughout the interview with Susanne.

A theme in about half the families was that these child care arrangements seemed to influence the mother's relationship to subsequent births. In 7 of the 11 situations in which siblings have been born, the mother played a much larger role in raising the second than she had the first. This led to the majority of second siblings feeling closer to their mothers, often echoing the closeness between the firstborn child and the father, and some competition in the struggle for the attention of the primary nurturing figure for both child and parent. Susanne's father said spontaneously of Amy and his wife's relationship, "They are *so* tight. She's going to have some separation troubles next year at kindergarten because of that." His wife playfully teased, "And you and Susanne didn't?"

As to the issue of generativity, each of the 15 children in the follow-up study had an ongoing commitment to growing, raising, or feeding something: plants (both house and garden) were watered, potted, propagated; pets were nurtured, fed, walked, even bred. In general, they all husbanded and shepherded a whole panoply of living things. Caretaking was valued as an activity in and of itself. Competence, spiced with some competitiveness with other propagators, was obvious in their caretaking skills and their pride in exhibiting their "progeny."[1]

It seems a short distance from *generativity* to *productivity*, the title on the marquis of latency. This developmental preoccupation seemed to dovetail especially well with these families because, as Helen's father said, "There are no free lunches in this family." Helen echoed this sentiment, "You know, there's a *lot* to do here, and either mother or father can make you do it. It wouldn't seem fair to me if they *both* didn't make us do it." Although there was the usual grousing about how

---

1. This is a particularly interesting version of the developmental line of caretaking in boys as put forward by John Munder Ross (1977).

unfair the work loads were in these two (or one and a half) career
families (since by now all the fathers were making some contribution to
the family treasury), nevertheless the loads were by and large dis-
tributed equally. *All* the children and their siblings had chores—the
younger, the more menial; however, none was wholly "make work."
There was a work ethic that was clearly expressed and espoused by the
children. The children also knew a lot about their parents' work—what
they did, where they did it, who their friends were, and why they did it.
Katelin, again describing her father's work, "He makes pots and plates
and stuff out of clay, and then he puts them in this box of brick stuff.
He's really good at it. He starts a fire in there and then he looks in. It
gets really hot, like a volcano, and, if you went in there, you would get
cooked. When his pots come out, they're gorgeous, so he charges a lot
of money for them." Describing her mother's work, "She writes a lot of
papers and grades a lot of papers and looks after people in her school,
but mostly she likes to type and write and think. I hope I have a teacher
like her when I'm big."

The products of the children's work, especially the creative work,
seemed surprisingly present in their homes. Susanne's father, a text-
book salesman, had carefully framed her best pieces of artwork and
hung them throughout the house, even in the place of honor in the
living room—above the mantelpiece. Katelin's artwork hung in the
living room and kitchen. As a 5-year-old, Allen had been especially
interested during his diagnostic play interview in birds with "big
beakers who like to bite noses." Now he was a devoted bird watcher and
a card-carrying member of the Connecticut Audubon Society. He had
his own spotting scope, and his pencil and watercolor bird renderings
were everywhere in his home. Helen's favorite rock and shell collec-
tions were displayed throughout the den and living room.

This shared, intimate pride in productivity was evocative of a latency
version of what Lora Tessman (1982) has called "endeavor excitement." Beginning in the second year of life, endeavor excitement is
directed toward the father during a period of increased autonomy and
individuation from the mother in the traditional family. It is an important forerunner of the energy later to be invested in work and love,
according to Tessman.

There were several observations, though by no means universal, that
made us think about the special effect on these children of having their
fathers' strength, power, and vitality so palpably present in the intimacy of the nurturing interaction and domain. There was something
scrappy and expectant about the social skills of these children, somehow more notable in girls (possibly because we still expect it less),

though certainly present in boys as well. Could it be more common as a personal style because it is some form of identification with the father's power and aggressivity, seemingly more palpable in his nurturing domain than in that of the mother's? This is noteworthy because the father's sense of power, strength, and vitality is integrated into the intimacy of the nurturing domain, not just as a disciplinarian or as an idealized world manager. The child feels a certain competence in his or her ability to make demands on the external social domain, identifying with a father who seems to be doing it comfortably in the nurturing domain.

Although it is ultimately impossible to factor out the positive identification with the father's nurturing capacities from that with the mother's capacities, an incident or two is worth sharing that convinces us that daughters, in particular, take some pride in identification with their fathers' power and vitality at a physiological level.

For Susanne and Amy, this had a particularly concrete anatomical focus. They had both been talking animatedly about their father's office in their house, how he was always on the phone, and how he loved to eat apples. Suddenly, the conversation stopped, and Susanne left the living room in a big hurry, yelling, "I'm getting the tooth!" Seconds later, she arrived breathlessly back in the living room, proudly bearing in her open hand her father's recently extracted molar. She and Amy both admired its size; Amy then brought the amusing scene to a conclusion by saying, "I have big teeth too."

Ultimately, of course, both mothers and fathers contribute to all developmental achievements in their children. But is the presence of so involved a father in these children's lives likely to predispose to androgynous gender identity? Happily, no evidence appears to date in the follow-up study. Happily, I say, because, as Rosemary Balsam (personal communication) points out, androgyny may serve as a defense against fully accepting one's femininity *or* masculinity.

As the longitudinal education of this researcher continues apace, I have come to see that it is easier for parents to share nurturing responsibilities during certain developmental epochs than in others. The period we discuss here certainly seems to be the most amenable yet studied. There is enough sublimation at work to permit children to use the better part of both parents. It provides easy access to the parents as real people, doing real things, for real reasons, and not merely trying to balance gratification and frustration. Katelin again articulates the benefits to her of this buffet of identifications. "When I grow up and I'm around 21, I'd like a little apartment to get started and enough money so that I could go shopping. I'm interested in being an art person who helps people. Maybe a secretary. I feel like a big shot when I'm in offices. Maybe that's it—an art secretary." I asked if she thought she might have a family. "My friend and I play that we're grown up, and we cook for our dolls and stuff like that. The 'kissy' stuff gets us excited when we talk about it, but I hope I don't have to do the mushy stuff, like Mom and Dad do." (To paraphrase O'Neill, ah—latency.)

There are a few patterns that appear in the father's behavior toward his children during this epoch that seem worthy of note before closing this preliminary examination. Although the father still knows a great deal about his children and even takes pride in knowing unique, if irrelevant, details of their lives, there is, in general, less parental competition during this phase. The postoedipal, posttriangular era allows for less conflict and frees more energy for doing what one values instead. Helen's father, "I have staying home down to a science. I'm really motivated to being home a lot." Helen's mother, "His ideas about the kids and home are better than mine. I really like work, and I'm good at it."

Interestingly, several of the men spontaneously reported that they felt less hunger for male companionship now that their sons and daughters were in this developmental era. Susanne's father recalled that, when she was about 2, he tried to find some men to talk to about how lonely he felt as a new father. Despite his own long-term abhorrence of bars and social drinking, he went bar hopping a couple of times. He felt even worse, "I don't need to do that any more; my kids are too normal for me to have to avoid them for any length of time."

Finally, the opportunity to rework conflicted longings and turn passive into active wishes for a more involved father continues: "The more experience I have loving Allen and being involved in his growing up, the more my old hurts about my father and his distance from me seem to heal. Funny—I thought it would be the other way around—you know, make it worse, rather than better. It's better the way it is between Allen and me." Saro Palmeri has reminded us that Spanish fathers address their male children as "Papi," or Daddy, at especially intimate moments (personal communication). The lesson begins early.

BIBLIOGRAPHY

BENSON, R. & HARRISON, S. (1980). The eye of the hurricane. In Greenspan & Pollock (1980), pp. 137–144.

BILLER, H. & WEISS, E. (1970). The father-daughter relationship and the personality development of the female. *J. Genet. Psychol.*, 116:79–93.

BORNSTEIN, B. (1951). On latency. *Psychoanal. Study Child*, 6:279–285.

CATH, S., GURWITT, A., & ROSS, J., eds. (1982). *Father and Child*. Boston: Little Brown.

CHUSED, J. (1986). Consequences of paternal nurturing. *Psychoanal. Study Child*, 41:419–438.

FREUD, A. (1936). *The Ego and the Mechanisms of Defense*. New York: Int. Univ. Press.

——— (1965). *Normality and Pathology in Childhood*. New York: Int. Univ. Press.

FURMAN, E. (1980). Early latency. In Greenspan & Pollock (1980), pp. 1–32.

GREENSPAN, S. I., HATLEBERG, J., & CULLANDER, C. (1980). A developmental approach to systematic personality assessment. In Greenspan & Pollock (1980), pp. 45–82.

——— & POLLOCK, G. H. (1980). *The Course of Life*, vol. 2. Bethesda: National Institute of Mental Health.

PROVENCE, S. & NAYLOR, A. (1983). *Working with Disadvantaged Parents and Their Children*. New Haven: Yale Univ. Press.

PRUETT, K. D. (1983). Infants of primary nurturing fathers. *Psychoanal. Study Child*, 38:257–456.

——— (1985). Oedipal configurations in father-raised children. *Psychoanal. Study Child*, 40:435–281.

——— (1989). The nurturing male. In *Father and Their Families*, ed. S. Cath, A. Gurwitt, & L. Gunsberg. Hillsdale, N.J.: Analytic Press, pp. 309–408.

RADIN, N. & GOLDSMITH, R. (1985). Caregiving fathers of preschoolers. *Merrill-Palmer Q.*, 31:375–383.

ROSS, J. M. (1977). Towards fatherhood. *Int. Rev. Psychoanal.*, 4:327–347.

RUSSELL, G. (1982). Shared-caregiving families. In *Nontraditional Families*, ed. M. Lamb. Hillsdale, N.J.: Erlbaum, pp. 139–171.

SARNOFF, C. (1976). *Latency*. New York: Aronson.

——— (1982). The father's role in latency. In Cath et al. (1982), pp. 253–263.

SCHECHTER, M. & COMBRINCK-GRAHAM, L. (1980). The normal development of the seven- to ten-year-old child. In Greenspan & Pollock (1980), pp. 83–108.

TESSMAN, L. (1982). A note on the father's contribution to the daughter's ways of loving and working. In Cath et al. (1982), pp. 219–238.

Some Refinements of the Separation-Individuation Concept in Light of Research on Infants

FRED PINE, Ph.D.

The separation-individuation concept, though clinically useful, has been called into question in a critique based on systematic infant research. While an effective rejoinder to the critique can be offered, the critique plus the rejoinder nonetheless require some modifications of the initial separation-individuation concept. Following a summary of the argument, I offer those modifications here.

THIS PAPER REFLECTS AN ATTEMPT TO BRING THE FORMULATION OF THE separation-individuation phase and process into line with the empirical research data on infant attachment and cognitive functioning that has accumulated in the last 25 years. Psychoanalytic theories of development need not be based solely on the findings of such research (having room for inferences back in time based on psychoanalytic treatments of children and adults, and also on observations of infants by psychoanalytically trained researchers); but psychoanalytic developmental theories should at least be consistent with and not contradictory to such research findings. In that spirit, I offer some modifications for a conceptualization of separation-individuation.

In extensive writings, Mahler (1968, 1972; Mahler et al., 1975) has outlined her conception of a separation-individuation phase and process. This conception has been critiqued, with varying degrees of sharpness and totality, on the basis of infant research which appears to demonstrate that humans are born with a degree of perceptual and cognitive sophistication too substantial for the infant ever to have been

Professor in the department of psychiatry (psychology) at the Albert Einstein College of Medicine/Montefiore Medical Center in New York.

in a phase where he or she failed to differentiate between self and mother (Peterfreund, 1978; Gaensbauer, 1982; Lichtenberg, 1983; Horner, 1985; Stern, 1985). I have, in turn, written what I believe to be a reasonably creditable rejoinder to that critique (Pine, 1986, 1990, 1992). Nonetheless, I believe that the combined infant research and critique do require refinements of the conception of separation-individuation that Mahler first offered, refinements that differentiate the process far more based upon individual variations in development. The refinements turn out to be small but significant. To me they represent a real gain, not only bringing the separation-individuation concept into line with empirical studies on infants, but also in line with a psychoanalytic understanding of all other phases and of the multiple functions of all behavior and thought.

It is my aim here briefly to review the earlier work, critique, and rejoinder en route to showing the necessity for the refinements.

THE BACKGROUND

Mahler's experience with very young, severely ill children led her to formulate a description of what she referred to as "symbiotic psychosis" of infancy (1952, 1968). This formulation grew out of an observed difference between certain children that she saw and others whose history and description were more consistent with Kanner's (1942, 1949) work on "infantile autism." Whereas Kanner's cases were reported never to have responded to human contact from the outset (e.g., no molding of the body, no social smile), the children Mahler described were reported to have shown normal development up to a point. At that point, something (usually identifiable) happened, often in the nature of a separation from the mother, and the infant's development seemed to cease its progress and, indeed, past achievements fell away. For various reasons (Pine, 1992), Mahler came to understand this as being caused by a rupture of the children's fantasy experience of oneness with mother (symbiosis), a rupture before he or she was emotionally ready for it, and (in predisposed children) panic, regression, and fragmentation were the result. Stark, panic-driven, and overwhelming clinging behaviors (linked to the symbiosis) were often seen, but *secondary* withdrawal into noncontact (autism) was also often seen and understood as a protective shield against the panic of loss of merger fantasy.

From this beginning, Mahler set out, with systematic observational research, to study how the normal child negotiates the task that the symbiotic psychotic child presumably failed at—that is, the move from symbiosis (I prefer the terms merger, or boundarylessness, or undifferentiatedness) to self-other differentiation and object relationship. The by now well-known result of that research was the formulation of a separation-individuation phase (from about 5 to 36 months) during which the main work of the separation-individuation process takes place. That work involves the achievement by the infant and child of an awareness of separate*ness* from mother (separation) and the taking on of its own individual characteristics (individuation), this latter, ironically, largely by identifications with the mother from whom the child is differentiating but who is taken inside and made into a part of the "me." It is also well known that Mahler understood this separation-individuation phase to be preceded by phases that she called "normal autism" (0 to 2 months) and "normal symbiosis" (2 to 5 months). The first of these, the normal autistic phase—also effectively challenged on the basis of later experimental infant research—is not essential to or even necessary for her main conception, and I shall not discuss it further here (but see Pine, 1981, 1992). Finally, by way of review, it is also well known that Mahler divided the separation-individuation phase into four subphases during which different aspects of the process take place. These are: differentiation, practicing, rapprochement, and the move toward object constancy.

Mahler's conception apparently proved highly serviceable clinically and, while its preoedipal and preverbal emphasis left the concept with many who either ignored or criticized it, her ideas nonetheless began to appear frequently in various theoretical and clinical discussions. In this scene, beginning in the late 1970s, a new critique emerged—one that was anchored in the burgeoning infant research findings regarding the competencies of the infant. As already indicated, its central proposition was that an infant, now shown through ingenious experimentation to have a surprisingly functional cognitive-perceptual-memorial apparatus practically from day one of life, simply could not be thought of as unaware of the mother-infant boundary and as experiencing himself or herself as merged with or undifferentiated from the mother. The many early indications of specificity of attachment (that is, behavioral preferences for mother over others) further demonstrated the infant's capacity for differentiated mental activity.

This overall argument is straightforward and compelling. It casts into doubt the whole existence of a symbiotic phase—one of infant-mother "dual-unity" (Mahler, 1968) in the infant's mind. And the separation-individuation *process,* which is after all the process of psychological work through which the infant moves out of symbiosis and into an awareness of self-other differentiation, loses its whole *raison d'être*. No symbiosis, no reason to grow out of it—as simple as that. Is anything salvageable? Is it worth saving? I think the answer to each question is a clear "yes," and the reasons for the salvage include both the effort to develop as finely differentiated a picture of infant development as possible, and to preserve (if appropriate) a developmental conception that has proven so serviceable clinically.

Elsewhere (Pine, 1986, 1990, 1992), I have proposed a rejoinder to the critique, one that is itself, I believe, as straightforward and compelling in its own way as is the critique of the symbiosis (merger, boundarylessness) concept. It is based on inference, as is everything we say about infant mental life, and so it can of course be incorrect. But I believe it to be a reasonable argument, and I offer it here briefly as a last piece of background before I turn to the revisions in Mahler's conceptualization that are required in the light of the critique and the rejoinder.

I propose that there are *moments* in the infant's day when merger or nondifferentiation from mother is in fact close to the reality of the infant's experience. My main candidates for such moments are the times when the infant, at first crying ravenously, is held in mother's arms and begins sucking at bottle or breast; gradually, body tonus relaxes, and the infant "melts" against the mother's body and gradually into sleep. The mix of wish and gratification, of inner memory image of the breast (or bottle nipple) and its actual presence, and the fact of bodily relaxation as the infant folds into the mother's body can all produce an *experience* of merger—not simply a wish or a fantasy. As for the infant's experimentally demonstrated perceptual and cognitive capacities for self-other differentiation, no one proposes that they are at their most acute at such times of ravenous crying, hungry sucking, and subsequent drowsiness. Although the capacity for differentiation may be present in the infant's quiet wakeful moments, an experience of near-merger may be the infant's reality at the moments I have described. There may be other mergerlike moments—say, of synchronous movement as mother walks with infant in arms, or mutual cooing—but the described moments are enough for my purposes.

Are these merger experiences (if momentary as I am suggesting, rather than characterizing the whole of the 2- to 5-month period of the normal symbiotic phase) sufficient to account for the significance of merger wishes in later life? I will answer this more fully when I come to the issue of individual differences in development, but for now I want to assert that the significance of developmental events is not strictly keyed to their temporal duration. Their affective significance—if great—can more than compensate for brevity. The instance of orgasm and its impact is the best example I can adduce for adult life. Its proportional importance to most far exceeds the amount of time spent in the midst of it.

But, one might ask, will not the infant's more "realistic" differentiated perceptions of mother-self separateness be the dominant ones? Won't they provide a stable anchor of perception and memory that corrects and erases the more fantastic merger experiences? Aside from the fact that those merger experiences may not be so fantastic—that is, they may be the reality of experience at times—there is no reason to believe that the more realistic (in adult terms) differentiated perceptions will automatically win out. They are not reliably dominant in all adults, even when the fact of self-other differentiation may be thought of as more securely established. In fact, if realistic perceptions were automatically the dominant ones, there would hardly be a need for psychoanalytic therapeutic treatment at all. But quite the reverse is the case. Psychoanalysis teaches how extraordinarily difficult it is (in areas of significant conflict) for objective reality to win out over the reality powered by wish and affect. Furthermore, whatever has thus far been demonstrated about the infant's cognitive capacities, no one has yet suggested that the infant has the capacity for a superordinate cognition that compares, contrasts, and/or reconciles divergent cognitive impressions, choosing one over the other. Rather a mix-up of multiple experiences is probably laid down in memory side-by-side—hence, differentiation *and* merger.

What I have done until now is present in summary form the essence of Mahler's symbiosis and separation-individuation concepts, the critique of these concepts based on experimental work with infants, and a rejoinder to that critique. But neither the critique nor the rejoinder leaves the original conception unaltered. I would like, in the remainder of this paper, to spell out their implications for three such alterations. I shall also examine a fourth proposed alteration, which I will find to be unnecessary; I shall begin with that.

SOME ALTERATIONS AND REFINEMENTS

The timing of the "symbiotic phase." Stern (1985), in particular, among the infant researchers, has proposed that the sequence that Mahler outlined should be reversed. He suggests, for reasons deriving from the infant research described earlier, that the infant has an awareness of self-other differentiation from the outset and that symbiosis (or merger) could only be a fantasy that emerges later on, at a time when fantasy formation has become possible. Thus, first the infant records "the facts"; and later develops "fantasies."

I have no problem with the idea that fantasy elaboration of experience is an ongoing process, much of it taking place "later on" (whenever that may be). My questions are: what is such fantasy formation based upon (in the realm of merger, undifferentiatedness, boundarylessness), and what is the timing of those phenomena upon which it is based?

I want to advance the view that merger experiences are among the "facts" recorded very early (in the first half year—Mahler's symbiotic phase). I have already given the basis for this argument, namely, that the nursing infant, body tonus relaxed, melting into the mother's body, can have direct experiences of oneness with mother. These would be quite different from the more differentiated experiences of the mother in wakeful moments of alert inactivity (Wolff, 1959), but they are experiences nonetheless, perhaps achieving even greater importance because of their contrast to the more differentiated perceptions of mother, but certainly achieving importance because of their affective significance. Or are we to say that the infant, now shown by the research data to have an active sensorium and cognitive capacity, records *nothing at all* mentally during these sucking/drowsy/low-tonus moments? I do not know what the basis for such an argument might be.

Even granting that the infant has "the facts" of mother-infant differentiation in the first half year, the emergence of separation anxiety and stranger anxiety at age 8 months suggests that the affective significance of these "facts" may first be registered (or be registered in new ways) at this time period. Thus, just as an awareness of differentiation does not rule out the presence of merger experiences, neither does awareness perceptually and cognitively guarantee that the emotional significance of such awareness—that is, its implications for the merger phenomenon—is already in place early on.

But there is in any event a second major reason for staying with the idea of the *early* (0 to 6 months) formation of the anlage of the *later* merger fantasies. We would expect that the infant's and the mother's experiences are matched timewise, not least because the mother's actions-upon-the-infant organize and orchestrate the infant's experience. Thus, as an example, we may say that the child enters the anal phase in the second year of life because neuromuscular development has brought him or her to the point where sphincter control is possible, and sensation is more fully experienced, and because the surrounding culture dictates the onset of efforts at toilet training in approximately that period; but we would also have to recognize the central role of the mother, whose actions and affects begin to convey to the child in the second year the importance of that area of his body and of sphincter control to *her,* and hence to them *both,* and hence to the *child.*

So too for symbiosis or merger. When the infant is very much a helpless organism, with frequent periods of limpness in the caretaker's arms or against her body, and when his or her communicative skills are undeveloped except for those affect displays built in by evolution—it is in this (early) time period that the merger issues are significant for *mothers,* and therefore, I propose, also for their infants. The mother who takes every opportunity to hold her infant close or who, to the contrary, cannot do this for fear of the intimacy or because the infant's imagined fragility will in either case activate, gratify, or frustrate vague longings for that intimacy, longings perhaps experienced on the skin surface or in the musculature as well. While it is true that mothers may respond *later* to their toddler's thrust for individuation and separateness by trying to hold them close (Mahler et al., 1970), it is in this *early* period that the intimacy with the infant's body is at its height—with all the wishes and conflicts that this closeness may arouse, variously in various mothers.

Here, then, in the infant's vaguely experienced nursing/drowsy/low-tonus moments of merger *and* in the affective significance given to this by maternal response lies the basis for formation of early and significant anlage of merger phenomena. The fact that these are probably vague and inchoate, that the infant may not give them more elaborated fantasy form until later on, does not alter the possibility (we can say no more than that) of early onset. Individual differences in the degree to which such experiences are present will, I suggest below, turn out to be crucial.

The concept of a phase. I shall be brief here, as I have discussed this elsewhere (Pine, 1981, 1990). The concept of a symbiotic phase implicit in all that I have discussed thus far, it should be clear, is very different from the concept Mahler initially advanced. *Moments* of merger are very different from a symbiotic totality, and the findings reported in the infant research literature certainly require this altered view. This presents a different view of what the infant is like in the first half of the first year. It is a complexly experiencing organism among whose experiences are brief, but sometimes affectively highly significant, experiences of merger. This revision preserves the significance of early merger experiences (with their later clinical consequences for some individuals), and yet does not contradict the infant research findings. Furthermore, in preserving a place for merger experiences in our understanding of development, the revision also preserves the basis for understanding the psychological tasks of the separation-individuation process. Symbiosis is, however, no longer seen as the totality of the infant's experience in the 2- to 5-month period, and this in turn forces a modification of our views of separation-individuation which I will address momentarily.

But first, one additional comment: Is this conception of the momentary nature of merger in the symbiotic phase a unique conception of a "phase" as we think of it in psychoanalytic developmental theory? I think not. No more does a child spend *all of his time* "merged" with mother in the symbiotic phase than he or she does being "oral" in the oral phase or "anal" in the anal phase or "oedipal" in the oedipal phase. In all phases the child is a multifaceted, cognitively complex being— far more so than our usual phase concept seems to suggest. Libidinal and aggressive urges, exploration and play, self and object experience, developments in ego and superego function are all part of all phases. The phase concept does not imply a single-minded totality of experience, but rather (a) a time when the psychological phenomenon of the named phase has an affective centrality that far outweighs its temporal spread, however brief or extensive; and (b) a time when the critical formative events in any particular area of development take place, again without regard to their momentariness or temporal spread. The proposed symbiotic phase, then, is the time of the critical formative events (built around the particular infant's merger experiences and the particular mother's affective involvement in them) that will affect the subsequent course of merger-separation phenomena in the separation-individuation phase and beyond. With modification of terms and content, the same holds true for all of the phases conceptualized in psychoanalytic thinking.

Individual differences. There is an implicit contradiction in our book (Mahler et al., 1975) and in writings on the separation-individuation process in general. It is nonproblematic, as I see it from my current standpoint, but I want to highlight it here for the sake of developing some additional modifications in the separation-individuation concept that I think are both fruitful and, once described, self-evident. The contradiction is this: the symbiotic phase is described as a *universal* experience that requires the separation-individuation process as the psychological work by means of which the child moves beyond merger to separateness, individuation, object constancy, and object relationship. On the other hand, the fact of *individual differences* in the child's movement through both of these phases (symbiotic and separation-individuation) stands out at every turn and is indeed the basis for the several case reports in the book. On the one hand, then, we have the universals of the phases and, on the other, the fact of wide individual variation. Apart from the vague (but nonetheless necessary) recognition of unknown constitutional factors that may affect such individual variation, most of our discussions are focused on experiential factors affecting individual differences. I would like here, in the light of the modified view of the symbiotic phase (in terms of moments of experience), to propose a basis for recognition of individual differences as *inherent* in the phase concept. The adventitious circumstances of individual experience are the means through which this inherent factor plays itself out.

Once we give recognition to the momentary nature of the merger experiences in development, we introduce the question of quantity, of more and less. The crucial question developmentally is not, however, how many moments of a particular formative experience a child has had, but how significant they have been in his or her emerging intrapsychic and interpersonal psychology. Symbiotic (merger) experiences are not like walking and talking where every child begins one way (i.e., not walking or talking) and ends another. Rather, it is like the other affectively variable and significant psychological phases which everyone passes through: the "passing through" is different for each, and hence the residues of the phase and their centrality for the person vary. The emphasis that follows is less on seeing, say, merger, a differentiation subphase, separation and stranger anxiety, the affective high of the practicing phase, the affective low of the rapprochement phase, the rapprochement crisis, and the development of object constancy as universals, but rather is on asking how central these are for a particular child and the origins of this centrality. This inevitable focus on individual differences in fact reflects the realities of our data wherein virtually every component of the separation-individuation process was seen to vary from child to child.

When we ask in which infant these (or any other phenomena) become more central, one overriding consideration comes immediately to mind. For the infant, a principal route through which a giant step is taken from momentariness of a phenomenon to its extended and lasting significance has to do with the intersect of the phenomena of some particular moment with highly emotionally laden issues of the mother's functioning. When the child's moment meets the mother's significant characterological issues or conflicts, a magnification of the moment is likely to take place. We can imagine many scenarios. A mother for whom an infant's melting into her body is a vital emotional necessity, who holds, and cuddles, and conveys her longing at such moments, will automatically—by her very response—magnify the psychological significance of those moments for the infant. Or another mother who responds with irritability and/or sadness to the child's later moments of separateness (say, a "no," or toddling off on his own) will imbue those moments with conflict and/or loss for the child, at times pulling certain predisposed children back into less individuated functioning. Such magnification of the significance of moments potentially occurs with respect to all developmental phenomena and actually occurs with at least some for every mother-child pair. For some it is the merger moments, for others separation, or oral intake, or anal stubbornness, or gender confusion, or triadic rivalry. What matters most in the caretaker's character and conflicts will come to matter in the child's moments, thus extending their significance beyond the moment, and will insure their spread into the child's character and conflicts. In such ways does psychogenic transmission between parent and child take place, building those significant individual differences in area and degree of pathology that we see developmentally and clinically.

The multiple functions of indicator behaviors. The last refinement of the separation-individuation process that I wish to address (like the emphasis on individual differences) seems to me totally self-evident once it is put into words and is (like the emphasis on individual differences) responsive to the fact of the more-and-less variable in this and all developmental areas. Just as we must say that the issues of merger, separation, and individuation are more central for some children than for others, so too must we recognize that certain behaviors considered to be markers and stepping stones in the course of the separation-individuation process serve functions related to separateness or individuation more for some children than for others. All behaviors have multiple functions (Waelder, 1930), and the extent to which they serve functions with respect to any specific area is a variable.

Let me take the behavior pattern that Mahler et al. (1975) called "coercion" as an example. When the child in the second year of life was insistently demanding that the mother do things as the child wished, analysts after Freud had no difficulty in seeing such behavior as a derivative of anal phase conflicts—stubbornness, control—played out in the mother-child relationship as it was around toilet training. When, in the course of our observational research on the separation-individuation process, we saw those same behaviors in what came to be called the rapprochement subphase of separation-individuation, we understood them differently. We thought of this as the child's effort, in the face now of his awareness of separateness (15 to 24 months), to deny and reverse that awareness. It is as though the child is saying: You *will* do as I wish, and by that I will make you still be part of me, an extension of me, subject to my omnipotent control and *not* a separate person.

Now what has happened? The child's behavior did not change. But what was seen as anal stubbornness was now seen as denial of separateness. The intrapsychic function of the behavior, played out in the mother-child interaction, was seen differently. This is not an "instead of," but an "in addition to." That is to say, (1) the behavior can be seen as serving multiple functions; and (2) it can serve more one function than another at any one time or for any one child. So, too, with other behaviors that we have pointed to as indicators of the child's progression through the separation-individuation phase.

Thus, most behaviors that emerge early in development are probably broadly biologically programmed and can come to serve functions with respect to separation-individuation *and everything else* that is going on developmentally—again more of this function than another for a particular child or at a particular moment dependent upon the particular individual history and the momentary psychodynamic situation. Just as this is true for the behavior pattern of coercion in the rapprochement subphase, it is true for increased wakefulness as the child moves into and through the normal symbiotic phase, the "customs inspection" of the mother's face and the emergence of the "peekaboo" game in the differentiation subphase, and the motor spurt and "refueling" behavior in the practicing period, all as examples.

To follow through just one more of these as an example, let us take the child's reaching toward and exploring the mother's face in the differentiation subphase (5 to 9 months). We need not assume that the child is doing that in order to figure out whether that person is part of the "me" or separate. Rather, it seems clear that such behavior is biologically programmed to emerge and then comes to serve functions with regard to the development of eye-hand coordination, affectionate attachment and skin stimulation, and awareness of separateness. How the latter? Because any touching of the mother's face produces a single sensation in the child's fingers, whereas any touching of the own body produces a double sensation (in the fingers and in the part of the body touched)—a sure indicator of the difference between other and self. These are just bits of "data" that the infant experimenter accumulates in the child's move to full awareness of differentiation. While such early-emerging behavior may be somewhat less individualized than later-emerging behavior, it is not hard to imagine one child in the second year for whom the coercing of mother is predominantly a "battle of the pot" and another for whom it is predominantly one of attempted omnipotent denial of separateness—depending on how the child's inner issues have developed to that point. Even the early (say, 12 months) motor spurt of the practicing phase, a biologically based development, for one child may carry the thrust of aggression, for another of turning passive to active, for yet another of diffuse discharge of tension, even though for all, but in varying degrees, it may bring the sense of magical, omnipotent, individuated selfness.

CONCLUDING REMARKS

The existence of a so-called normal symbiotic phase (a period for the infant of experienced merger, boundarylessness, and lack of differentiation from the mother) has been called into serious question via the results of research on the infant's apparently remarkable cognitive-perceptual functioning which seems to guarantee early awareness of self-other differentiation. The conception of a separation-individuation phase and process would have the rug pulled out from under it were the critique allowed to stand unmodified. If no symbiosis, then no need to move beyond it via a separation-individuation process. As simple as that. Yet both the clinical utility of the concept of separation-individuation and the value of developing an increasingly refined conception of infant mental development dictate an attempt to respond to the critique and preserve what is of value in the separation-individuation concept. I do that here, summarizing the separation-individuation concept, the critique from the infant researchers, and my own rejoinder to that critique.

Nonetheless, both the critique and the rejoinder force a reexamination of the separation-individuation concept, and I have undertaken that here.

1. The question of *timing* of a normal symbiotic phase does not require alteration, given both the infant's (inferred) early experience of merger (especially during nursing/drowsy/low-tonus moments) and the likelihood that the *mother's* intrapsychic issues regarding merger and differentiation are most active with the very young, maximally helpless, as yet relatively unformed infant.

2. The concept of a symbiotic *phase* requires significant revision. The revision involves seeing the merger experiences as momentary ones, not an ongoing state. Nonetheless, they are affectively significant and, for some child-mother pairs, exceptionally significant and conflicted. The focus on moments does not, however, differentiate this phase from any other. A phase is reconceptualized as the time in which the significant formative events in any developmental area take place, without regard to the momentariness or extent of the presence of the particular phenomena involved.

The final two modifications of the separation-individuation concept are really two sides of a single coin, both involving the recognition of individual variability.

3. *Individual differences* in the degree to which merger and separation-individuation issues are central to mental life are the rule, not the exception. For some, movement through the 6- to 36-month period is significantly, and even primarily, about the achievement of awareness of separateness, these children presumably being ones where these issues are significant in the caretaker so that parental inputs create a magnification of these issues for the child. For other children, given the awareness of separateness side-by-side with experiences of merger from the start of life, the separation-individuation task may be less conflictful and proceed more in the background, while other issues take center stage.

4. In line with the above, the marker behaviors which we (Mahler et al., 1975) have singled out as indicators of the course of the separation-individuation process, all have (like all behaviors) *multipotentiality of intrapsychic function*, so that for one child these reflect central psychic work on separation-individuation and for another much less so.

A rejoinder to the critique of symbiosis and a refinement of the conception of the separation-individuation process can, I believe, produce a conception that (a) is not inconsistent with the findings of infant cognition research; (b) is informative regarding one significant aspect of the full range of developmental phenomena; and (c) is preservative of and even adds to the clinical utility of the separation-individuation concept.

BIBLIOGRAPHY

GAENSBAUER, T. J. (1982). The differentiation of discrete affects. *Psychoanal. Study Child*, 37:29–66.

HORNER, T. M. (1985). The psychic life of the young infant. *Amer. J. Orthopsychiat.*, 55:324–344.

KANNER, L. (1942). Autistic disturbances of affective contact. *Nerv. Child*, 2:217–250.

———— (1949). Problems of nosology and psychodynamics of early infantile autism. *Amer. J. Orthopsychiat.*, 19:416–426.

LICHTENBERG, J. (1983). *Psychoanalysis and Infant Research*. Hillsdale, N.J.: Analytic Press.

MAHLER, M. S. (1952). On child psychosis and schizophrenia. *Psychoanal. Study Child*, 7:286–305.

———— (1968). *On Human Symbiosis and the Vicissitudes of Individuation*. New York: Int. Univ. Press.

———— (1972). On the first three subphases of the separation-individuation process. *Int. J. Psychoanal.*, 53:333–338.

———— PINE, F., & BERGMAN, A. (1970). The mother's reaction to her toddler's drive for individuation. In *Parenthood: Its Psychology and Psychopathology*, ed. E. J. Anthony & T. Benedek. Boston: Little-Brown, pp. 257–274.

———— ———— ———— (1975). *The Psychological Birth of the Human Infant.* New York: Basic Books.

PETERFREUND, E. (1978). Some critical comments on psychoanalytic conceptualizations of infancy. *Int. J. Psychoanal.*, 59:427–441.

PINE, F. (1981). In the beginning. *Int. Rev. Psychoanal.*, 8:15–33.

———— (1986). The "symbiotic phase" in the light of current infancy research. *Bull. Menninger Clin.*, 50:564–569.

———— (1990). *Drive, Ego, Object, and Self.* New York: Basic Books.

———— (1992). The Mahler era in psychoanalysis. *Psychoanal. Inq.* (in press).

STERN, D. N. (1985). *The Interpersonal World of the Infant.* New York: Basic Books.

WAELDER, R. (1930). The principle of multiple function. *Psychoanal. Q.*, 5:45–62, 1936.

WOLFF, P. H. (1959). Observations on newborn infants. *Psychosom. Med.*, 21:110–118.

PSYCHOANALYTIC
THEORY

Thinking through the Hungry Baby

Toward a New Pleasure Principle

CHARLES D. LEVIN, Ph.D.

Freud's metapsychological paradigm and his conception of the neonate were closely linked. The vignette of the "hungry baby" epitomizes Freud's pain-centered, pragmatic understanding of primary motivational forces. Within the range of mainstream psychoanalytic theory, this point of view has remained essential, although in recent decades it has been supplemented in important ways by a more object-centered, moral perspective on character development. But psychoanalysis still lacks a positive metapsychological formulation of pleasure as a motivation in its own right. This paper explores the problem in the light of recent infant research and of Hartmann's systematic reflections on metapsychology.

THE CONCEPT OF FANTASY WITH WHICH WE WORK AS ANALYSTS CAN BE traced to Freud's theory of hallucinatory wish fulfillment as described in *The Interpretation of Dreams*. Freud's belief that psychic life begins with the drive-induced play of mental imagery (perception, memory, fantasy) in the first year of life has been challenged in the light of recent evidence from neonatological research (e.g., Peterfreund, 1978; Lichtenberg, 1983). I support Freud's original insight that very early

---

Psychoanalyst in private practice; postdoctoral fellow, département de sociologie, Université de Montréal; visiting professor, comparative literature, McGill University.

This paper was written during tenure of a Social Science and Humanities Research Council of Canada Doctoral Fellowship 1984–88. Earlier versions were presented to the Canadian Psychoanalytic Society, Montreal, March 1989, and the Annual Congress of the Canadian Psychoanalytic Society, Banff, Alberta, June 1990. It was awarded the D. C. Levin Memorial Essay Prize (Canadian Psychoanalytic Society), 1989. I would especially like to thank Christine Ury for all that she has done in connection with this paper.

memory traces provide the material for the dynamic evolution of the internal world. Present-day research makes it abundantly clear that Freud grossly underestimated early sociability; but in his understanding of the origins of intrapsychic life, he implicitly granted the neonate some measure of perception, cognition, and memory which can now be defended on the basis of contemporary experimental evidence. In the following discussion of these questions, I hope to demonstrate that Freud's thought experiment about the hungry baby remains surprisingly relevant to us today, as a starting point for a radically revised metapsychology.

It can be argued that the hallucinatory gratification of the drive, which Freud attributed exclusively to primary process thinking, presupposes some activity of the ego, since memory is usually described as an ego function (Schur, 1966). The important question is when the requisite cognitive functions come into play. Following Piaget (1937), popular psychoanalytic theory denies the infant sufficient perceptual and memory capacities to warrant Freud's original hypothesis. Winnicott (1962), for example, doubted that the hungry baby situation could apply until the end of the (primary undifferentiated) holding stage of development. In line with this, Lichtenberg (1987) states, "it seems unlikely that calming comes about in the awake infant as a result of conjuring up hallucinatory wish-fulfillment images of a breast. A more likely source of calming is actual sensory soothing by a caretaker or self action (thumb-sucking), or . . . the cued recall of the lived experience" (p. 315).

However, what Freud called hallucinatory gratification is, in essence, cued recall of lived experience (though Freud assumed that the baby confuses memory with perception). In my view, Freud's hypothesis is still a plausible one, if we assume that it pertains to affectively overdetermined (but not all) sectors of infant experience (Pine, 1981). Unfortunately, both the theorists and the critics of primary undifferentiation, in their attempts to make the concept of primary narcissism more logically consistent from a *cognitive* point of view, have tended to treat the most significant part of Freud's account as expendable: namely, his emphasis on the affective *memory* of the experience of pleasure in the genesis of psychic activity.

Whatever the eventual outcome of these debates,[1] it seems to me that

1. In the discussion which follows, I have presupposed the arguments and conclusions of a number of neonatological researchers who have adduced grounds for asserting the presence in early infancy of retentive memory (Rovee-Collier and Lewis, 1982; Rovee-Collier and Hayne, 1987), three-dimensional and social perception (Bower,

the more significant shortcoming of Freud's metapsychology lies not in its implications for perception but in the theory of affect: namely, his emphasis on the avoidance of pain as the motive for object experience and relationship. If we take seriously the research of Emde (1989), for example, who states, "Emotions are fundamentally social" (p. 45), then we are obliged to reconsider the role of the hedonic axis in the constitution both of the internal and the interpersonal worlds. I believe that the real problem with psychoanalytic metapsychology is that it lacks a genuine pleasure principle, and in my efforts to develop this idea, I have taken courage from Hartmann's (1958) observation that "We cannot consider adaptive a relationship to the world in which we take cognizance of the world only in so far as it causes pain" (p. 43); and also these remarks by Freud (1924):

> Pleasure and unpleasure . . . cannot be referred to an increase or a decrease of a quantity (which we describe as 'tension due to stimulus'), although they obviously have a great deal to do with that factor. It appears that they depend, not on this quantitative factor, but on some characteristic of it which we can only describe as a qualitative one. . . . Perhaps it is the rhythm, the temporal sequence of changes, rises and falls in the quantity of stimulus. We do not know [p. 160].

THE HUNGRY BABY

In chapter 7 of *The Interpretation of Dreams* there is a passage where the newly developing concept of the pleasure principle crystallizes in the vivid image of a hungry baby. The phrase "hungry baby" does not reappear in Freud's writings, but it has come to serve as an epithet for the basic model of psychoanalytic metapsychology. It was anticipated in Freud's Project (1895) and was elaborated subsequently in a variety of contexts, notably Freud's (1911) "Formulations on the Two Principles of Mental Functioning." Rapaport (1951) has suggested that the fundamental observation underlying the "conceptual model of psychoanalysis" takes the following schematic form: "restlessness [in infant]—appearance of breast and sucking—subsidence of restlessness" (p. 225). According to Freud (1900), the "first structure" of the psyche "followed the plan of a reflex apparatus, so that any sensory excitation impinging on it could be promptly discharged along a motor path." The efforts of the psychic apparatus are initially "directed towards

---

1975; Atkinson and Braddick, 1981; Spelke and Cortelyou, 1981; Butterworth, 1982; Aslin, 1985; Meltzoff and Moore, 1985), and cognitive self-object differentiation and object permanence (Wishart and Bower, 1984; Spelke, 1985; Butterworth, 1987).

keeping itself so far as possible free from stimuli" (p. 565). This idea took on the status of a necessary biological postulate—the "Constancy Principle"—and Freud (1915) defined the nervous system in terms of it: as "an apparatus which has the function of getting rid of the stimuli that reach it, or of reducing them to the lowest possible level; or which, if it were feasible, would maintain itself in an altogether unstimulated condition" (p. 120). This means that any stimulus, internal or external, is a potential impingement on the regulatory balance of the apparatus. As sources of discomfort, however, internal bodily stimuli, such as hunger, differ from external sources of irritation, such as bright lights and loud noises. The latter are usually temporary: they can be reduced (by turning away, withdrawing, going to sleep) or shut out by the stimulus barrier. But the force of the vital needs (*die Not des Lebens*) does not diminish spontaneously, and "no actions of flight avail against them" (1915, p. 119).

Freud gave another reason for distinguishing between the external stimulus and the internal *instinctual* drive: that the unpleasant effect of the drive can be diminished only through what Freud calls "satisfaction." If a hungry baby is not fed, the pressure of the stimulus (hunger) on the apparatus will increase, and this increase of innervation is what Freud defines as "unpleasure." Conversely, a decrease in the force of the stimulus—the *satisfaction* of the drive—constitutes "pleasure." Such is the famous "pleasure principle" (originally called the "unpleasure principle") which, in combination with the Constancy Principle, forms the ground plan of the psychic apparatus.

Freud's next move was brilliant. In effect, he asked: what happens when the drive has yet to be gratified? What goes on inside the baby when the mother doesn't come? His answer to this question presumes that the infant has already had an "experience of satisfaction." Previous quenchings of the drive—when the mother did come—will have included a perceptual element. The memory traces of these experiences of satisfaction will inevitably become associated with the stimulus of the drive itself. In consequence, the drive, upon resurgence, will be in a position to trigger a new element—the mnemic image of satisfaction—and thus to "re-evoke the perception itself, that is to say, to re-establish the situation of the original satisfaction" (p. 566). In short, the arousal of a vital need gives rise to the *wish* for its fulfillment, and this in turn provokes "regression" to the corresponding memory trace, which is thereby "cathected," or charged with psychic intensity. The memory trace acquires a "perceptual identity" with the actual experience of satisfaction as sensed in the past. No breast or bottle actually appear; but the baby has an experience of the satisfaction of the drive. This is what Freud meant by "psychic activity." The infant's wish fulfillment, its fantasized reproduction of the memory of gratification, is the first component of a subjective, internal world, the psychic dimension in which thinking "takes place." As Rapaport (1950, p. 261) later put it, "The hallucinatory image is the archetype of thought." Or according to Wolff (1967, p. 307), the "*hallucinatory wish fulfillment* is the precursor of veridical thought and constitutes the primary (or primitive) model of ideation in psychoanalysis."

"Nothing," said Freud (1900), "prevents us from assuming that there was a primitive state of the psychical apparatus . . . in which wishing ended in hallucinating" (p. 566). But such a blissful state cannot last indefinitely. The memory trace, no matter how pleasant, is no match for the drive; it will sooner or later be overwhelmed by the pressure of the internal stimulus. And so this primary type of thought process must of necessity evolve into a "secondary process," the mental activity associated with the practical achievement of the drive aim. When the cathected mnemic image does not succeed in reducing the unpleasure of the organism, the infant will return to crying, but this time with psychic purpose. The motor discharge will be aimed at a specific object; moreover, this object will be distinguished in some minimal sense from the mental image of the object, since the cathexis of the latter has been abandoned in favor of "specific action," and thus "reality testing" will have begun. The baby cries again, and eventually the mother comes. As Freud explains, "Thought is after all nothing but a substitute for a hallucinatory wish" (1900, p. 567; see also A. Freud, 1953, p. 13).

With this observation, Freud carries us into the realm of the "principles of mental functioning," which he divided into two: the *pleasure* principle and the *reality* principle:

> A new function was now allotted to motor discharge, which, under the dominance of the pleasure principle, had served as a means of unburdening the mental apparatus of accretions of stimuli, and which had carried out this task by sending innervations into the interior of the body (leading to expressive movements and the play of features and to manifestations of affect). Motor discharge was now employed in the appropriate alteration of reality; it was converted into *action* [1911, p. 221].

As Freud emphasized whenever his attention was focused on the relation between the two principles, the rise of the second, the reality principle, should not be taken to imply that the first, the pleasure principle, has been destroyed, or even deposed. The pleasure principle has devolved into the reality principle so that the second is really the continuation of the first by other means (as in Clausewitz's famous dictum). In Freud's own lucid account, the difference out of which the reality principle evolves is essentially a practical one—a matter of expediency.

> Just as the pleasure-ego can do nothing but *wish,* work for a yield of pleasure, and avoid unpleasure, so the reality-ego need do nothing but strive for what is *useful* and guard itself against damage. Actually the substitution of the reality principle for the pleasure principle implies no deposing of the pleasure principle, but only a safeguarding of it [1911, p. 223].

The pleasure principle remains intact—on this point, Freud was consistent: it always retained its primacy over the reality principle in his thought. The view that the pleasure principle necessarily takes ultimate precedence over the reality principle derives from the fact that the pleasure principle continues to supply the motive, while the reality principle merely introduces a change of means. The reality principle can legislate the abandonment of specific objects—for example, it can indicate that the hallucinated gratification of the drive is ineffectual, and should be relinquished if satisfaction is to be achieved; but it must point the way to adequate substitutes, and these must conform to an ultimate aim: the reduction of unpleasurable drive tension (the Constancy Principle).

To the extent that the concept of the reality principle represents in Freud's thought primarily the pragmatic adjustment of the dictates of the pleasure principle, it really signifies the adaptation of the pleasure principle to the "external world." According to this interpretation, activities based on the pleasure principle are simply evolving in the light of experience. As Hartmann (1939) pointed out, it is unnecessary to characterize this type of development as a true change of function, i.e., as a reorientation from pleasure to reality. A version of "reality" is always in play, and unless we start from the assumption that the pleasure principle originally functions in complete isolation from anything we might conceivably deem to be real, including the somatic demand of the drive itself, we are obliged to reinterpret much of the behavioral domain conventionally ascribed to the emergence of a new psychic regime—the reality principle—as nothing more than a pragmatic extension—an increasingly practical implementation—of the pleasure principle. Hartmann (1939) expressed this point very clearly:

> Psychoanalysis has impressed upon us how much the pleasure principle disturbs adaptation, and this can easily lead us to underestimate its significance in the mastery of the external world . . . the mental apparatus must search the external world for pleasure possibilities as soon as

its needs exceed a certain measure and can no longer be satisfied by fantasy. The turning to reality can also be a protection against anxieties aroused by fantasies and may serve to master anxiety. In these two cases the turning to the external world and the necessity to acknowledge it are still completely under the sway of the pleasure principle [p. 41f.].

But Hartmann's formulation, as it stands, might just as well be turned around. Once it is acknowledged that it is on the basis of the pleasure principle itself that the infant gives up on the fantasy of satisfaction, and seeks the real breast, there no longer seems to be any strong reason to invoke two different principles to explain this development. My conceptual analysis of the hungry baby model leads to the unexpected discovery that the two principles not only presuppose each other—they are in significant respects interchangeable at this stage of psychological development. The essential function of both is the same, viz., to cause the nervous system "to undertake . . . activities by which the external world is so changed as to afford satisfaction to the internal source of stimulation" (Freud, 1915, p. 120). However, insofar as the ultimate aim of the drive is satisfaction in reality, we must assume the logical—if not the temporal or ontogenetic—priority of the reality principle. The pleasure principle, as Freud defines it, and as Hartmann later amends it, is really conceived in the image of the reality principle and its pragmatic criteria: it is *already* the reality principle in undeveloped form.

WAITING FOR GRATIFICATION

There is no doubt that in Freud's account, the reality principle is inseparable from the pleasure principle. Not only does Freud come very close to stating this explicitly; it is an inescapable inference. We have seen that the hungry baby's hallucinated gratification is inevitably a disappointment; it cannot satisfy. At best, regression to the mnemic image of satisfaction will serve to delay the impact of frustration. But the unpleasurable accumulation of excitation in the baby must be such that, given the Principle of Constancy, the baby will abandon its fantasized wish fulfillment for the real breast at the first opportunity, and (under favorable conditions) the baby undoubtedly does this with pleasure. Thus, the mechanism of the pleasure principle leads quite naturally to a realistic choice, and supplies every necessary motive for the baby to distinguish between fantasies and reality.

In fact, the metapsychological issue is not the conflict between pleasure and reality, as the names of Freud's two principles and two egos seem to imply; nor is it the distinction between the imaginary breast and the real one, which the infant easily makes in practice on the basis of the "pleasure principle," as Hartmann pointed out. Preference for the real breast (as opposed to the mental image of it) does not require a "concept" or "representation" of "reality" in the Kantian or Piagetian mentalistic sense. To the extent that the reality principle is explained by the evolution of the drive, the two principles are indistinguishable, and we might just as well say that the drive operates on the reality principle as on the pleasure principle—that is, it aims for satisfaction.

What makes Freud's account interesting for us now is that it raises questions extending beyond the hungry baby. The problem posed implicitly by Freud concerns the relation between the drive and the object, which cannot be accounted for within the logic of the Constancy Principle. The psychologically significant distinction between the two principles of mental functioning is not the difference between fantasy and reality (which in its rudimentary forms can be explained well enough in terms of conventional learning theory), but the difference between demanding immediate gratification and being able to tolerate delays in satisfaction of the drive. As Freud (1911) says, "the substitution of the reality principle for the pleasure principle implies no deposing of the pleasure principle, but only a safeguarding of it. A momentary pleasure, uncertain in its results, is given up, but only in order to gain along the new path an assured pleasure at a later time" (p. 223).

This point was also stressed by Hartmann: it implies that the real meaning of the reality principle is not reality testing as such, but the capacity to withstand the pressure of the drive, to sustain a measure of emotional equilibrium, until such time as satisfaction can really be achieved. But Freud did not explain how such a capacity could be derived metapsychologically. He simply assigned it as a feature of the reality principle. There is no doubt that the ability to absorb drive pressure would distinguish the reality principle sharply from the pleasure principle. But does this ability really belong to the *reality* principle as Freud defined it? It would appear that it cannot—at least not if the reality principle represents only a modification of the pleasure principle. As Hartmann (1939) stated, "The ability to renounce an immediate pleasure-gain in order to secure a greater one in the future cannot be derived from the pleasure principle alone; not even memories of painful experiences suffice to explain it" (p. 42).

What Freud did not directly address, in his explanation of the capacity for deferral of gratification, is the possibility that it implies an emotional attachment which is not entirely reducible to the motive of drive reduction—or the Principle of Constancy—which governs the pleasure and reality principles alike. Hartmann also avoided this implication—or rather, he met it only halfway. Although he recognized the

difficulty in Freud's account of the relationship between the two principles, he retained Freud's assumption that attachment to the object is
essentially "anaclitic"—that it "leans on" or derives from the need-
gratifying function of the object. This means that the infant's attachment to the object is based essentially on the calculation of practical
advantage (and expediency): it results from the development of the
pleasure principle into the reality principle, and cannot be one of the
preconditions of the reality principle in this limited sense. In consequence, Hartmann could not directly address the question of the
baby's emotional relation to the object in the early history of the drive.
Instead, he concentrated on the cognitive aspect of the problem: he
posited that in addition to the pleasure principle, there must be *two*
kinds of reality principle: the narrow pragmatic one, which derives
from the pleasure principle in the manner Freud postulated, but which
cannot explain the rise of the capacity for deferral of gratification; and
a broader, cognitive reality principle, which "would historically precede and hierarchically outrank the pleasure principle" (p. 44). It
would be the latter which forms the basis of anticipation and deferral,
orients the baby toward realistic solutions, and "can even regulate the
possibilities of pleasure gain" (p. 44).

The problem that both Hartmann and Freud were avoiding is the
fact that although the ability to put off demands for gratification will
one day yield great *practical* benefits, it cannot at the outset be characterized as an essentially cognitive or pragmatic achievement; it is an
emotional development which in some ways goes beyond the question
of "reality" in either the cognitive or the practical senses of that term. If
the hungry baby learns to be just a little more patient, this is not likely to
be because he or she discerns some obvious advantage, such as a more
prompt feed. On the contrary, the evidence seems to suggest the opposite: that the relation between the mother and the child is not a
matter of who wins the struggle over somatic demands, but rather a
question of how they negotiate an overall psychosomatic and rhythmic
fit (Tronick, 1982). The infant's increasing capacity to tolerate delay is
not based on practical considerations; in fact, if the mother ignores the
baby's crying, on the theory that a quick response to distress would only
be a reinforcement of the crying behavior, the baby will actually tend to
cry more, rather than less, as the first year of life unfolds (Bell and
Ainsworth, 1972). Moreover, it would be rather far-fetched (and a
genuine example of the adultomorphic fallacy) to assume that the baby
learns to wait quietly for mother's breast because he has calculated, on
the basis of expediency, that a feed is more likely if he does not give in
to the pressure of hunger right away.

Leaving aside constitutional factors and innate temperamental differences, we can say that the baby comes to scream less when he is hungry if he has a satisfying emotional relationship with the mother (Ainsworth and Bell, 1977). To be able to wait is to trust the object's good intentions, and this implies that the baby is willing to grant his relation to the object a certain priority, even in fantasy, over the pressure of the drive to achieve satisfaction. It means that the "aim" of the drive has become (or is already) more than pleasure through reduction of tension (i.e., the reactive avoidance of pain), but also some other aspect of the object, some unconsumable or inchoate dimension of the "other"—an *aesthetic* dimension, if you will—as an important additional source of pleasure which compensates for the destabilizing effect of hunger-drive pressure. If we accept this, then we must try to define pleasure not only in terms of reduction of stimulus, but also in terms of increase and anticipation of stimulus—in other words, we must either abandon or relativize the Constancy Principle; and we must assume that even in the case of the very young baby, the term "stimulus" may legitimately refer to processes psychologically much more complex than the experience of hunger and its gratification.

The fact is that putting off gratification has little to do with giving up hallucinations in favor of external reality. At the very minimum, we should expect that the "reality principle" in this other sense of Freud's—the sense of being able to wait, to tolerate deferral of gratification—depends precisely on the baby's faith in the object, his *belief* in the memories of satisfaction, and hence perhaps also on his capacity to *fantasize*. According to this view, what Freud calls a regression to the mnemic trace, or "hallucination," is not necessarily a return to a more primitive mode of psychic functioning; it may represent the development of an internal world in which the baby is learning to entertain himself with "hallucinations" while he waits for the "reality" he wants to materialize. Thinking (symbolization) in this primitive sense would appear to be something that develops actively in relation to the object, rather than only negatively as a secondary defense against the non-satisfaction of the drive.

PAIN

Freud's early metapsychological reasoning (1895–1900), when examined closely, offers only slim grounds for asserting the primacy of pleasure in the psyche, and affords little insight into the nature of libido, or what he later (1920) called Eros (Compton, 1981). The overriding emphasis is on the regulation and diminution of pain. Even within the perspective of the structural model, Freud (1923) speaks, for example, of "The id, guided by the pleasure principle—that is, by the perception of unpleasure" (p. 47). As we have seen, this view of the somatic forces at work within the psyche, whose representatives Freud deemed to be *unconscious,* was influenced to some extent by the convenient and illustrative logic of hunger. Hunger is by no means a simple experience, but (if we ignore the cultural development of taste and the oral and anal constellations of psychosexual development) the psychological effects of hunger are in the main readily accessible to consciousness; and the method of satisfaction is a fairly straightforward matter of *consumption.* This cannot be said of the "sexual instincts" at any time of life. As a rule, Freud's metapsychological formalization of the drive concept fails to do justice to the sense of significance and complexity with which his otherwise less theoretically strict references to libido, sexuality, Eros, and pleasure are laden. In the five existing metapsychological papers, Freud rarely touches on the problem of psychosexual development, and makes no mention of the oedipus complex. The issue of sexual desire in particular was always held apart from consideration of the drives in general.

If it is true that the psychoanalytic understanding of sexuality has suffered from difficulties in conceptualizing the drive, this may have resulted in part from the convenient but misleading habit of lumping the many different kinds of pleasure together, and particularly the forms of satisfaction (Schur, 1966), at the metapsychological level, in order to make them conform to the Constancy Principle. Indeed, Freud (1915, p. 123) held that the drives are "qualitatively alike," distinguishable only with respect to their source, whose study "lies outside the scope of psychology." This perspective effectively ruled out the possibility of a metapsychological distinction between the various drives.

It would be wrong to say that Freud reduced metapsychology to the model of hunger. But there would be some justice in arguing that all the central features of the drive theory can be traced to a sort of amalgam of two easily observable physiological phenomena. The first would be the satisfaction of hunger, as we have seen; the second would be the male sexual orgasm, which clearly illustrates the mechanism of pleasurable bodily discharge. In general, every drive is conceived as a somatic *source* of tension with a certain *impetus* to be discharged through achievement of an *aim,* satisfaction, which is gained by consumption of an *object.* At the most basic level of drive economy, this model tends to cast the psyche in a passive role: the emphasis is on gaining pleasure, rather than making it, and pleasure itself is understood primarily as a kind of relief. The possibilities of finding pleasure in the imaginative discovery of an object, or of creating pleasure through the construction of an object, or of elaborating pleasure through a form of interaction with an object (what Kant described in his *Critique of Judgment* as "purposiveness without a purpose" and "the free play of the understanding and the imagination"), are not categorically excluded; but they have no clear metapsychological status, since they are treated by definition as secondary derivative modifications (e.g., through sublimation) of the tension pattern of the drives.

The *object* of the drive would be the pole around which the potential for an *active* pleasure principle (i.e., pleasure seeking as a primary motivational factor) is clustered. But the object for Freud was not in the main a dynamic concept. The activity of drive-functioning comes chiefly from the drive's somatic source, its impetus (energy or force), and its aim (satisfaction); yet, when taken by themselves, in relation to a static object, these dimensions of the drive are only dynamic in a *reactive* sense, because they are defined predominantly in terms of the means-ends rationality of flight/pursuit, and motivated less by gains in pleasure than by discharge of unpleasure. The object—and therefore the potential within the organism for pleasure as an end in itself, rather than as a by-product of the escape from pain—had, for Freud, a metapsychologically secondary status. Of the four constituents of the drive, he held the object to be "what is most variable about an instinct and is not originally connected with it [the instinct], but becomes assigned to it only in consequence of being peculiarly fitted to make satisfaction possible" (1915, p. 122). (Indeed, with the introduction of the death drive, Freud effectively eliminated the object concept altogether, defining innervation itself as primordially painful, and conceiving of the *pure* drive as an unalloyed expression of the overriding *aim* to extinguish *all* stimulation.)

Freud did, in fact, make a concession on these points. He noted that the object can become the focus of "a particularly close attachment of the instinct" which he described as a fixation. During psychosexual development, there are many potential objects of fixation, not least the parts of the own body. Nevertheless, the evidence suggests overwhelmingly that primary caretakers are the most important objects of such fixations, and Freud was well aware of this fact. In his metapsychological discussions of the drive, however, Freud ignored the possibility that the infant is capable *not only* of taking pleasure *from* the object, as in the satisfaction of hunger, but also of taking pleasure *in* the object, and then of *elaborating,* rather than just consuming, this pleasure, in *interaction* with the object, and in temporary disregard of the Constancy Principle (see Brazelton et al., 1974; Trevarthan, 1977;

Stern, 1985). In other words, Freud did not grasp in its full significance the "symbolic" dimension of the preverbal infant's psychological existence (and the extent to which healthy *drive* satisfaction itself probably depends upon *symbolic* satisfaction at a very early age indeed).

This was the problem that the object relations theorists were struggling with: the origins of psychic activity in the relation to the object (though not necessarily in interaction with the external object). In the process of developing this new perspective, Klein, Fairbairn, and Winnicott transformed both of the physiological metaphors underlying Freud's metapsychology—hunger (consumption) and orgasm (discharge): the helplessness and the excitement of the infant—into symbolic relations with the object (rather than energic relations to the aim) of the drive. Metapsychology became, especially in the works of Klein and Bion, a problematic of orality and anality, a reflection on "object hunger" and the "evacuation" (into the object) of dystonic psychic states. But this restoration of the object by no means settled the question of pleasure which Freud had raised. Its consequence was not to place the experience of pleasure on a new and more secure metapsychological footing, but to reinforce its displacement in favor of the emphasis on pain already implicit in Freud. This is particularly clear in the Kleinian school, where Fairbairn's dictum that the drive is object-seeking is interpreted mainly in the light of primitive defenses against psychic pain. (Unfortunately, Fairbairn also understands object-seeking in opposition to pleasure-seeking.)

It is well known that the evolution of Freud's thought (1914, 1917, 1923) foreshadows these developments. After 1914, the relation to the object began to acquire more significance in light of the structural model which was emerging. Of course, the theme of bliss dominated Freud's description of the neonate: the infant was like a protoplasm or an unhatched egg, "a system living according to the pleasure principle" (1911, p. 220n.); psychic life was tinged by "oceanic feeling," and infantile sexuality was autoerotic and polymorphous perverse. But these were all images of an isolate whose objects were nonexistent, inconstant, or "assigned." As soon as Freud considered the psychodynamic function of the object in infantile life, the picture changed. To be sure, Freud held that the mother (or the father) was the "first love object"; but he also wrote, "Hate, as a relation to objects, is older than love. It derives from the narcissistic ego's primordial repudiation of the external world with its outpouring of stimuli" (1915, p. 139). The hungry baby had become the *angry* baby.

Klein wrote of the need to "internalize the good object" as an antidote to the "death instinct," and Bion wrote of the infant's catastrophic states and the mother's reverie. It is not so difficult to reconcile these points of view with Freud's account of the hungry baby's regression, in which it turns out that "Thought is after all nothing but a substitute for a hallucinatory wish" (1900, p. 567). All three of them were theorizing about origins of mental activity in terms of psychosomatic responses to pain, and this reflects Freud's enduring view that the self-contained or egglike quality of the nascent psyche can only be breached by need—and the pain to which it gives rise—which seduce the infant into an affective submission to the pleasure-providing object. Thus, although the broad and often unacknowledged influence of Klein has been to increase our appreciation of the (internal) object in our understanding of psychodynamics, object relations theory still works within the parameters of the Constancy Principle, disguised in the form of the infant's flight to the object (internal or external) in pursuit of more tolerable and stable states of the self. The essential difference between Freud and Klein is that Freud conceived the modification of the pleasure principle into the reality principle as a practical achievement on behalf of the otherwise hapless drive, whereas Klein tended to view it as a moral victory for the abused object. Both of these points of view are essential to clinical practice and to general psychoanalytic psychology, but the attempt to squeeze them both into the vocabulary of the hungry baby model and the two principles of mental functioning has only led to confusion and theoretical discord.

PROVISIONAL CONCLUSION

On the basis of the foregoing considerations, I propose to mate the pleasure and the reality principles, in the economic and regulatory senses of those terms, and to call them, together, the *pain principle*. The pain principle would cover not only withdrawal from stimuli, but any stimulus-seeking activity originating in an unpleasurable current, including sublimation in the classical sense.

What Hartmann described as the "reality principle in the broader sense" (not derived from the [un]pleasure principle), should be conceived in terms of the various sensory-cognitive (*ego*) functions, which (as Hartmann intimated, and much subsequent infant research has confirmed) are present from birth as a human biopsychological *Anlage*.

So far as the capacity to defer drive satisfaction is concerned, it would make sense to count this among the attributes which belong to an *object principle* (using the term "object" in the psychoanalytic rather than the Piagetian sense). However, if we are to accept the idea of an object principle independent of the pain principle, we must bear in mind that emotional development is probably not contingent on object relations alone, but also on the way in which the latter intersect with the pain principle and the rudimentary ego, which may be influenced by internal or constitutional as well as environmental factors. In general, the affective system is not reducible to the functioning of any *one* of the constituents of Freud's (1915) definition of the drive. Like perception (both enteroceptive and exteroceptive), cognition, motor development, language development, and the drives themselves, it has a quasi-autonomous psychobiological base.

It is important to be able to see development in psychodynamic terms, but the explanatory scope of this point of view can be exaggerated. As Hartmann (1939) pointed out, not all psychological functions can be "derived" from conflict over drives and needs. "The ego is not merely a resultant of other forces" (p. 39). In my view, psychic activity needs to be understood as much in terms of the relationships between the various mental functions as in terms of their apparent (phylo)genetic origins one from the other. *Object perception and object-relating do not "derive" from drive frustration.*

This way of grouping metapsychologically what we already know clinically and developmentally (pain principle, ego, object principle) has several advantages: briefly, it dispenses with the metaphysical implications of atomism and essentialism—Freud's tendency to derive all of psychic life from the vicissitudes of *one* phylogenetically *primary*, functional principle—and replaces it with a more realistic, multi-genetic model of the psychic apparatus (the psyche conceived as an ongoing interaction and growth of psychological capacities); and it diminishes the confusing effect of introducing references to reality into metapsychological discourse, where "reality" may mean any number of degrees and kinds of relation to the environment (and the self). This formulation also conforms, in some important respects, to Schur's recommendation that we distinguish the pleasure principle from the unpleasure principle. Finally, it leaves room for consideration of a primary autonomous (but not necessarily conflict-free) *aesthetic* orientation to the world, to go along with the fundamentally practical point of view formulated by Freud in terms of the pain principle, and the essentially moral one developed by Klein in terms of the object principle.

The aesthetic dimension of psychic life has been discussed in various ways by Winnicott (1971), Milner (1950), Ehrenzweig (1967), and Meltzer and Williams (1988), among others; and seems to me to have been hinted at by many working in the experimental tradition of infant psychology—certainly Werner and Kaplan (1963), with the concept of "physiognomic" perception, but also Bruner (1983), with his ideas on learning as play, for example, and Brazelton et al. (1974), Stern (1985), and Trevarthan (1977), with their observations on the primary inter-subjective, kinesthetic "dance" of early relationships.

Aesthetic experience can be conceived as the most basic form of symbolic process, in which the inevitable interplay of modalities, functions, and capacities will yield specific qualities of self and/or interactional memory (Levin, 1989). It is of course fruitful to think about the aesthetic dimension in terms of the primary process in the broadest sense possible; but there is also reason, as I take Meltzer and Williams (1988) to be suggesting, to believe that aesthetic experience is constitutive of the internal world. As a primitive symbolic process, it qualifies as one of the basic media in which internal objects subsist. Clinical attention to this "layer" of experience may eventually lead to a more satisfactory formulation of the *pleasure principle* along lines independent of the problematic of the hungry baby.

Of course, any suggestion of a metapsychology which does not conform to the Constancy Principle is necessarily speculative—but no more so, I believe, than Freud's ultimate example of constancy itself: the concept of the death instinct. As Freud (1920) said, "It is surely possible to throw oneself into a line of thought and to follow it wherever it leads out of simple scientific curiosity" (p. 59). The worst that could happen is that it would lead us "beyond the pain principle."

SUMMARY

In his brilliant thought experiment about the hungry baby, and in subsequent metapsychological papers, Freud tended to equate mental pain with stimulus innervation. This encouraged a reduction of ontogeny to phylogeny, and the subordination of developmental theory to metapsychological axioms. In spite of his awareness of the complexity of both human sexuality and infantile object relations, Freud could not account for the infant's primary relatedness and stimulus-seeking behavior in metapsychological terms because he was working with concepts of "reality" and of "pleasure" which were really just logical variations of the *un*pleasure principle. I propose that psychoanalytic theory and practice would benefit from a multigenetic theory of development. I also suggest that although Freud elucidated the *pragmatic* and Klein the *moral* dimensions of the psyche (the pain principle and the object principle), an *aesthetic* point of view still needs to be worked out (the pleasure principle).

BIBLIOGRAPHY

AINSWORTH, M. D. S. & BELL, M. (1977). Infant crying and maternal responsiveness. *Child Develpm.*, 48:1208–1216.

ASLIN, R. N. (1985). Effects of experience on sensory and perceptual development. In Mehler & Fox (1985), pp. 157–183.

ATKINSON, J. & BRADDICK, O. (1982). Sensory and perceptual capacities of the neonate. In Stratton (1982), pp. 191–220.

BELL, S. & AINSWORTH, M. (1972). Infant crying and maternal responsiveness. *Child Develpm.*, 43:1171–1190.

BOWER, T. G. R. (1975). Infant perception of the third dimension and object concept development. In *Infant Perception*, ed. L. B. Cohen & P. Salapatek. New York: Academic Press, pp. 33–50.

—— (1979). *Human Development.* San Francisco: W. H. Freeman.

BRAZELTON, T. B., TRONICK, E., ADAMSON, L., ALS, H., & WISE, S. (1974). Early mother-infant reciprocity. In *Parent-Infant Interaction*, ed. R. Schaffer. Amsterdam: Elsevier, pp. 137–154.

BRUNER, J. (1983). *Child's Talk.* New York: Norton.

BUTTERWORTH, G., ed. (1982). *Infancy and Epistemology.* New York: St. Martin's.

—— (1987). Some benefits of egocentrism. In *The Child's Construction of the World*, ed. J. Bruner & H. Haste. London: Methuen, pp. 62–80.

COMPTON, A. (1981). On the psychoanalytic theory of instinctual drives. *Psychoanal. Q.*, 50:190–237, 345–392.

EHRENZWEIG, A. (1967). *The Hidden Order of Art.* Berkeley: Univ. California Press.

EMDE, R. N. (1989). The infant's relationship experience. In *Relationship Disturbances in Early Childhood*, ed. A. J. Sameroff & R. N. Emde. New York: Basic Books, pp. 33–51.

FREUD, A. (1953). Some remarks on infant observation. *Psychoanal. Study Child*, 8:9–19.

FREUD, S. (1895). Project for a scientific psychology. *S.E.*, 1:283–397.

—— (1900). The interpretation of dreams. *S.E.*, 4 & 5.

—— (1911). Formulations on the two principles of mental functioning. *S.E.*, 12:213–226.

—— (1914). On narcissism. *S.E.*, 14:3–66.

—— (1915). Instincts and their vicissitudes. *S.E.*, 14:111–140.

—— (1917). Mourning and melancholia. *S.E.*, 14:237–260.

—— (1920). Beyond the pleasure principle. *S.E.*, 18:7–64.

—— (1923). The ego and the id. *S.E.*, 19:3–66.

—— (1924). The economic problem in masochism. *S.E.*, 19:157–170.

HARTMANN, H. (1939). *Ego Psychology and the Problem of Adaptation.* New York: Int. Univ. Press, 1958.

KANT, I. (1790). *Critique of Judgment.* New York: Macmillan, 1951.

KNIGHT, R. P. & FRIEDMAN, C. R., eds. (1954). *Psychoanalytic Psychiatry and Psychology.* New York: Int. Univ. Press.

LEVIN, C. D. (1989). An essay on the symbolic process. Ph.D. dissertation, Concordian Univ.

LICHTENBERG, J. D. (1983). *Psychoanalysis and Infant Research.* Hillsdale, N.J.: Analytic Press.

——— (1987). Infant studies and clinical work with adults. *Psychoanal. Inq.,* 7:311–330.

MEHLER, J. & FOX, R., eds. (1985). *Neonate Cognition.* London: Lawrence Erlbaum.

MELTZER, D. & WILLIAMS, M. G. (1988). *The Apprehension of Beauty.* Strath Tay, Scotland: Clunie Press.

MELTZOFF, A. N. (1982). Imitation, intermodal coordination and representation in early infancy. In Butterworth (1982), pp. 85–114.

——— & MOORE, M. K. (1985). Cognitive foundations and social functions of imitation and intermodal coordination in infancy. In Mehler & Fox (1985), pp. 139–156.

MILNER, M. (1950). *On Not Being Able to Paint.* London: Heinemann, 1971.

PETERFREUND, E. (1978). Some critical comments on psychoanalytic conceptualizations of infancy. *Int. J. Psychoanal.* 59:427–441.

PIAGET, J. (1937). *The Construction of Reality in the Child.* New York: Basic Books, 1954.

PINE, F. (1981). In the beginning. *Int. Rev. Psychoanal.,* 8:15–33.

RAPAPORT, D. (1950). On the psychoanalytic theory of thinking. In Knight & Friedman (1954), pp. 259–273.

——— (1951). The conceptual model of psychoanalysis. In Knight & Friedman (1954), pp. 221–247.

——— & GILL, M. M. (1959). The points of view and assumptions of metapsychology. *Int. J. Psychoanal.,* 40:153–162.

ROVEE-COLLIER, C. & HAYNE, H. (1987). Reactivation of infant memory. In *Advances in Child Development and Behaviour,* ed. H. W. Reese. Orlando: Academic Press, vol. 5, pp. 185–238.

——— & LEWIS, P. L. (1982). Learning, adaptation, and memory in the newborn. In Stratton (1982), pp. 147–190.

SANDLER, J. & ROSENBLATT, B. (1962). The concept of the representational world. *Psychoanal. Study Child,* 17:128–148.

SCHUR, M. (1966). *The Id and the Regulatory Principles of Mental Functioning.* New York: Int. Univ. Press.

SPELKE, E. (1985). Perception of unity, persistence, and identity. In Mehler & Fox (1985), pp. 89–113.

——— & CORTELYOU, A. (1981). Perceptual aspects of social knowing. In *Infant Social Cognition,* ed. M. E. Lamb & L. R. Sherrod. Hillsdale, N.J.: Lawrence Erlbaum, pp. 61–84.

STERN, D. N. (1985). *The Interpersonal World of the Infant.* New York: Basic Books.

STRATTON, P. M., ed. (1982), *Psychobiology of the Human Newborn.* New York: Wiley.

TREVARTHAN, C. (1977). Communication and cooperation in early infancy. In *Before Speech*, ed. M. Bullowa. Cambridge: Cambridge Univ. Press, pp. 321–347.

TRONICK, E., ed. (1982). *Social Interchange in Infancy*. Baltimore: Univ. Park Press.

WERNER, H. & KAPLAN, B. (1963). *Symbol Formation*. New York: Wiley.

WINNICOTT, D. W. (1962). Ego integration in child development. *The Maturational Processes and the Facilitating Environment*. New York: Int. Univ. Press, 1965, pp. 56–63.

—— (1971). *Playing and Reality*. Harmondsworth: Pelican.

WISHART, J. G. & BOWER, T. G. R. (1984). Spatial relations and the object concept. In *Advances in Infancy Research*, ed. L. P. Lipsitt & C. Rovee-Collier, vol. 3, pp. 57–123.

WOLFF, P. H. (1967). Cognitive considerations for a psychoanalytic theory of language acquisition. In *Motives and Thought*, ed. R. R. Holt. New York: Int. Univ. Press, pp. 300–343.

On Narcissistic Defenses

CHARLES HANLY

Child observation, scholarship on pre-Homeric Greeks, and a clinical study of the loss of reality in a severely neurotic patient are used as evidence for a narcissistic form of projection that can be differentiated from projection as a defense against dangerous drive demands.

THE PURPOSE OF THIS PAPER IS TO BROADEN AND REFINE OUR UNDER-standing of projection and denial. Until recently, I had assumed that these defenses were completely understood when we conceived of them as a means of rendering an unwanted aggressive or libidinal impulse unconscious by altering perception or by substituting a fantasy for perception. But an accumulation of impressions over many years and puzzlement about a clinical issue have led me to think that a more complex formulation may enable us to get at a better approximation of these defensive processes.

The first group of impressions concern the mental lives of children. We are all familiar with projection in the lives of children. A 2-year-old, in crisis because of the birth of a sibling on account of intense, jealous rage caused by memories of pleasures lost in a painful weaning from the breast, experiences a powerful wish to get rid of his infant brother. This wish, despite its potential for pleasure, is highly painful. To some extent he loves his brother and identifies with him, but, much worse, he knows that he should love his brother as his parents do. Even the disappointing remnant of love left to him will be lost forever if he harmed the baby. He is caught in a conflict. The struggle triggers a change. His fear of becoming a monster, hateful in the eyes of his parents, has vanished. He is a good boy again. He is curious about his brother. He can touch him without fear. And at night he cannot go to sleep after having been tucked into bed, in the usual way, without

Training analyst at the Toronto Psychoanalytic Institute and professor of philosophy at the University of Toronto. This paper was completed during my tenure as Erik H. Erikson Scholar at the Austen Riggs Center.

recurrently calling out to his parents because of the terrifying tigerlike animal that lurks in the dark under his bed or in the closet of his bedroom. He is afraid that it will spring on him and tear at him with its fierce teeth. The child's world has become "inhabited" by a frightening, mysterious creature of unknown origin.

This new state of affairs is expedient in two respects despite the fact that the unwanted intruder in the child's world is indifferent to parental assurances that he does not exist. By exposing the child to the fear of an external object, the projection removes (renders unconscious) his fear of himself and reduces the consequent risk of his withdrawal from the parents upon whose love and approval he must depend. This fear serves as a motive, acceptable to the child, for calling his parents to him to give him protection and comfort. For it is such reassurances that may, in due course, tame the beast. If no remedy is found, if the child's hallucinatory defense arouses only impatient, angry reactions in his parents, the developmental dilemma for the child is this: a flaw will be incorporated into his ego and superego development (Hanly, 1984) that will correspond to his fixated aggressive need to find threatening, helpless objects upon which he can vent his latent rage. Such a need can contribute to a predisposition to become prejudiced as an adult. The flaw in ego and superego development renders the displacement of aggression involved in prejudice ego-syntonic by making it appear justified by reality. It is one source of this ego and superego flaw that will be the focus of the observations and reflections that follow.

Projection of this kind has long been familiar to psychoanalysis. Freud first described the process in 1894 in a letter to Fliess. The question I want to raise is whether there is another type of projection, which can be and needs to be differentiated from it, which has a pathogenic potential for ego and superego development comparable to and accompanying the potential for pathogenic drive development of fixated aggression and libido. Here is another example of childhood psychic defense—an instance of denial.

When my two oldest daughters were 5 and 3, I took them to visit Santa Claus at the local shopping mall. Upon our return, the eldest announced to me, "Santa Claus isn't real, is he?" When I asked her how she knew, she told me that she had seen the man under the mask. In her pride of discovery she wanted to know if she could tell her sister. My wish to protect the younger from premature disillusionment struggled for a moment with my preference not to protect a fantasy with an untruth. But the child had been listening to our conversation with wide-eyed attention. The cat was already out of the bag. I gave my permission, whereupon the following conversation ensued.

THE ELDER: Louise, you know, there really isn't a Santa Claus.

THE YOUNGER (with incredulity): Santa Claus doesn't bring toys at Christmas?

THE ELDER: No.

THE YOUNGER: Santa Claus doesn't come in a sleigh?

THE ELDER: No.

Whereupon the younger, concluding her questioning with a laugh of triumph at the absurdity of her sister's idea, said, "You mean the reindeer just pull Santa Claus along the ground?" Faced with this stalwart defense by the younger of her world of fantasy, the older sister turned away with a sigh of resignation at the failure of her effort at education to reality. I need not have been concerned about her disillusionment. Forces stronger than parental authority or sibling observation were at work preserving her enchantment until she would be ready, like her older sister, to abandon it.

Evidently, the younger child preferred a fantasy of her own to a reality—an instance of denial. To be sure, culture and society facilitate the fantasy, but the cultural and social factors serve rather than create the need that gives rise to the substitution. The denial involves more than an intellectual preference by the child for her image of Santa Claus sustained by perceptual avoidance. On the contrary, the child enthusiastically availed herself of every opportunity to see Santa Claus. Her perceptions of him were as self-evident and convincing to her as would be, in due course, her perception of the reality. And it is not only that her perceptions failed to yield a sufficiently articulated object to enable her to differentiate the man from the mask; her perceptions offered her the sight of a magical, ubiquitous figure endowed with the capacity to create and a will to provide all the objects of her desires. Here we come upon a projection of the urgent wishes of a child onto an object that becomes endowed by the projection with the capacity to satisfy them. Where have we come upon this kind of transformation of experience before? In dreams, of course, the manifest content of which, even in the case of the naïve wish-fulfillment dreams of children, always involves a measure of distortion insofar as it always represents the wish as being fulfilled. The projection transforms a helpless longing into an expectation of satisfaction by providing a perception of the means for realizing it. It gives the child a megalomanic grasp of the world and its events. It is the manic equivalent of the paranoia-forming projection described above.

We come upon a first difference between this preoedipal form of denial and denial during and after the onset of the oedipal stage. The small boy who marches off to kindergarten, carrying his father's old briefcase and wearing his discarded tie, is enacting a fantasy of being as big as his father and of being able to do what his father does. By means of the self-aggrandizing fantasy, he seeks to deny the reality of the differences. In this case, however, the denying fantasy is premised on the boy's perception of the difference which offends his sexual ambitiousness and causes him anxiety. One would be gravely concerned about the mental development of a child at this stage who not only acted in this way but who could not actually perceive the differences between himself and his father, whereas we have no concern about a preoedipal child who is unable to perceive the difference between the masquerade and the person. Nevertheless, these types of projection are episodic. They are set in motion by unrequitable wishes. However, there remains this important difference: the projection involved in the "misperception" of the Christmas fairy is phase-appropriate, it does not arise out of an infantile calamity, and it will correct itself with normal growth. Perhaps we are looking at a different kind of projection.

Let us consider one further example from the observation of children. A 3-year-old, in picking up her father's watch from a table, lets it drop on a tile floor, arousing in the father an apprehension that she might have damaged it. He picks it up, places it back on the table, mildly reprimands his daughter, and cautions her about how easily watches can be broken. She in turn goes up to the watch, wags her finger at it admonishingly (which her father had actually not done to her), and tells it to be a good watch, to stay on the table and not fall down on the floor, " 'cause you could break yourself"—uttered with a solemnity fitting the occasion and with an air of worldly wisdom. The child had effortlessly, naturally, and without guile transferred the relation she had just experienced with her father onto her relation to the watch. In this she identified herself with her father as the admonisher and herself with the watch as the admonished. Tacitly expressed in the resulting behavior is the assertion that it was not she who had dropped the watch, the watch had fallen; if anyone was awkward or naughty, it was the watch or, at least, it had to accept its full share of blame. In this way the child was protecting herself from feelings of shame about being awkward or feelings of guilt about being naughty.

In addition to the projection that maintains impulses in an unconscious state, there is the projection that maintains a veil over the mechanical, inanimate, material nature of the object by investing it with the animate life with which the child is familiar in herself and in her primary objects. This more primitive projection facilitates and, in this way, contributes to the choice of the projection that sets up the drive defense. The narcissistic projection renders the drive projection's alteration of perception ego-syntonic. In order to be able to admonish the watch, in this example, the child first had to perceive and believe the watch to be fundamentally the same as herself—she had to project her own psychic life upon it. About this assertion, there is nothing novel. It has long been recognized that children form such projections, but they have been treated as consequences of the projections that are defensive against drives and as sharing in their episodic nature. I would propose that there is a second type of projection, narcissistic projection. This projection generates an a priori schema or template according to which objects and the world are construed perceptually. It is phase-appropriate during the first stages of infantile development and normally dissolves during the oedipal stage and its resolution. It contributes to the characteristic preference of small children for projection, denial, isolation, and splitting as defenses against drives. It serves as the cornerstone upon which the magical "world" of the child is built up.

The child's ideas of substance and causality are informed by the perceptual experiences that are laid down by narcissistic projection. Piaget (1930) has studied cognitive aspects of the development of the concept of causality in children. The history of ideas can identify a broadly similar, although more complex, development in the concepts of substance and causality in the history of philosophy and science from the pre-Socratic philosophers of ancient Greece to modern times.

My thesis can, then, be stated in another way. The magical world of infancy is not simply the sum of the projections, denials, isolations, and splittings that are demanded by phase-characteristic drive conflicts. It owes its origin to intrapsychic conflict to be sure, but also, in a fundamental respect, to a conflict with the world. Children, quite apart from their need for defenses that can help them master the demands of their instinct life, require protection, given their prolonged helplessness, against an awareness of the indifference of the world to their welfare. The magical world of infancy is constructed upon a narcissistic defense which denies (veils from perceptual awareness) the indifference of the inanimate world as well as the animate and larger social world. Narcissistic projection maintains a homeostatic condition which is optimal for the growth and exploration that is necessary if the condition of helplessness is to be reduced. In retrospect, then, we may entertain the possibility, at least, that in the case of the child who was afraid of being attacked by an animal, there was in addition to the facilitation provided by the dark itself a narcissistic investment of the dark which made it into the habitation of a menace that could successfully mimic real existence. It is this narcissistic investment that gives to infantile thought its omnipotence. It is this projection that brings about the otherwise strange identity between dream and reality in the world of the child. This phenomenon of early development has been perceptively studied from the point of view of its characteristic evolution and the role of parenting by Ferenczi (1913) and by Winnicott (1971). Winnicott focuses our attention, as does Ferenczi, upon the subtly, seemingly paradoxical, dialectic of development whereby it is, in part, as a result of the phase-appropriate maintenance of narcissistic illusion in the child that its dissolution can take place.

But at this point questions arise: cannot these phenomena be adequately accounted for by means of the greater part played by primary process thinking along with the inevitable cognitive and experiential limitations of the mentality of children? Why introduce an additional hypothesis which seems to contravene the Occam's razor, *entia non sunt multiplicander?* To be sure, cognitive and experiential limitations play their part in these phenomena of childhood. The world is discovered afresh (or, sadly, not) by children as they grow. At first the world of matter and physical forces lies beyond the child's ken both intellectually and perceptually. This state of affairs undoubtedly facilitates the formation of the child's psychically animated and teleological experience of inanimate objects, but the facilitation of something does not bring it about. The possible is much larger than the actual. Moreover, children are not merely diminutive, inexperienced, and untutored adults with undeveloped capacities for perception and thought, although adults whose childhood remains heavily repressed tend to treat them as though they were. Eighteenth-century family portraits often convey this impression. In the faces of these children there appears a pathetic, fragile, precocious maturity and a dry, lifeless sobriety generated by their only being imitations of adults they cannot be. Absent, among other things, is the exuberance (or dread) of the child's life in a world animated by illusions formed by narcissistic projection made possible, but only possible, by the child's immaturity.

That primary process thought activity plays an important role in this process cannot be doubted. Displacements, condensations, use of thinking by means of images rather than by means of language provide essential keys to understanding the genesis of the child's "world." Below, I shall use Freud's (1900) idea of formal regression to link pathological narcissistic projections to primary process as he linked dreams to primary process. But primary process is the vehicle of the pleasure principle. Its tendency is only accidentally self-preservative. In itself, it is a stranger to anxiety, although its actions are modified by anxiety.

But the processes designated by "narcissistic projection" are defensive processes mobilized by anxiety. Hence, although primary process thought contributes in essential ways to narcissistic projection, it is neither identical with it nor the explanation of it. Parallel arguments arise in relation to the correct understanding of ancient Greek experience to which I now turn.

The second group of impressions derive from the study of the ancient Greeks. The animistic world view of the pre-Homeric and Homeric Greeks is often understood to have been a system of beliefs—a first attempt at an explanation of nature—based on analogies with human relations which were most immediately at hand and therefore first seized upon in the effort to make experience intelligible. Animism, in this view, was an intellectual construct—a theory about nature and the forces at work in it. In this view, there is the implicit assumption that ancient man's experience of nature—his perceptions of objects— was no different than the experience of modern man. This implicit assumption has been made explicit and given an elaborate theoretical justification in the structuralism of Levy-Strauss (1962), but I agree with the views of his predecessor, also a French cultural anthropologist, Levy-Bruhl (1910), that animism was rooted in and originated in the perceptual experience of our ancient ancestors.

This thesis is borne out by a literal reading of the text of Homer's *Iliad*. In the powerful, opening council scene Achilles is about to draw his sword to kill Agamemnon, the commander-in-chief of the Achaean forces, when he is confronted by the goddess Athene. Achilles is being carried away by rage because Agamemnon has forced Achilles to give him his captive paramour Briseis after Agamemnon had been obliged by Calchis, their high priest, to return his paramour, who was the daughter of a Trojan priest of Apollo, in an effort to cure a pestilence that was decimating the Achaean camp. Athene admonishes Achilles to put up his sword and offers him substitute gratifications if he does. The Homeric poets are at pains to report that the others at the council did not see Athene—only Achilles did. They describe a man undergoing a hallucination. Achilles' dialogue with his conscience is conducted as between two persons. His conscience is not experienced by him as an inner voice, however impersonal and at odds with his impulse—it is experienced as a being addressed by a mother figure. The hallucinated figure plays the part of the parent, who serves as an auxiliary ego and conscience for the small child.

The difference between the child and the adult in ancient times seems to have been the substitution of precariously internalized and idealized parental figures for the real parents—a maturational process

that fell short of the consolidation of a superego as a part of the ego,
even if an unconscious part. Those scholars who treat the account of
the gods in the *Iliad* as a dramatization of a set of abstract theological
beliefs have to explain away as poetic license passages in which the
poets themselves treat these experiences quite literally. Homer's descriptions of the gods go well beyond the allegorical poetic machinery
which traditional scholars have wanted to make it out to be. What
Homer appears to be describing is a form of experience in which the
identifications that form the nucleus of the superego have not been
internalized. They remain attached to their original, narcissistically
aggrandized objects, the images of which retained a high potential for
projection. This reading is also justified by the evidence reported by
Dodds (1963) that even later than the Homeric period ancient Greeks
experienced their dreams as events that occurred outside the boundaries of their own egos which their sleeping minds had been able to
witness, as though a part of the psyche had escaped its proper boundaries and lived a life of its own in nature. A remnant of this way of
experiencing dreams is alluded to by Socrates when, during his impris-
onment while awaiting death, he recalled a dream in his youth in which
a priestess had appeared to him and admonished him to make music.
He had believed that his vocation as a skeptical philosopher would
make good his fate, but he had lately taken to writing poetry in case he
might have been in error.

Again, in the *Iliad,* there is an account of how the Trojan soldiers
became frightened and recoiled in terror as from a tabooed object
when a snake landed in their midst as it fell from the grasp of an eagle
flying over them. A priest to whom they reported the ill omen confirmed their worst fears. The snake represented Agamemnon, the
eagle Hector, the Trojan leader, and it signified that Hector would fail
in his attempt to assault and destroy the Greek camp. Hector, when
apprized of this news, claimed a higher authority for his confidence in
victory—the promise of Zeus, no doubt in an oracular dream or in a
waking hallucinatory experience, the text does not say.

These sorts of experience are typical of animistic cultures. The point
I wish to make about them is that the experience of nature upon which
an animistic culture can thrive requires that the inherent nature of
objects must be obscured by a projection of psychic qualities upon
them. In order for the ancients to react to the behavior of animals, the
breaking of weapons or other artifacts, disease, etc., as described by
Homer, the character of their perceptions must have denied them
access to a perceptual and hence to an intellectual awareness of the
inherent irrelevance of the flight of a bird and the fate of a snake, to the

outcome of human events. In order for natural events to become symbolic messages that could reveal the fate-disposing intentions of the gods, there had to be at work a pervasive projection onto nature through which it acquired a divine and demonic psychic character. In my example, I assume that the Trojan soldiers did not dare experience their own terror and helplessness in the face of the battle their leader was insisting they must fight. It was required to assume an existence outside the boundaries of their egos. A chance natural event offered those who shared a common situation, and a common denied despair, a form of experience through which their wish to move Hector to abandon his ambition might be realized. The hypothesis that I am proposing to account for the characteristic phenomenon of animism is a pervasive narcissistic projection preserved into adulthood by the cultural, social, and psychological conditions of that time.

The self-alienation consequent upon this projection is illustrated in the reconciliation of Achilles with Agamemnon which led to Achilles' return to the battle. Instead of acknowledging his vengefulness toward Achilles and the adverse consequences that followed from it as his own, Agamemnon solemnly attributes them to Zeus. He had been the passive vehicle of "a Power that takes complete command, Ate, the eldest Daughter of Zeus, who blinds us all, accursed spirit that she is . . . flitting through men's heads, corrupting them, and bringing this one or that one down" (*Iliad*, p. 356). The use of projection by the great archaic king to alienate responsibility is not basically different psychologically from its use by the child who scolds a watch.

The forms of experience to which these projections give rise are adaptive and expedient given the circumstances of extreme helplessness shared by our ancient ancestors and modern children when confronted by external and internal danger. When survival is threatened, an illusory hope or assurance is better than despair. In this respect narcissistic projection can serve the same purpose as Freud's (1926) postulated stimulus barrier. Narcissistic projection in childhood is biologically adaptive insofar as it protects a transitional period during which the child's capacities for a more adequate relation to reality can develop. It allows for a first circumscribed differentiation of subject and object. It allows for a measure of independence from parents. The same can be said of the adaptive value of the animism of our ancient ancestors. Animism is still phase-appropriate for children, and it was the best way of experiencing life and nature available to the ancients as they made the transition from dumb animal to *homo sapiens*. Of modern adult life the same cannot be said.

What is the source of the difference between patients who are able to tolerate conflict and those that are driven to enact it? What is the difference between, for example, a patient who suffers the symptoms of an unconscious family romance fantasy but does not act it out and one who does? I want to present something of the analysis of such a patient in order to consider whether or not the idea of a pervasive narcissistic projection would help in understanding the more severe forms of neurosis involved.

The patient, a professional man recently graduated from university in his late 20s, appeared to be obsessional. During his assessment interviews he spoke in rather flat measured tones with an air of painstaking attention to relevant details in his carefully constructed account of his circumstances and history. Upon entering with a courteous, rather formal greeting, he would carefully hang up his jacket on the hooks provided and seat himself, taking special precautions against disturbing the creases in his trousers in a posture rather uncomfortably maintained throughout the somewhat tense, but otherwise unexceptional interviews. He was the eldest of two children of a poor European immigrant family to the U.S. where he had grown up in a slum. He saw his father as a failure in the small shop he had established—the object of criticism by a discontented mother. He described his mother as demanding and aloof, lacking in comfortable affection, taking pride in the furnishing of their home, which she had acquired through savings from her employment and kept covered with protective plastic. He remembered having been given a puppy when he was a small child and his mother forcing him to give it up when it had soiled the rug in the living room. Yet he prided himself in his importance to his mother who let him know of her derogating attitude toward his father. He felt called upon to do something exceptional with his life. He had been married, divorced, and now lived with a divorced woman of his own age and profession with two children from her previous marriage. He had recently come to Toronto where, despite difficult economic conditions in his field, he had secured a solid junior, but appropriate, position in an excellent firm, but he was fearful that he might lose his job. He felt somewhat depressed. There were uncertainties and dissatisfactions about his girlfriend. That she was a little taller than he was one of several banal-seeming complaints that he had about her. He looked forward to the analysis as something he had long felt much in need of and which he highly valued. I did not even remotely surmise at the time what lay ahead for both of us or what lay hidden in this bit of ingratiation. These initial interviews took place in July and since I was planning an August vacation, I thought it best to start the analysis in September.

By the time my patient attended his first analytic session, his circumstances had radically altered. He had been fired. He was without employment. The obsessional veneer was in tatters. He felt humiliated and depressed as well as wronged and enraged. Mr. L. believed that he had been "in on the ground floor" of a new branch office of the firm—the first professional to be hired—that he should have been promoted as the operation grew and new personnel were added. Instead, a director arrived and more appointments were made at his level. He believed, perhaps correctly, that one of these recent arrivals was preferred to him by the director whom he had come to hate and look upon as an incompetent. He began to see how the director's incompetence was causing mistakes in the development of the first major project upon which the group had embarked. He came to believe that it was his duty to try to rescue the operation. He wrote a lengthy report to the owner of the firm denouncing the director as an incompetent, detailing his mismanagement of the project, outlining a plan of his own to save the day, and offering his services to direct the operation. For these efforts, he had been summarily dismissed. The project, one that was well known to the public, continued on its way to a successful completion.

The analysis gradually revealed intense, rivalrous, pseudooedipal ambitions at work in a family romance fantasy. He was to come to a new country, as his father had once done, but, unlike his father, he was to become a towering success and make his fame and fortune. He identified the owner of the firm for which he worked as the family romance father who would give him his start. The transference was centered upon the same unconscious identification. Behind his superficially saccharine courtesy concerning the importance of the analysis to him as we parted for the summer there was growing an intense narcissistic fantasy of me as the grandiose, benign parent who would see to it that his wishes were, at last, gratified. This transference found its way into dreams with the recurrent theme of a powerful figure who enabled him to accomplish some exceptional feat sometimes including bettering his benefactor. It emerged in a transference fantasy. He knew that he was a control case. Through his genius at being a patient, so the fantasy went, he would make me into a brilliant analyst. I would quickly become wealthy and famous and give him his rightful due—acknowledgment, acclaim, and royalties on my fees for life, thus making him rich and famous too. Here we come upon the prototype for these fantasies in the transition from primary narcissism to the first form of object love in which the grandiosity of primary narcissism is invested in the mother and by extension in the father. This same narcissistic template organized his love relations. He idealized the woman with whom he had formed a common-law relation in the same fashion. He expected her to set him up in his profession, to which she also belonged, and became enraged with her when she showed every indication of having professional and life interests of her own that were not dedicated to promoting him.

Can the sequence of events be formulated as follows? Mr. L. came to Canada to make his fame and fortune. What constituted fame and fortune for him was still largely determined by unresolved infantile ambitions. After an initial success, he began to despair of realizing his aims. Disappointing events at work caused him to become worried that he would suffer another in a series of defeats. He sought therapy. The conclusion of the contract for analysis had precipitated a regression to the early narcissistic organization described above. This regression aroused in him the elational conviction that success was, at last, in hand and it released a narcissistic projection that both inhibited his capacity to test the reality of his situation and caused him to see real flaws in the operation of the business where there were only things that disappointed his burgeoning ambitions. He became persuaded that he had the evidence he needed to make his case to the owner. And so he did. And so he once again encountered a humiliating defeat.

Here we come to a crucial point in the argument. How are we to account for the acting out of the family romance fantasy? Need we appeal to a regression to an early stage of narcissism and to a narcissistic projection? Is it not sufficient, and more economical besides, to assume that this man's family romance fantasies had become exceptionally intensified. The hypercathexis of the fantasy had caused him to overlook things he should have been paying attention to, had interfered with his judgment, etc. To be sure, these things had taken place. And to be sure, the intensification of this fantasy had a decisive influence on his motivation. For a full and correct understanding of Mr. L.'s situation, however, it is necessary to take something else into account. There appears to have occurred what one might call a shrinking or impoverishment of his experience—a reduction of it to the standpoint of his own ego and its interests. He could no longer take the standpoint of another person—his director, the owner, his rival—as a point of orientation to gain a perspective on his situation that was not dominated by his own needs, ambitions, and expectations. If the director asked his rival to undertake a particular piece of work, it had to be because he preferred him and could not be because it happened to be expedient. A host of indications of reality of this sort were no longer available to him. They could no longer stimulate self-doubt. His perceptual contact with these realities was broken and replaced with a flood of impressions that made his grand design seem not only correct but urgent. In this respect, this adult's perception of reality was no different from the child who could not yet perceive the man behind the mask or the Homeric warrior who trembled in terror at the sound of the thunder of an approaching storm not only, or primarily, because of the dangers of the storm, but because he heard in it the anger of a god.

Many patients suffer from the demands of a family romance fantasy, but they are able to contain its derivatives without acting them out. Mr. L. was unable to do so. I wonder if this difference could not be explained by a regression to a narcissistic stage of childhood and the narcissistic projection that is characteristic of it. These processes are not independent. It is the increase in the intensity of the object-libidinal fantasies that causes the ego to undergo both the impoverishment of its self-critical capacities and the intensification of its grandiosity involved in the narcissistic regression. The narcissistic regression then becomes the ally of the object-libidinal and aggressive fantasies in the acting out.

Freud (1900) identified three types of regression: topographical, temporal, and formal. Formal regression is defined as "where primitive methods of expression and representation take the place of the usual ones" (p. 548). If to this one were to add "primitive methods of perception," one would have included what I have been referring to as narcissistic projection or a regression to narcissistic projection. Freud (1924a, 1924b) called our attention to the loss of reality in neurosis, even when it involves only the substitution of a fantasy for reality and to the continuity between this state and the much more disturbed one that occurs when the perception of reality is altered by a fantasy. One can locate three points on this continuum: at the upper end, a fantasy is substituted for reality, but the capacity to test reality is not impaired; in the middle, a fantasy is substituted for reality, and the capacity to test reality is impaired, although its perception has not been otherwise altered, i.e., hallucinatory disturbances of perception do not occur; at the lower end, the perception of reality is altered by fantasy to the extent that it becomes hallucinatory.

The ego state of the patient described above could be located toward the lower end of the middle group. His perceptions of objects and events were not hallucinatory, but they were so dominated by his unconscious aggressive and libidinal aims and by grandiose ego ideals that their intrinsic nature was veiled by subjective meaning. He had, as it were, himself created the mask behind which he could not see the man. This patient acted upon his unconscious family romance fantasy when others do not—both because of the strength of the fantasy and because of a regression to narcissistic ego functioning which altered his perceptual awareness so that he took the conscious ideas and wishes deriving from the fantasy to be viable ambitions. And so he pursued them in the world to his own undoing.

When Freud reintroduced the concept of defensive process in 1926, he pointed out that repression is only one of the potentially pathogenic ways in which the ego manages conflict. He concluded, "It may well be that before its sharp cleavage into an ego and an id, and before the formation of a super-ego, the mental apparatus makes use of different methods of defence from those which it employs after it has reached these stages of organization" (p. 164). My hypothesis is that narcissistic projection and denial are such prestructural defensive processes. Like the early libidinal organizations, they are not originally pathogenic, nor are they pathogenic in the circumscribed regressions to them in dreams, play, and art. They become pathogenic when the ego is forced to have recourse to them in confronting the realities of everyday life.

Narcissistic projection and denial can be differentiated from their drive equivalents because they occur in the absence of drive conflict in the lives of children and as they probably did in the lives of ancient peoples. However, my observations agree with Grunberger (1971, 1989) insofar as he preserves integral links between narcissistic and object libido. They do not agree with Kohut's (1971, 1977, 1978) theory of narcissism which first severs and then reverses these links (see also Goldberg, 1988). There is, however, a point of similarity in the self-psychological notion of a selfobject insofar as the self or ego, in narcissistic defenses, makes the object over according to its own needs. There is also a point of similarity with Klein's (1946, 1955) idea of projective identification (see also Grinberg, 1990) insofar as narcissistic projection involves an identification of the object with the self, rather than an identification of the self with the object. But the concept of narcissistic projection as developed here does not presuppose a death instinct, nor does it presuppose Klein's postulated infantile instigators of projective identification. According to my hypothesis, narcissistic projection would develop whether or not infants had to defend themselves against the bad parts described by Klein. Geleerd (1965) has described the continuing normal use of narcissistic projection in adult life using the idea of "denial in the service of the need to survive" (p. 123). A. Freud (1936) has described the restriction of the ego which results from a reliance upon the denial of an unpleasant reality but does not consider narcissistic projection as such. Kris (1979) explores the narcissistic factor of denial in fantasy. These views are consistent with the hypothesis of this paper which postulates that drive conflict and a regression to narcissistic defenses are codeterminants of severe neuroses (see also the discussion of regression in psychoses by Arlow and Brenner, 1964). But perhaps, more importantly, this account of narcissistic defense may be viewed as a development and elaboration of Annie Reich's (1953, 1960) observations on regression, narcissistic identification, and narcissistic object relations in her seminal papers on pathological forms of self-esteem regulation.

If one adopts the narrow definition of projection recommended by Anna Freud (Sandler, 1985) as "the externalization of a disowned impulse in one's self onto another, an impulse which is felt to be coming back at oneself" (p. 143), then narcissistic defenses, as described here, should not be classified as projections for in them there need be no projection and reversal of an endangering drive demand as one finds, for example, clearly present in the child's fear of an attacking jungle animal under her bed discussed above. In contrast, the child who "sees" Santa Claus to be real, the child who "sees" an artifact as animated by mischievous and obedient volitions, the ancient Greek who experiences his conscience addressing him from a hallucinated figure, or the modern adult, struggling with exaggerated ambition, who perceives opportunities for self-advancement in a situation that offers nothing better than ordinary possibilities, are perceptually altering reality in order to render it ego-syntonic. These phenomena could be classified as externalizations rather than projections, if one were to generalize from Anna Freud's account of externalization in the transference (1965, p. 41).

Whatever one's view of this taxonomic question which is still much in dispute (Sandler, 1985; Sandler and Perlow, 1987), the process that I have labeled narcissistic projection has two salient points in common with projection in the narrow sense that makes me want to exercise the "licence to use projection and externalization interchangeably" (Sandler, 1985, p. 145). Its mechanism shares with projection in the narrow sense the alteration of the perception of reality. (The phenomena that I have considered are instances of very large classes of phenomena that suggest that narcissistic projection involves global, as distinct from local, alterations of perception and that drive-conflict-motivated projection may depend upon it for its efficacy.) The pathogenic effect of narcissistic projection is the same as the effect of drive-motivated projection—an interference with reality testing. At the same time, the data that I have considered from child observation and classical cultural history are consistent with Anna Freud's suggestion that externalization refers to normal developmental processes, although I prefer to use the term projection. However, I have suggested—and I believe

Anna Freud would not have disagreed—that what I am calling narcissistic projection has an inherent potential for serious pathogenesis when fixation of ego development occurs or when a formal regression to this childhood stage of ego functioning occurs in an adult. In the final analysis, any terminology will serve that enables us to draw the correct distinctions and to make accurate conceptualizations of the phenomena. What I have termed narcissistic projection is motivationally and structurally different from projections that defend against threatening drive demands. If one considers these differences to be more important taxonomically than the similarities I have used as a basis for a choice of terms, and if the term "externalization" is used to mark these differences, I have no quarrel with the choice for narcissistic projection, and externalization would either be synonymous or narcissistic projection would be an important species of externalization.

What was the pathogenic combination of factors in the case of acting out described above? There was a provocative current situation. The patient found himself in a new job, in a new country—a circumstance that posed for him the question of success or failure. He had been in this situation before in graduating from high school, in the armed forces, and at university. Each time he had contrived failure. And he had a secret liability. He had graduated and held a degree in his field, but his degree was flawed for he had paid others to write a major thesis required for graduation. He now needed this knowledge in his employment. Success was defined for him by his unconscious, narcissistically compromised, oedipal ambitions. His ego ideal required of him a stunning success that would make him powerful and wealthy for life, universally admired for his genius. His sexuality and aggression and his ego ideal urgently demanded what his ego could not possibly accomplish. In seeking to satisfy these demands, the ego had to deny its own flaw. His ego regressed. This regression was facilitated by his new relationship to his analyst. On the surface the analysis was intended to help him succeed, according to his real abilities and opportunities, but the relationship was, of course, immediately enlisted unconsciously in the regression. The analyst was to provide him with the Excalibur he needed to triumph at last. His unconscious fear of this dependency and its meaning was such that it propelled him into action in the hope that he would be able to pay the analyst one last visit upon his return to report that he no longer needed analysis. In this transference there is evidence of an unconscious perception of the analyst by the patient that answers to the description of a narcissistic projection or denial. The analyst and what he can realistically offer had vanished in the patient's fantasy in the way in which the person disappears in the masquerade under the rapt gaze of an excited child.

It must be evident that this clinical account has been greatly simplified in order to focus attention upon its narcissistic aspects. For example, in addition to the patient's fear of dependency in the transference there was also a negative oedipal fear of passivity which contributed to his desperate striving after phallic grandiosity. In the transference this conflict aroused a fear of the unconscious wish to be dominated and penetrated by the analyst, which was compounded with and intensified his fear of my finding out about his having once presented the work of others as his own. This factor also contributed to his acting out. But his cheating was itself motivated by a despair about his own competence that was at once narcissistic, aggressive, and sexual. These factors are conjunctive rather than alternative, although their relative importance will vary with the severity of the neurosis. The ego ideal, while functionally and developmentally differentiated from the ideal ego (Hanly, 1984), retains potential connections. This potential is actualized in the form of magical ideas concerning the efficacy of moral conduct even in a mature adult who has a well-established, agnostic, positivistic view of the world when threatened with real helplessness. Narcissistic defenses are not isolated from other defenses in the lives of people, just as narcissistic libido is not disconnected from object libido.

Narcissistic projection and denial have a holistic, seamless quality which uniformly suspends reality testing in favor of subjectively determined meanings or in favor of objectively determined meanings which happen to or have been contrived to cohere with the demands of urgent preferences. This seamless quality makes the effects of narcissistic projection akin to the postulated effects upon experience of Kant's synthetic a priori forms which, like projection, also have their source in the human mind. It is also akin to the music of the spheres of the ancient Pythagoreans who, on mathematical and cosmological grounds, postulated that the heavenly spheres made perfect harmonies as they rotated, which could not be heard because they never ceased or began or varied in any way. The care that a good mother gives her child sustains the child's illusion of omnipotence on the side of reality as Ferenczi (1913) so well described; she preserves the monad, as Grunberger (1989) would say, as do the cultural and commercial Christmas and other festival masques. The willing suspension of disbelief that occurs normally and necessarily in the theater, if the theater is to be enjoyed, has this same global quality. If anything in the spectacle or a distraction from the audience breaks the "spell," the illusion ceases and one is only watching actors play their parts. The pomp and circumstance of religious and civic rituals and ceremonies have a similar character in adult life. It was this narcissistic spell that King Lear broke in his "mad" ravings and meditations on the heath. Formal regression in dreams has the same effect until more anxiety than we can tolerate arouses the sleeping reflection that it is only a dream or, if intense enough, arouses us altogether (Freud, 1900). Children, in whom reality testing remains relatively undeveloped because of their continued reliance on narcissistic projection in their waking lives, often need to call upon the reassuring presence of their parents to whom this ego function is vouchsafed when they have dreams in which anxiety prevails. This narcissism is defensive in its function insofar as it protects against painful experiences of helplessness from within and without. It is activated by signal anxiety, as are other defensive processes. If this hypothesis of narcissistic defenses is sound, it should add to our clinical capacity to understand the more severe neuroses in children and adults in which reality testing is badly compromised as well as to further our understanding of the contribution that narcissism has made and continues to make to life generally.

BIBLIOGRAPHY

ARLOW, J. A. & BRENNER, C. (1964). *Psychoanalytic Concepts and the Structural Theory.* New York: Int. Univ. Press.

DODDS, E. R. (1963). *The Greeks and the Irrational.* Berkeley: Univ. California Press.

FERENCZI, S. (1913). Stages in the development of the sense of reality. *First Contributions to Psycho-Analysis.* London: Hogarth Press, pp. 213–239.

FREUD, A. (1936). *The Ego and the Mechanisms of Defense.* New York: Int. Univ. Press, 1966.

——— (1965). *Normality and Pathology in Childhood.* New York: Int. Univ. Press.

FREUD, S. (1895). Extracts from the Fliess papers: Draft H. *S.E.,* 1:177–397.

——— (1900). The interpretation of dreams. *S.E.,* 4 & 5.

——— (1924a). Neurosis and psychosis. *S.E.,* 19:149–153.

——— (1924b). Loss of reality in neurosis and psychosis. *S.E.,* 19:183–187.

——— (1926). Inhibitions, symptoms and anxiety. *S.E.,* 20:87–175.

GELEERD, E. R. (1965). Two kinds of denial. *Drives, Affects, Behavior,* ed. M. Schur. New York: Int. Univ. Press, 2:118–127.

GOLDBERG, A. (1988). *A Fresh Look at Psychoanalysis.* Hillsdale, N.J.: Analytic Press.

GRINBERG, L. (1990). *The Goals of Psychoanalysis.* London: Karnac Books.

GRUNBERGER, B. (1971). *Narcissism: Psychoanalytic Essays,* tr. J. S. Diamanti. New York: Int. Univ. Press, 1979.

——— (1989). *New Essays on Narcissism,* tr. D. Macey. London: Free Association Books.

HANLY, C. (1984). Ego ideal and ideal ego. *Int. J. Psychoanal.*, 65:253–261.

HOMER. *The Iliad,* tr. E. V. Rieu. Hammondsworth: Penguin Books, 1950.

KLEIN, M. (1946). Notes on some schizoid mechanisms. *The Writings of Melanie Klein,* 3:1–24. New York: Free Press, 1975, pp. 1–24.

——— (1955). On identification. Ibid., 3:141–175.

KOHUT, H. (1971). *The Analysis of the Self.* New York: Int. Univ. Press.

——— (1977). *The Restoration of the Self.* New York: Int. Univ. Press.

——— (1978). *The Search for the Self,* 2 vols. New York: Int. Univ. Press.

KRIS, A. (1979). Persistence of denial in fantasy. *Psychoanal. Study Child,* 34:145–154.

LEVY-BRUHL, L. (1910). *Fonctions mentales dans les societes inferieures.* Paris: Alcan.

LEVY-STRAUSS, C. (1962). *La pensee sauvage.* Paris: Plon.

PIAGET, J. (1930). *The Child's Conception of Physical Causality.* New York: Harcourt, Brace.

REICH, A. (1953). Narcissistic object choice in women. *Psychoanalytic Contributions.* New York: Int. Univ. Press, 1973, pp. 178–208.

——— (1960). Pathologic forms of self-esteem regulation. Ibid., pp. 288–311.

SANDLER, J. (1985). *The Analysis of Defense.* New York: Int. Univ. Press.

——— & PERLOW, M. (1987). Internalization and externalization. *Projection, Identification, Projective Identification,* ed. J. Sandler. Madison, Ct.: Int. Univ. Press, 1987, pp. 1–12.

WINNICOTT, D. W. (1971). *Playing and Reality.* New York: Basic Books.

Did Dora Have an Oedipus Complex?

A Reexamination of the Theoretical Context of Freud's "Fragment of an Analysis"

RACHEL B. BLASS, M.A.

A careful review of the Dora case refutes the commonly held view that it reflects Freud's adoption of his classical oedipal model. Through Dora, Freud examined some of the theoretical and emotional underpinnings of the seduction theory and began a complex and very gradual move toward an oedipal model, never reaching his classical formulation. The transitional nature of this case allows for an understanding of some of Freud's difficulties in adopting the oedipal model and the considerations that, nevertheless, eventually determined the move. How and why this was overlooked in all later studies of the case has important implications for the process of development of psychoanalytic theory and the writing of its history.

DORA AND THE POSITIVE OEDIPUS COMPLEX

JONES (1953), COMMENTING ON FREUD'S "FRAGMENT OF AN ANALYSIS," asserts, "The comparison, or rather the contrast, between Freud's early case histories in the 1895 *Studies on Hysteria* and this beautiful little

Department of psychology and student counseling services, Hebrew University of Jerusalem. This research was supported in part by a fellowship from the Smolen Foundation, Sigmund Freud Center, Hebrew University of Jerusalem.

I wish to thank Prof. Bennett Simon for our discussions which inspired the present paper, his support which contributed to its materialization, and his helpful comments which enriched it.

monograph composed six years later is illuminating. . . . The almost clumsy groping in the one, and the confident penetration in the other, could let one well believe that they proceeded from two different men" (p. 364). Subsequent analyses tend to support this position. It was no longer Freud the novice of the outdated seduction theory that had to be contended with. It was now the Freud of fantasy, dream, wish, and transference, all centering around the newly self-discovered oedipal constellation with which the authors must take issue.

Thus Erikson (1962) in the first actual critique of the case points to Freud's undivided concern with "genetic truth" and the better understanding of the unconscious, to the neglect of "historical truth," which is of utmost importance for a developing adolescent such as Dora. Furthermore, for Erikson, Freud's "genetic truth" centered on "psychosexual and oedipal" formulations (p. 461). Freud's assignment to the father of the role of the "hoped-for protector of his daughter's inviolacy" is seen to be a somewhat surprising exception to Freud's general tendency to limit the girl's concerns to libidinal wishes to be seduced by the father, the need to repress such wishes, and the desire to find appropriate substitutes for him. Following Erikson, others have criticized Freud's inappropriate treatment of adolescent transference (Adatto, 1966) and his overwhelming of the adolescent ego with adult oedipal interpretations (Schlessinger, in Lindon, 1969; Blos, 1972).

In the mid-1970s a renewed interest in technique led to more detailed analyses of Freud's interactions with Dora (Langs, 1976; Muslin and Gill, 1978). The view that Freud adhered to a positive oedipal model, however, remained constant. Freud, it is contended, saw the nucleus of Dora's disturbance and the basis for her love for, and rejection of, Herr K. in her repressed sexual longings for her father. In line with this the authors assumed, moreover, that Freud considered Dora's transference to be founded on early real and fantasied experiences with *parental* figures (e.g., Kanzer and Glenn, 1980, chaps. 1 to 5). Some of the studies of Dora's transference turn our attention to two new questions: one pertains to the place of the countertransference, the other to the role of the mother in the transference. Freud's unawareness of both his libidinal, oedipal strivings in relation to his young patient and his negative countertransference arising especially in response to her rejection of these strivings receive extensive notice (e.g., Glenn, 1980; Bernstein, 1980). With regard to the role of the mother, Freud's *neglect* of this important component of the oedipal constellation is discussed (e.g., Lewin, 1973).

In more recent years Freud's oedipal understandings of Dora are counterposed to various forms of preoedipal and early oedipal understandings (Blos, 1979; Krohn and Krohn, 1982; Kohon, 1984). Blos (1979, p. 488), for example, speaks of Freud's "pursuing with single-mindedpertinacity the positive oedipal theme" throughout Dora's analysis, a pursuit which resulted in the de-emphasis of the importance of the preoedipal issues of adolescence. In a similar vein Krohn and Krohn (1982) inform us that "Freud conceptualized Dora's pathology as representing primarily positive oedipal conflicts" (p. 558). Here it is the understanding of Dora in terms of her phallic-oedipal constellation (Nagera, 1975) that is purportedly neglected. In these reviews the preoedipal and early oedipal mother is considered central to Dora's dynamics. Accordingly, Freud's remarks regarding Dora's libidinal attachments to the major female characters of her drama, Frau K. and the governesses, have been adduced as evidence for Freud's latent appreciation of the mother's role (Blos, 1979). The assumption that Freud was working from within an oedipal framework in which libidinal attachments are necessarily considered to be substitutes for and founded on intrafamilial precursors allows for such an interpretation of Freud's views.

Other reviews of Freud's analysis of Dora have come from feminist circles (see Bernheimer and Kahane, 1985). Freud's purported focus on oedipal fantasy usually is introduced in the context of a critique of his obliviousness to the actuality of Dora's seduction. Freud's understanding of Dora in terms of oedipal fantasy is viewed as the product of his mistaken abandonment of his early theories which ascribed to incest and actual seduction the most prominent pathogenic role.

In a more general way, however, most reviews of the Dora case see in it a sharp break, in the main a positive one, from his earlier theory of seduction. Krohn and Krohn (1982) reflect the prevalent sentiment in their description of Dora's case as the first to be presented in the "psychoanalytic phase as opposed to the preanalytic phase of his work" (p. 556). Likewise, the historian Peter Gay (1988) discussed the Dora case under the heading of "A Problematic Debut." Slipp (1977) and Spiegel (1977) pointed to Freud's overemphasis of fantasy to the neglect of interpersonal factors and actual seduction. They tie these to Freud's recognition of the failure of his seduction theory. Accordingly, examinations from the historical perspective tend to be directed toward the study of the relationship between the oedipal framework Freud worked with in Dora's analysis and those that evolved in the course of the following 90 years.

Careful study of the transition from the seduction hypothesis to oedipal dynamics does not confirm the radical change described or assumed by the various reviewers. Such a study suggests that the abandonment of this hypothesis involved a gradual and complex process. At the time of Dora's analysis, as well as at the time of its publication approximately five years later, Freud's ideas concerning the oedipal dynamics and their role in normal and pathological development had not reached the consolidation ascribed to them in each and every one of the later studies of the case. While some support for the gradual abandonment of the seduction hypothesis may be found in the analytic literature (Compton, 1985; Laplanche and Pontalis, 1968; Levin, 1978; Schimek, 1987), there is a complete and striking absence of studies examining the place of this hypothesis in Freud's analysis of Dora. The following pages, which contain a detailed exposition of the various propositions that Freud put forth in his theoretical explanations of Dora's dynamics, provide the context for the exploration of the above contentions. Implications for the understanding of the underlying issues that Freud was struggling with through his analysis of Dora and how and why these issues were overlooked or distorted will then be addressed.

FREUD'S UNDERSTANDING OF DORA'S DYNAMICS

Freud's understanding of the dynamics underlying Dora's clinical picture gradually unfolds in the course of his case presentation. A variety of etiological propositions emerge with the relative significance of each within the overall scheme of pathology never clearly stated. Through awareness to the diverse, unusual, and confusing nature of Freud's propositions, the elucidation of the underlying issues is made possible. In what follows I present Freud's various propositions regarding Dora's dynamics in chronological order. In this way the gradual development of his ideas, the inconsistencies that emerge through their evolvement, and their incongruencies with the broader oedipal framework become apparent. My description is based on Freud's statements in his presentation of Dora's clinical picture (pp. 15–63) and his analyses of Dora's dreams (pp. 64–111).

THE CLINICAL PICTURE

I have chosen not to deal with Freud's propositions concerning the secondary motives and gains that play into the construction of the neurotic symptom. These propositions which appear throughout are in my view important, but run in a separate line alongside the development of Freud's ideas regarding the primary determinants of hysteria.[1] Also, while certain propositions are presented by Freud as more specific to Dora than others, I as a rule have refrained from entering into the specifics of her case, preferring rather to present Freud's basic propositions in a more skeletal and general form.

Proposition 1: Psychic Trauma. Freud's initial explanation of Dora's pathology is described in the context of the model of hysteria he proposed in *Studies on Hysteria* (Breuer and Freud, 1895) and later amended (Freud, 1896a, 1896b, 1896c). As Freud explains, "The experience with Herr K.—his making love to her and the insult to her honour which was involved—seems to provide in Dora's case the psychical trauma which Breuer and I declared long ago to be the indispensable prerequisite for the production of a hysterical disorder" (p. 26f.). In accordance with this theory, the trauma which occurred when Dora was 16 years old would lead to pathology only if it came into association with an earlier repressed trauma. Thus, in Dora's case, Freud proceeds to seek out an earlier trauma. He ultimately comes upon a sexual event dating back two years earlier—Herr K.'s kiss in the doorway when Dora was but 14 years old. Freud informs us that this event was "just the situation to call up a distinct feeling of sexual excitement in a girl of fourteen" and that she "kept it a secret till her confession during the treatment" (p. 28). Freud here wavers as to whether the earlier event was registered without being fully experienced, or whether it was experienced as unpleasurable. Freud ultimately adopts the latter possibility. He then, however, is faced with the recurrent problem of why the opportunity for sexual discharge, which according to his then prevalent model is by definition pleasurable, should be met with such a negative response. Freud seems to claim that such a reversal of affect constitutes the very core of pathology in the hysteric. He asserts that he "should without question consider a person hysterical in whom an occasion for sexual excitement elicited feelings that were preponderantly or exclusively unpleasurable" (p. 28). But Freud soon resumes his search for the ultimate etiological factor responsible for the development of such an abnormal sexual response system.

Proposition 2: Repressed Love for the Seducer. In this proposition Freud shifts away from his earlier formal explanations of neurosis. It is not a

---

1. The interplay of external and internal causative factors and the environmental collusion which are reflected in "secondary gain" touch upon some basic etiological questions Freud was struggling with in Dora's analysis but are beyond the scope of this paper.

trauma inflicted by the seducer, Herr K., that is responsible for Dora's symptoms, but rather her forbidden longings for him, the symptoms being symbolic expressions of these longings and libidinal wishes. This proposition is an advancement over its predecessor in that it takes into account the broader emotional picture and intrapsychic desires and wishes. It does, however, in many ways resemble Freud's earliest (and never wholeheartedly adopted) formulation of hysteria as the result of the repression of "incompatible ideas" (see the cases of Lucy R. and Elisabeth von R. in the *Studies on Hysteria*). The present proposition also suffers from the many shortcomings of that early formulation. Most notable is the absence of a theoretical framework that would explain why from the economic point of view repression would take place in the face of this very specific incompatibility (i.e., only when sexual ideas were involved). This shortcoming determined Freud's turn to the next proposition.

Proposition 3: The Somatic Origin. Freud maintains that at the basis of every hysterical symptom there is an organic determinant. At first Freud seems to ascribe equal significance to the psychical and the somatic spheres in the determination of hysteria, suggesting that while the psychical determinants are the most important for therapeutic purposes, from a theoretical point of view the somatic origin is essential. But then Freud proceeds to downplay the necessary role of the somatic or organic factor. Only a "compliance" of the physical organism is required. This "compliance" allows for the expression of the repressed ideas of longing and libidinal wishes in the form of bodily symptoms (p. 40f.). Freud thus returns once again to what it is that is longed and wished for.

Proposition 4: Sexual Fantasy and the Father. This proposition contains two components, one that sexual fantasy must be involved, the other that in Dora's case the father is the object of the fantasy. Freud presents the sexual component much more hesitantly than ever before or thereafter in his published writings. He states: "According to a rule which I had found confirmed over and over again by experience, though I had not yet ventured to erect it into a general principle, a symptom signifies the representation—the realization—of a phantasy with a sexual content, that is to say, it signifies a sexual situation. It would be better to say that at least *one* of the meanings of a symptom is the representation of a sexual phantasy, but that no such limitation is imposed upon the content of its other meanings" (p. 46f.). It may be seen from this passage that Freud's hesitancy pertains not only to the ubiquity of the sexual determinant but to its basic nature as well. As Freud struggles to find the exactly appropriate term with which to define the sexual factor—

i.e., whether as a "representation," a "realization," a "phantasy with a sexual content," or a "situation"—Freud's uncertainty about whether the ultimate origin of the sexual fantasy is to be seen in an actual or an imaginary event shines through.

The second component of this proposition, namely, that the father is the object of the fantasy is not a necessary one. At this point Freud's assertion that Dora's symptoms (e.g., her cough) are to be associated with her relationship with her father is not necessary. It was the "wearisome monotony" with which Dora kept repeating her complaints against her father that led Freud to suspect that her symptoms "might have some meaning in connection with her father" (p. 46). The conjunction of the chance connection with the father and Freud's "rule" of the necessary involvement of sexual fantasy is the only reason presented here for Freud's later interest in pursuing Dora's sexual-affectionate ties with her father.

Before proceeding to his subsequent propositions Freud digresses to elaborate on some implications of his assertion regarding the necessary involvement of sexual fantasy. Freud asserts: "There is never any danger of corrupting an inexperienced girl. For where there is no knowledge of sexual processes even in the unconscious, no hysterical symptom will arise; and where hysteria is found there can no longer be any question of 'innocence of mind' in the sense in which parents and educators use the phrase" (p. 49). This passage demonstrates once again Freud's uncertainty as to the actuality behind the fantasy. Whether it is the girl or whether it is only her "mind" that cannot be deemed inexperienced and innocent (and hence cannot be corrupted) is never made completely clear in this context. In addition, this passage accentuates the very sharp contrast between the theoretical position Freud is trying out and the theoretical position he ostensibly set out to support, that of his works of 1895–96. Whereas there it was the absence of sexual knowledge and experience that preconditioned neurosis, here it is their presence in relation to the repressed events that constitutes the necessary prerequisite.

Proposition 5: Unconscious Sexuality and the Motive Force. Freud's previous proposition provided an explanation in terms of content or quality. It suggested that repressed sexual fantasy determined the symptoms which were considered fantasy enacted in symbolic form. In this proposition Freud turns to the quantitative factor: from whence the energy that leads to the formation of the hysterical symptom? Freud says, "The motive forces leading to the formation of hysterical symptoms draw their strength not only from repressed *normal* sexuality but also from unconscious perverse activities" (p. 51). Freud's understanding of sexuality at this point appears more complex than his earlier formal view of it as a somatic, genital, striving (see Draft G, in Freud, 1985). In line with his essays on sexuality (1905b) Freud suggests that sexual development takes place through a series of stages, each characterized by the predominance of an erotogenic zone and aim. Optimal normal development results in the sublimation of the force associated with the earlier aims. Accordingly, while the pervert displays inhibited development, the neurotic's behavior is the product of the early aims retaining their force in a repressed and unconscious form. These aims together with the "normal" repressed genital sexuality are what provide the qualitative fantasy with the necessary, complementary, energetic factor or motivational force. Freud illustrates this proposition in his interpretation of Dora's throat symptoms in terms of oral fixation. Later Freud confronts the cause of the early sexual fixation.

Proposition 6: "Reactive Reinforcement": The Father, the Seducer, and the Sexual Motive Force. While Freud presents this proposition in one complex interweaving of ideas, I will single out three of its major components.

A. Reactive Reinforcement. This concept is unusual in that (1) it makes a solo appearance in all of Freud's writings; (2) in this appearance, it is given a fairly significant role; (3) no special mention is made either of the debut or of the exit of this concept. Freud writes: "Contrary thoughts are always closely connected with each other and are often paired off in such a way that *the one thought is excessively intensely conscious while its counterpart is repressed and unconscious.* This relation between the two thoughts is an effect of the process of repression. For repression is often achieved by means of an excessive reinforcement of the thought contrary to the one which is to be repressed. This process I call *reactive* reinforcement" (p. 55). By applying it to hysteria, and more specifically to Dora's case, Freud suggests that Dora's intense love of her father, which was seen to be responsible for several of her symptoms (proposition 4), is itself a "reactive symptom" (p. 58), arising in attempts to suppress intense feelings of love for her seducer, Herr K. As Freud explains: "In this way I gained an insight into a conflict which was well calculated to unhinge the girl's mind. On the one hand she was filled with regret at having rejected the man's proposal, and with longing for his company and all the little signs of his affection; while on the other hand these feelings of tenderness and longing were combated by powerful forces, amongst which her pride was one of the most obvious. Thus she had succeeded in persuading herself that she had done with Herr K.—that was the advantage she derived from this typical process of repression; and yet she was obliged to summon up her infantile affection for her father and to exaggerate it, in order to protect herself against the feelings of love which were constantly pressing forward into consciousness" (p. 58).

The question arises why in hysteria there is a special propensity toward the employment of this mechanism and why its employment has such negative effects. Freud's answer is presented in the following passages.

B. Fixated Infantile Sexual Affection for the Father. Freud suggests that the hysteric is particularly inclined to use the mechanism of reactive reinforcement because she has at her disposal especially intense latent feelings of love for the father. The intensity of the love is such that it retains its primary sexual nature. These feelings for the father which are similar to, and thus an appropriate substitute for, those felt toward the seducer, can readily be invoked when the conflictual feelings for the latter appear. These remarks are in need of further elaboration.

At an earlier point Freud had suggested that it was Dora's sexual fantasies in relation to her father that were responsible in part for some of her symptoms (see proposition 4). There it was Freud's empirically derived rule of the ubiquity of sexual fantasy in hysteria that necessitated this assumption. The father was not singled out; many figures in and outside the immediate family were potentially etiologically significant, and in relation to all of them the involvement of a sexual motive was assumed essential. With the proposition of reactive reinforcement Freud returns once again to the elucidation of the affectionate father-daughter relationship. This time, however, what was previously seen as chance affection now becomes a universal bond. While Freud does not yet speak here of an "oedipus complex" per se, he does refer, citing his first published mention of it in *The Interpretation of Dreams,* to a "sexual attraction . . . felt between parents and children" which typically appears at an early age and which has been poetically described in the "legend of Oedipus" (p. 56). It is very important to take note, however, that Freud's ideas regarding the subsequent normal development of this infantile attraction differs considerably from his later renderings of it. Freud contends, in sharp contrast to his later writings, that when this attraction to the parent persists past infancy in the form of an underlying "sexual inclination," pathology is implicated, this later "sexual inclination" being seen as a manifestation of "a fixation of this rudimentary feeling of love" (p. 56).

Given such a model of drive development, the fact that only neurotics can invoke sexual ideas in relation to the father in order to facilitate the repression of other conflictual ones can now be understood. Only neurotics have actually retained the universal affection for the parent in its primary sexual form. Along a similar line, the negative effects of invoking the sexual ideas in relation to the father may be understood in terms of its involving the surfacing of latent pathology. For the more complete understanding of hysteria, what now remains is to elucidate the factors that have determined the child's fixation to his earliest expression of love.

C. The Source of the Fixation: Early Sexual Actuality. Freud's disclosure of his views on the factors which determine the fixation to the early, sexual, form of affection for the parent is marked by a certain reluctance. He states: "At this point certain other influences, which need not be discussed here, come into play, and lead to a fixation of this rudimentary feeling of love or to a reinforcement of it; so that it turns into something (either while the child is still young or not until it has reached the age of puberty) which must be put on a par with a sexual inclination and which, like the latter, has the force of the libido at its command" (p. 56f.). Yet in a footnote to these remarks, Freud takes the opportunity to express his position on the nature of these very influences: "The decisive factor in this connection is no doubt the early appearance of true genital sensations, either spontaneously or as a result of seduction or masturbation." This brief and downplayed statement has far-reaching implications. It points to Freud's underlying contention that the source of the fixation of the infantile sexual affection, and hence the ultimate source of neurosis, lies in an actual event. The nature of this actuality—self-induced genital stimulation or such stimulation generated by a seducer—corresponds in part to that which Freud specified in his earlier, supposedly abandoned, model of the psychoneuroses—the seduction model.

Freud's focus on actuality was not only downplayed but was also ambivalently held. This may be seen in what happens as he turns to apply his ideas on fixation more specifically to the elucidation of Dora's case. It then becomes gradually apparent that it was not necessarily an act of sexual contact but more likely one of excessive emotional dependence that was primarily responsible for the fixation. "The nature of her disposition had always drawn her towards her father, and his numerous illnesses were bound to have increased her affection for him." Furthermore, the father in turn had admired Dora to an excess and had "made her his confidante while she was still a child" (p. 57).

Proposition 7: "Reactive Reinforcement" and Homosexuality. Freud suggests that the intensified love for the father facilitates not only the repression of conflictual feelings experienced toward the seducer but the repression of undesirable homosexual feelings as well. As in the case of the seducer, no theoretical conjectures constraining who is to be chosen as the object of homosexual desire are specified. As in relation to the father, the fixation of early sexual libido (this time homosexual libido) allows for its resurgence. Freud is not completely clear on this point, but it would appear that a three-step process is being proposed. First there is a suppression of sexual libido directed toward men; as a result there is an upsurge in unconscious fixated libido directed toward women; and finally there is an upsurge of fixated sexual energy specifically tied to ideas of love for the father in an attempt to repress the two other forbidden loves.

THE DREAM ANALYSES

If one follows Freud's interpretations of Dora's dreams, the attempt gradually to uncover the gamut of dynamic propositions that had been hypothesized on the basis of the clinical material becomes apparent. The father, the seducer, homosexual strivings, early fixations, and the precipitants of these fixations, all interplay as Freud strives toward comprehensive understanding. But in the course of this interpretative process, Freud, confronted with certain recurrent stumbling blocks, is obliged to go beyond the limits of his original propositions.

In the first dream Freud's initial interpretations center on the underlying love of the seducer (Herr K.), with a secondary focus on the attempts to repress it through reactive reinforcement. "The dream confirms," Freud explains to Dora, "what I had already told you before you dreamt it—that you are summoning up your old love for your father in order to protect yourself against your love for Herr K. But what do all these efforts show? Not only that you are afraid of Herr K., but that you are still more afraid of yourself, and of the temptation you feel to yield to him. In short, these efforts prove once more how deeply you loved him" (p. 70).

Two additional temptation-reducing factors are brought into play. One relates to the use of an *emotional* aspect of the father's love as a source of support in the face of temptation. The father also *protects* the daughter from her malintentions toward the seducer. Freud writes: "The essence of the dream might perhaps be translated into words such as these: 'The temptation is so strong. Dear Father, protect me again as you used to in my childhood'" (p. 73). The other factor relates to the disgust felt during the sexual encounter with the seducer. This too is understood as a defensive maneuver aimed at countering the upsurge of sexual love. But Freud remains perplexed and apparently disturbed by the response of disgust and returns to it with different explanations on several occasions.

At this point, however, Freud's interpretations take a sharp turn. Through a series of complex reversals of Dora's accusations that her luetic father transmitted his illness to her, Freud arrives at the conclusion that it was Dora's masturbatory practices that were responsible for her neurosis. The masturbation appears to be given a more direct role in the formation of the neurosis than Freud previously proposed (proposition 6, point *C*). He informs Dora "that she was now on the way to finding an answer to her own question of why it was that precisely she had fallen ill—by confessing that she had masturbated, probably in childhood" (p. 76). Theoretically this is explained as follows: "Hysterical symptoms hardly ever appear as long as children are masturbating, but only afterwards, when a period of abstinence has set in; they form a substitute for masturbatory satisfaction" (p. 79).

In his final interpretation of Dora's first dream Freud attempts to tie together all his different strands of thought. Some additional ideas emerge in the process. He contends that Dora "summoned up an infantile affection for her father" so that it might protect her against her present affection for a stranger (p. 86). This idea is familiar, but as Freud explains Dora's need for protection a new proposal emerges. "There was a conflict within her between a temptation to yield to the man's proposal and a composite force rebelling against that feeling. This latter force was made up of motives of respectability and good sense, of hostile feelings . . . jealousy and wounded pride . . . and of a neurotic element, namely, the tendency to a repudiation of sexuality which was already present in her and was based on her childhood history. Her love for her father, which she summoned up to protect her against the temptation, had its origin in the same childhood history" (p. 88f.). The nature of this neurotic element is described in the following comment: "if Dora felt unable to yield to her love for the man [who was her tempter], if in the end she repressed that love instead of surrendering to it, there was no factor upon which her decision depended more directly than upon her premature sexual enjoyment and its consequence—her bed-wetting, her catarrh, and her disgust" (p. 87). This new variation on the theme of masturbation is abstruse. While we may understand Freud's contention that masturbation can lead to fixation of the infantile affection, it is difficult to understand why masturbation would be an ultimate cause for the rejection of a seducer. For this it is necessary to integrate several of Freud's partial answers. In child masturbators there persists long past the abandonment of onanistic practices an intensified desire for masturbatory satisfaction. Later sexual excitation awakens this desire. One's moral stature, however, necessitates its repudiation (p. 87f.). The moral child masturbater, when seduced in adulthood, will respond with substitutive hysterical symptoms on the one hand, and will reject the seducer on the other. Freud apparently suggests that this moral repudiation of masturbation may become intimately associated with a sense of disgust with oneself and more specifically with one's genitals. This disgust is projected onto the sexuality of the seducer and reinforces the tendency to reject him (p. 84). While in Dora's case very specific circumstances determined the feelings of disgust, Freud apparently considered the affective counterpart of the hysteric repudiation of sexuality to be universal.

In this complex understanding of Dora's dream, the mother plays a fairly minor role. She is the subject of Dora's jealousy which arose with the defensive reemergence of infantile love for the father.

Freud's understanding of the second dream, like that of the previous one, puts much emphasis on Dora's relationship with Herr K., but there are two fundamental differences. First, Dora's internal conflict is no longer seen to be derived from her specific history of prolonged masturbatory practices. It is not a conflict between morality and the perverse desire to masturbate (which is aroused with sexual excitation) that Freud now considers to have led to Dora's repression of sexual excitation and her consequent rejection of Herr K.'s advances and the appearance of accompanying symptomatology. The central conflict is presented as a young woman's conflict between sexual interest, desire, and curiosity, and social and moral prohibitions which look upon these disapprovingly. The more painful hysterical symptoms are understood as a form of self-inflicted punishment for the expression of sexual interest.

The second major innovation is that the *frustration* of the sexual desire can itself be a source of pathology. The rejection of the seducer comes with the recognition that his propositions may not be completely sincere. The desire for revenge and the hope of regaining his attention and affection now serve as motivating factors (p. 105f.). The neurotic "slap in the face," rather than the neurotic disgust, is the focus of Freud's explanatory efforts.

Freud proceeds to a comprehensive framework for neurosis founded on the interplay between the more general conflict about sexuality and the frustration of sexual desire. The conflict leads to the rejection which brings in its course the frustration by the seducer and the related symptomology. But were the seducer to pursue his love, the neurotic would be obliged to reject him ever more forcibly. Apparently the continued pursuit would intensify the threatening internal conflict. Freud frames all this in terms of an opposition between fantasy and reality: "Incapacity for meeting a *real* erotic demand is one of the most

essential features of a neurosis. Neurotics are dominated by the opposition between reality and phantasy. If what they long for the most
intensely in their phantasies is presented to them in reality, they none
the less flee from it; and they abandon themselves to their phantasies
the most readily, where they need no longer fear to see them realized"
(p. 110).

THEORETICAL CONTEXT AND UNDERLYING ISSUES

THE NONOEDIPAL CONTEXT OF DORA'S CASE

If one follows Freud's propositions concerning Dora, it becomes immediately apparent that an oedipal constellation is not what lies at the
heart of Dora's hysteria, nor does it lie at the heart of Freud's ideas on
pathology in general. The oedipal drama is mentioned, but at this
point Freud considers the unconscious retention of the infantile sexual
affection for the father to be a manifestation of pathology, not a feature of normal development; and the retention of this sexual force is,
on the whole, associated with an actual event—masturbation or seduction (proposition 6C). More importantly, the emergence of the love for
the father is considered to be a secondary feature. It is primarily presented as a defensive maneuver aimed at the repression of the primary
conflict which is experienced in relation to the seducer. Complicated
relations with one's father are clearly not presented as a prerequisite of
neurosis. Thus both in terms of the quantitative force and of the
qualitative content it is apparent that Freud has not yet arrived at an
oedipal formulation. This is further attested to by Freud's explicit
statements that in Dora's case he was primarily interested in providing
evidence that would "substantiate" his views put forth in 1895 and
1896 (e.g., p. 7).

While Freud had not yet arrived at his oedipal formulation of the
etiology of the neurosis, his ideas were headed that way. In the course
of his case presentation the gradual move from the seduction theory to
a model of neurosis based on rudimentary notions of the oedipus
complex may be noted.

THE SEDUCTION THEORY BACKGROUND

To understand the transitional context in which Dora was analyzed
and the issues Freud was struggling with it is important to recognize
the complex nature of the seduction theory and the history of its development and abandonment. Opposing this recognition are two psychoanalytic myths. One myth is that the seduction theory is a simple and

conceptually primitive theory positing an immediate relationship between actual seduction and incest and neurosis. Related to this myth is the idea that this theory was "confirmed" on the basis of the patients' verbal reports which were assumed to be true and which were accepted at face value. The second myth is that the seduction theory was suddenly and completely abandoned in 1897, primarily as a result of Freud's recognition of the centrality and power of oedipal fantasy.

These analytic myths were dispelled as the theory of seduction emerged as a sophisticated one, attempting to resolve essential theoretical questions (Blass and Simon, 1992a, 1992b; Simon, 1992; Simon and Blass, 1990). It appeared, moreover, that Freud continued to be perplexed by these questions, to examine them, and perhaps to ascribe to some of the basic tenets of the seduction theory far past the time he is alleged to have abandoned that theory. I summarize some conclusions regarding these issues.

1. The Four Distinct and Complex Formulations of the Seduction Theory. There is no one seduction theory per se. There are rather four different etiological formulations of neurosis in which the idea of seduction plays a central role. The very meaning of seduction differs considerably in these formulations. In the first (Breuer and Freud, 1895), sexual seduction is assigned to the broader category of traumatic events. When the excitation of a traumatic event is, for whatever reason, prevented discharge through the associative pathways, its later reawakening by an associatively linked event, i.e., the precipitating event, results in the release of the early excitation through hysterical symptomology. Freud heavily emphasized the defense against unpleasure as the major factor in the prevention of discharge, but was stymied by the selective employment of the defensive mechanism. In the second formulation, first noted in a letter to Fliess on February 7, 1894, Freud posits that traumas are defended against and are pathogenic only when they are associatively linked to an even earlier, specifically sexual trauma which occurred in the patient's prepubertal period. Freud's third formulation, most fully elaborated in the *Project* (1895) and three different essays in 1896, has generally been referred to in the analytic literature as *the* seduction theory (Sadow et al., 1968; Schusdek, 1968; Stewart, 1967; Sulloway, 1979). This formulation centers on the idea of the "deferred action" of memories of infantile seduction. The prepubertal sexual trauma is described as a *nonexperienced* event of genital stimulation. This unusual phenomenon is theoretically feasible by way of Freud's postulation that the prepubertal period is a presexual one. When the memory of the event of genital stimulation is revived in the postpubertal period through an asso-

ciatively linked event, i.e., sexual seduction, its charge is then experienced for the very first time. The intensity of this later primary experience of the early seduction is traumatic and therefore invokes defense. The fourth formulation (December 6, 1896) was made public by Freud only in some of his recantations of the seduction theory many years later. The major innovation is that neurosis is no longer considered to be the result of just any early seduction; rather it is the result of an incestuous one perpetrated by a perverse father.

While the actual event of seduction is prominent in all the formulations, complex internal mechanisms were also essential. Support for this view may be found in a recent study by Schimek (1987) who ultimately concludes, "Reconstruction and interpretation already played a major part in the original theory; so did the role of internal psychological factors . . . [such as] conflict and repression . . . the external trauma was only the starting point . . . of a lengthy and complex process which could eventually lead to neurosis" (p. 961).

2. The Basic Questions. The following theoretical questions underlie many of the propositions of the seduction theory.

A. What is the ultimate and universal origin of the motive force behind the neurotic symptom? Freud moves from the position that the motive force is the intense excitation of the external world set up within the individual in such an immediate form that it cannot be "worn away," to the position that it is sexual excitation dissociated from the individual's experiential world, due to the environment's premature stimulation of the organism that serves as the pathological force.

It is important to note that fantasy and internal drives are in no way incompatible with such a theory. Internally motivated sexual and self-preservational drives and their ideational representation, the wish, are postulated as well. If not gratified, these internal motives will lead to unpleasure, but they are not the source of pathology. Pathology, according to the seduction theory, is the product of the intervention of the external world. The external world creates the individual's basic conflicts by inserting or arousing motives that run counter to the organism's natural and age-appropriate strivings (Friedman, 1977).

B. What is the ultimate and universal origin of the specific form and ideational content of the neurosis? In brief, Freud sought to determine not only the ultimate source of pathological motivation but also to reveal the ultimate factor that determines the uniformity in which this motive manifests itself. While intense stimulation is itself the source of pathology, additional factors of a qualitative kind come into play. Most notable among them are the specifics of the setting in which the stimulation took place. These inherent components of the memory of the pathogenic event serve as templates for the later expression of the pathogenic force and determine the specific form of pathology.

Freud's interest in this additional dimension grew as he developed his theory and became increasingly focused on a single universal factor. His final hypothesis that the father is in *all cases* the perpetrator of the seduction is to be understood in this context.

C. What is the source of repression? Throughout the formulations of the seduction theory Freud struggles with the question of how and why certain kinds of intense stimulation are prevented discharge and hence become, together with the memories to which they are attached, pathogenic structures. Although Freud's formal conceptualizations become increasingly sophisticated, he continues to maintain the simple and theoretically inadequate notion that the social and moral inacceptability of certain ideas and memories leads to their repression. While the conceptually sophisticated notions were intimately tied to the quantitative factor, i.e., the motive force, the more intuitive and theoretically deficient one was tied to the qualitative factor, i.e., the specific content of the neurosis.

3. Confirmation and Bias. Confirmation of the various formulations was, according to Freud, obtained primarily from patients' verbal reports, their reproduction of early events in the course of treatment, and on the basis of the clinical success of the treatment. Contrary to common belief, Freud was not naïve regarding the reliability of such evidence. From the start Freud struggled with issues of the trustworthiness of the patients' reports, the effect of suggestion, the verification of the permanence of cure, and issues relating to the existence of alternate explanations. But he puts forth a convincing argument in favor of the validity of his evidence as well as of the a priori likelihood of his theories (e.g., Freud, 1896c).

Careful study reveals that it was not the evidence alone or even primarily that guided the evolution of his seduction theory. Nor did contradicting evidence do much to shake this theory. Discrepancies between the available clinical data in 1896 and Freud's theoretical formulations at that time attest to this (Schimek, 1987). Freud's own private complaints concerning the absence of sufficient confirmatory evidence (e.g., letter to Fliess, May 30, 1896) for the very formulations which he publicly professed to be clinically proven are further testimony. A predilection for certain kinds of solutions as well as biases of a more personal nature not only led Freud to his discoveries but also to maintain them in the presence of refuting evidence. The personal bias becomes more noted in Freud's presentation of his "paternal etiology" formulation of the seduction theory. The seductiveness that emerges from Freud's reports of the "forceful" and "penetrating" interpretations which he bestows upon his disbelieving female patients points in this direction. Moreover, Freud later admitted that his analysis revealed to him that his earlier, supposedly inevitable conclusion that his own father was the "prime originator" of his neurosis was "no doubt . . . an inference by analogy from myself unto him" (1985, p. 268). In a broader sense, however, Freud's preference at this time for formulations which posit a clash between the external world and the individual's internal strivings, and which place the responsibility for the perverse and immoral sexual motives on the external environment, are what ultimately determined the course of his theoretical formulations (Laplanche and Pontalis, 1968).

4. The Abandonment. In his letter to Fliess of September 21, 1897 Freud lists four reasons for abandoning his seduction theory—his failure to bring a single case to conclusion; the unlikelihood that there exists such a high incidence of seductive fathers; the theoretical impossibility of distinguishing between actuality and affectively cathected fantasy; and the recognition that the unconscious can never be fully tamed by consciousness and hence treatment could never be complete. Inasmuch as Freud was aware of these arguments throughout—and some of them stand in sharp contrast to his explicit statements at earlier points—it is likely that additional factors influenced his admission of failure at this time. It has been suggested that Freud's appreciation of the power and centrality of the oedipal fantasies in his self-analysis led him to the recognition that the patients' reports of seduction were actually derivatives of their own oedipal fantasies (Kris, 1954, p. 34; Jones, 1953, p. 322). Careful examination of Freud's letters and especially of the way in which he later shunned his early formulations and anyone who dared to support them leads to the supposition of an additional course of events. The confrontation with his own oedipal fantasies which included seductive fantasies involving the "daughter" led Freud unconsciously to suspect the effect these fantasies had on his theory, his method, and his relationship with his young female patients. He saw that the patients' reports of their fathers' acts were in accord with his own seductive fantasies directed toward his patients, and thus were likely to be fantasy. But he also became more in touch with his fear that his seductive fantasies were having a real seductive effect on his patients and the kind of material they produced. Ultimately he came to doubt the truth of his theories and the truthfulness of his patients.

These doubts did not lead to an immediate abandonment of the theory. After a brief period of uncertainty and even despair Freud returned to tackle his basic questions regarding the neuroses with formulas which placed a greater emphasis on fantasy and its symbolic transformation but which also retained many fundamental elements of the seduction theory. In his inquiries into the internal origin of fantasy Freud also addressed the question of responsibility. His formulations that attributed pathology to external sources had dealt not only with etiology but also with blame for the girl's sexuality (see letter to Fliess, January 3, 1897, entitled *Habemus papam*). With the realization of the error in belittling the primary etiological role of fantasy there arose questions of responsibility both for the girl's seductive behavior and for the unjust accusation of the male participant. Were fathers, Freud himself included, indeed completely wrongly accused? Are the daughters and their newly discovered primal sexual fantasies responsible? And if not the daughters, then who? These questions as well as questions of personal responsibility for having believed, and in fact suggested, to his patients that they were seduced in childhood, continued to concern Freud for many years.

THE TRANSITIONAL CONTEXT OF DORA'S CASE

Through Dora's analysis Freud gradually passes from the seduction theory to a theory of neurosis that centers on intrapsychically originating moral conflict and on the early childhood events that make it pathogenic. In this transition four basic trends are outstanding. The clearest trend can be seen in relation to the motive force. Here infantile sexuality gradually replaces excessive excitation of the external world (proposition 1) as the ultimate source of pathogenic energy. Freud states that the fixation of the infantile drives determines their acting as a pathogenic agent (e.g., proposition 5), but what determines their fixation? Freud turns outward once again, away from his newly found internal force, as he suggests that some actual event of genital stimulation is responsible (proposition 6C). His wish to downplay the effects of external actuality and to retain the inherent internalness of his theory is reflected in his gradual move from a proposition that seduction acts as the most significant sexually stimulating event to a proposition that masturbation does (e.g., the first dream analysis).

A much more complex process takes place in regard to Freud's question of the source of the ideational content of the neurosis. Here Freud's focus is on fantasy. The fantasy behind the neurosis is no longer considered an immediate product of an actual event in the external world (as in proposition 2), but Freud encounters considerable difficulty as he attempts to determine its internal origin. At first he suggests that the infantile drives not only supply the fantasy with its motivational *force,* but that these drives have a formative effect on its specific nature as well (propositions 4 and 5). But infantile drive development was not at this point associated with any specific or fixed object(s) (Compton, 1985). The drives cannot adequately explain the universal appearance of the father in fantasy, or the complexity of feelings associated with that fantasy. Freud's subsequent conception of reactive reinforcement may be regarded as his ultimate solution of this problem. According to this conception, the fantasy emerges as a product of the convergence of infantile sexual drives with sexual love felt for the father during early childhood (proposition 6). In effect, two diverse sources—infantile drives and a sexual attitude toward the father inherent to childhood—underlie the pathological fantasy. These sources remain distinct and when joined together provide the setting for neurosis—a fact that markedly distinguishes this proposition from Freud's later oedipal ones. The joining together of infantile sexuality with an early loving attitude toward the father may, however, be regarded as an important step on Freud's way toward his later conclusion that the oedipal fantasies are necessarily inborn.

Freud's transition toward the oedipus complex can also be noted in his ideas on repression. With the introduction of his idea of infantile sexuality, Freud's most formal conceptualization of repression based on the notion of a presexual period had to be discarded. In its place Freud reintroduced his earlier and more intuitive conception of repression as related to conflictual ideas (proposition 2). But in reintroducing this conception Freud gradually develops a more comprehensive framework which explains why only conflictual ideas of certain kinds of content are repressed. Freud contends that the association of a conflictual idea (in relation to the seducer) and an earlier highly charged idea (in relation to the father) will result in the repression of the conflictual one, with the other idea assuming prominence in its place. Here reactive reinforcement allows for a conception of repression that integrates Freud's ideas on motive force with his growing recognition of the centrality of specific kinds of content.

With specific ideational contents assigned a formal and major role within this model Freud secures a context for the elaboration of ideas on the nature of normal conflict and its relationship to repression and pathology. He could now take one more important step forward. Freud assigns the individual's conflict over the pathological desire for masturbatory satisfaction a major theoretical role (first dream analysis), and from there ultimately shifts to the position that normal or appropriate sexual strivings are themselves a source of conflict, guilt, and repression (second dream analysis). The focus becomes the normal moral conflict and the necessity of its repression. But here too it may be seen that Freud is one very major step away from the theoretical framework of the oedipus complex in which the moral conflict and the primal libidinal tie to the father are bound together in a single integrative formulation.

The final major trend in Freud's transition to his oedipal model relates to the issue of responsibility. Dora is assigned an ever-increasing share of responsibility for her wishes, fantasies, and ultimately for her neurosis. In the end, the moral offensiveness of her desire for masturbatory satisfaction lies at the foundation of her neurosis. Concomitantly, the responsibility of external objects, namely, "the seducer" and "the father," is gradually reduced. In relation to the father this move requires considerable effort. Aware of the painful implications for Dora of some of the less appealing sides of her father's character (p. 33f.), Freud consistently maintains the distinction between the source of distress and the source of neurosis. No matter how miserable Dora's father was, he did not, according to Freud, make her sick. In addition, Freud tends to highlight the father's more positive features (most notably the protection he provides Dora from her wish to yield to the threat of seduction). And Dora's hostile and sexual feelings toward her father are considered complex transformations of feelings toward others or from some other period of life. Thus, Freud's shift away from the seduction theory conception that others are primarily responsible for the individual's fantasies, wishes, and neurosis results in a conception that the individual brings upon himself his or her own neurosis. Accordingly, environmental effects are minimized and the father emerges not only as a nonseductive character but as a guardian from seduction. In Freud's later oedipal formulations the father is given a much more substantial and permanent role within the girl's fantasy world. Consequently, the father's potential influence on the development of pathology is increased without detracting from the role of the girl's own wishes.

THEORETICAL CONCLUSIONS

As Freud realized the deficiencies and limitations of his seduction theory, he directed his major efforts to the elucidation of an internal force that could act as the source of the motive behind neurosis. To this end Freud introduces the idea of the individual being endowed from birth with infantile sexual drives. This turn inward involves a very difficult step. Internal forces had been hypothesized from the start.

Wishes, fantasies, dreams, and various other ideational transformations of these forces appear in Freud's very earliest writings. What is
new and problematic is not only the suggestion that the sexual force
exists from infancy, but that an *internal* force disrupts the individual's
harmonious existence. The basic conflicts within man are no longer
products of the interference of the environment (Rapaport, 1960, p.
18); they are products of contradictions and oppositions between the
individual's internally originating strivings. But with all the basic forces
coming from within Freud is faced with the question: what is the specific factor that determines pathology? When does conflict produce
pathology, not only normal distress? Freud answers this question by
means of fixation. When infantile drives retain their initial force, later
conflict will result in pathology. What Freud is in effect suggesting here
is that the antithesis between infantile strivings and mature demands
sets the scene for pathogenic conflict. In the absence of sublimation,
pathology ensues.

Remaining solely within his model of infantile sexual drives, Freud is
forced to return to the idea that an actual event of genital stimulation is
the ultimate source of the neurosis. The economic nature of his model
requires the postulation that fixation is based on such an excitatory
event. Freud's gradual focus on masturbation (rather than on seduction) may be seen as an attempt to incorporate genital stimulation and
retain the notion of the internal origin of neurosis.[2]

But in this understanding of masturbation, Freud introduced another etiological factor. Not only genital stimulation was inherently
pathogenic but certain associated ideas had to be considered necessary
prerequisites to neurosis. Two sets of ideas are prominent: ideas of
morality connected with the self-indulgent act of masturbation, and
then later with the idea of sexual desire in general; and the idea of the
object, i.e., the father (as in the oedipal legend), to which the infantile
drives become fixed when excessively stimulated in childhood. Uncertain about the relationship of these ideas, Freud examined various
possibilities. Gradually he established fantasy as a primal source of
motivation. That is, in addition to fantasies that are derivatives of some
more primal motive, such as bodily need or external trauma, there are
fantasies, associated with the ideas of morality, with sexual drives, and
with the object of these drives, that themselves are highly charged and
serve as motivating forces.

2. The centrality of the concept of masturbation to Freud's formulations has not
received due consideration. The intermediate space between internally and externally
effected sexuality in which "masturbation" lies and its being prototypical of self-
sufficiency determined, in part, Freud's lifelong focus on this concept.

Freud believed that the originally motivating ideas and fantasies developed only under pathological circumstances. In this way he could maintain a distinction between normal and pathogenic conflict, and also provide an explanation for the special nature of the symptoms derived from the latter. For example, the specific constellation of excessive concern with the father and disgust with the seducer could now be understood (through reactive reinforcement) in terms of conflict over sexuality founded on an underlying fantasy of sexual love for the father. Since this fantasy is derived from an association between *fixated* infantile drives and *fixated* infantile attitudes toward the father, it explains why this is not an ubiquitous reaction to sexual advances.

The complex tie between drive and fantasy that Freud struggles with emerges from his interest in discovering *the* ultimate source of neurosis, and the inadequacy of a purely quantitative explanation (e.g., in terms of sexual excitation) in this regard. This drive-fantasy tie also emerges from Freud's struggle with the question of responsibility. With his insight that the origin of neurosis is not necessarily associated with an actual event of seduction, Freud sought to assign the girl personal responsibility for her fantasies and actions. Her intrapsychic fantasy, supplied by her fixated infantile drives, fixated as a result of her perverse sexual desires, lay at the foundation of her neurosis. It is interesting that in ascribing responsibility to the patient, Freud not only *facilitates* the transition to his later oedipal formulations, but also *inhibits* it. The focus on the girl's responsibility was intimately tied to the complete absolution of the father. To achieve this end, all of the girl's hostile and loving feelings for the father were considered transformations of feelings for some other figure. As a result, the idea of "the father" as an inherent component of the girl's inner fantasy world could not emerge.

At the time of Dora's analysis, its writing up, and its publication, Freud was not yet prepared for the final move to his classical oedipal model. This move involves the postulation that the intrapsychic fantasy in relation to the father is not a pathological product used in the service of defense against conflictual drives, but rather is a normal phenomenon, reflecting the individual's inherent conflict and exerting a constant influence on the expression of the drives. This is not readily postulated. First, it involves the ascription of a primordial status to the oedipal fantasy. The oedipal model assumes that the triadic dynamics which motivate and shape the individual is an inborn structure, uniting within it both force and content. Freud's concern with origins demanded, however, that an answer to the question of how such structures arose be provided before such an assumption was wholeheartedly adopted. It was not until 1913 that Freud, through his phylogenetic hypothesis of *Totem and Taboo,* presented his most consolidated explanation of the source of the "original fantasy" (Laplanche and Pontalis, 1968).

A second factor inhibiting the shift to the oedipal model is the fact that a normative oedipus complex complicates the source of pathology. If the very existence of the fantasy cannot be considered a major determinant of pathology, then Freud is obliged once again to look for an environmental cause. As we have seen, however, Freud had just moved away from his seduction theory and wished to avoid this. Later, formulations that integrated environmental factors with innate fantasy were more acceptable to Freud, but even then a certain reluctance to ascribe a central role to environmental factors may be discerned. Freud's later interest in "libidinal types," which he hoped would "bridge the gulf between the normal and pathological" (1931, p. 217) is reflective of his ongoing struggle with this issue.

Finally, Freud had to arrive at some conceptualization of the factor responsible for the repression of the girl's libidinal drives toward her father. For this, considerable elaboration of the primal oedipal fantasy was necessary. In fact, it was only in 1925 that it became sufficiently elaborate. Freud's move to the classical oedipal model was made possible at a much earlier date only by his shifting the focus of theoretical conceptualization to the analyses of his male patients. After Dora, the only female patient extensively discussed is homosexual (Freud, 1920), a fact which provided a special context for the understanding of her repudiation of her libidinal strivings in relation to her father.

The shift to the oedipus complex was not only an unnecessary move, but it could be carried out only with greatest difficulty. The questions or issues that stood in the way of the oedipal model at the time of the abandonment of the seduction theory continued to perturb Freud for quite some time. It may be claimed, in fact, that these issues remain unresolved to this day (Simon, 1991). Furthermore, the shift demanded that Freud's highly speculative, phylogenetic hypothesis become a cornerstone of his theoretical framework.

THE OEDIPAL INTERPRETATION OF DORA

In the light of my present analysis the fact that Dora's case has been traditionally described as Freud's exemplar of oedipal dynamics is in need of explanation. In terms of *how* such an interpretation could be suggested two factors are outstanding. One is the lack of distinction by the reviewers between the clinical-dynamical level and the theoretical level. On the clinical-dynamic level, for example, Freud maintained that Dora loved both her father and Herr K. and that the love for one would appear in the place of the other, but this does not warrant the conclusion that Freud had postulated an oedipal model and that the love for Herr K. was a substitute oedipal attachment. In the literature on Dora, however, such conclusions are frequently encountered. In the absence of a clear distinction between the clinical and theoretical levels the assumption prevails that Freud's interpretations of the clinical material and one's own are presented within the same basic theoretical context. The resultant distortions are noted. Kanzer (1980), for instance, in his description of Freud's analysis of Dora's dream states: "Everything in the dream called for reversal. He [Freud] applied this rule to Herr K., insisting that Dora wished love making from him as once from her father" (p. 77). Freud's actual remarks in this context point, however, in a different direction. What Freud insisted upon was that Dora was "summoning up [her] old love for [her] father in order to protect [herself] against [her] love for Herr K." (1905a, p. 70).

The second factor is the neglect of inconsistent theoretical formulations or their reinterpretation in terms of more familiar ones. Freud's conception of reactive reinforcement is of particular interest. Only two authors take note of Freud's interpretations that emerge from this conception. Krohn and Krohn (1982) quote from the interpretations, mention their being highly surprising, especially "in light of his [Freud's] own discoveries of the childhood origins of neurosis" (p. 558), and then immediately return to discuss conventional formulations. The meaning of the surprise is neglected. Kohon (1984) deals with the concept of "reaction" more concisely. He notes Freud's view that "Dora's love for her father [was] . . . a 'reactive symptom'" and then informs the reader that it "makes more sense" to think of it in more conventional oedipal terms (p. 81). As a consequence of the neglect of reactive reinforcement and the prominent etiological role it ascribes to the seducer independent of the father, other concepts must be reinterpreted as well. For example, in Dora's case the meaning of the concept of transference is based on an early and idiosyncratic formulation which allowed Freud to distinguish between "father transference" and "Herr K. transference." But once the "reactive" relationship between father and Herr K. is obliterated, this unique meaning cannot be recognized and the concept of transference is assumed to mean what it did in Freud's later uses of it. One consequence of this is that Freud is mistakenly attributed with acknowledging his failure to take note of the "father transference" (e.g., Muslin and Gill, 1978, p.

317), while what Freud actually acknowledged was only his neglect of Dora's "transference" to him which originated in her relationship to Herr K. (1905a, p. 118).

The tendencies to focus on the clinical material, to neglect unfamiliar theoretical conjectures, and to reinterpret in the light of one's own framework always exist. In fact, from the start psychoanalysis has been characterized by a tension between the pull away from "grey theory to the perpetual green of experience" (Freud, 1924, p. 149), and the opposing attraction to procrustean beds which could accommodate the ever-growing body of clinical data and allow for their immediate theoretical conceptualization. That the Dora case has erroneously and consistently been presented as *the* case of Freud's oedipal understanding of hysteria raises the question of the purpose of the employment of these tendencies specifically in this case. *Why* was it necessary to reinterpret Freud's analysis of Dora as an oedipal analysis? The answer to this question relates to the desire to maintain a coherent and consistent conceptualization of the development of psychoanalysis. Bennett Simon and I (Blass and Simon, 1992a; Simon, 1992; Simon and Blass, 1990) have contended that psychoanalysis has developed a myth concerning the abandonment of the seduction theory. This myth describes a simple process whereby Freud comes to realize the error of his early theories and then promptly and completely discards them in favor of his "true" classical models centering on oedipal fantasy. The value of this myth was found to lie in its concealing some of the more "wild" processes of confirmation that went into the actual development of Freud's early theories. The reinterpretation of the Dora case as an oedipal analysis may be seen to be an appendix to this myth. It "demonstrates" that the first extensive case report following Freud's alleged final abandonment of the seduction theory in 1897 is, indeed, a purely oedipal one, but also takes the myth one step further in that it proceeds to conceal some of the more problematic theoretical maneuvering that went into the move to the oedipal model. By presenting Dora's analysis as taking place within an already existent oedipal framework, the theoretical necessity of Freud's controversial phylogenetic hypothesis is blurred and the theoretical difficulties with the determination both of the role of environmental factors and the source of repression in the female oedipus complex are put aside.

Powerful motives are involved in putting aside the complex and controversial factors that went into the early development of psychoanalytic theory. While new clinical data are taken into account and radical innovations are considered, it is, as a rule, the bridge to the basic tenets of the traditional formulations that makes room for the novel.

This is particularly true in the Dora case. As theoreticians wish to present new ideas concerning adolescence, female sexuality, and transference, interest in this early case is revived (Jennings, 1986). This reliance on the early traditional formulations can interfere with our capacity to explore and question these formulations. The proposition that the oedipal model has been with us from the earliest days of psychoanalysis proper and that it guided Freud in all his analyses may be seen in this context to be an attempt to preserve that foundation. The reviews of Freud's analysis of Dora accentuate this proposition.

Preserving the foundations of psychoanalytic theory through the reinterpretation of its development has its price. By acknowledging the actual history of our ideas, no matter how disillusioning or perhaps just confusing the immediate results may be, we have the opportunity to strengthen the underpinnings of the theory and clarify the factors that truly serve to validate the theoretical propositions. Thereby we also do justice to our patients, as we recognize the limitations of our theoretical conceptions in readily accommodating the complexity and diversity of their existence. Dora exemplifies this complexity. In Freud's presentation of Dora's case, as he struggles to mold his theoretical formulations to encompass the many dimensions she reveals to him, we are given a special opportunity to observe psychoanalysis in creation.

BIBLIOGRAPHY

ADATTO, C. (1966). On the metamorphosis from adolescence into adulthood. *J. Amer. Psychoanal. Assn.*, 14:485–509.

BERNHEIMER, C. & KAHANE, C., eds. (1985). *In Dora's Case: Freud, Hysteria, Feminism.* New York: Columbia Univ. Press.

BERNSTEIN, I. (1980). Integrative summary: On the reviewings of the Dora case. In Kanzer & Glenn (1980), pp. 83–91.

BLASS, R. B. & SIMON, B. (1992a). Freud on his own mistake(s). In *Psychiatry and the Humanities*, 12:160–183.

―――― & ―――― (1992b). Theory, evidence, and confirmation in the development and abandonment of Freud's seduction hypothesis (in preparation).

BLOS, P. (1972). The epigenesis of the adult neurosis. *Psychoanal. Study Child*, 27:106–135.

―――― (1979). *The Adolescent Passage.* New York: Int. Univ. Press.

BREUER, J. & FREUD, S. (1895). *Studies on Hysteria.* S.E., 2.

COMPTON, A. (1985). The development of the drive object concept in Freud's work: 1905–1915. *J. Amer. Psychoanal. Assn.*, 33:93–115.

ERIKSON, E. H. (1962). Reality and actuality. *J. Amer. Psychoanal. Assn.*, 10:451–474.

FREUD, S. (1896a). Heredity and the aetiology of the neuroses. *S.E.*, 3:141–156.
——— (1896b). Further remarks on the neuro-psychosis of defence. *S.E.*, 3:159–185.
——— (1896c). The aetiology of hysteria. *S.E.*, 3:189–221.
——— (1900). The interpretation of dreams. *S.E.*, 4 & 5.
——— (1905a). Fragment of an analysis of a case of hysteria. *S.E.*, 7:3–122.
——— (1905b). Three essays on the theory of sexuality. *S.E.*, 7:*S.E.*, 125–243.
——— (1913). Totem and taboo. *S.E.*, 13:1–161.
——— (1920). The psychogenesis of a case of homosexuality in a woman. *S.E.*, 18:145–172.
——— (1924). Neurosis and psychosis. *S.E.*, 19:149–158.
——— (1925). Some psychical consequences of the anatomical distinction between the sexes. *S.E.*, 19:243–258.
——— (1931). Libidinal types. *S.E.*, 21:215–220.
——— (1950). Project for a scientific psychology. *S.E.*, 1:283–397.
——— (1985). *The Complete Letters of Sigmund Freud to Wilhelm Fliess*, ed. J. M. Masson. Cambridge, Mass.: Harvard Univ. Press.
FRIEDMAN, L. (1977). Conflict and synthesis in Freud's theory of the mind. *Int. Rev. Psychoanal.* 4:155–171.
GAY, P. (1988). *Freud: A Life for Our Time*. New York: Norton.
GLENN, J. (1980). Freud's adolescent patients. In Kanzer & Glenn (1980), pp. 23–47.
JENNINGS, J. L. (1986). The revival of "Dora." *J. Amer. Psychoanal. Assn.*, 34:607–635.
JONES, E. (1953). *The Life and Work of Sigmund Freud*, vol. 1. New York: Basic Books.
KANZER, M. (1980). Dora's imagery. In Kanzer & Glenn (1980), pp. 2–83.
——— & GLENN, J., eds. (1980). *Freud and His Patients*. New York: Aronson.
KOHON, G. (1984). Reflections on Dora. *Int. J. Psychoanal.*, 65:73–84.
KRIS, E. (1954). *The Origins of Psychoanalysis*. New York: Basic Books.
KROHN, A. & KROHN, J. (1982). The nature of the Oedipus complex in the Dora case. *J. Amer. Psychoanal. Assn.*, 30:555–578.
LANGS, R. (1976). The misalliance dimension in Freud's case histories. *Int. J. Psychoanal. Psychother.*, 5:301–317.
LAPLANCHE, J. & PONTALIS, J.-B. (1968). Fantasy and the origins of sexuality. *Int. J. Psychoanal.*, 49:1–18.
LEVIN, K. (1978). *Freud's Early Psychology of the Neuroses*. Pittsburgh: Univ. Pittsburgh Press.
LEWIN, K. (1973). Dora revisited. *Psychoanal. Rev.*, 60:519–532.
LINDON, J. (1969). A psychoanalytic view of the family. *Psychoanal. Forum*, 3:11–65.
MUSLIN, N. & GILL, M. M. (1978). Transference in the Dora case. *J. Amer. Psychoanal. Assn.*, 26:311–328.
NAGERA, H. (1975). *Female Sexuality and the Oedipus Complex*. New York: Aronson.

RAPAPORT, D. (1960). *The Structure of Psychoanalytic Theory.* New York: Int. Univ. Press.

SADOW, L., GEDO, J. E., MILLER, J., & POLLOCK, G. H. (1968). The process of hypothesis change in three early psychoanalytic concepts. *J. Amer. Psychoanal. Assn.*, 16:245–273.

SCHIMEK, J. G. (1975). The interpretations of the past. *J. Amer. Psychoanal. Assn.*, 23:835–865.

———— (1987). Fact and fantasy in the seduction theory. *J. Amer. Psychoanal. Assn.*, 35:937–965.

SCHUSDEK, A. (1968). Freud's "seduction theory." *J. Hist. Behav. Sci.*, 2:159–166.

SIMON, B. (1991). Is the Oedipus complex still the cornerstone of psychoanalysis? *J. Amer. Psychoanal. Assn.*, 39:641–668.

———— (1992). Incest: See under oedipus complex. *J. Amer. Psychoanal. Assn.* (in press).

———— & BLASS, R. B. (1990). The history of incest in psychoanalysis. Read at the Israel Psychoanalytic Society.

SLIPP, S. (1977). Interpersonal factors in hysteria. *J. Amer. Acad. Psychoanal.*, 5:359–376.

SPIEGEL, R. (1977). Freud and the women in his world. *J. Amer. Acad. Psychoanal.*, 5:377–402.

STEWART, W. A. (1967). *Psychoanalysis: The First Ten Years.* London: George Allen & Unwin.

SULLOWAY, F. G. (1979). *Freud: Biologist of the Mind.* New York: Basic Books.

Attachment and Separateness

A Theoretical Context for the Integration of Object Relations Theory with Self Psychology

RACHEL B. BLASS, M.A. and
SIDNEY J. BLATT, Ph.D.

The aims of attachment and of separateness, and their experiential counterparts within the overall sense of self identity, guide the individual throughout the life cycle. Multiple forms of relatedness, based on varying degrees of self-object differentiation and instinctual drive involvement, enable the individual to establish and consolidate a sense of self both as a cohesive and autonomous entity and as inherently attached to others through loving relationships. This theoretical orientation provides a context for integrating Kohut's major conceptual contribution with classical object relations theory. The essence of this integration requires resolution of the challenges that Kohut's concept of "selfobject" poses to conventional understanding of the relationship between relatedness and self development.

RECENT THEORETICAL FORMULATIONS HAVE SOUGHT TO DEFINE THE INterface between Kohut's formulation and classical drive and object concepts of psychoanalysis (Friedman, 1980; Goldberg, 1989; Kitron, 1991; Pine, 1989; Segel, 1981; Wallerstein, 1983). These efforts have taken place within a more general climate of reconciliation between

Rachel B. Blass is in the department of psychology and student counseling services, Hebrew University of Jerusalem. This research was supported in part by a fellowship from the Smolen Foundation, Sigmund Freud Center, Hebrew University of Jerusalem.

Sidney J. Blatt is in the departments of psychiatry and psychology, Yale University, and the Western New England Psychoanalytic Institute and Society.

divergent theoretical frameworks in contemporary psychoanalysis. Not only has the theory of object relations become an essential facet of classical analytic theory (Greenberg, 1990), but opposing conceptions of object relations theory are being brought together within broader integrative models. These models, which consider the "I" or the "self" in relation to the "we," as defined by the relatedness to others (Emde, 1988; Lichtenberg, 1983; Stern, 1977, 1985, 1988), constitute potential integrations of "separateness" and "attachment" object relational theories of psychological development. Within this context, we posit a dialectical model of attachment and separateness in the development of self identity (Blatt, 1990; Blatt and Blass, 1990, 1991). An examination of Kohut's concepts from the perspective of our attachment-separateness dialectic model of development focuses both on self and relatedness from a developmental perspective. Our goal is to delineate and elucidate some of Kohut's basic conceptual innovations that are relevant to the understanding of personality development.

The Attachment-Separateness Developmental Model

Personality development throughout the life cycle involves two fundamental developmental lines—that of attachment and of separateness (Blatt and Shichman, 1983; Blatt and Blass, 1990, 1991). The attachment line considers the quality of the individual's relationships—the capacity to form and maintain stable relationships and the ability to integrate these into a sense of self in relation to another person. The separateness line considers the development of the individual as a self-contained and independent unit. Individuation, differentiation, and autonomy are developmental achievements that lead to a stable sense of self as separate with a clear sense of goals and values. The relationship between these two developmental lines is intimate and complex, with the individual's overall self identity emerging as a product of "an ongoing dialectic between the self as separate and the self as experienced in its attachments to objects" (Blatt and Blass, 1990, p. 115).

Previously (Blatt and Blass, 1990) we defined the specific stages and affective and functional components of the two development lines of attachment and separateness and their interrelationship through a revision of Erikson's eight-stage epigenetic model of development (1959, 1963, 1968). These formulations enabled us to extend our understanding of the processes of internalization and integration through which psychological development occurs. The examination of the interface between our attachment-separateness model of development and Kohut's self psychology requires further clarification of certain aspects of our model and a more precise definition of our central concepts and terms.

1. *Aim and experience.* All approaches to psychological development conceptualize the individual as coming into being both through *experiences* of interaction with significant others and through *experiences* of separateness. Different theories can be distinguished, however, by what they consider to be the central goal or *aim* of psychological development: either aims of attachment or of separateness.

By postulating basic aims in terms of two fundamental developmental lines throughout the life cycle, we stress in our model that the meaning and quality of self experience is determined by the dialectic between attachment and separateness aims. When separateness aims such as the control of the other or autonomy predominate, drive satisfaction will be experientially distinct from when the predominant aim is attachment (e.g., a need for intimacy). Gratifying drive-related experiences and resolution of various inevitable drive-related conflicts can enhance the development of attachment and the sense of self as separate. Both experiences of drive satisfaction and of object-seeking can be in the service of the two superordinate aims (separateness and attachment).

2. *Attachment and relationship.* Relationships may include "attachment" and/or "separateness" components. When the separateness aim predominates, the relationship is marked by a functional use of the object in the service of the preservation or gratification of the sense of self as separate. The object is recognized insofar as it contributes to this aim. Classical concepts of narcissistic relationships, beginning with Freud's (1914), clearly reflect the underlying separateness aim. When the attachment aim predominates, the central quality of the relationship focuses on the existence and integrity of the other being an inherent component of the experience. Recognition or acknowledgment of the other can occur at different levels of development, but is always with an awareness of the object beyond its providing self functions and its gratifying self needs. Only such relationships should be considered "attachments." Attachments express the individual's innate and lifelong needs for human contact (Balint, 1937, 1968; Benedek, 1952; Bowlby, 1969–73; Ribble, 1943; Rollman-Branch, 1960)—to be responded to by the other and in turn to be responsive or pleasing to the other (G. Klein, 1976; Suttie, 1935). Later transformations of such needs and wishes include selfless concern (Winnicott, 1963), nonreducible needs for intimacy and mutuality (Erikson, 1959, 1963), and a sense of belonging (G. Klein, 1976, p. 229). The classical view of "true object love" as involving the "perception of and reaction to the object as

a separate individual with his own needs, desires, and reactions" (Pulver, 1970, p. 330) ignores the possibility that the other may be used for enhancement of the self as a separate and self-contained entity or become an object of true attachment. The term "object love" should pertain only to special qualities of relatedness (e.g., basic trust, concern, intimacy, mutuality, as well as their infantile precursors) associated with attachments to the object throughout the life cycle. These attachments may also secondarily serve separateness aims, and the gratification of separateness aims may eventually lead to attachment. We maintain, however, that the distinction between relationships based primarily on attachment aims and those based primarily on the aims of the separate self, allows for a more sensitive approach to the different ways in which various theoretical models conceptualize the basic nature and role of relationships in psychological development.

3. *Separateness and differentiation.* Classical separateness theories (e.g., evolved by Mahler and A. Freud) describe separateness as emerging from relationships with objects which become progressively more differentiated. Early formative relationships allow for the "hatching out" from the undifferentiated symbiosis, and later relationships reflect the individual's capacity for maintaining distinct and differentiated self-object boundaries in relational or interpersonal contexts (Mahler, 1963; Settlage, 1980). The approach of a separateness theory is founded on an immediate association between separateness and differentiation. But once separateness is recognized as one of two developmental aims and the predominant role of the attachment aim is acknowledged, it becomes apparent that there actually is a distinction between separateness and differentiation. The attainment of separateness requires various kinds of relationships, which at different points in development vary in degree of differentiation of self and object. It is "the early mother-child unit and not its breaking up [that constitutes] the primary condition for identity in man" (Lichtenstein, 1977, p. 72). The internalization of the undifferentiated relationship and ongoing involvement in such relationships directly determine and sustain the individual's sense of self identity as a separate and self-contained entity.

Paradoxically, the individual's sense of self identity as a self-contained unit depends in part on a loss of the boundaries of that unit; a sense of self as separate is experienced within a state of self-object fusion. This paradox is resolved through an examination of two aspects traditionally associated with symbiosis (Blass and Blatt, in preparation). One aspect relates to merger—the "oneness" of the self and object reflecting the most intimate tie between the individual and the maternal object. It is the special attachment experience of union that is significant (e.g., Balint, 1937, p. 101f.; David, 1980, p. 92).

The other aspect of symbiosis relates to narcissistic fusion. Here the lack of differentiation of self and object involves the omnipotent experience of the other as part of oneself. The self is extended in such a way that it expands to include the need-satisfying maternal part object and thus preserves the experience of self-sufficiency and integrity of primary narcissism (e.g., Gruenberger, 1979; Mahler, 1952; Mahler et al., 1975; Parens, 1980). Thus in symbiosis the undifferentiated state seems to be linked to two experiential components, one related to the aim of attachment and the other in the service of enhancing separateness and self-sufficiency. "The very extremeness of the symbiotic relation . . . becomes the very source of the emergence of human identity" (Lichtenstein, 1977, p. 72). This original experience of undifferentiation is normally retained throughout life, manifesting itself at various times and to varying degrees in undifferentiated relationships with others.[1] "Even as an adult man cannot ever experience his identity except . . . within the variations of a symbiotically structured Umwelt" (p. 73). Control, illusions of self-sufficiency, continuous gratification of self-needs, and the very experience of an expansive self are some of the partial aims that are immediately attained when the separateness aim predominates within the undifferentiated relational context.

This distinction between separateness and differentiation contributes to a fuller appreciation of the undifferentiated relationship in the formation and maintenance of self identity and to the evaluation of Kohut's theoretical contributions.

KOHUT'S THEORETICAL CONTRIBUTIONS AND THEIR LIMITATIONS

Kohut set the basic framework of his theoretical formulations through the introduction of the developmental line of "narcissism" as complementary to that of "object love" and through the related innovation of the "selfobject." To appreciate Kohut's contributions to knowledge about psychological development, as well as their limitations, it is necessary to understand what he was introducing in articulating a new

---

1. We (Blass and Blatt, in preparation) distinguish between undifferentiation as a source and manifestation of severe pathology (e.g., Blatt and Wild, 1976) and normal aspects of undifferentiation (e.g., Grotstein, 1983, 1984; Rose, 1972; Silverman et al., 1982).

developmental line. According to his official version (e.g., Kohut 1971, pp. 3–6, 25f.), what distinguishes the line of narcissism from that of object love is a functional qualitative factor. That is, what is presumed to distinguish narcissism and object love is the degree of differentiation of the self and object within the relationships associated with each developmental line. As Ornstein (1978, p. 66) explains, while both narcissism and object love are forms of object relations, they denote distinctly different qualities of relationship in the psychoanalytic sense. Object love involves relationships in which there is a complete differentiation of self from object ("true object" in the classical sense); such an object is related to with full recognition of separateness. Narcissism, in contrast, involves relations in which there is a lack of differentiation, or only partial differentiation of self from object (hence the new term "selfobject") (p. 62). While this official position is maintained throughout (Coen, 1981),[2] two other factors seem to be of equal importance in the definition of the narcissistic and object love developmental lines. One factor is the instinctual basis of the relationship, and the other is its self-cohesive role. It is only the true object that is "cathected with object-instinctual investments" (Kohut, 1971, p. 51) and it is only the "selfobject relation that early on maintains the cohesiveness of the developing self" (Ornstein, 1978, p. 103). Ultimately what emerges is a model in which instinctual object cathexis is relegated to distinct objects, and self cohesion is considered to be formed solely on the basis of certain kinds of nondifferentiated relationships. Clearly then instinctually based object relations are not in and of themselves thought to be meaningful contributors to self cohesion (Tolpin, 1979). Such relationships, however, are thought to be at the foundation of object love. Here Kohut (1971) maintains that love for the object is not a primary phenomenon but rather emerges in the course of development toward separateness (p. 220). In these formulations Kohut retains the classical view of object love and introduces narcissism as an additional dimension which has not been fully recognized or carefully studied in its own right.

Kohut's model both limits and expands our understanding of the processes of psychological development. Kohut restricts the scope of his contributions by recognizing the two basic forms of relatedness—object love and narcissism—and by defining these formations by three independent criteria—degree of differentiation, involvement of in-

---

2. This position is maintained throughout despite Kohut's later statements regarding the differentiation of the mature selfobject. To explain how these apparently contradictory statements are held simultaneously is beyond the scope of this paper.

stinctual drives, and contribution to self cohesion. There are, however, many different forms and shades of relationships that can emerge from the complex interactions between Kohut's three defining criteria. For example, undifferentiated relationships can serve the aim of attachment rather than the aim of the cohesion of the separate self, or instinctual drive experiences (libidinal and aggressive) are essential to the formation of such cohesion.

Kohut's contributions are also restricted by his neglect of attachment. Both Kohut's view of the individual's *experience* of attachment to the other (within the context of object love) and his view of the emergence of the individual's sense of an autonomous self are founded on the primacy of a separateness aim. Maturity is defined in terms of the self's "'more mature' *usage* of others"; the development of capacities for concern and sharing are not addressed (Bacal, 1990, p. 209). Moreover, Kohut's writings become increasingly disinterested in the entire realm of object love and associated experiences of attachment. As Kohut turned his focus almost exclusively on "the primary psychological configuration . . . [of] the experience of the relation between the self and the empathic selfobject" (1977, p. 122), development along the line of object love gradually became a "nonspecific effect" of narcissistic processes (Ornstein, 1978, p. 66; Kohut, 1982, 1984).

Kohut further constricts the scope of his contributions by linking self cohesion and development to the establishment of a positive sense of self-esteem. The term "narcissism," which at different times has been used to refer to both cohesion and esteem (Moore, 1975), provides a context for the linkage. Developments related to grandiosity and idealization are ultimately considered to be the major determinants of self cohesion; and the attainment of positive experiences in these areas are considered to be the individual's major partial aims. Kohut's description of the bipolar self highlights the way his focus on self-esteem limits the attainment of self cohesion to a very narrow set of developmental processes. The individual's development throughout the life cycle is viewed in terms of "transformations of archaic grandiosity and exhibitionism into the central self-assertive goals, purposes, and ambitions" on the one pole, and "transformations of archaic idealizations into the central idealized values and internalized guiding principles" on the other (Ornstein, 1978, p. 99).

Despite these limitations of Kohut's formulations, his concentrated focus on the specific self-selfobject relationships of the separate self leads to elaboration of certain neglected processes and to major theoretical contributions. Three basic contributions are noteworthy:

1. *Object relationships and the narcissistic aim.* The developmental line of

self as separate encompasses multiple concurrent developmental processes (Blatt and Blass, 1990, 1991). The establishment of autonomy, initiative, industry, generativity, and their integration into a comprehensive and integrated sense of self as separate require that the individual participate in and experience a variety of events both within the relational context and outside of it, involving both drive and nondrive influences. Kohut's study of the self cohesion that takes place through the consolidation of self structures related to grandiosity and idealization describes an important strand of the separateness line. This "narcissistic" strand joins and interacts with other separateness elements such as that of self integration through the development of ego controls or the establishment of a secure sexual identity. Kohut elaborates the specific forms of relationships that are necessary for the attainment of "narcissistic" aims. His detailed study of the needs for mirroring and idealizing relationships broadens our understanding of object relations. These relationships are based primarily on the capacity of the object to provide the necessary mirroring and idealizing self-regulatory functions and are characterized by the experience of the object not only as subservient to the self but as an integral part of it. These object ties describe noninstinctual relationships in which the individual does not actually *relate to* the object (i.e., the selfobject) or becomes *attached* according to our definition of attachment. While the relationship is intense, the object is not experienced as having any real existence of its own (Kohut, 1971, p. 3; Kohut and Wolf, 1978; Ornstein, 1978, p. 60).

2. *Separateness and undifferentiation throughout the life cycle.* Kohut's formulation also clarifies how the needs for narcissistic relationships endure in various transformations throughout the life cycle (Goldberg, 1983; Kohut, 1983; Ornstein, 1983). Kohut (1980) stresses that we live in "a matrix of selfobjects from birth to death" (p. 478) and that "people maintain lasting selfobject relationships throughout life as part and parcel of normal growth and development" (Goldberg, 1983, p. 298). Classical theory has always recognized to some extent the lifelong need for relationships of various kinds, but Kohut's conception of the ongoing matrix of the self-object relationships increases our awareness that the individual's *sense of separateness throughout the life cycle* involves relationships in which the individual experiences the other as an integral part of himself (Ornstein, 1978, p. 60). As Grotstein (1984, p. 202) explains, "The concept of the self-selfobject relationship predicates that the boundary of the self (the I) transcends I's body to include the body of the other." This transcendence is not of the attachment kind but rather, as Grotstein goes on to explain, involves processes of "projective identification from the separate self." For Kohut, fusion

only relates to self expansion. Concepts of "union" and "merger" of attachment fall outside the realm of the self-selfobject relationship (Tolpin, 1979, p. 223). Mergerlike experiences of boundary loss—what Greenacre (1957, p. 67) refers to as a "love affair with the world"—are, for example, reframed by Kohut (1966, p. 261) as "narcissistic experience[s]" of "an expanded self which includes the world." Once again we see how Kohut fails to recognize that the ultimate tie to the object can be based on other motives in addition to narcissistic ones.

3. *Modification of the theoretical context.* Kohut adds a fundamental theoretical assumption in his proposition that throughout the life cycle the existence of the self as a cohesive entity is intimately tied to the existence of an empathic environment of responsive selfobjects (Goldberg, 1983, p. 298). Basic theoretical concepts of development can readily encompass the idea that the individual's growth and well-being depends on the existence of supportive others. But traditional developmental concepts are unable to accommodate the formulation that ongoing existence of others is experienced as an inherent and integral component of the individual's cohesive sense of self separate and autonomous. Traditional conceptualization places the individual's self identity as a stable configuration of internalizations or as a gestalt of the affective and functional structures developed in the course of the maturation process. These concepts presume a sharp "inner-outer" dichotomy. Self identity is considered only in terms of what is "taken in" to the self as opposed to what is "left outside." These concepts do not, however, have the capacity to encompass the notions of self and self identity that are experienced exclusively *within* the relationship. The experience of self cohesion within the context of the self-selfobject relationship requires a rethinking of our fundamental concepts of development.

Kohut, in this regard, does not explicitly introduce a *formal* modification of the theoretical context. In his focus on his new concepts of "transmuting internalizations" and "optimal frustration," and their roles in the structuralization of the bipolar self, he retains the classic orientation to self identity. Despite this classical framework, Kohut latently struggles to conceptualize the self as experienced within its ongoing relationships to selfobjects (Bacal, 1990, p. 200). This struggle is often expressed through the dilemma of whether the selfobject is considered an intrapsychic experience and structure or an interpersonal event. Kohut maintains that the selfobject is both an inner structure and an experience which takes place between people. Kohut's difficulties in formulating the self in a relational context become apparent in this dual focus (e.g., Kohut, 1983, p. 390ff.). Ultimately

Kohut admits that his formulation involves "a violation of the rules of logic" and a "terminological and conceptual inconsistency" (p. 391). While Kohut fails to overcome these difficulties, his struggle with them is an important contribution because it highlights the necessity for modifying the basic theoretical context so that it can encompass the notion of self as existent within the relationship.

Numerous efforts in recent years attempt to make the necessary theoretical modifications. These attempts, to a large degree inspired by Kohut's latent struggle, have resulted in the elaboration of the theoretical space intermediate between the intrapsychic and the interpersonal (Grotstein, 1983, 1984; London, 1985; Modell, 1984, 1985). As Loewald (1978, p. 501) explains, the experience of the self in its relation to the selfobject "could not be called an intrapsychic structure." Such organizations "are experienced by the persons involved as taking shape and having force *between* them. They are neither internal nor external; and this is so despite the fact that an internal world, an intrapsychic id and ego of significant consolidation are established." Loewald goes on to suggest that self organizations or functions of this kind are best conceptualized as "psychic process-structures which are not intrapsychic but in an intermediate region" (p. 502).

SUMMARY AND INTEGRATION

Our analysis indicates that the importance of Kohut's conceptual contributions lies in the questions he poses to conventional understanding of the relationship between relatedness and self development. Kohut's concept of the selfobject relationship contains the essence of these contributions in that it points to the subservience of certain forms of object relationships to the self-enhancing narcissistic aims throughout life and to the importance of the ongoing experience of an undifferentiated self and object in the attainment of that aim. Conventional views of an antithesis between close relatedness and narcissism and between separateness and undifferentiation cannot fully encompass Kohut's innovative formulations. Kohut's formulations lead not only to further elaboration of the conventional views of relatedness, narcissism, and an expanded range of separateness aims, but also to a broadening of the basic psychoanalytic conceptual model. This is reflected in the sharp differences that are found in the interpretations of Kohut's writings. Some reviewers, for example, claim that Kohut failed to acknowledge the role of object relations in self development, stressing the lack of true recognition of the object inherent in Kohut's narcissistic relationships (e.g., Modell, 1985, p. 71). Other reviewers, however, have pointed to the close bond inherent in these relationships and ultimately have depicted Kohut's model as an object relations theory, primarily concerned with attachment (Bacal, 1987, 1990; Seinfeld, 1990).

Through an examination of the role of attachment and separateness in the development of self identity, it becomes apparent that Kohut's concern with the cohesion of the self is primarily a concern with the self as a separate and self-contained entity. Kohut's concern with relationships is a concern with certain forms of undifferentiated and non-sexual relationships and the way in which they contribute to the consolidation of the separate self. Thus a theoretical model of attachment and separateness reveals the specific domain of Kohut's contributions and points to the necessity of integrating them within a more comprehensive developmental model that also recognizes the importance of attachment, differentiated relationships, and the role of instinctual drives. Such an integration of Kohut's innovations allows us to appreciate more fully the role of the undifferentiated selfobject relationship in the development of the cohesive self not only as a separate entity, but also as attached to others through loving relationships. We can also appreciate more fully how sexual and differentiated self-object relationships effect the narcissistic strand of development. From this theoretical perspective we can now see how normal development includes the experience of controlling and self-expanding instinctual relationships and mirroring by another who is recognized and loved in his own right.

A major proposition of this integrative model is that dichotomies of drive and self, and of object love and narcissism, that pervade Kohut's work do not truly reflect the nature of these functions and processes. Kohut's (1975, p. 754) related dichotomy of the Guilty Man and the Tragic Man, which distinguishes between a conception of the individual "as in conflict over his pleasure-seeking drives" and that of the individual as "blocked in his attempt to achieve self-realization," is equally limited. The attainment of self realization entails conflict every step along the way. Self realization is based on optimal supply of self and relational gratifications and their inevitable and appropriate denial or limitation, as the individual's innate needs and capacities gradually unfold (Behrends and Blatt, 1985; Blatt and Behrends, 1987). This approach, characteristic of object relational developmental perspectives in general (as seen in the works of theorists such as A. Freud, Loewald, and especially Erikson), is not antithetical to "dynamic" conflict-oriented perspectives. Rather, "dynamic" perspectives complement the developmental framework by highlighting the manifold tensions inherent in both the provision and limitation of the gratifications and nutriments necessary for healthy self development. The supply of empathy, for example, is not always normatively nonconflictual. In childhood, the mother's empathic response, an interaction which may be understood in terms of both the attachment or the separateness aims, also takes place within an oedipal context. Beyond the supply of the needed self nutriment itself, the empathic response by the mother has meaning in terms of that inherently conflictual relational context. Furthermore, the intimacy and oneness experienced through the empathic response may be in conflict with the child's need to experience himself as differentiated within the relationship. The experience of empathy may also fall within the conflict between the child's innate progressive developmental impetus and his regressive pull toward fulfillment and gratification of needs in early and familiar forms. Finally, there is the tension between the aim of attachment and the aim of separateness. At times the supply or gratification of the child's needs that emerge from one of these two dimensions contradicts the child's needs that arise in relation to the other. The wish for empathy as an expression of an attachment aim, for example, may oppose the child's wish to be incomprehensible, obscure, and thus separate. The complexities of the developmental process are best understood by relating not only to the kinds of self needs that emerge in its course, but to the various kinds of motivations and dialectical tensions that underly them. Throughout the life cycle, identity is attained and maintained not only through the vicissitudes of narcissism—the focus of Kohut's efforts— but also through the appropriate gratification of conflictual needs that serve the individual's aims of both separateness and attachment.

BIBLIOGRAPHY

BACAL, H. A. (1987). British object-relations theorists and self psychology. *Int. J. Psychoanal.*, 68:81–98.

——— (1990). Does an object relations theory exist in self psychology? *Psychoanal. Inq.*, 9:197–220.

BALINT, M. (1937). Early developmental states of the ego. In *Primary Love and Psychoanalytic Technique*. London: Hogarth Press, 1952, pp. 90–108.

——— (1968). *The Basic Fault*. London: Tavistock.

BEHRENDS, R. S. & BLATT, S. J. (1985). Separation-individuation and internalization. *Psychoanal. Study Child*, 40:11–39.

BENEDEK, T. (1952). The functions of the sexual apparatus and their disturbances. In *Studies in Psychosomatic Medicine*. New York: Ronald Press, pp. 373–406.

BLASS, R. B. & BLATT, S. J. (1991). Attachment and separateness in the experience of the symbiotic relationship (in preparation).

BLATT, S. J. (1990). Interpersonal relatedness and self definition. In *Repression and Dissociation*, ed. J. L. Singer. Chicago: Chicago Univ. Press, pp. 299–335.

——— & BEHRENDS, R. S. (1987). Internalization, separation-individuation, and the nature of therapeutic action. *Int. J. Psychoanal.*, 68:279–297.

——— & BLASS, R. B. (1990). Attachment and separateness. *Psychoanal. Study Child*, 45:107–127.

——— ——— (1991). Relatedness and self definition. In *Interface of Psychoanalysis and Psychology*, ed. J. Barron, M. Eagle, & D. Wolitsky. Washington, D.C.: American Psychological Assn. (in press).

——— & SHICHMAN, S. (1983). Two primary configurations of psychopathology. *Psychoanal. & Contemp. Thought*, 6:187–254.

——— & WILD, C. M. (1976). *Schizophrenia*. New York: Academic Press.

BOWLBY, J. (1969–73). *Attachment and Loss*, 2 vols. New York: Basic Books.

COEN, S. J. (1981). Notes on the concepts of selfobject and preoedipal object. *J. Amer. Psychoanal. Assn.*, 29:395–411.

DAVID, C. (1980). Metapsychological reflections on the state of being in love. In *Psychoanalysis in France*, ed. S. Lebovici & D. Widlocher. New York: Int. Univ. Press, pp. 87–110.

EMDE, R. N. (1988). Development terminable and interminable. *Int. J. Psychoanal.*, 69:23–42.

ERIKSON, E. H. (1959). *Identity and the Life Cycle*. New York: Int. Univ. Press.

——— (1963). *Childhood and Society*, 2nd ed. New York: Norton.

——— (1968). *Identity, Youth, and Crisis*. New York: Norton.

FREUD, S. (1914). On narcissism. *S.E.*, 14:67–102.

FRIEDMAN, L. (1980). Kohut. *Psychoanal. Q.*, 49:393–422.

GOLDBERG, A. (1983). Self psychology and alternative perspectives on internalization. In *Reflections on Self Psychology*, ed. J. D. Lichtenberg & S. Kaplan. Hillsdale, N.J.: Analytic Press, pp. 297–312.

——— (1989). A shared view of the world. *Int. J. Psychoanal.*, 70:16–19.

GREENACRE, P. (1957). The childhood of the artist. *Psychoanal. Study Child*, 12:47–72.

GREENBERG, J. R. (1990). Object relations theory in perspective. *Psychoanal. Inq.*, 10:254–269.

GROTSTEIN, J. S. (1983). Some perspectives on self psychology. In *The Future of Psychoanalysis*, ed. A. Goldberg. New York: Int. Univ. Press, pp. 165–201.

——— (1984). Some perspectives on empathy from others and toward oneself. In *Empathy*, ed. J. Lichtenberg, M. Bernstein, & D. Silver. Hillsdale, N.J.: Analytic Press, vol. 1, pp. 201–215.

GRUENBERGER, B. (1979). *Narcissism*. New York: Int. Univ. Press.

KITRON, D. (1991). Narcissism and object love as separate but dependent developmental lines. *Psychoanal. Study Child*, 46:325–336.

KLEIN, G. S. (1976). The vital pleasures. In *Psychoanalytic Theory*. New York: Int. Univ. Press, pp. 210–238.

KOHUT, H. (1966). Forms and transformations of narcissism. *J. Amer. Psychoanal. Assn.*, 14:243–272.

—— (1971). *The Analysis of the Self*. New York: Int. Univ. Press.

—— (1975). Remarks about the formation of the self. In *The Search for the Self*, ed. P. Ornstein. New York: Int. Univ. Press, pp. 737–770.

—— (1977). *The Restoration of the Self*. New York: Int. Univ. Press.

—— (1980). Summarizing reflections. In *Advances in Self Psychology*, ed. A. Goldberg. New York: Int. Univ. Press, pp. 473–554.

—— (1982). Introspection, empathy, and the semi-circle of mental health. *Int. J. Psychoanal.*, 63:395–407.

—— (1983). Selected problems of self psychological theory. In *Reflections on Self Psychology*, ed. J. D. Lichtenberg & S. Kaplan, Hillsdale, N.J.: Analytic Press, pp. 387–412.

—— (1984). *How Does Analysis Cure?* Chicago: Univ. Chicago Press.

—— & WOLF, E. S. (1978). The disorders of the self and their treatment. *Int. J. Psychoanal.*, 59:413–425.

LICHTENBERG, J. D. (1983). *Psychoanalysis and Infant Research*. Hillsdale, N.J.: Analytic Press.

LICHTENSTEIN, H. (1977). *The Dilemma of Human Identity*. New York: Aronson.

LOEWALD, H. W. (1978). Instinct theory, object relations, and psychic structure formation. *J. Amer. Psychoanal. Assn.*, 26:493–506.

LONDON, N. J. (1985). An appraisal of self psychology. *Int. J. Psychoanal.*, 66:95–107.

MAHLER, M. S. (1952). On child psychosis and schizophrenia. In *The Selected Papers of Margaret S. Mahler*, 1:131–154. New York: Aronson, 1979.

—— (1963). Thoughts about development and individuation. *Psychoanal. Study Child*, 18:307–324.

—— PINE, F., & BERGMAN, A. (1975). *The Psychological Birth of the Human Infant*. New York: Basic Books.

MODELL, A. H. (1984). Self psychology as a psychology of conflict. In *Psychoanalysis: The Vital Issues*, ed. G. H. Pollock & J. Gedo. New York: Int. Univ. Press, vol. 2, pp. 131–148.

—— (1985). The two contexts of the self. *Contemp. Psychoanal.*, 21:70–90.

MOORE, B. E. (1975). Toward a clarification of the concept of narcissism. *Psychoanal. Study Child*, 30:243–276.

ORNSTEIN, P. H. (1978). The evolution of Heinz Kohut's psychoanalytic psychology of the self. In *The Search for the Self*, ed. P. Ornstein. New York: Int. Univ. Press, pp. 1–106.

—— (1983). Discussions of papers by Drs. Goldberg, Stolorow, and Wallerstein. In *Reflections on Self Psychology*, ed. J. D. Lichtenberg & S. Kaplan. Hillsdale, N.J.: Analytic Press, pp. 339–384.

PARENS, H. (1980). Psychic development during the second and third years of life. In *The Course of Life*, ed. S. I. Greenspan & G. H. Pollock. Washington: National Institute of Mental Health, vol. 1, pp. 459–500.

PINE, F. (1989). Motivation, personality organization, and the four psychologies of psychoanalysis. *J. Amer. Psychoanal. Assn.*, 37:31–64.

PULVER, S. E. (1970). Narcissism: the term and the concept. *J. Amer. Psychoanal. Assn.*, 18:319–341.

RIBBLE, M. A. (1943). *The Rights of Infants*. New York: Columbia Univ. Press.

ROLLMAN-BRANCH, H. S. (1960). On the question of primary object need. *J. Amer. Psychoanal. Assn.*, 8:686–702.

ROSE, G. J. (1972). Fusion states. In *Tactics and Techniques in Psychoanalytic Psychotherapy*, ed. P. Giovacchini. New York: Aronson, pp. 170–188.

SEGEL, N. P. (1981). Narcissism and adaption to indignity. *Int. J. Psychoanal.*, 62:465–476.

SEINFELD, J. (1990). *The Bad Object*. New York: Aronson.

SETTLAGE, C. F. (1980). The psychoanalytic theory and understanding of psychic development during the second and third years of life. In *The Course of Life*, ed. S. I. Greenspan & G. H. Pollock. Washington: National Institute of Mental Health, vol. 1, pp. 523–539.

SILVERMAN, L. H., LACHMAN, F. M., & MILICH, R. H. (1982). *The Search for Oneness*. New York: Int. Univ. Press.

STERN, D. N. (1977). *The First Relationship*. Cambridge, Mass.: Harvard Univ. Press.

——— (1985). *The Interpersonal World of the Infant*. New York: Basic Books.

——— (1988). Affect in the context of the infants' experience. *Int. J. Psychoanal.*, 69:233–238.

SUTTIE, I. D. (1935). *The Origins of Love and Hate*. London: Kegan Paul.

TOLPIN, M. (1979). Discussion of "The sustaining object relationship" by H. B. Levine. *Annu. Psychoanal.*, 7:219–225.

WALLERSTEIN, R. S. (1983). Self psychology and "classical" psychoanalytic psychology. In *Reflections on Self Psychology*, ed. S. Lichtenberg & S. Kaplan. Hillsdale, N.J.: Analytic Press, pp. 313–338.

WINNICOTT, D. W. (1963). The development of the capacity for concern. *Bull. Menninger Clin.*, 27:167–176.

Winnicott's Antitheory and Winnicott's Art

His Significance for Adult Analysis

GERALD I. FOGEL, M.D.

The significance of Winnicott's work for the theory and practice of adult analysis is examined. Winnicott's most valuable contribution was to discern important new clinical phenomena. This is a crucial aspect of theory development, but not the same as explicating new theory, and partly accounts for the difficulty integrating his ideas with traditional psychoanalytic theory. Winnicott left the theoretical revisions possibly necessitated by his discoveries for others to accomplish, and some of this new work is discussed and synthesized. The nature of Winnicott's discoveries, especially the phenomenological field of transitional or intermediate experience, is elusive to define, and is also related to his clinical stance and his attitudes to theory for the purposes of clinical work. His work demonstrates the limits of theorizing and of our theories, and also an attitude toward theory that facilitates clinical and theoretical progress. He also provides conceptual language to discuss what is often called the art of psychoanalysis. Both the value and limitations of studying Winnicott are considered.

MANY HAVE POINTED OUT HOW DIFFICULT IT IS TO EXPLAIN WINNICOTT'S theory systematically or to integrate his work with traditional psychoanalytic theory. I believe it is impossible to do so, at least in the usual sense, for several reasons. First, his major contribution was to discern new *phenomena;* he described new data of experience. This is a crucial aspect of advancing psychoanalysis and often leads to extensions and

Training and supervising analyst, Columbia University Psychoanalytic Center for Training and Research. Associate clinical professor of psychiatry, Columbia University College of Physicians and Surgeons.

revisions of theory. But Winnicott neither did nor wished to do this theoretical labor himself. The new or modified theories possibly necessitated by his work must be accomplished by others. Second, the most important phenomenon he discerned was the experiential field of transitional experience, and this phenomenological field, which comprises the essence and ground of most of his discoveries, is by its nature quite difficult to define precisely. Third, these new phenomena rest upon and only exist in Winnicott's own work in relation to the theories of others, and therefore can be partly characterized as a way of reframing these established theories, placing them in a new perspective. Finally, his clinical stance challenges the theorizing function itself, and his implicit theoretical stance parallels his clinical stance.

Although I will refer to selected aspects of Winnicott's theory and its relation to the theories of others, I will not attempt a systematic explication or integration. Instead, I will concentrate on two separate, but closely related aspects of his work. One is the field of transitional phenomena and experience, for I believe that here is an important essence of all of Winnicott's discoveries. The other is his theoretical and clinical *stance*—his *attitude* to theory and his ideas regarding the appropriate relation of theory to practice, of theorizing to experience, and of ideas *about* reality to reality itself. I refer, by the way, to Winnicott's "antitheory" in my title in an ironic sense, for he believed in and used traditional analytic theory, and he had, at least implicitly, a distinct theoretical perspective of his own. I wish to emphasize as strongly as possible, however, that his stance and these transitional or intermediate area experiences sometimes bring into sharp focus limits and dangers which are inherent in the dominant psychoanalytic theories of our time and constraints which may sometimes be imposed on developmental processes and therapeutic work by theorizing and by abstracting from experience.

It is because I deal primarily with Winnicott's significance for the theory and practice of adult analysis that I speak not of transitional *objects* but of transitional *phenomena* and the intermediate area of *experience*. Winnicott uses the terms "intermediate" and "transitional" interchangeably when referring to such experience. He formally introduced the transitional object in 1953, but was preoccupied with it throughout his subsequent work. In the introduction to *Playing and Reality* (1971), he says that he is always reluctant to give examples or definitions, because such pinning down inevitably leads to an "unnatural and arbitrary" process, "whereas the thing that I am referring to is universal and has infinite variety" (p. xii). Here are two more quotes from the paper where he reflects upon this universal thing:

The transitional object is *not an internal object* (which is a mental con-cept)—it is a possession. Yet it is not (for the infant) an external object either [p. 11].

This intermediate area of experience, unchallenged in respect of its belonging to inner or external (shared) reality, constitutes the greater part of the infant's experience, and throughout life is retained in the intense experiencing that belongs to the arts and to religion and to imaginative living, and to creative scientific work [p. 16].

Notice that Winnicott is in the mind—in psychic reality—whether he refers to a transitional object or to transitional experience. This "thing"—experience, object, or phenomenon—is neither completely external nor internal *as we perceive it psychically*, yet it is real mental experience and refers to real things. I think Winnicott believes that this thing he is so interested in is illusion, is play, yet, though it cannot be reality tested in the ordinary sense, is the only thing that is real or worthwhile in life. What *is* this "thing"? Again, here is Winnicott (p. 113): *"If play is neither inside nor outside, where is it?"*

These experiences or phenomena which are so difficult to locate and define are closely related to his theoretical and clinical stance. In its very essence, Winnicott's thought undermines and challenges (though in a characteristically gentle and pixieish way) the theorizing function as we have ordinarily defined it and therefore all prior psychoanalytic theories. Theories ordinarily explain, but Winnicott is more interested in grasping or describing the nature of personal experience, not its causes or its components. Almost everything he deals with refers to a relational or existential *process* with special stress on the field which "contains" that process and the factors which promote and sustain it. The important variable in Winnicott is usually whether this process, be it theoretical or clinical, is vital and authentic or not, true or false, actual or not, real. He is usually not concerned with a *content* variable. Prior psychoanalytic theories have organized the *contents* of experience, and their basic data always contain discrete whole or part subjects and objects. Winnicott is happy to use other people's theories, categories, or techniques, but he takes them as givens, has little to add to them by logical extension. His basic data is the total existential and relational field in which subjects and objects exist. Clinically, he teaches what attitude to take to patients; theoretically, what attitude to take to theo-ries for purposes of clinical work. The newly articulated clinical phe-nomena which interest him fall between the cracks of earlier theories, and are relevant, I believe, to what is often called the art of psycho-analysis. I will return to this art aspect.

Taken as a whole, Winnicott creates not a theory, but an antitheory.

He tackles the ineffable, attempts to characterize or reveal the very essence of experience itself, when this experience is humanly meaningful experience. This is where meaning and human reality are created, where its difficult-to-reconcile contradictions can never be nailed down once and for all. His metaphors enchant and often persuade, but always resist exact definition. We are in the land where all the world can be found in a grain of sand, of symbolic realization, of negative capability, and the spontaneous gesture, of human immanence and the willing suspension of disbelief—where symbol, reality, and illusion all arise, but *before* we abstract and define or explain them.

A crucial paradox must be kept in mind, however. His clinical and theoretical approach shows the limits of theorizing, makes clear the necessity to let go of our attachments to our theories—all of our preexisting meaning structures—for the sake of creative learning and spontaneous growth. He is therefore a revolutionary, a true liberator. Yet, though it is mostly implicit, he also has a deep appreciation for theory and the necessity and inevitability of theorizing in human life, and, importantly, respect for cultural traditions and traditional psychoanalytic theory. His own observations, if not exactly explicitly anchored in these theories, more or less take traditional theoretical categories for granted, and also imply (though he never quite fully spells them out) possible new theoretical categories. So he believes in knowing and doing things in objectively real space and time, not merely feeling or being spontaneous in transitional space. A Winnicottian true self is neither empty of contents, inchoate, nor passive in relation to life. He shows us (1971) that there is no being without doing, just as there is no meaningful doing without being. There is paradox in every corner of Winnicott, but as this small sample of Winnicottian phrase making shows, also a grave possibility for mischief and mystification. Although Winnicott himself may be enigmatic and paradoxical, he is usually clear and direct, and it is hard to catch him in a contradiction or denying any of the hard realities of human life. Many others who try to explain him or to do a so-called Winnicottian psychoanalysis, however, fall into mystification and confusion or naïve and excessive poetic license, idealize being at the expense of doing.

My chosen perspective and Winnicott's nature demand that I go for the essence and risk that sort of foolishness here. But Winnicott was more than elusive essence. Although "the facts" never will add up to Winnicott's essence, they can be stated and placed in historical context. I will remind you of some of the phenomena that Winnicott discerned.

Winnicott made notable contributions in the areas of early personality development, adult personality and psychopathology, and the analytic situation and process. Like the ideas of many good psycho-analytic thinkers, most of his ideas have application in all of these areas. I think of Winnicott as having that quality which Freud admired so much in Charcot—the Charcot he quoted as having once said that "Theory is good, but it does not keep things from existing." Brücke was Freud's ideal for scientific rigor, disciplined and rational thinking. Charcot was Freud's model for the gift of "sight," for concentrated attention upon the thing itself, for the ability to absorb oneself so completely in an experience or phenomenon that it finally "speaks"— reveals its essence directly, by intuition. Winnicott, as Charcot and Freud, had this gift of "sight." When men of such special gifts have the marriage of creative imagination and external reality that characterizes the transitional experience, what is revealed to them often becomes obvious at once to others. They provide the new raw data that make subsequent theoretical advances possible.

I will merely list some of the things Winnicott saw that now seem so obvious to us that we not only take for granted they are real phe-nomena, but also think they must always have been there: the *good-enough mother; primary maternal preoccupation;* the *facilitating environment; transitional objects* and *transitional phenomena;* the significance of *illusion, space, potential space, symbolism, paradox,* and *play;* the *true* and *false self;* the important positive role of *disillusion* and *aggression* in the separation-individuation process; new aspects of the close relationship of *psyche and soma* in normal development and health; the *capacity to be alone; ego relatedness* and *ego coverage;* the *capacity for concern;* the *use of an object; communicating and not communicating; hate in the countertransfer-ence;* and many more. Others have extended his ideas, especially those that apply to the analytic situation and process, such as the *holding* or *containing function* of the analyst and the analytic situation, the notion of *analytic space,* and the *good-enough analyst.*

THE THEORETICAL CONTEXT—FREUD AND KLEIN

What are the theories that are thrown into a new perspective by Win-nicott? They are those of Freud and Melanie Klein, of course, whose ideas are always present, though often only implicitly in Winnicott's work. I believe he agreed with and took entirely for granted most of their views. He spoke of both with deep respect and gratitude. He was uniquely placed historically and personally in relation to the Anna Freud-Melanie Klein controversies in England in the '40s. He was analyzed by a Freudian, James Strachey, and a Kleinian, Joan Riviere, and considered both experiences important and productive. Klein supervised him for six years and referred one of her own children to him for analysis. Although he came to disagree with some of her ideas, his understanding of what is necessary for the achievement of mature object relations and an individuated personal self rest solidly in Klein's theory. While he usually used his own language, he took for granted the central significance of internalized object relationships, especially preoedipal, dyadic ones, and of part objects, primitive aggression, and guilt and reparation in the individuation process. Regarding the depressive position, he said (1965, p. 176): "This is Klein's most important contribution, in my opinion, and I think it ranks with Freud's concept of the Oedipus complex. The latter concerns a three-body relationship and Klein's depressive position concerns a two-body relationship—that between the infant and the mother."

Oversimplifying considerably, I characterize his differences with her as theoretical and temperamental. Theoretically, he found himself unable to accept Klein's theory of the paranoid-schizoid position: both her notions of innate sadism and envy as primary drives and of the existence of self-object discrimination—an autonomous, differentiated fantasy life—in the earliest months of life. Temperamentally, he was a healer, not a fighter, and was sensitive to what he came to characterize as the facilitation of innate developmental tendencies; this and his pediatric experience helped him realize that some of the primitive aggression he saw in his patients was caused by interference with this natural process, both in development and the analytic process. I do not think he denied the depth or ubiquity of this aggression, but he believed that such "impingements" were often a significant factor in causing this aggression. Very severe impingements cause the paranoid-schizoid picture, and this is always pathological, never normal.

In addition, he believed that theories—other people's *ideas* about reality—could be used in this manner, as impingements that a patient or developing child could not defend against, could only reject blindly and destructively, or comply with, thereby creating a caricature of human responsiveness, and therefore a caricature of the spontaneity which he considered to be the essence of psychological health. He thought that some Kleinians used their theories this way, and thus could not hear the responses of their patients which could have demonstrated the limits of the theories or of the people using them. Kohut (1971) later made the same claim about Freudian orthodoxy in America. Whether in reaction to American intellectualism or English deep confrontations, the result could be narcissistic rage (Kohut, 1972). This iatrogenic phenomenon, based on the analyst's insufficient knowledge, overvalued theory, or unacknowledged countertransference, was often wrongly taken for a confirmation of the insensitively applied theory—a self-fulfilling prophecy. Winnicott and Kohut had other things in common besides their historical whistle-blowing functions, though I think Winnicott was the more subtle and significant thinker.

Winnicott enriched and extended Freud and Klein without rejecting their essential findings. Developmentally, Klein (1945) demonstrated a world beyond Freudian oedipality, of the significance of the pre-oedipal and how the preoedipal shapes and remains alive in the oedipal. Winnicott went beyond Klein, showed us a world of mental life, presumably in the earliest period of infancy, that exists before self-object discrimination exists, but where subjectivity is nevertheless present, though absolutely dependent on what he called the environmental provision—the actual relationship to the mother. This phase also shapes and lives on in subsequent phases.

To Klein's clinical and theoretical guide to preoedipal character syndromes in adults and the significance for all patients of "primitive" (dyadic) fantasy, conflict, and defenses, Winnicott added what he called the third part of mental life. Neither differentiated objective thought nor emotional and magical subjective thought, he named this realm transitional or intermediate. He tried to demonstrate and explain the origin and fate in development of certain subjective and intersubjective mental states, experiences in which subjects and objects are undifferentiated psychically and related to each other ambiguously. He maintained that such experiences should not always be viewed as evidence of regression, defenses against object-instinctual conflict, or attempts to deny objective reality. Clinically, Klein extended Freud's work by elucidating the complex world of internalized object relations, the intrapsychic and interpersonal play of transference and countertransference, deepening our understanding of the psychoanalytic process.

Winnicott expanded Freud and Klein further still, by studying the qualities and significance of the field as a whole, of personal space and potential space, the limits and possibilities for shared space, the characteristics of the analytic frame, the containing or holding function, the so-called matrix of transference and countertransference, the "stuff" of experience itself, the sometimes ineffable ground without which all these figures, triadic or dyadic, cannot exist in any humanly meaningful way. Winnicott could see that if we were too attached to our theories or any other preconceived notion or expectation of a patient, we could hinder, rather than facilitate, clinical progress—and theoretical progress as well. Thus an important aspect of the analytic attitude is highlighted—the necessity to attend without being hindered by any fixed categorical content.

One might say that, for Winnicott, Freud represents the paternal principle—moral law, rationality, objectivity, the world of similarity and difference—where secondary process is expected ultimately to prevail; Klein the maternal principle—talion law, emotionality, subjectivity, the world of split and part objects, of primitive identifications and projections—where primary process is always given its due. Winnicott then represents the principle that is difficult to name, because it has no fixed categories of mental content and cannot be reduced to either of the other two. Perhaps we can catch aspects of it by referring to a principle of original unity or original innocence—the realm of technical neutrality, Bion's realm beyond memory or desire, sacred or self-reflexive space, unconditional positive regard, human immanence, suchness. We find ourselves on ground that somehow gives significance to and cannot be separated from mental content, yet cannot be reduced to that content. Thus we move from triadic to dyadic to holding function.

SOME THEORETICAL IMPLICATIONS

This third principle or frame of reference for all mental life—this holding function—is easy to understand as a derivative of infant-mother care, but difficult to grasp in its significance for all human life. It is easy to imagine why an infant or very damaged patient needs to be "held," but not so easy to acknowledge and understand this holding factor in relation to higher mental organizations and levels of function. Winnicott found a way to characterize this aspect of human experience that refers to adult as well as infantile functioning, that responsibly contains both reality and fantasy, and functions as a possible resting and growing space, not only as a hiding place. It is partly characterized by a creative tension between subjective and objective, between inner and outer reality.

I find Winnicott's essence in his never-ending quest to demonstrate—more by revelation than by explanation—this transitional or intermediate realm. His talent for discerning this experiential field played an essential role in all of his subsequent discoveries as well as his legendary clinical acumen. Discerning is not the same as establishing new conceptual premises, providing new theory, but this is powerful and influential discerning indeed. He sometimes called this intermediate area the *basis* of all experience, by which I think he meant all *personal* and *personally meaningful* experience. As the transitional object is the first "not me possession," so a person's personal experience must also be possessed, before it can be truly lived and only then possibly understood, and this is so at every developmental level.

Klein deepened our notion of psychic reality, the world of fantasy, by insisting we need not always take the external world—so-called objective reality—into account. Winnicott says there is another realm, one that may even be the essence of personal experience. It can neither be reduced to internal reality—pure subjectivity—nor can it be reduced to external reality—objectivity—but partakes of each. It cannot be reality tested in the empirical sense; its existence depends on our agreeing to regard it as privileged, special, not to be questioned as to inside or outside. He calls it an illusion, but this is where his most basic and easily misunderstood paradox lay. Because although it is a so-called illusion, many of the important things in life and possibly all of the meaningful and uniquely human ones are to be found there— culture, imaginative living, creative scientific work, and so forth. It is the only way reality can become *meaningfully* real to us. Calling it an illusion is Winnicott's concession to Freud and science, a whimsical bow to our sacred cow, objective reality.

Philosophic and contemplative traditions have always pondered the mystery of human self-awareness. Many have noted that our scientific and technological age has tended to idealize rationality and reason, sometimes failed to note that, despite the advantages of scientific method for mastering and controlling our world, it cannot account for the entire realm of human potential and mastery. Existential and relational variables—*process* variables—exist that elude a physicalistic model. Object relational and self-psychological schools have been the major recent contributors within psychoanalysis to challenge such models, though we now see that this critique of logical positivism has existed in every corner of the natural and social sciences and the humanities in recent years.

Winnicott offers a potentially unifying perspective by claiming that moments of self-awareness in health may transcend subjectivity and objectivity. He points out that what has the appearance of truth may mock human life, be lifeless and static or vicarious and compliant, lacking personal meaning, spontaneity, realness, actuality. By staying so clearly within *psychic reality*—the realm of human experience—he does not elevate subjectivity at the expense of objectivity. He presents us with a conundrum, however, because important aspects of human experience cannot be entirely contained by our traditional theoretical categories. The intermediate area of experience eludes them, is an essence, and is neither completely inner nor outer. We are in theoretical land ordinarily occupied by primary narcissism, so-called objectless or oceanic states, which are usually conceptualized as states of merger or symbiosis, yet asked to consider that such phenomena be regarded as possible aspects of health. It should be possible, Winnicott implies, to discern patterns, characteristics, and qualities of the whole psychical system which reflect healthy development, are reducible neither to subjectivity nor objectivity, and which do not *necessarily* imply infancy or severe psychopathologic states.

One must read more Winnicott than the transitional object paper to comprehend the range of phenomena and levels of function contained in the intermediate area, or its qualities and characteristics that permeate Winnicott's work. Others have tried to place these phenomena theoretically or to develop new theory to take them into account. From an enormous literature, I can present only a few pertinent examples. Relying on conceptions of Hartmann's and Rapaport's ego psychology, Coppolillo (1967) postulates that transitional experience is that in which neutralization, aim inhibition, and compromise formation occur, where optimal autonomy from both inner drives and outer stimulation or impingement exists, so that regression in the service of the ego can occur, and a resultant psychological growth and adaptive mastery. Because the transitional object concept has been so captivating, many think of transitional or intermediate *experience* as an aspect of early life, an early infantile stage. In fact, it is a universal experience of human living of which, in infancy, the transitional object is a vehicle.

Metcalf and Spitz (1978) also consider regression in the service of the ego, but from a developmental perspective. Spitz believed that the transitional object phase represented a third critical organizer of psychic life (along with the earlier smiling response at 3 months and stranger anxiety at 6 to 8 months), one which correlates with Mahler's phases of separation-individuation. They speak (p. 100) of a "concatenation" of important capacities which emerge at this point in development; they include, among others, "the development of memory, of libidinal object constancy, and of the capacity for symbolization." With Winnicott, they note that the "inception and unfolding of symbolic thinking" are at issue here, and therefore "one of the foundations for the unique human mental activities of dreaming, fantasy, and creativity." The transitional object period is on the way from "recognition memory" to "evocative memory," and the transitional object is a "quasi-need," a "prosthesis for evocative memory" on a developmental path from the "recognition of a sign gestalt to evocation through a volitional act of mentation" (p. 106).

I believe that the flexibility and reliability of this facilitative intrapsychic "space," which "contains" our capacity to imagine, dream, and be aware of and profit from it (and ultimately to assume personal responsibility for it), are tested by the inevitable course of further development—the always increasing and increasingly complex internal and external tasks which are well known to us all. Paradoxically, this experiential mode is required for and is also a product of further integration and synthesis. It must remain available or be implicitly constant or within stable limits, if individuation and higher levels of mental organization are to be accomplished. And it must depend less and less for its existence on an "environmental provision," become increasingly autonomous, as higher developmental levels are attained.

Its reliable presence reflects a stable and autonomous ego organization and is a measure of ego strength. In "good-enough" health, autonomy is a self-reflexive system, which, like the Mahlerian space "between" mother and child for which the mother is responsible, requires monitoring and management of extraordinarily complex internal and external realities, utilizing communicatory feedback reliably and flexibly, in an eternal process which continually evolves and changes. An individual must determine, for example, whether to advance to the unfamiliar, return to the familiar, let go of or rely on automatized modes of experience and behavior, and assess whether overall conditions allow for creative challenges and strategic retreats, or require more urgent adjustments. The capacity to use relationships and activities flexibly to augment the individual's own capacity for "ego coverage" is also one more among countless additional factors.

None of this is new, but as an important component of what we ordinarily conceive as a structured system, an intrapsychic "space" that cannot be reduced to any part or parts of the structure, or regarded as the sum of the structure's parts, is an unusual but interesting metaphor. To conceive of such a metaphorical space may be sensible, however, if one considers, for example, the ways in which aspects of ego strength actually manifest themselves in the analytic setting. Assessment, prediction, and definition are notoriously difficult when we consider analyzability, or how we know when a psychoanalytic situation or process or a transference neurosis is reliably in place or how to sustain and develop it, or how some of us make good-enough predictions of outcome during an analysis, or develop criteria for a successful termination. The qualities that guide us in such matters reflect existential and relational gestalten—process variables reflecting properties of the whole organization and of the ways in which all the parts interact in relation to all of the other parts, intrapsychically and interpersonally. No single variable or particular arrangement of variables can ever claim to be *the* criteria to nail down or define such a process. This is why these phenomena are so difficult to study empirically, despite the empirical *sound* of such terms as ego "functions" or "regulations," which softly imply that precise measurement and deterministic prediction might be possible. The elusive characteristics of Winnicott's transitional space are strangely and strikingly analogous to the *clinical* ego of analytic process.

In his monograph on sublimation, Loewald (1988) shows the relation of some of his ideas to Winnicott's. Loewald claims that what he calls "true symbolism" is always found in what he calls "true sublimation," and both of these are linked to his concept of internalization and the innate human tendency to strive for higher levels of mental organization, for psychological growth. He explicitly equates these phenomena to Winnicott's transitional experience. In effect, these are mental states in which integration and unification may be attained without defensive alteration or any sacrifice of discrimination and differentiation. Similarity and difference, separateness and relatedness are reconciled in a higher symbolic linkage, resulting in a higher level of mental organization. While it is true that the symbolic function is inevitably exploited for defensive purposes in psychic life, classical psychoanalysis has tended to deal with symbolism only in such narrow or reductive terms. In a way that would not be natural to Winnicott, Loewald uses his philosophical background, speaks of such things as "the root and playground of both reality and illusion" that "makes possible the distinction, as well as the confusion, between inner and outer reality" (p. 71), and of states that "represent way stations from indeterminacy to determinacy or from the ineffable to effable" (p. 72).

Winnicott often speaks of play and other transitional experiences as existing in real time and space, but also of having the character of being special or privileged, intimating time out of time. Although Loewald challenges the use of spatial metaphors in structural theory, time figures prominently in his thinking about the major psychic structures. He speaks, for example (1980), of the ego's function of creating "presence," and of a "living" past and future as inherent in vital, healthy psychic structures. For Loewald "psychic time" is a crucial concept, but one that exists in psychic reality and is not equivalent to linear-historical objective clock time. As with Winnicott, the truth of objective space-time is not denied, but its preeminence and exclusivity as standards to judge human psychic reality are denied. In psychic reality, time and space have crucial aspects that elude a deterministic model. Kaplan (1991) points out that just as distance is a variable of work in physics, time is a variable of work in psychology. He believes that by allowing more time for certain processes to occur, such as the differentiation between perception and apperception in reality testing, Winnicott demonstrated the developmental opportunity that an allowed illusion embodies.

Pattern, form, arrangement, flexibility, and movement are some of the components of complex, nonlinear dynamic systems like the human mind and the subsystems that comprise it. Nonlinear conceptions of space and time may be among the additional factors crucial to consider in a self-reflexive system. Taking into account such factors allows one to say what one knows is true: mature psychic structures are more flexible but also more difficult to define and elusive to grasp *as structures* in the physicalistic sense. The easiest structures to describe in an actual patient on the model of physicalistic structures are primitive, archaic ones; they are visible because they are reified: automatized, rigid, simplistic, nonreflective. In Freud's metaphor, for example, the ego and the superego, in health, merge into each other.

Winnicott's descriptions of the mother bringing to the baby precisely what the baby is able to create, of children's play and adult creative living and interplay, of stages of growth in the capacity to be alone, of the crucial supportive function and facilitative power of "ego coverage," or an analytic "hold"—these all give us an intuitive glimpse into the profound and universal presence and power of these experiences. It also reveals their profoundly fragile nature and the paradox that must be sustained, which requires there be no challenge to the ambiguity between reality and fantasy that is necessarily part of their living fabric. By speaking of the reality of these experiences, we risk linguistic confusion, as we are accustomed to using the term for objective, external reality. Perhaps actuality is the better term. With this usage, we may conceive that the mind *creates* actuality in a symbolic "actualizing" marriage of what is created and what is found, out of imagination and event, and therefore brings the quality of being real to personal experience.

Winnicott comments frequently on the central significance of symbol creation and symbol usage in these experiences. Although his intuitive skill in this area is beyond question, his scholarly knowledge regarding the symbolic function in human thought does not appear to be extensive. The relationship of his work to a psychological theory of symbolism and the relationship of this psychology to cultural, historical, aesthetic, and philosophical issues have only just recently begun to be developed. The philosopher Richard Kuhns (1983), for example, has used some of Winnicott's ideas in a scholarly and beautifully written book in which he presents a theory of culture and art utilizing modern psychoanalytic principles. Cultural traditions function as vehicles for what he calls "enactments." Like transitional objects and phenomena, cultural enactments serve both a personal and social function—a meeting place for subjective, personal psychic reality; for intersubjective, shared, communal psychic reality; and for objective and adaptive shared social purposes.

WINNICOTT'S ART

I turn to some of the specific ways that Winnicott demonstrates what attitude we should take to patients and to theory for purposes of clinical work. I said earlier that he illuminates aspects of psychoanalysis that often fall between the cracks of theory, that comprise the art of psychoanalysis. Most believe that psychoanalysis at its best is both science and art, but not all notice that even our best theories cannot illuminate this elusive but crucially important art aspect. Winnicott provides an example of and also conceptual language to talk about our art. Clinically, for example, we often refer to tact and timing to convey the many factors necessary to consider in deciding when and how to interpret or be effectively silent—how to use our theories and the theories we construct during clinical work. Winnicott (1971) says:

> Interpretation outside the ripeness of the material is indoctrination and produces compliance. A corollary is that resistance arises out of interpretation given outside the area of the overlap of the patient's and the analyst's playing together. Interpretation when the patient has no capacity to play is simply not useful, or causes confusion. When there is mutual playing, then interpretation according to accepted psychoanalytic principles can carry the therapeutic work forward. *This playing has to be spontaneous, and not compliant or acquiescent* [p. 59f.].

Many routine clinical judgments contain innumerable operant variables at a given moment, some of a subjective and intuitive nature. I have already referred to analyzability, stages of analysis, and evaluations of outcome. But what of the moment-to-moment work? How does one know when the "as if" position is reliably present, when the patient has the capacity to experience and observe? How does one know when the content of a dream is "ripe," or if the associations to it are compliant or resistant or if they are vital and therefore deepening of the material? What about those times when the associations are actually vital and useful but also defending against the transference? And by whose criteria do we determine what is "vital"? By what or whose criteria can one determine the stage, depth, or quality of an analysis?

One way to approach such questions is to admit that in an actual clinical situation some *analysts* are better than others at answering such questions. One of the important skills involved is the capacity to recognize transitional or intermediate experience, intuitively to appraise Winnicott's "play" factor. It may be that only experience and self-analysis improve this skill, not the further mastery of more abstract theoretical concepts. Being able to know when and whether psychic reality is real, live, and meaningful at a given moment may depend on the individual art of intuitively recognizing and responding to the transitional mode—its presence, absence, or potentiality. In effect, the analyst must be able to know when he hears the right stuff, the real thing, or to sense its immanence.

Further, the ability to resonate or function effectively in psychic reality is not theory-specific. A Freudian's theoretical touchstone and clinical special skill might be insight and the observing ego, a Kleinian's that of meaningful and fearless emotional interpersonal engagement, and a Winnicottian's the recognition and provision of accurate attunement. But the most experienced, talented, and well-analyzed practitioner in any school will naturally be aware of all these factors, though each might conceptualize the factors differently. A good Freudian might, for example, tactfully and patiently *clarify* instead of interpret, and not even know that a Winnicottian would appreciate his intuitive empathy. Or he might in a "timely" fashion *confront* the patient with his resistance to the treatment or the transference and be doing a good-enough Kleinian interpretation of the projective or introjective manipulation of the personal relationship.

Clinical subtleties such as these are always fascinating, but it is difficult to find a way to say something about them that is general, true, and does not sound banal. When most people talk about actuality or the true self, however, that is what usually occurs—banality, tender-minded sweet talk, or naïve, well-meaning pseudowisdom. But when Winnicott does it, one senses that he has captured a pervasive and crucial phenomenon, and found a way to talk about it that is down to earth, sensible, and does not idealize intangibles at the expense of hard-won clinical-theoretical conceptions.

I turn to Winnicott's attitude toward theory for purposes of clinical work. He shows that just as a person can construct a personality with all the right content—oedipal complex, depressive position, whole and part objects, whatever is supposed to be there—and fool himself and sometimes his analyst into believing he is describing or living a real life, one can also possess an elegant theory and be unaware that sometimes, in *practice*, one has no access to, does not truly possess, the data of experience which is the theory's only purpose to serve. Just as there are true and false selves, there are, in practice, true and false theories, theories that are useful or not for various purposes and in various contexts. The distinctions between them may be subtle and subjective. A theory may be true in some contexts and not in others. It may be true but disavowed. It may be true, but applied or misused for distorted or false purposes. The ironies and ambiguities are diabolical and endless. The difference between psychological mindedness and psychobabble is not always obvious, and it cannot be looked up in any book.

Further, reading Winnicott is a continual demonstration of how one may use a theory one has mastered to see old things in a fresh way, or to see phenomena against the backdrop of mastered theory confidently to stretch oneself regarding those things that cannot easily be contained in it, or how to use multiple theories to cast familiar phenomena in new and interesting lights. There are several passages in "The Capacity to Be Alone," for example, in which Winnicott (1965) discusses the Freudian primal scene from the point of view of mastering the hate of Kleinian maternal separation and of bringing that primal scene into the service of masturbation. In this context this refers to a meaningful Winnicottian fantasy for which there is personal responsibility, not a mere physical erotic act. He then provides further perspectives on the same psychological process by approaching it from the point of view of Klein's good internal object. It is one of the neatest examples of integrating apparently different theories and of integrating theory with practice that I have ever seen. Winnicott is full of such examples.

CONCLUSION

Do I consider myself a Winnicottian? I deeply appreciate and respect his work, but the answer is probably no. I found myself more immersed in and celebratory of his work at earlier stages of my career, and the more I know, the less I find I need him to explain what I do, or to teach analytic practice and theory. The best route to the proper evaluation and use of Winnicott is probably via experience in and mastery of one of the more traditional traditions. The things he talks about may be the most important things, but they are also the easiest things to talk about, and the capacity to talk well about them does not always correlate with actual analytic knowledge or skill. Probably more nonsense has been written in Winnicott's name than in that of any serious analytic thinker I know. Like Kohutian analysis, Winnicottian analysis may be the easiest to learn, but the hardest to do well. I suspect that many of Winnicott's most ardent and vocal admirers deny the years of devotion to and mastery of Freudian and Kleinian theory and practice that was necessary before Winnicott became a good Winnicottian. One can be a natural or intuitive artist and put good art or attunement in one's technique at any level of competence or experience, but one cannot be a fully realized artist until one has mastered completely the usually mundane-by-comparison technical components of one's art, and one cannot learn these from Winnicott.

An analyst walks a perilous path when he talks mostly of spontaneous gestures and true selves, uses words like actuality or realization, or organizes his thinking about theory or technique mainly on the basis of recognizing and working with such phenomena. Winnicott had a special and rare gift. But few psychoanalysts *as psychoanalysts* can claim any expert knowledge regarding such things as the nature or "basis" or "ground" of all experience. This is the proper domain of poets, philosophers, and theologians. Generally, psychoanalysts are no better qualified than anyone else to declare what is real or meaningful, or what characteristics or values comprise grounded and healthy psychological life. One analyst's accurate attunement or "frame" intervention is often another's countertransference. When we do good-enough analysis, we ordinarily may safely leave such judgments to the patient. But it is naïve to think that such factors are not deeply implicated in psychoanalytic theory and practice, so we must not deny their existence because we cannot easily integrate them in our theories or because of our ideal of not imposing ideas or values on our patients. They are ordinarily less useful as basic building blocks for theory, however.

Since I believe such things are the main event in Winnicott, I can understand the frustration and even condescension he elicits in the more tough-minded of analytic thinkers. In such a realm as the intermediate zone, concise definitions and means to obtain objective verifications of important concepts and principles are lacking.

There are good Winnicottians working within every theoretical tradition, however, though some of the best do not know that this is what they are. This is because one can learn tact and timing and the appropriate limits and proper usage of theory by working within many different traditions. One does not have to have read Winnicott to know that theory is good, but it does not keep things from existing. But Winnicott can widen the scope and deepen the work of any analyst— make one more aware of what one does, and of the relation of what one thinks to what one does, of the actual ambiguity and range of the phenomena which our theories attempt to organize. There are astonishing clinical and theoretical pearls. And Winnicott has no equal at demonstrating that, in the right hands, the necessarily serious business of doing and thinking about analysis is, at its best, also play—eternally and nonclimactically just plain fun.

In summary, I turn to Winnicott for wisdom, for inspiration and play, for clinical and theoretical perspective, for his Mozartian laughter in the face of the wonder and terror of human existence, and envy of his capacity, in my fantasy, to dance eternally and effortlessly in transitional space. Finally, I read him to deepen my capacity to see what he saw, whatever it is and however elusive. Although I respect and work within the same traditional theoretical traditions he did, I half expect that whenever and in whatever form the next psychoanalytic revolution occurs, and if someone can ever spell out all of the theoretical *implications* in what he saw, Winnicott may turn out to have been a theoretical prophet. Who can say?

BIBLIOGRAPHY

COPPOLILLO, H. (1967). Maturational aspects of the transitional phenomenon. *Int. J. Psychoanal.*, 48:237–246.

KAPLAN, D. (1991). Personal communication.

KLEIN, M. (1945). The oedipus complex in the light of early anxieties. In *Contributions to Psycho-Analysis*. London: Hogarth Press, 1948, pp. 339–377.

KOHUT, H. (1971). *The Analysis of the Self*. New York: Int. Univ. Press.

———— (1972). Thoughts on narcissism and narcissistic rage. *Psychoanal. Study Child*, 27:360–400.

KUHNS, R. (1983). *Psychoanalytic Theory of Art*. New York: Columbia Univ. Press.

LOEWALD, H. W. (1962). Superego and time. In *Papers on Psychoanalysis*. New Haven: Yale Univ. Press, 1980, pp. 43–52.

———— (1988). *Sublimation*. New Haven: Yale Univ. Press.

METCALF, D. & SPITZ, R. A. (1978). The transitional object. In *Between Reality and Fantasy*, ed. S. Grolnick, L. Barkin, & W. Muensterberger. New York: Aronson, pp. 99–108.

WINNICOTT, D. W. (1953). Transitional objects and transitional phenomena. *Int. J. Psychoanal.*, 34:89–97.

———— (1965). *The Maturational Processes and the Facilitating Environment*. New York: Int. Univ. Press.

———— (1971). *Playing and Reality*. New York: Penguin Books, 1974.

CHARACTER

The papers in this section were presented at the colloquium on "Maturational and Experiential Determinants of Character" at the Anna Freud Centre, London, October 26 and 27, 1990.

What Does Psychoanalysis Have to Contribute to the Understanding of Character?

HERBERT J. SCHLESINGER, Ph.D.

While character is an indispensable term in psychoanalytic discourse, it is not primarily a psychoanalytic term. The psychoanalytic theories of neurosis and development are built around the idea of the "complementary series." While psychoanalysis has powerful theories about the "accidental" complement, it only recognizes the "constitutional" complement, and psychoanalysis has nothing to say about it. Current research may shed more light on this latter component and also provide the data for future psychoanalytic theorizing about character and personality.

CHARACTER IS A TERM IN THE PUBLIC DOMAIN. IT IS NOT PRIMARILY A psychoanalytic term. In everyday usage it has three major meanings (in addition to alluding to the personages of literature). We use it to tag an idiosyncratic person, as in "the most unforgettable character I ever met," to acknowledge another's trustworthiness, e.g., "He has a fine character," and to refer to the enduring aspects of personality, e.g., "What do you expect, that's his character."

Psychoanalysts find the term indispensable and use it frequently, observing two of the usages of the term more or less as does the man in the street. We also have appropriated it to describe a form of psychopathology, and styles of personality organization that are distinctive but not necessarily pathological. I would like to consider first the two usages that analysts share with the man on the street, and then the

Alfred J. and Monette C. Marrow Professor of Psychology and Director of Clinical Training, Department of Psychology, Graduate Faculty, New School for Social Research, New York. Training and Supervising Psychoanalyst, Columbia Center for Psychoanalytic Training and Research, New York.

special diagnostic sense, which we will see amounts to an elaboration and specification of one of the popular usages.

Let us consider first character as the enduring aspect of personality. When the man in the street uses the term about an acquaintance, it generally implies that he has learned that he can expect nothing better from that person; one has to be resigned to the hard fact of character, and abide with it. Unlike the analyst, the man in the street is not in the business of attempting to alter character. But the experienced, hardened, or "burned" analyst may also feel he has come to the end of his resources when he invokes "character" to account for the obdurateness of resistance, that is, to explain why hoped-for developments have not occurred. Both parties have encountered persistent, if not permanent, aspects of personality, and for both the context of discovery was disappointment.

But character, in the sense of the enduring aspects of personality, also has positive connotations. We hold certain persons in great respect, even awe, just because their characters remained firm so that they could prevail under the most adverse circumstances. In short, character is an indispensable term which recognizes that while man is highly adaptable, well equipped to survive (if he does not destroy himself, which of course begs the question), he has (or ought to have) certain relatively immovable internal commitments, a hierarchy and organization of goals and purposes, and a range of permissible and efficient modes of achieving them. These qualities permit others to predict his behavior, that is, to count on his response in a wide range of circumstances. When we speak approvingly of a person in this regard, we say he has integrity, perhaps a certain nobility of character. When we do not approve, the same traits can be described by such terms as "stubbornness," "rigidity," and "ideologically fixed."

I alluded to man's capacity for self-and-other destructiveness, a capacity that sadly seems to be enduring, and which probably also should be assigned at least in part to character. These tendencies may lead to behavior that is maladaptive to self and others, measured at least against the standard of physical survival. And the behavior may be such as to bring public denunciation or praise, sometimes both. Analysts will remind me that this issue should properly be referred to the drives, to a possibly constitutional excess of aggression. But does not that assignment beg the question? Would not the excessive endowment of aggression be considered properly as an aspect of character?

The issues I have just touched upon have preoccupied the major novelists and dramatists of (at least) Western culture. I refer to the relationship between character and fate. For instance, was it a central issue in Oedipus's character or a flaw in his character that led to his downfall? Did Sophocles intend us to learn something about humanity in general, or only about a particular and inadequate man? Is the key to Oedipus's tragedy his failure to heed the ancient admonition, "know thyself"? Not even knowing who his parents were was a serious cognitive lapse for a man who was hardly stupid. He had, after all, passed with flying colors the comprehensive examination posed by the Sphinx. Or was it Oedipus's impulsiveness, his penchant to dispose instantly of strangers who dared to block his path and to lust after comely widows? Or was it his hubris, to think that he, by fleeing Corinth, could evade the fate revealed to him by the oracle. The Greeks would have favored one other option, that Oedipus's fate had long ago been sealed by the curse laid on the house of Atreus because of the sins of an ancestor.

Consider also that the complex we name after Oedipus might better have been named after his father. It was Laius, after all, who, fearing the oracle's prophesy that a newborn would usurp his throne and bed, had his son put out on the mountainside to die. Laius too tried to evade his fate, but it caught up with him nevertheless, as it caught up with Oedipus. Recall that when we first meet Oedipus, he is a young man full of virtuous intent who has earned his leadership of Thebes by valor and by important public works. He had done his best to spare his parents their predicted fate and was wrong only in his belief that he was no longer a danger to them.

We may choose among several explanations of Oedipus's downfall, not all of them competing. The modern legal mind, laying great stress on conscious intent, might even exculpate Oedipus altogether, since he did not and could not know what he was doing; it was all a setup. And yet in the denouement, Oedipus did not avail himself of this "out," though he was aware of its factual basis. Instead, he took full personal responsibility for what he could hardly have avoided, and indeed had striven mightily to prevent.

The traditional psychoanalytic view has taken the Oedipus story as capturing a universal truth about mankind (or at least, malekind). As a function of man's lengthy childhood dependency and the concurrent (but often unevenly paced) courses of development of the sexual and aggressive drives and the sense of reality, the male child's first passionate attachment is to his mother, while his first beloved rival is his father. The successful passage through this rocky strait, or "resolution" of the oedipal conflicts, has been thought to determine the subsequent health of the personality. Failure to navigate it, and in consequence repressing the conflicts, could lead to repeated resurgences of the original impulses of the nursery years in incongruous adult contexts, where the compulsive playing out of unremembered childhood fantasies could only spoil realistic life opportunities. But this built-in developmental hazard, with its predisposition for later trouble, does not in itself fully capture the psychoanalytic view of character. The term came to be used loosely. Not unlike its ordinary usage, it referred to relatively fixed and therefore expensive ways of dealing with the unresolved complex, chiefly by living out one or another of the fantasied roles and solutions available to the infant mind, such as persisting in phallic strivings to attract the beloved mother, or resigning oneself to permanent loss as the rejected suitor submissive to the victorious father. A number of common "frozen nonsolutions" to the oedipal problem have been elevated to the status of "character types" (Freud, 1916).

The term has also been used to describe characteristic ways of behaving that seemed to derive from earlier developmental calamities, from frozen nonsolutions to (unresolved) "preoedipal" conflicts. Taking their names from the psychosexual stages at which fixations took place, the terms "oral" and "anal" character came into common usage (Freud, 1908), and later the "narcissistic" characters (Freud, 1930). Character thus came to be used, much as in the lay sense, to describe common patterns of traits that are exaggerated variants of normal behavior, such as the "stubborn" or oppositional character, or overscrupulous or obsessional character, or optimistic and pessimistic characters. Theoretical rationales for these conditions were more or less loosely derived from misadventures at one or another psychosexual stage or other developmental vicissitudes.

While Freud (1905b) supposed quite early that personality could be explained fully only by reference to a "complementary series" in which factors of constitutional endowment are balanced against factors in experience and development, most psychoanalytic contributors have focused on experiential or developmental factors. Recently, the constitutional aspect of the genetic point of view has received increased attention as methods of investigating behavioral genetics have improved, and as molecular biology has demonstrated a degree of success in pinpointing some genetic determinants of major psychoses and several major forms of personality disorder.

I have focused on character as an expression of psychopathology, a defect in personality as it might result from distorted development. Does psychoanalysis have anything to say about the normal development of character? It is, of course, a strength of psychoanalytic theory that it has a single theory for normal and pathological development, viewing pathology as exaggeration or restriction of the normal rather than as categorically different. I shall concentrate on an attribute we hope to find in "normal" character, moral dependability. I believe it is what we mean when we speak of someone as "having character," or possessing integrity. Moral dependability can be warped or absent to a pathological degree in conditions that carry such dire labels as "psychopath" or "sociopath." These labels indicate persons with little capacity to delay gratification, little moral compunction, and even little ability to consider the consequences to self or others of yielding instantly to temptation, and little capacity for empathy with others. They often turn to crime, but as criminals they fortunately are not too successful. They fill our prisons and learn little from that or other experiences. For the most blatant of these conditions, recent molecular genetic and epidemiological studies have implicated a degree of genetic vulnerability and transmission, a plausible constitutional factor. While psychoanalysis has always made room for the influence of "constitution," it has no theory about this factor.

An exaggeration of moral dependability can also become pathological. Some "tragic heros," and occasional lesser public figures, demonstrate this flaw when they persist in an originally honorable commitment long after it has become clear to all, including the hero, that the literal fulfillment of the oath, vow, or promise would no longer serve the originally intended purpose and might even destroy the intended beneficiary and himself (Schlesinger, 1980).

The traditional psychoanalytic view of the development of conscience and moral sensibility has been linked to the outcome of the oedipal struggle. The superego, a new structure that Freud (1923) called "the heir of the Oedipus complex" (p. 48), emerges as evidence that the resolution of the conflict was accomplished by internalizing, or identifying with, the unbeatable father, according to the pragmatic advice, "If you can't lick 'em, join 'em." The internalized father, his values and sense of right and wrong (as understood by the child), was seen as forming the core of conscience and a guide to moral behavior. Much would depend, in this view, on the fantasied character of the father, rather than on his actual psychological makeup, and on the actual and fantasied relationship between father and son.

I will not enter here into the lively debate about whether what we call superego might best be thought of in itself as a pathological development, a structured, and to that extent rigid, outcome that is at odds with the requirements of an integrated conscience. The different implications of the concept of the superego and the concept of the integrated conscience for a theory of character would deserve fuller discussion than I can attempt here. I will note only that the theory of the superego attempts to account for the culmination of lines of development in cognition, emotion, and personality that began much earlier. An explanation of conscience and character in terms of oedipal dynamics alone would have to take for granted many earlier developmental achievements.

I propose that we could take the defining act of moral integrity to be the ability to be true to a value or purpose even when it is no longer convenient, to fulfill a commitment despite how one's feelings for the "other" may have changed—in short, to keep a promise and to be true to one's word. Thus, character formation would seem to rest on the earlier accomplishment of several developmental and maturational tasks. These would have to include as a minimum the acquisition of a sense of time and especially the awareness of the continuity of the sense of self and relationships (perhaps better, self-*in*-relationships) over time (Schlesinger, 1978).

I use the term "sense of self" here to imply relatively firm boundaries, or clear distinctions, between representations of self and of others. Being aware that one lives in mutually gratifying interdependency with these "others," and having the ability to empathize with their emotional positions, would seem vital to the development of a dependable moral outlook (Schlesinger, 1980). One must also be firmly aware of one's place in a social context and appreciate the degree to which one's actions would support or destroy that context. To keep a promise requires that one be able to remember value received at that later time when one must redeem one's word. To be governed by internalized standards would seem to require that these several core aspects of personality had already become structured. The implication I would like you to draw is that the emergence of character, in this sense, rests not only on the successful resolution of a specific psychosexual conflict, but also on the concurrent or earlier development and maturation of cognitive and social skills that lead to an integrated sense of self-in-context.

These earlier achievements of development that I believe underlie morality are, of course, necessary for all aspects of mature living. By themselves, and even with successfully internalized standards, they do not guarantee "correct" behavior. What they do guarantee is emotional awareness of conflict and an "honest market" in which proper weight can be given to issues of convenience, preference and the existence of competing interests. Even with full awareness and after agonizing deliberation, it is still possible to behave wrongly by certain appropriate standards. It is also possible to take a stand that is morally correct from one (generally internal) point of view and to behave badly from a public or societal point of view, or to satisfy one's moral obligation to one party and fail another to whom one can be viewed as equally obligated.

Freud (1905a) stated at one point, "What is moral is self-evident."[1] But mature persons of consequence (and I include here the full range of tragic heroes) are rarely held up for our awe or admiration when they are about to make an easy moral decision. The easy decisions are made automatically without awareness either of conflict or of moral risk, as a function of what one might term an integrated conscience. The easy decisions are "self-evident." Again I touch on issues that have provided the major themes of serious literature, themes that also are central to our clinical and theoretical concerns.

I asserted at the outset that character is not primarily a psycho-analytic term. Since psychoanalysts use the term frequently, that statement may need some explication. I base my argument narrowly on the proposition that the psychoanalytic theories of neurosis and of development are closely intertwined. In these theories, the governing concept is conflict, primarily unconscious conflict. Character, as a concept, cannot be derived systematically from these theories. In spelling out these theories, Freud did not claim to have the key to all of human experience. Quite early, he saw that psychoanalysis was a *psychology* and that its explanatory power would have to depend upon the degree to which the phenomenon to be explained was a function of constitution on the one hand and experience on the other. You recall, Freud saw constitution and experience as complements and viewed their role in development and neurosis as complementary (Freud, 1905b). Thus it is only the experiential side of the equation involving learning, not the constitutional side involving maturation, that psychoanalysis is uniquely suited to address.

Many of the phenomena included in the notion of character can also be described with such terms as "personality," "temperament," "constitution," and "style." We see the effects of conflict on character, and we also see the effects upon character of more or less successful efforts at resolving conflict, to the extent that these efforts have shaped or distorted personality development, or have left scars or lacunae of one kind or another. But character itself, apart from its neurotic coloration or distortion, is not *caused* by conflict or by unsuccessful efforts at conflict resolution, as are neuroses. Unlike neurosis, character or personality cannot be fully explained in terms of compromise formation,

1. Translated in the *Standard Edition:* "As to morals, that goes without saying" (p. 267).

although Freud (1908) and Abraham (1921, 1924, 1925) early defined several character types based on libidinal fixation.

Freud and his early followers exploited the explanatory power of conflict in an attempt to account for the development of memory and thinking, the shift from primary to secondary process, and the development of a sense of reality. These explanations too were tempered by the recognition of the complementarity of constitution and experience. I believe that Freud recognized this limitation upon the explanatory power of psychoanalytic concepts quite early, perhaps as early as when he abandoned the project to develop a scientific psychology (Freud, 1950), that is, a biological psychology.

Many years later, Heinz Hartmann (1939) gave explicit form to these earlier understandings in referring to a "conflict-free sphere" of the ego. We recognize that taken literally, this term is an oxymoron; there is no portion of the ego that categorically is free of conflict. The term stands for the recognition that key psychological functions or capacities that conventionally are assigned to the ego in the structural model were not formed by or caused by conflict. But, as we know to our sorrow, they soon enough enter into conflict or are made use of in conflict resolution.

We know now through observations of children and experimental work with infants that many of the earlier theories about the derivation of the sense of reality and the development of object relations through conflict and compromise formation are not true (or, at least, not wholly true). At least we know now that infants recognize an external world and develop the sense of an "other" earlier than could be explained by reference to a theory based on conflict and conflict resolution.

I hope I have established at least to your partial satisfaction that I have some reasons for asserting that character is not primarily a psychoanalytic term. As psychoanalytic theorizing focused on understanding the various distorting effects of misguided conflict resolution on personality development and personality organization, recognition grew that there are large groups of patients whose stable, chronic psychopathology is not easily captured by gross distinctions between neurosis and psychosis. Increasingly we have articulated groups of so-called character disorders. Recent efforts to distinguish between borderline and narcissistic personality organizations, not just as personality disorders, also represent steps toward developing a psychoanalytic theory of character. The most recent group of theoreticians interested in this area, among whom Kernberg (1976) and Kohut (1971) are prominent, hardly represent the beginning of this development. One would have to look back to the work of Wilhelm Reich

(1949) and his followers, and particularly Hellmuth Kaiser (Fierman, 1965), on the one hand and Melanie Klein (1932) and her followers on the other. I mention Melanie Klein in this context because her efforts to define paranoid and depressive "positions," which are misguided from many points of view, also represent an effort to discern principles of coherence in personality development (i.e., "points" of personality organization).

Thus, one could say that while psychoanalysis, almost from its very beginning, was concerned with understanding certain character traits, it did not have a theory of character. We still do not have one (Abend, 1983; Baudry, 1983). The theory of neurosis, linking symptom formation to areas of intrapsychic conflict and stages of psychosexual development, came nearly to its present state quite early. It is a relatively recent development that our interest in character has turned from discovering the psychosexual origins of certain character traits toward seeking principles around which personality could be said to be organized, principles that could comprehend adaptation as well as defense, and that could account for the stability, resilience, and coherence of character. These principles would necessarily have to refer to constitutional and genetic "givens" and the vicissitudes of their maturation, as well as to the facts of normal and deviant psychological development. Whether the ultimate form of reference will turn out to be the "complementary series" suggested by Freud or some more complicated algorithm, I will not venture to guess. But I suspect that whatever its form, future theory will give more weight to the maturation of constitutional factors than we are now accustomed to give them in our thinking about normal and pathological development.

BIBLIOGRAPHY

ABEND, S. M. (1983). Theory of character, panel report. *J. Amer. Psychoanal. Assn.*, 31:211–224.

ABRAHAM, K. (1921). Contribution to the theory of the anal character. In *Selected Papers on Psycho-Analysis*. London: Hogarth Press, 1948, pp. 370–392.

——— (1924). The influence of oral erotism on character-formation. Ibid., pp. 393–406.

——— (1925). Character-formation on the genital level of the libido. Ibid., pp. 407–417.

BAUDRY, F. (1983). The evolution of the concept of character in Freud's writings. *J. Amer. Psychoanal. Assn.*, 31:3–31.

FIERMAN, L. B., ed. (1965). *Effective Psychotherapy*. New York: Free Press.

FREUD, S. (1905a). On Psychotherapy. *S.E.*, 7:257–268.

—— (1905b). Three essays on the theory of sexuality. *S.E.*, 7:125–243.

—— (1908). Character and anal erotism. *S.E.*, 9:167–175.

—— (1916). Some character-types met with in psycho-analytic work. *S.E.*, 14:309–333.

—— (1923). The ego and the id. *S.E.*, 19:3–66.

—— (1930). Civilization and its discontents. *S.E.*, 21:59–145.

—— (1950). Project for a scientific psychology. *S.E.*, 1:283–397.

HARTMANN, H. (1939). *Ego Psychology and the Problem of Adaptation.* New York: Int. Univ. Press, 1958.

KERNBERG, O. F. (1975). *Borderline Conditions and Pathological Narcissism,* New York: Aronson.

KLEIN, M. (1932). *The Psychoanalysis of Children.* New York: Delacorte Press/Seymour Lawrence, 1975.

KOHUT, H. (1971). *The Analysis of the Self.* New York: Int. Univ. Press.

REICH, W. (1949). *Character-Analysis.* New York: Orgone Institute Press.

SCHLESINGER, H. J. (1978). Developmental and regressive aspects of the making and breaking of promises. In *The Human Mind Revisited,* ed. S. Smith. New York: Int. Univ. Press, pp. 21–50.

—— (1980). Mature and regressive determinants of the keeping of promises. In *The Course of Life,* ed. S. I. Greenspan & G. H. Pollock. Washington: National Institute of Mental Health, vol. 3, pp. 129–147.

Maturational and Experiential Components of Character Formation

DUNCAN McLEAN, BA, MB,
B Chir, MRC Psych.

A character, my dear sir, can always ask a man who he is, because a character really has a life of his own, a life full of his own specific qualities, and because of these he is always someone. While a man—I'm not speaking about you personally, of course, but a man in general—well, he can be an absolute 'nobody.'
LUIGI PIRANDELLO, *Six Characters in Search of an Author*

This paper explores the concept of character from the point of view of its use both in everyday language and in psychoanalytic literature. It also examines, with clinical illustrations, some of the complex interactions of maturation and experience in the formation of character.

AS PSYCHOANALYSTS, WE MAY SEE THIS LAST QUOTE, IN WHICH "CHARacter" is portrayed as having a firm identity distinct from "man," as an obvious projection. Indeed, in psychoanalysis the concept of character has always threatened to disappear in vague generalizations. It has been suggested that it can be dispensed with altogether and that the fixed structures of an individual's mind can be defined in terms of the structural theory of id, ego, and superego. Recently, however, Baudry (1989) has argued convincingly, as have others in the past, that it remains an indispensable concept despite its diffuseness.

In common English usage "character" has a number of interrelated

Associate member of the British Psychoanalytic Society; psychiatrist to the Anna Freud Centre; consultant psychotherapist, King's College Hospital, London.

meanings, some of which inform the psychoanalytic concept more than others. Most importantly—and I refer here to its etymological origins in the Greek for *engrave*—it identifies something stable or fixed about an individual. Within this meaning character is seen as something that endures over time and is supposedly independent of changing situations or circumstances. It is the essence of an individual, albeit imperfectly reflected through behavior. Commonsense observation as well as analytic practice tend to support this notion. We like to think that we know people and that they do not change. Also, as psychoanalysts, we focus on psychopathology which by definition tends to be rigid or fixed, but this fixity may be more apparent than real. Character, which includes the idea of a response or adaptation to the environment, may have only a relative stability. The whole area of social psychology is important here since we know how differently people may behave under the impact of differing social circumstances. Experiences even later in life can bring about profound and fundamental changes in people. What remains the same are elements of an individual and not that to which character refers: their summation.

Another related meaning of character in common usage has to do with the inner qualities of an individual, usually of a positive kind. A man of character has virtues such as courage and determination. As psychoanalysts we are mistrustful of these evaluations, knowing that they may be based as much on defensive reaction formations as on sublimations.

In whatever terms character is described, however, it is virtually impossible to avoid the impression that one is making value judgments, as some aspect of character delineates every individual's adaptation to his environment, and such adaptation may or may not be considered successful. This may be one reason why psychoanalysts have tended to shy away from the subject.

A further meaning of character—and this by no means exhausts the various nuances of this word—is that which distinguishes a particular individual from his fellows. A "character" tends to be someone markedly different from others, even if in a somewhat exhibitionistic sense. In this last sense character becomes a concept indispensable for psychoanalysis. There is rarely sufficient discrimination within the id, ego, or superego of an individual to do more than highlight a particular aspect of their functioning. The concept of character thus serves as an important transition between overt behavior on the one hand and internal structure on the other. If we can see this character structure as the synthesizing aspect of the way the internal world adapts to the environment, then it becomes an essential starting point in explorations of the inner world. Baudry (1989) has usefully discriminated between behavior, character traits, and character organization, where there is a hierarchy, in ascending complexity, of whatever lies behind observable behavior.

One might say that it is character traits which have the most meaning in psychoanalysis, since such a concept groups together a number of elements in a personality under the dominance of an underlying psychic organization, but does not attempt to encompass the total functioning of the person. This is the approach Freud took in some of his observations on character. However, in "Character and Anal Erotism" (1908), one of the few papers directly on character by Freud, he went somewhat beyond this and viewed the traits of orderliness, parsimony, and obstinacy as being unified by reaction formation to the underlying anal drive. Here, one might say, are the beginnings of a typology of character based in this instance on the libido theory. It was Abraham (1923, 1924, 1925) who took this particular line of thinking further and described the influence of oral, anal, and genital drive derivatives on the formation of character. Interestingly, it remained the impact of anal drive derivatives that proved the most revealing and informative, and one might speculate why this was so. Like all typologies though, useful as they are at times, one feels that a limited number of concepts have been stretched too far. The other issue of note is that in the early formulations about character formation, it is the maturational aspects that are emphasized.

Freud, in 1931, attempted another typology of character. He divided people into erotic, obsessional, and narcissistic types, with subtypes as combinations of these. It is the overall relation between libido and internal and external structures that gives character its particular stamp. This is, in effect, a typology based on his structural theory, with a dominance in the personality structure whether of id, superego, or ego. Freud did not explore the etiology of these different dispositions. Character was described in terms that left open the question of its evolution.

The development of character was explored more explicitly in Freud's 1916 paper on "Some Character-Types Met with in Psychoanalysis." Of the three parts to this paper, "The Exceptions," "Those Wrecked by Success," and "Criminals from a Sense of Guilt," the last two refer to the impact on development of the superego in relation to the oedipus complex in the formation of character. Maturational development is highlighted, although implicit in the formation of the superego is the question of identifications and thus an important experiential dimension. "The Exceptions" is a particularly interesting pa-

per because it considers the complex interplay between innate maturational factors and experience. Freud highlighted the way in which
certain individuals granted themselves licenses in life because of the
disadvantages they had experienced. The licenses granted can extend
from relative immunity to the reality principle, to permission to ignore
the strictures of the superego. The disadvantages perceived range
from obvious physical deformity, to a woman's sense of injustice at not
possessing a penis; and though he highlighted physical disadvantages,
Freud included all those grievances an individual may bear against
what his environment has failed to provide him with in early life. The
adaptation to these real or imagined disadvantages is in part a model
for the narcissistic injuries that have such an important influence on
character.

Edith Jacobson (1959), elaborating on Freud's paper, stressed that
physical beauty as well as deformity could have an effect on the development of women. She thus brought in the influence of a perceived
advantage on the development of character. Although Jacobson and
Freud confined themselves mainly to the effects of physical attributes,
their considerations can be seen as a model for the way in which maturation and environment may interact. As the ego develops in the child,
the environment, represented largely by the parents, is constantly responding in a way that highlights advantages or disadvantages. For
example, on the one hand, bed wetting or temper tantrums and, on the
other, the capacity for affect recognition or reading skills may in one
family attract considerable attention, while in another they go relatively unnoticed. Self representations are therefore laid down in a
manner which are obviously as much a consequence of object responses as they are of object identifications.

Subsequent considerations take us into the development of character to which object relations theory and self psychology have added
important dimensions. However, I wish to return to some of the earlier
considerations of character, and in particular the approach to it
through resistance. With the emphasis on symptom formation, character was sometimes viewed in a global and value-laden way, so that
individuals were good or bad, worthy or unworthy. It was soon recognized, however, that resistance was an approach to character: resistance in its various manifestations was the habitual manner in which
an individual responded to situations, analysis included. In this sense,
resistance was to early analysts an equivalent concept to that of character; and even Freud recognized that every analysis was a character
analysis to the extent that resistances had to be overcome.

In the structural theory, resistances are divided according to the different agencies of the mind, so that there are superego and id resistances as well as subdivisions of the ego resistances of repression, transference resistance, and secondary gain. By elaborating on the different forms of resistance, one could arrive at an overall functioning of the individual's character. It was Reich (1945) who took this conceptualization the furthest, and there was no doubt that he greatly extended the technique of character analysis by concentrating on resistances in this way, but he tended to see both resistance and character in a pejorative light and as enemies to be overcome in the furtherance of analysis. The adaptive aspects of character, especially those manifested through the development of the ego, were to come to the fore later and to preoccupy a number of leading analysts, in particular, Heinz Hartmann and Anna Freud.

Adaptation must be central to any theory of character since one face of character is always turned to the external world. Anna Freud's book, *The Ego and Mechanism of Defense* (1936), is clearly central to this issue. Although some defenses may be exhibited only under special circumstances, such as in symptom formation, there is an aspect of each individual's ego that is characterized by the habitual use of a certain pattern of defense. Defense mechanisms are a means of dealing with impulses aroused by external stimuli and, as with the concept of character, they are close to observable behavior. This may in part explain why psychiatrists have taken to defense mechanisms more fully than to other psychoanalytic concepts.

There are many analysts who would see the delineation of defense mechanisms as central to any psychoanalytic description of character, but defenses are only one aspect of the ego, and they are particularly related to the resolution of conflict.

Anna Freud gave credence to both maturational and experiential factors in the defense mechanisms. Identification with the aggressor in particular, was seen, as were other defense mechanisms, as being influenced by the quality of early object relationships. On the other hand, it is clear that she thought that maturational factors were equally important. For example, in 1966, she speculated that it was the early maturation of the ego and the premature development of reaction formations that laid the groundwork for a later obsessional formation.

Another of Anna Freud's concepts, that of developmental lines, seems closely connected to the concept of character. Both concepts center on a description of external attributes which may point the way toward an elaboration of internal factors. The concept of developmental lines is particularly applicable to children in whom adaptation is constantly changing. Because character is a relatively static concept it is used only tentatively with children and is much more frequently applied to adults. Certain characteristics of children, however, such as shyness or passivity, may be exhibited early and remain relatively unchanged, so that, at least retrospectively, one might see them as fundamental to character. It is equally true, though, that on occasion quite radical transformations may take place in later development, such as adolescence, so that the overt behavior of the individual becomes quite the opposite of that seen in him as an infant. An example, probably by no means uncommon, is that of an adolescent boy who at puberty had become aggressive and occasionally violent with his parents, and who was in constant conflict with them, while prior to adolescence he had been exceptionally compliant and passive in relation to his parents' demands. I doubt that one would have been able to predict this change; conversely it is equally common to see individuals who remain passive even in adolescence.

This transformation in adolescence is seen to occur as the result of a maturational factor, as the increased drive pressure brings about the demand for a complex set of readjustments, including the push toward autonomy. Yet adaptation must have as much to do with the impingements of reality as with those of the drives, and the work of Hartmann in particular elaborated on this.

Heinz Hartmann (1939) identified the complex set of conditions needed to understand ego development. In considering adaptation, he stressed those aspects of development that were outside the realms of conflict and pathology. He arrived at such concepts as the conflict-free sphere of the ego and preconscious automatisms that must be considered an important facet of character.

In addition, Hartmann addressed, more explicitly than previous authors, the interaction between hereditary and experiential factors in development. He defined maturation in a manner that I am inclined to follow, that is, in terms that are exclusively related to the hereditary givens of an individual. Importantly, however, he pointed out that the maturation processes "are not completed at the time of birth and there is growth in the sense of maturation outside of the mother's body also. This maturation, though we know little about it in many areas, must be recognized as an independent factor in addition to learning by experience, by memory, by exercise, by automatization, by identification, and by other mechanisms" (p. 103). Hartmann saw maturation as unfolding biological propensity, but we are almost as much in the dark as he was about what this actually constitutes. If one takes an attribute such as shyness, which could hardly be considered to exist at birth, it seems that recent studies by developmental psychologists have shown that it is markedly determined by hereditary factors. As analysts, apart from the consideration that maturation is important, this does not take us very far. Shyness in an individual may develop out of a whole number of different factors and could be related to guilt on the one hand, or annihilation anxiety on the other. We need more specific knowledge of the maturational factor that may underpin such attributes, and we then need to understand how it may interrelate with experiential factors.

At this point I will give a brief clinical example. This case is instructive because it poses a number of questions about the impact of maturational factors on development. Toby was 8 years old when he was brought to the Anna Freud Centre for assessment. His parents wanted to know whether psychotherapy had anything to offer him. He had in fact been very extensively assessed previously, from the age of 3 years on, because of delay in language development; Toby had at that time only a few words and stereotyped phrases. All but one of the assessors had given the opinion that he had a receptive aphasia. I will come back to the one dissenter later.

When seen at the Centre, Toby's disturbance was clinically indistinguishable from that of other children who might be diagnosed as having a borderline disturbance. There were delays and distortions in nearly all aspects of his development, with marked instinctual infiltration of all psychic structures. He was excitable, impulsive, and overactive. His interests were infantile. He had, for many years, been obsessively interested in food, constantly preoccupied with where, when, and what he was to eat. More recently, he had moved on to an obsessive interest in Paul McCartney and his records, in which there seemed to be some exhibitionistic identification. Ego structures seemed weak, and he was easily overcome with frustration or anxiety. His defenses were primitive, and he often used denial or obsessively repetitive behavior, much as a 2-year-old might in dealing with anxiety-provoking situations. In addition, there was a concreteness and rigidity about his thinking that was quite striking. For example, he would not go to the toilet in a strange place because, with the lid down, it looked as if the toilet had an evil smile. His superego was also primitive. There was very little concern or awareness of the needs of others, and his ego ideal had still highly unmodified idealized aspects.

There seemed to be nothing in his environmental background that could account for such a disturbance. His parents were rather ordinary, if somewhat overanxious, middle-class professional people. It seemed difficult to disagree with the previous assessors that it was some missing maturational factor in relation to language acquisition which had caused this profound disorganization in development. It was not a question of Toby's general intelligence; a number of tests had shown him to have average intelligence. His rather poor performance on the verbal scales was made up by superior performance on the performance scales. Yet there was some reason to doubt the notion of a receptive aphasia since, as the one dissenter among his earlier assessors had noted, Toby had, from a relatively early age, been able to produce long sequences of sentences in a parrotlike fashion. He could, for example, quote verbatim from adult programs he had heard on television. Toby's difficulty seemed to be related to an inability to play with language and use it flexibly and symbolically. Here, however, we become lost in vague generalizations since we do not know what specific maturational factors may lie behind the capacity to play—in language or in any other domain.

This case seems to suggest—I would think with a degree of probability—that a number of serious developmental abnormalities are caused by maturational deficits which lead to quite serious characterological deformations later in life, but we do not yet know in any clearly definable way what these maturational deficits might be. The other question of interest is the interaction between maturational and experiential factors. In the case of Toby, the supposed maturational deficit led to consequences in development that had many secondary effects. For example, at the simplest level, Toby was not unaware that his behavior was viewed as exceptional, and there were many indications that his self-esteem was under some pressure. Other aspects of development were interesting to note as well. It appeared, for instance, that Toby was progressing through the various instinctual phases of development, though in a delayed way. It seemed that at about the age of 7 there was an upsurge in phallic narcissistic interests and concerns, and at the age of 8 some indication of a move into oedipal interests. We often think of instinctual phase progression as being a maturational factor, but perhaps it is not. On the other hand, it may be that maturational factors are triggered by certain developmental phases. We do know that triggering of maturation by experience is an important factor in development. The maturation of the visual or auditory apparatus is triggered by experience, though it seems that there are certain "windows" of time in which this triggering can take place. If the experience is delayed too long, then certain capacities are lost forever.

This case would nowadays not be considered a neurotic disorder, but psychoanalysts have until relatively recently conceptualized character mainly on the basis of the neurotic model. Fenichel (1945) constructed a quite elaborate typology of character based upon the structural model. Character pathology was seen primarily as neuroses of character. He used the type and quality of defense as the main means of subdividing different character types, so that sublimatory types were normal, and reactive types which showed some degree of pathology were divided into phobic and obsessional ones. He admitted though that this was unsatisfactory; his chapter on character disorders considered character from a whole series of different structural points of view, although in essence he started from a number of different characterological attitudes; he thus reverted to a way of seeing character as a halfway point to describing internal structure. Although he considered the importance of impulse, and not just defense, in the formation of character—and hence its role in such conditions as delinquency—he did not really stray far from the conflictual model. The idea of ego arrests, whether maturationally or experientially caused, was not considered. Recently, Yorke et al. (1989) argued for the retention of the concept of character neurosis. This does seem useful in delineating a group of disorders of character that are equivalent to symptom neuroses and have the same structural components—apart, that is, from the fact that in a character neurosis the disability is ego-syntonic, and regression is not a central feature. The difference in the etiology of the character and the symptom neuroses is something which a number of people have considered but have been unable to explain satisfactorily. It has been suggested, though, that the distinction between the two is more apparent than real since a transmutation from one to the other can easily occur.

The early distortions of character formation have on the whole been more extensively studied by the object relations theorists and self psychologists. Kohut and Kernberg have described serious character pathology in greater detail, as well as adding to an understanding of its etiology. For example, Kohut (1971) highlighted the impact of empathic failure in distorting early ego identifications and self representations. It was Kernberg, however, who addressed the question of character most directly. In 1968, he started off with the classical formulations of Fenichel and added a particular dimension from his own view of object relations theory. This, in effect, divided character pathology into three different levels of high, intermediate, and low, the high level roughly approximating to a neurotic character disorder and the low level to borderline organizations. The levels of pathology were considered in terms of the relative maturity of defenses, object relationships, superego, etc., so that, for example, defenses in low-level character pathology would be characterized by the primitive defenses of splitting and projection. In effect, low-level character pathology was seen as having much greater instinctual infiltration of all psychic structures; in particular, he viewed aggression as disruptive to the development of more mature functioning. To my mind, Kernberg's classification is the most satisfactory that I have discovered, but, like other object relation theorists, the very way in which the metapsychology is formulated appears to give a heavy bias toward experiential factors in development. Although these theorists may well argue that the description of internal object relationship does not preclude the existence of maturational factors, these seem to be barely considered. There is a tendency from this point of view to see all development as a consequence of the impact of early relationships. If maturational factors are regarded at all, it is in gross terms such as heightened aggressivity, and all the potentially subtle factors of ego maturation are effectively ignored.

I take character to be a useful fiction. It is the habitual patterning of an individual's activities and responses as seen by an observer. In adult life, when development is largely completed, it becomes, given stable social circumstances, relatively fixed. As a consequence, in an everyday way, once we have got to know someone, we feel we can rely on our knowledge of how they will behave. We count on certain people to be intelligent, reliable, entertaining, as well as on others as being fickle, morose, or taciturn. Character, like behavior in general, follows Waelder's (1930) principle of multiple functioning and can therefore be analyzed in a whole variety of ways, e.g., as subserving the reality or pleasure principle, the drives, defensive needs, superego injunctions. In terms of an assessment of the components of maturation or experience which have brought about this synthesis, the very idea of "components" oversimplifies the enormous complexity of the way these two factors interact in development to bring about the end point of character.

Development has inextricably interwoven these factors, and I believe one can do no more than point to the elements of each that may have been influential. The problem here is that the psychoanalytic method is a much better tool for examining the impact of experience than of maturational factors. The latter may be explored by the psychoanalytic observation of children, but is also the province of developmental psychologists. The understanding of maturational processes is generally not specific enough to be very informative about individual differences. For example, language development as a maturational process is currently understood in general and global terms, so only if there is a gross disturbance in this sphere would it reflect on a child's development. As suggested before, there are studies, such as that on shyness, which show that certain individual differences in people are based on maturational processes. Almost any adult trait, such as sociability, tendency to depression, general intelligence, can be subjected to statistical analyses that suggest that they are in part hereditary, but we do not know the specific elements which are inherited. Has it something to do with the drives or with the ego? If, for example, it has to do with the ego, then of which particular capacity? While we do not know the answer to these questions, we may assume that maturation does have a profound impact on individual development, comparable to that of experience, and, in a similar way, reverberates throughout the process of development.

Seen from the side of experience, we can map out this interaction much more clearly. Psychoanalysis has been paramount in the exploration of this area and has viewed it from numerous perspectives, such as the impact of early mother-infant care, the importance of traumatic experiences, the processes of mirroring and identification. In particular, psychoanalysis has been able to demonstrate the importance of the timing of experience in development and the way that this resonates through the subsequent developmental process. I now turn to the following case as an example.

Mr. N., in his late 20s, came to analysis because of a relatively severe symptom. A year before starting his analysis he had developed panic attacks and, like many people with this symptom, he had at first thought he had a physical illness, characterized by intense fear, sweating, overbreathing, and palpitations. In addition, he had one unusual feature, and that was a sensation of numbness or frozenness in his mouth that was unlike the usual paresthesia associated with overbreathing; this feature would remain even when his panic subsided. He consulted his general practitioner who told him that he had a psychological disorder.

An understanding of his symptom was arrived at relatively quickly, but despite this there was a persistent feeling in both the patient and in me that his analysis had never really got off the ground. His panic subsided in the first months, but what came to be much more the focus of the analysis was his character development, and in particular the way in which he used his intellect.

Mr. N. was a poet who had written and published extensively. He obviously had a very superior intelligence and phenomenal memory. He could recall long passages from plays or poems read many years previously. Although he was mildly pleased with this ability, he appeared to be largely unaware of his exceptional gifts, and it was characteristic of him to disregard or devalue his capacities.

A year before the onset of his panic attacks he had met a young woman, Miss T., who was a librarian. His experience with women before this had been meager and had usually ended painfully. His previous girlfriend had been the first woman to whom he had given himself passionately, only to have the affair end abruptly under the impact of two events that shook him deeply: he had made this woman pregnant, resulting in an abortion; and shortly after this he had to leave for a time during which she was unfaithful to him.

With Miss T. he had at first thrown himself into the new relationship with some feeling, but difficulties had soon arisen. His new girlfriend had talked to him about her past, and had referred to two male mentors who had been particularly important to her. These had not been sexual relationships, but nevertheless Mr. N. became very jealous and consciously decided to withdraw a large part of his affection from Miss T. Although he continued his relationship with her, one of the consequences of his withdrawal was that he lost all sexual interest in her. He attached little significance to this, and it was some time before he revealed that he and his girlfriend had ceased to have a sexual relationship. It was also some time before the quality of their relationship was revealed. Miss T. lived in France and so they only met on weekends. It became apparent that although he was industrious and hardworking during the week, he would, when with his girlfriend, collapse and effectively be mothered by her when they were together.

The panic attacks started shortly after the withdrawal of his affection; the very first attack occurred at a time when he had successfully completed a project to organize a poetry festival. He had been in charge of a number of people for the first time, and it was while feeling exhausted after the successful completion of this project, and about to board an aeroplane to return home, that his first attack had occurred.

The oedipal implications of this will be lost to no one. In some respects the precipitants of his neurosis had some very classical features, and indeed the patient was himself aware of this, having read Freud extensively in his early 20s. He was able to refer to particular papers which he considered to have a bearing on his condition.

The high intellectual attainments of his adult life were at some remove from his own upbringing, which had been a modest one. His father was a motorcycle policeman and was presented to me as a caricature. He was a bad-tempered bully who considered any emotion other than aggression to be effeminate. Mr. N. was terrified of his father's rages and vividly recalled his red face and bulging veins when he had been particularly splenetic over the antics of left-wing intellectuals and students whom he had been watching on television. Mr. N. lived in terror that his father's displeasure and scorn might be directed at himself, and fearfully tried to avoid any provocation of his father. He felt his father had little interest in him and particularly during his adolescence had become increasingly disappointed at the way his son was turning out. Mr. N., in adult life, still feared his father, though he recognized that he was not as critical as Mr. N. had perceived him to be.

His mother was presented as a much more shadowy figure. Mr. N. was an only child, but did not know why. He assumed it was because he was a very difficult baby; there were family stories about his incessant crying. His conscious feelings about his mother were rather limited. He had romantically tinged memories of reading comics at about the age of 4, while his mother worked in the home. He recalled a sense of security and of being well cared for and loved. By the time he was a teenager, however, he was convinced that, as with his father, he was a disappointment to his mother, and he despaired of pleasing her. He now saw her as being impossible to communicate with; he claimed that if he told her anything about his current life, she would ignore him and continue her endless, trivializing patter about the minutiae of her life.

These brief details about his background and the manner in which his symptom arose, all accord with a diagnosis of a neurotic disorder with an unresolved oedipal conflict, but elaborating on these issues did not seem to get anywhere. Although his panics had subsided, little else in his life changed. There was a growing awareness that despite outward appearances his life was very impoverished, and that there was a disturbing lack of affective resonance with other people. In particular there was no affect to give weight to the insights formulated and a near-absolute resistance to any transference. Mr. N. disclaimed any feelings about myself whatsoever, and would even share a mild sense of puzzlement as to why this should be. Although there were some elements of transference recognizable in his dreams, he could never acknowledge this on anything but an intellectual level, and I felt that he refused any empathic contact with me. It was therefore through this resistance, in a time-honored fashion, that his analysis was drawn into a deeper consideration of his character.

He had told me early in the analysis that his daydreams were rarely sexual, but had for many years been spun about a central theme in which he worked with unremitting dedication, in a garret or some other isolated place, to produce a work of art such as a novel. It was of central importance to this fantasy that all achievements were entirely the result of his own efforts, and that he was to be seen as a person without parents both intellectually and actually. Of course, a great deal was condensed into these fantasies. For example, working hard meant repudiating his mother's taunts during adolescence that he was lazy and would never come to anything, as well as repudiating and defending against his own very strong passive wishes. What I wish to concentrate on, however, is the development of his interest in writing, which has always remained central to his conception of himself.

As a baby, between the ages of 18 and 21 months, he developed a severe gastroenteritis, which necessitated hospitalization and temporary isolation. He was visited infrequently by his parents, who could only gesture to him through a glass door. He had no recollection of these events and reported only what he had learned from his mother. Just prior to his hospitalization his mother's sister had been admitted to a hospital to give birth to his male cousin (later to become a source of chagrin to him, since his own mother unfavorably compared their development). While his aunt was in the hospital, his mother wrote to her, and he had observed this. While he was in the hospital, his mother told him, he had demanded paper and pencil from the staff and had attempted to "write" letters to his mother. These letters were of course meaningless scribbles, but there was little doubt that his language development was well advanced and there was an intention to communicate on paper. It is interesting to note that on arrival home he announced that he wished to be back with the doctors—a wish fulfilled by his analysis.

For this precocious little boy the trauma of his separation must have come at a time when a number of important maturational factors were at work. It will have coincided with a period of rapid language development, perhaps particularly so because of his high intelligence. The acquisition of language skill is important for mastery at many developmental levels, but the circumstances of its original acquisition may give a particular stamp to its functions and uses ever after. For example, there must be considerable differences between the child who is only too readily understood; the child whose first articulations are ignored; and the child whose acquisition of language opens up an exciting new world of interaction with others. In fact, one might see a simple paradigm for the optimal way in which experience and maturation may interact, namely, the importance of an adequately frustrating as well as stimulating environmental experience.

Toward the end of his second year he had only recently overcome the peak of his omnipotence. In parallel with this would be the beginnings of self representations and self-sustaining introjects which took some account of the need for an object. Viewed from these perspectives, it seems that the meaning of language, and particularly the written word, had a double and paradoxical implication for Mr. N. On the one hand, it was an attempt to reach and contact his mother; on the other, it became a symbol of his denial of his need for a mother and represented something that he believed could be self-sustaining. This paradox could be seen in a number of aspects of Mr. N.'s later character. For example, he could show great insight when discussing literature and when understanding the subtle feelings and motivations of those involved in a dramatic plot. I was constantly surprised, however, by his emotional blindness in everyday interactions with others in which, because his own needs had to be repudiated, the simplest expressions of being liked or disliked would be misinterpreted.

His interest in literature and other art forms could be traced from very early days. At about the age of 4—again testifying to his precocious skills—he was an avid reader of comics. He remembered being not only interested in the daring escapes of the heroes but also in their romantic attachments. By the age of 6, he had read and become an expert in a whole range of mythologies, particularly Nordic ones. In retrospect, he was able to recognize that it was the eschatological, end-of-the-world mythologies which interested him most. Clearly by this time his use of fantasy in literature encompassed many complex developmental issues, but he both attempted to deal with, and at the same time cover over, the original trauma of his hospitalization.

At puberty, his imagination took a sharply unpleasant turn. He began to have horrifying nightmares in which he was buried alive, or in which his body was putrefying and being eaten by worms. His isolation with gastroenteritis clearly figured here. His response was to develop an interest and expertise in horror movies; and this counterphobic maneuver enabled him to attain some mastery.

Not surprisingly, during his adolescence he became a voracious reader of literature, of which, with his exceptional memory, he had an encyclopedic knowledge. He passed exams easily, gaining a scholarship to read English at university. His career stumbled, however, when he failed to complete his Ph.D. In fact, although he amassed a great deal of material, he never even started his thesis, and this failure was still very painful to him. His inability to write his Ph.D. thesis can be seen from a number of perspectives, but it recalls both a sense of futility in the capacity to communicate and a concomitant failure to establish a properly creative or authorial voice. His writings, which he himself disparaged unfairly for being trivial, were witty and erudite, but somehow seemed to lack a center. It was as if the opinion maker or creator was completely obscured and, in fact, Mr. N. turned this into a virtue by making it a rule never to use the first person singular in a piece. He rationalized this as being in the interest of style, but it reflected in fact a profound inhibition.

This case is in many respects typical of a symptom neurosis. The trauma of the early hospitalization created a fixation point to which Mr. N. regressed under the impact of anxieties at the oedipal levels. He was unable to compete with other men, in part because phallic introjects were flawed and he was constantly threatened by the feeling of being useless and "full of shit." He was also terrified of any critical attack by either a man or a woman, and with the latter would rapidly regress to the dependent and ambivalent relationship where withholding played a large part. He felt inadequate with women and with good reason, because he was incapable of giving them much either sexually or affectionately.

The reasons for citing this case were to highlight how this early fixation became an organizer of his later character development as revealed through the analysis of his resistance. As an adult Mr. N. was highly intellectual and devoted himself to literature, but he was also inhibited both professionally and personally. He was unable to develop his creative gifts fully as a writer, and in intimate relationships could not tolerate recognizing his own needs and impulses. As a consequence his life even before the onset of his neurosis was relatively impoverished. He was unable to recognize or tolerate his own affects, and relationships to others were shallow. He often felt bad about himself and considered himself inadequate both as a writer and an individual. These adult characteristics could in part be traced back to his early trauma. It was one of the gratifying aspects of analysis that traumas often acted as organizers which allowed more clarity than did the impact of other experiences through development. Even with a trauma though, to give some focus to experiential components in development, the equally important aspect of maturational factors cannot be ignored. The style and manner in which Mr. N. reacted to his hospitalization and its subsequent elaborations in his personality must have been influenced by constitutional aspects of drive and ego at each point of development. When other experiential aspects are considered, things become even more complex. Psychoanalytic studies have examined the effect of early mothering in the first year of life and also the continuing impact of object relations in producing identifications and self representations, but because these experiences are so diffuse and are spread over a long period, it becomes even harder to unravel maturation from experience.

While Freud (1937) looked at the issue from the aspect of treatability, he highlighted as unknown the strength of maturational factors such as drive intensity and ego abilities or deficits. He said, "In cases of what is known as character-analysis . . . it is not easy to foresee a natural end, even if one avoids any exaggerated expectations and sets the analysis no excessive tasks. Our aim will not be to rub off every peculiarity of human character for the sake of a schematic 'normality', nor yet to demand that the person who has been 'thoroughly analysed' shall feel no passions and develop no internal conflicts. The business of the analysis is to secure the best possible psychological conditions for the functions of the ego; with that it has discharged its task" (p. 250). In many ways we are not much further forward than Freud in unraveling these issues, since we rarely know what maturational limits may be set to an individual's ego. It seems likely that in the future we may become better able to identify individual maturational deficits, for example, to know that an individual has a constitutional propensity toward shyness, and then be able to map out, through an analytic reconstruction, the way in which this propensity interacted with experience. It would be very revealing to be able to do this in a manner similar to the way traumatic components can now be analyzed.

BIBLIOGRAPHY

ABRAHAM, K. (1923). Contributions to the theory of the anal character. *Int. J. Psychoanal.*, 4:400–418.
——— (1924). The influence of oral erotism on character formation. *Int. J. Psychoanal.*, 6:247–258.
——— (1925). Character-formation on the genital level of the libido. *Int. J. Psychoanal.*, 7:214–222.
BAUDRY, F. (1983). The evolution of the concept of character in Freud's writings. *J. Amer. Psychoanal. Assn.*, 31:3–31.
——— (1984). Character: a concept in search of an identity. *J. Amer. Psychoanal. Assn.*, 32:455–477.
——— (1989). Character, character type, and character organization. *J. Amer. Psychoanal. Assn.*, 37:655–686.
FENICHEL, O. (1945). *The Psychoanalytic Theory of Neurosis.* New York: Norton.
FREUD, A. (1936). The ego and the mechanisms of defense. *Writings*, 2.
——— (1965). Normality and pathology in childhood. *Writings*, 6.
——— (1966). Obsessional neurosis. *Int. J. Psychoanal.*, 47:116–122.
FREUD, S. (1908). Character and anal erotism. *S.E.*, 9:169–175.
——— (1916). Some character-types met with in psycho-analytic work. *S.E.*, 14:311–333.
——— (1931). Libidinal types. *S.E.*, 21:215–220.
——— (1937). Analysis terminable and interminable. *S.E.*, 23:209–253.
GIOVACCHINI, P. (1972). *The Treatment of Characterological Disorders.* New York: Science House.
HARTMANN, H. (1939). *Ego Psychology and the Problem of Adaptation.* New York: Int. Univ. Press, 1958.

JACOBSON, E. (1959). The "exceptions." *Psychoanal. Study Child*, 14:135–154.

KERNBERG, O. F. (1968). A psychoanalytic classification of character pathology. *J. Amer. Psychoanal. Assn.*, 18:800–822.

———— (1983). Character analysis. *J. Amer. Psychoanal. Assn.*, 31:247–271.

KOHUT, H. (1971). *The Analysis of the Self*. New York: Int. Univ. Press.

NUNBERG, H. (1956). Character and neurosis. *Int. J. Psychoanal.*, 37:36–45.

PANEL (1983). Theory of character. S. M. Abend, reporter. *J. Amer. Psychoanal. Assn.*, 31:211–224.

———— (1958). The psychoanalytic concept of character. A. Valenstein, reporter. *J. Amer. Psychoanal. Assn.*, 6:567–575.

PIRANDELLO, L. (1921). *Six Characters in Search of an Author*. London: Methuen.

REICH, W. (1945). *Character Analysis*. New York: Orgone Institute Press.

STEIN, M. (1969). Analysis of character. *Psychoanal. Q.*, 38:168–170.

STERBA, R. (1951). Character resistance. *Psychoanal. Q.*, 20:72–76.

WAELDER, R. (1930). The principle of multiple function. In *Psychoanalysis: Observation, Theory, Application*. New York: Int. Univ. Press, 1976, pp. 68–83.

YORKE, C., WISEBERG, S., & FREEMAN, T. (1989). *Development and Psychopathology*. New Haven: Yale Univ. Press.

Confronting Dilemmas in the Study of Character

SAMUEL ABRAMS, M.D.

Distinctive dilemmas in the psychoanalytic study of character are described. What they are and how they have been addressed illuminate the past achievements and some of the future directions of clinical research.

THERE ARE SEVERAL OVERLAPPING DILEMMAS IN THE STUDY OF CHARacter. When examined in sequence, they demonstrate the achievements in the psychoanalytic understanding and management of pathological traits. They also provide a perspective on further challenges. The colloquium on "Maturational and Experiential Components of Character" provided an unusually rich opportunity to consolidate established positions and examine new directions.

Description and Conceptualization. The first dilemma is one that is typically encountered in any scientific enterprise. It is the dilemma of selecting the most useful scheme for classifying information. When is it more advantageous to approach the study of character from a descriptive category and when from a conceptual one?

Freud (1908), by correlating certain traits and anality, instantly demonstrated what is attractive about a conceptual category. Such an approach offered clinicians an immediate linkage between manifest and latent. This way of assimilating data shaped much of his work on character from then on (Baudry, 1983) and influenced many others who followed. Analysts moved from a typology initially informed by instinctual drives to one shaped by unconscious fantasies, or derived from solutions to central conflicts, or cast from outgrowths of the

Clinical professor, department of psychiatry, New York University School of Medicine.

This is an expanded version of comments made at the 1990 colloquium on "Maturational and Experiential Determinants of Character" at the Anna Freud Centre, London, England, October 26 and 27, 1990.

object-interaction system. Some traits were viewed as intimately linked to certain fundamental pathological disorders (e.g., Alexander, 1930; Brenner, 1959; Frosch, 1970, 1988; Robbins, 1982; Kernberg, 1970). These diverse typologies made character, in Baudry's (1984) felicitous phrasing, a concept in search of an identity.

In spite of these complex and often conflicting schemes of classification, conceptual categories lured clinicians. The attraction was instant bridges between observable phenomena and the sources of disorders without having to relinquish preferred orienting perspectives.

However, the implicit disadvantage of such an approach consistently surfaced. Ordering along conceptual lines may prematurely foreclose further inquiry. The belief that something is already known tends to shut off research interests, just as in the clinical situation an analyst's hasty certainty can encumber the task of joint discovery.

An empirical approach, such as McLean (1992) and Schlesinger (1992) promote, minimizes this danger. Each suggests that character traits are best approached descriptively and both like the word "enduring." Character traits are features of individuals that are engraved, essences that are relatively stable or fixed. Character traits shape predictable ways of behaving that abide over time, a behaving that affects other persons, tasks, and principles.

At the colloquium, the first dilemma, a dilemma of choosing the more felicitous system of classification, was settled in favor of empiricism, thereby keeping the range of inquiry as wide as possible. However, preferred orienting typologies lurked everywhere. Character as a *concept* is constantly in quest for an identity; but as an empirical phenomenon it is neither divisive nor controversial.

The second dilemma is less free of divisiveness. It can be described as the *Normal-Pathological Dilemma*. In spite of its usefulness as a starting point, a merely descriptive approach in itself may be limiting for distinguishing normal from pathological traits. "Normal" and "abnormal" already imply a category based on premises that need to be made explicit. Both Schlesinger and McLean warn that such premises invariably introduce the thorny question of values. From an empirical point of view alone, it might be possible to assemble a system of explicit values that satisfactorily distinguish normal from abnormal. Schlesinger summarizes some useful possibilities. He suggests traits are pathological when they feature "self-and-other destructiveness" or are "maladaptive."

Destructiveness seems to be a self-evident premise, however difficult it might be to demonstrate at times, but adaptation is a more conceptually based one and therefore more subject to ambiguities. From such a framework, a trait is pathological if it encumbers adaptation, normal if it facilitates it or is at least neutral in this regard. Within this framework, for example, Schlesinger argues that "moral dependability" is a feature of normality.

One difficulty with this approach is that adaptation is readily confused with mere adjustment and normal and abnormal too easily linked to good and bad. From the standpoint of the leaders of small or large social units, for example, adjustment is usually good and opposition is bad. Converting the politics of good or bad into clinical assessments of normal and abnormal is a dangerous sport, although regrettably it is an active sport even within some psychoanalytic circles. Under certain circumstances, the ability to resist prevailing standards might be far more valuable if it also proves stressful and symptomatic. For some moralists and for all revolutionaries, opposition to prevailing standards is normal, the failure to do so is pathological.

Excessively compelling traits also draw the clinician's attention. It is true that character is engraved and enduring, but more or less engraved or enduring, implying at least a certain degree of flexibility. Enduring is not the same as compelling. If an independently spirited person cannot tolerate the necessary reliance on others during an acute illness, most clinicians would be inclined to view such dogged autonomy as pathological.

Destructive, maladaptive, and excessively compelling behaviors are useful terms, widely embraced by psychiatrists and psychoanalysts alike. However, Freud offered an approach for distinguishing normal and abnormal character traits that is uniquely psychoanalytic. The approach is derived from its methodology.

In analysis we require patients to establish a particular relationship with us and engage in a cooperative task, one devoted to discovering the various unrecognized sources of their behavior. Freud discovered that once we embark on the task, we come upon abiding traits in our patients that interfere with that cooperation or with that pursuit. He designated that phenomenon as a resistance due to character. His classificatory scheme was elegantly simple. Traits that encumber the psychoanalytic process are pathological, those that facilitate it are not. This has proven to be an altogether parsimonious, pragmatic, and inspired solution.

Both Herzog (1991) and McLean (1992) give splendid confirmatory illustrations. Herzog describes a patient whose way of relating interferes with the analysis and also proves to be a major unrecognized obstacle in her life outside the analysis. In McLean's case a man who cannot entirely own his feelings so that he cannot fully absorb what has happened to him as a child also is discovered to be compelled to write in the third person; he cannot even assume ownership of his professional work. This becomes evident to both of them because his personal analytic narrative has also been a third person description rather than an individually possessed experience. Thus, Herzog and McLean validate the Freudian view. Character traits discernible as obstacles within the analytic work may be designated as pathological; what impedes analysis also encumbers a patient's capacity for work and love.[1] This is an entirely satisfactory solution, provided we remain mindful of the premise that underlies this category. We must also recognize that this limits some of our generalizations about normal and pathological characters since some traits do not participate in the psychoanalytic situation as readily as do others. Another caution: a premise that ties "normality" to success in the psychoanalytic situation conveys the additional hazard of elitism, i.e., the best "normality" of all is the capacity for analysis. This would be an unwise and perhaps dangerously parochial perspective.

From a clinical and an analytic point of view, the second dilemma seems satisfactorily resolved. However, on confronting the third of the dilemmas, we come upon some important exceptions to the positions established in the first two.

The Child and Adult Dilemma. Descriptively, character traits are repetitive, predictable expressions of behavior that abide over time, distinctive features that specifically define a person. But abide over how much time? Are character traits continuous from childhood throughout adulthood? The answers at the colloquium were yes and no.

The phrase, "enduring over time," underscores continuities, a favored perspective of analysts who search the past for determinants of the present. Both McLean and Herzog illustrate what we usually expect to encounter in that search, traits that originate in childhood and continue into adulthood. Experienced clinicians, however, recognize that this is not always so. During the colloquium, Robert Gillman described an Irish beauty whose spontaneity and exuberance during childhood were rudely interrupted in latency, and Harold Blum reminded us of the powerful changes of character *usually* expected in

1. During the colloquium, Arthur Valenstein recalled papers written some time ago describing failures in the analysis of allegedly "normal" people. These "normals," so judged upon the basis of the usual psychiatric clinical criteria, were unable to engage the analytic relationship or the task. Psychoanalytic research demonstrated that the so-called "normal" traits that allowed them to conform so well in life proved fundamentally "pathological."

adolescence. Some adults report (sometimes with relief, sometimes with anguish) how similar they have always been since childhood in one respect or another, while others recall (sometimes with relief, sometimes with anguish) how different they have become. The premise that guided us in settling the first dilemma must be amended: character traits abide over time—more or less, yes and no. Discontinuities occur; what is their source?

The child-adult dilemma requires an additional framework for it to be engaged, the theory of the developmental process. The developmental process is based on several assumptions. (1) During growth there is an underlying maturational blueprint that guides an expectable sequence of progressive hierarchical phase organizations. (2) These stages are characterized by the appearance of novelties, new ways of thinking, new ways of feeling, new adaptive repertoires. (3) The appearance of such novelties implies the presence of transformational activities. Consequently, each advanced phase or stage ushers in the potential for changes in traits of character.

This recognition of expectable changes during childhood and adolescence signals a significant difference between children and adults. Traits of children are inclined toward change; traits observed in adults are likely to be truly engraved. This fact not only poses a challenge for the way we solved our first dilemma, but it makes the approach to differentiating normal and abnormal more complex.

An informal comment by Albert Solnit demonstrated the intricacies of the dilemma more precisely. He recalled that Anna Freud had noted that adolescents cannot participate in the analytic situation, at least within the model of revival and transference consolidation that proves so fruitful for adults. The requirement of reactivating the past through memories and the medium of transference conflicts with the developmental need in adolescents to search for the novel and to turn objects into ideals. A paradox: in terms of developmental needs, an adolescent who behaves according to the adult model is behaving pathologically.

This demonstrable exception to the Freudian principle that settled the second dilemma is useful because it requires us to integrate the developmental process in the study of character. This also requires us to recognize that clinicians sometimes serve a conceptual master other than the analytic process. In children and adolescents behavioral traits that advance the developmental process are normal—not pathological—even though they sometimes obstruct advances in the analytic process.

The Maturational and Experiential Dilemma. This is a dilemma of sources. The developmental process, a concept that proved useful for engaging the adult-child dilemma, proves serviceable in this area as well.

The terms "maturation" and "experience" may not be the best labels to categorize sources, because these words have ambiguous meanings even within psychoanalysis and in addition tend to polarize the issues. Perhaps a more neutral designation is preferable, e.g., nature and nurture or disposition and the environment, although the tendency toward polarizing persists even with these terms.

What of character is attributable to disposition and what to the environment? Herzog (1991) focuses upon temperament—clearly dispositional—and its effect over time. McLean (1992) describes the effect of precocious or retarded speech, also dispositional, and, he, like Herzog, documents its effect over time.

Herzog speaks of character traits as residues of past relationships. He specifically focuses on those influenced by temperament. This view of character is not quite determined by the environment itself (i.e., by the actuality of offerings), but already reflects the interaction of an inherent temperament with figures in the surround. In effect, he suggests that every object interplay is influenced by temperament. Equipment shapes the quality of interactions. McLean also approaches the issue of traits as a residue of past relationships, but his understanding is somewhat different. He describes a traumatic event in a child's life, specifically the effect of a hospitalization and illness. He places such actualities within an experiential category and contrasts it with phase conflicts that he judges to be maturational (or dispositional). He is more inclined to isolate and polarize maturation and experience, while Herzog blends and integrates.

Psychoanalysts have historical precedent for such polarizing. A hundred years ago hysteria was first experiential (a consequence of seductions) and subsequently maturational, i.e., an expression of inherent fantasies.

This proclivity to polarize the outside and the inside to establish categories of understanding is not limited to psychoanalytic circles. Researchers into infectious disease who orient themselves outward become microbe hunters, those who turn inward become immunologists, although both groups examine the same kind of phenomena. Some historians organize the past as a reaction to a series of actualities, others to the natural emergence of forms of social organizations.

The problem is compounded where the study of character is concerned because a system of values easily encroaches upon any assessment of behavior. In and outside of the clinical situation, the search for explanations often turns into a hunt for responsibility and the need to assign blame rather than define causes.

How can we best understand the interaction between dispositional and environmental influences? Can the inherent shape experiences? Can actualities impact upon dispositional leanings?

There is a complex of cyclic reverberations between the inherent and emerging structures and the often erratic and always variable range of stimuli that abound in the course of growth. There is no way to recognize stimuli without a recording structure, and structures that cannot register stimuli have no usefulness. A tree that falls in an empty forest does not make a sound; it only creates waves. Waves can only be converted into sounds by a complex auditory organ designed to do so. Waves need ears to be experienced as sounds; ears deprived of waves record nothing. The environment exists only to the degree that we are able to process it; and it is equally true that disposition is only actualized within the context of relationships and events.

This perspective places the search for essences into a different context.

In the beginning such a search led psychoanalysis to instinctual drives and the recognition of the centrality of conflict. Initially traits of character were linked to underlying drive-defense components—the first essence.

Then Freud told us that the self was the product of abandoned object relationships. Character was redefined as the expression of abiding structures derived from earlier interactions—a new essence. For some, this proved so remarkable a discovery that drives and defense, if not entirely discarded, were promptly relegated to a secondary position.

In recent years, the neonatologists have demonstrated constitutional variations and the infant researchers have discovered a rich mine of temperamental differences. They suggest that the transactions that form the basis of early object relationships and the paths of drive and defense are both influenced by temperaments. You will rarely hear a clearer description of such influences as in the papers by Herzog and McLean. Temperament appears to be another essence.

Drives, the object-interaction system, and equipmental factors are three major psychological realms. Within each of these realms, there is a sequence of development over time, a sequence informed by maturation and experiences. The goal of mental growth is through greater differentiation, and the path is a discontinuous one. All three realms are encompassed by an overriding developmental process that conveys each and assembles all into coherent organizations. The assembling and reassembling yield products of great variability; some of those products we designate as traits of character. In this model, traits that are empirically similar may derive from quite different sources. We have no reason confidently to link a trait a priori with one or another of the subordinate realms.

This newest essence has the advantage, not demonstrable in the earlier ones, of pulling all the other discoveries together rather than discarding any. However, it has the disadvantage of enhancing the complexity of psychoanalytic work considerably. The disadvantage of greater complexity is partially compensated by the opportunities for fresh research in the organization of drives, relationships, and apparatuses. The dilemma of maturational and experiential sources can only be engaged by extending our conventional models of understanding.

The Therapeutic Dilemma. This involves the distinction between therapeutic action in analysis through veridical interpretations as contrasted with results attributable to experiences generated between the participants.

To what degree is effective management of disorders of character a consequence of new insights through integration and to what degree is it a result of effecting changes in representational structures through generating experiences within the therapeutic interaction? For some, this question quickly reduces itself to a polarity between protagonists of conflict resolution on the one hand and modifying the self and object representational system on the other. This clinical dilemma might be described as the integration-interactive dilemma.

Herzog clearly paid attention to an integrative approach; he helped his patient, Dr. K., by having her understand a feature of temperament that influenced the way she behaved with people and especially with the way she behaved with him. He not only interpreted meanings, he also interpreted structures. However, he also focused upon another activity with his patient, an activity that he labeled a play experience between them, an experience that also had therapeutic impact. For Herzog, the treatment requires both integration and interaction. It is not clear whether these two approaches are always so easily coordinated.

Herzog also described an expanded use of reconstruction. He reconstructed not only past actualities but also the influence of temperament upon the perceiving instrument. Reconstruction for most analysts usually means looking for what *really* happened out there, e.g., the Wolf-Man's actual confrontation with the parental primal scene, the birth of a sibling, a maternal depression, etc. It has been at least 15 years since I first heard Peter Neubauer propose that reconstruction requires not only attempting to understand what a child was exposed to but the way the events were perceived and experienced. Such perceiving and experiencing, he added, depend upon temperament and the prevailing level of developmental organization. I have always felt this position to be highly useful. Its clinical applicability was demonstrated convincingly by Herzog.

Summary

1. Descriptive-Conceptual Dilemma. It is usually more valuable to approach a phenomenon empirically at first rather than with a preformed conceptual framework.

2. Normal-Pathological Dilemma. When we attempt to assess the value of a phenomenon, it is necessary to have at least a minimal preformed conceptual framework, and it is wise to know the premises upon which the framework is constructed.

3. Child-Adult Dilemma. When we come upon a glaring exception to a prior position, we must either alter the original view or broaden our conceptual framework. When an exception is made the center of attention, it provides the opportunity to increase the range of inquiry and understanding. The child-adult dilemma brings the theory of the developmental process into sharp relief as a valuable addition for differentiating and comprehending normal and pathological traits of character.

4. Nature-Nurture. Polarizing comes naturally, as do automatic shifts into preferred ways of viewing phenomena. Nature or nurture almost never exists in isolation. Harmonizing, organizing, synthesizing, integrating the influences of nature and nurture are the tasks of all people during their development and the tasks of psychoanalysts in attempting to understand growth and development.

5. The Therapeutic Dilemma. Does the study of character pose any special technical issues? Probably not, nor does the study necessarily illuminate the theory of therapeutic action in any distinctive way. Conflict resolution seems immutably tied to insight, promoting experiences tied with changing object representations. Coordinating rather than polarizing these and other positions may best address this dilemma.

BIBLIOGRAPHY

ALEXANDER, F. (1930). The neurotic character. *Int. J. Psychoanal.*, 11:292–311.

BAUDRY, F. D. (1983). The evolution of the concept of character in Freud's writings. *J. Amer. Psychoanal. Assn.*, 31:3–31.

——— (1984). Character: a concept in search of an identity. *J. Amer. Psychoanal. Assn.*, 32:455–477.

BRENNER, C. (1959). Masochistic character. *J. Amer. Psychoanal. Assn.*, 2:197–226.

FREUD, S. (1908). Character and anal erotism. *S.E.*, 9:169–175.

——— (1916). Some character-types met with in psycho-analytic work. *S.E.*, 14:311–333.

FROSCH, J. (1970). Psychoanalytic considerations of the psychotic character. *J. Amer. Psychoanal. Assn.*, 18:124–156.

——— (1988). Psychotic character versus borderline. *Int. J. Psychoanal.*, 69:334–358.

HERZOG, J. M. (1991). Temperament and transaction. *Bull. Anna Freud Centre*, 14:184–196.

KERNBERG, O. F. (1970). Psychoanalytic classification of character pathology. *J. Amer. Psychoanal. Assn.*, 18:800–822.

McLEAN, D. (1992). Maturational and experiential components of character formation. This volume.

ROBBINS, M. (1982). Narcissistic personality as a symbiotic character disorder. *Int. J. Psychoanal.*, 63:457–474.

SCHLESINGER, H. J. (1992). What does psychoanalysis have to contribute to the understanding of character? This volume.

CLINICAL
CONTRIBUTIONS

Narcissistic Disorders in Children

PHYLLIS BEREN, Ph.D.

This paper discusses children who initially may seem suitable for psycho-analytically oriented treatment but who do not respond in the anticipated manner. Such difficulties in treatment may suggest the presence of a narcissistic disorder. Clinical material from a latency-aged girl is presented to demonstrate the typical difficulties encountered in maintaining a working relationship with such children, and the special frustrations and countertransference issues that are apt to arise. A set of criteria is proposed to help in the diagnosis of a narcissistic disorder, and a treatment approach is suggested.

IN THE PAST TWO DECADES A GREATER UNDERSTANDING OF CERTAIN pathological conditions in adults has been gained by the elaboration and expansion of the theory of narcissism. These theoretical formulations have influenced our diagnostic assessment and our clinical technique with adult narcissistic disturbances (Reich, 1953; Kohut, 1966, 1968, 1971, 1972; O. Kernberg, 1967, 1970, 1975; Modell, 1976; Bach, 1985). In the literature on assessment, diagnosis, and treatment of children, mention has been made of narcissistic defenses (Mahler and Kaplan, 1977), but until recently little attention has been paid to the possibility of an already existing narcissistic disorder (Bene, 1979; Bleiberg, 1984, 1988; Egan and P. Kernberg, 1984).

This paper looks at some of those children who at first glance seem ideally suited to psychoanalytically oriented treatment but who do not respond in the anticipated manner to our therapeutic interventions. For example, some child cases end in a therapeutic stalemate or fall considerably short of the treatment goal, despite what appears initially to be a relatively benign diagnosis and a good therapeutic prognosis. It

Member, Institute for Psychoanalytic Training and Research and The New York Freudian Society. Supervisor and faculty, The Institute for Child, Adolescent and Family Studies. Instructor, New York University School of Social Work doctoral program, where an earlier version of this paper was given in November, 1990.

sometimes also appears that standard psychoanalytic technique, such as the analysis of defense and interpretation of unconscious conflict, may have little positive effect and instead may make some children only more resistent and defensive or even disorganized. Certain children also present the therapist with unusual countertransference reactions which may take the form of feeling bored, ineffectual, or doubtful about the usefulness of the treatment. These feelings may in turn lead to finding reasons for lessening the frequency of sessions, changing the modality of treatment, or terminating the treatment altogether.

A number of authors have written about the "corrective emotional experience" as a special therapeutic technique for certain developmental disorders (Alpert, 1957; Berger and Kennedy, 1975; A. Freud, 1968, 1976; Weil, 1973). When clinicians need to deviate from standard analytic technique by the use of the "corrective emotional experience," they may sometimes be treating children who suffer from a narcissistic disturbance. Likewise, cases in which the reported focus is on the countertransference of the therapist and his or her difficulty in establishing and maintaining a standard analytic atmosphere and working relationship may also indicate a narcissistic disturbance in the child (Bornstein, 1948, 1949; Kabcenell, 1974; Kay, 1978).

I want to illustrate these considerations with the case of Jane, who was 8½ years old when she entered therapy. The main complaint of her parents was that she did not make an effort in school and had difficulty completing her work. At home she had tantrums every day, usually about wanting her mother to buy her something special. The parents found her exceedingly demanding and unreasonable. She had difficulty being alone and occupying her time and instead wanted to be entertained. She often complained that her parents were nicer to her two older sisters than they were to her. Unlike their middle daughter whom the parents described as an easy and wonderful baby, Jane from early on seemed difficult to satisfy and was exceptionally clingy. While Jane had friends and liked to have other children around her, she was disappointed that the popular girls did not choose to socialize with her. One way that Jane seemed to differentiate herself from her sisters and mother was to dress in what she thought to be the fashion of the times: like a punk teenager. She expressed both envy and disparagement of her sisters and felt the parents favored them. Jane did not acknowledge having any problems and viewed her need for treatment as totally her mother's desire. All she would grant is that her mother called her tantrums "the fit of the day." She herself had no idea why she had tantrums. She denied any problems in school, even though her school reports were very poor. She blamed everything on the teachers playing favorites.

For half the duration of her treatment, which lasted four years, Jane continually denied her unhappy and painful feelings or her role in any of the difficulties in school and at home. I have discovered this to be common in children with narcissistic disorders, who tend to have little or no objective self-awareness. Over the course of treatment Jane disliked and resented it if I tried to empathize with what she might feel. For example, when she complained one day how unfair it was that her sister had been given some new furniture for her bedroom and her parents refused to do the same for her, I said that this must make her feel angry and disappointed. Jane screamed at me, "Don't tell me how I feel, no one knows except me." Or she yelled at me that I could not read her mind if I attempted to make some interpretation of her defensive stance. The most benign intervention or interpretation always was rejected or, worse yet, caused her to become very hostile followed by a refusal to talk to me.

This high level of guardedness, denial of problems, and lack of empathy in such children can pose difficulties for the therapist, making it hard to feel that a mutual working relationship has been established. Although many of these children may complain about coming to therapy, they will come dutifully and appear engaged in the session if they are not relating directly to the therapist. In contrast, the classical theory of child analysis suggests that in order for a child to benefit from therapy, he or she must perceive, experience, or acknowledge a problem. For example, in Berta Bornstein's well-known case of Frankie (1949), to be discussed later, the teachers were instructed that once Frankie made a positive attachment to them, they were to inform him that his mother could not longer stay with him in school. When he protested that he could not remain alone, they were asked to tell him that there was someone he could talk to who would help him stay in school. "This pre-analytic phase was designed to create a conflict in the child between his symptom and reality. . . . By our pre-analytic scheme we hoped to produce in him insight into his need for help, without which no psychoanalytic treatment can make any progress" (p. 184). This implies that a child has to have a number of well-developed ego functions such as a capacity for insight and self-awareness to benefit from an analytic approach. The ability to admit to problems and perceive one's own part in them presupposes a relatively well-developed sense of self. The narcissistic children's sense of self is usually less developed, more vulnerable, and more dependent on outside approval. It is as if their sense of self is still in the process of formation and more dependent on the admiration of others and their own grandiose fantasies. Such children have a tendency to feel easily injured and, in response to these perceived slights, to react with a good deal of anger. It would be unlikely that such children could easily admit to problems or see the purpose of treatment, since they often externalize their problems. Frequently, the treatment itself may be experienced as a narcissistic injury.

While it is beyond the scope of this paper to give a detailed account of Jane's therapy, I have chosen to discuss a few aspects which I feel highlight some of the difficulties in the treatment of a narcissistic child. Many of the sessions had a very formulaic quality to them. Jane often came in with a snack which she proceeded to eat, giving it her full attention. While she was eating she read the contents on the package and rationalized that it did not contain too many calories, since she was concerned about how she looked and was in fact considerably over-weight. When I said that I knew she was worried about her weight, she denied this. Once the eating ritual ended, she entered the second stage of her therapy session. She walked around the room in what appeared to me to be an aimless fashion, usually doing some strange foot stepping while bouncing her head and snapping her fingers. Because she wanted me to guess and would not say what she was doing, it took me a while to figure out that she was trying to imitate the rock star David Byrne of the Talking Heads. Having guessed correctly, I was rewarded by learning a little more about her. Her desire and pleasure in having me guess contained a deeper meaning which she was unwilling to analyze or understand and which felt to me as if it were one more example of her controlling behavior. What she did confess was her desire to be a rock star. She clearly wanted to have an audience and she wanted to use our sessions for me to be her audience and to admire her imitations and give her my undivided attention. She had no interest in interacting with me. She was content to have me watch her eat and then perform. I might add that it is this type of demand on the therapist that may engender countertransference feelings of being bored and exploited. It is also the behavior of a much younger child who wishes the mother to admire everything she does. Another example of this need for an admiring audience was her bringing her recorder to play in sessions. In reality she was not very accomplished because she spent very little time practicing. One had the clear sense that she believed she could be whoever she wanted to be just by wishing it. Thus she could eat all the cake and candy she wanted and still be thin and beautiful. She could be a teenager like her middle sister, and she could be a star.

This was a further indication of her poorly developed sense of self, her shaky identifications, and the omnipotence of her thought. Thus she could also disregard reality by insisting that she was doing fine in school when in fact she was not. This disregard for reality by children who otherwise might appear normal in their reality testing and judgment is not unusual in children with narcissistic disorders. Sometimes parents will complain that these children lie or make up stories. In Jane's case her near total denial of her poor school functioning was a narcissistic defense she used because she could not tolerate admitting she was not good at something.

Another example of how her reality testing and judgment became compromised in the service of maintaining a kind of grandiose self was in her total disregard for the rules of the game. In contrast to the usual strict adherence to rules by latency-aged children, Jane seemed unaffected by them. Thus in playing checkers or some other board game, Jane made up the rules as she went along. When I tried to understand how she came to play this way, she insisted that it was how she played with her friends. When I tried gently to suggest that perhaps some children played one way and other children another, she told me I was wrong and that her way was right. Her manner of playing was so difficult to follow and was so controlling that it made me feel confused and manipulated. It was as if there was no way to play with her other than to allow myself to be used as an extension.

There were, however, moments when I intuitively sensed Jane to be more amenable to hearing what I said about her near failing in school or the fights with her mother and sisters. I had come to learn that she was better able to tolerate my interventions if I used some humor or made a joke. Thus, I would preface my intervention with, "Jane, you know that the only reason I am saying this is because it's my job. That's what therapists are supposed to do, to talk about the things nobody wants to talk about—but what can I do, it's my job; and if I didn't do that, I would be out of a job." This was often received with a big smile. She then allowed me to say, "I know how you hate it when I suggest you might feel a certain way about something, because your mother is always telling you how she thinks you feel and that makes you so angry." Jane could respond to this and say, "You bet!" and give me examples of fights where her mother insisted on seeing things her own way. Over time she came to be less guarded with me as she came to feel that I was her ally. The issue of how she played checkers was approached again. I asked her who taught her how to play and she responded that her uncle had. Again I used humor. I said, "Jane, I have some very bad news for you that will make you very upset because you will think I'm a terrible person for what I'm going to say about your uncle." Her eyes opened wide and I went on to say, "Your uncle all these years has taught you the wrong way to play checkers. I know you like your uncle and how hard this must be for you." She responded by smiling and went on to ask me how others played. In this way I managed to get around her feeling narcissistically injured by having to admit that she did not know something. It was alright if someone else was ignorant, but not she.

It might be questioned what in this interchange made it possible for her to react differently. First, I should note that she in fact had certain problems with other children. She could only be friends with those girls whom she could boss and manipulate. She desperately wanted to be accepted by the more popular girls, but they rejected her because in many ways she was immature. It would have been very difficult for her to find many children who would play board games the way she did. She would also have had a hard time admitting that she did not know how to play. Thus I gave her an opportunity to turn to me for some assistance without having to lose face. I had learned that a precondition for her hearing what I said was for me to devalue myself in some fashion so that I did not appear smarter than she. Earlier in the treatment she had frequently played a teacher who gave me tests for mental retardation. The need for me to be the retarded, devalued child was enacted with her rather than interpreted. As unconfrontive as this was, it must have taken us almost two years to arrive at this point. Later in the treatment I was able to analyze the transference from the standpoint that she needed to devalue me as she did her mother as well as her father and sisters. Further, her need to have me devalued was also interpreted as a reflection of how she felt about herself. At the time that she was able both to hear and accept my interpretation, her struggle with her mother lessened and she began to relate in a more satisfying manner with her father.

It is not uncommon for narcissistic children to take a very long time to gain some trust. Because the work is so slow and the play so repetitive and often controlling, the session may appear to move slowly and both child and therapist may at times feel bored and restless.

When the narcissistic child complains of being bored, it is often an expression of dissociated feelings of emptiness and oral longing or of repressed anger. Boredom leads them constantly to search for external stimulation or gratification, expressed in demanding requests for new toys, new clothes, or other diversions. The narcissistic child often expects the therapist to admire her new clothes, new possessions, or her performance, and not to intrude herself in any manner.

The narcissistic child's level of object relationship is different from that of a neurotic child. The narcissistic child's self and object constancy and self-other representations are not as fully developed, and the child often does not view the therapist as a person in her own right. The therapist's reaction to the child's aloofness and apparent lack of emotional connection may be to feel used rather than useful, so that an induced countertransference ensues. This may take the form of boredom, restlessness, or discouragement, and may reflect her own hopelessness and repressed anger at her inability to connect with the child as well as an induced response to the child's provocations.

When a child's play and behavior in treatment is excessively controlling, the child may also be showing the therapist that she herself feels controlled, powerless, and helpless. This controlling behavior also reflects the child's disbelief in the give-and-take of a relationship and her conviction that she can rely only on herself to get what she feels she needs. The therapist who does not understand this motivation may instead try to work in a more confronting manner or bring herself forcefully into the transference, but this often results in the child becoming more defensive, angry, or withdrawn.

I believe that the roots of this disorder lie in the early relationship with the mother and in particular in the inherent contradictions of the anal rapprochement subphase as described by Mahler et al. (1975). While the child is becoming increasingly more independent, she is at the same time also demanding the mother's constant involvement. As the child becomes more aware of her separateness from mother and exercises this, there is still an attempt to coerce the mother into functioning as a dual unit. The child can no longer maintain her delusion of parental omnipotence and gradually realizes that her love objects are separate individuals with their own personal interests. She must gradually and painfully give up the delusion of her own grandeur, often by way of dramatic fights with mother, which Mahler calls the "rapprochement crisis." It is also in the anal rapprochement stage that objective self-awareness begins to develop and that the affect of shame becomes associated with anality and later with phallic strivings as the drives come into conflict with parental demands and prohibitions.

In the course of this developmental stage there are especially difficulty demands on the parents to be emotionally present for the child, while at the same time setting limits and maintaining empathy with the child's struggles. The parents of narcissistic children usually have great difficulty responding to them in a comforting, supportive, or appropriate manner based on the child's developmental needs. The Furmans (1984) describe a group of parents who for various reasons, perhaps their own depression or self-preoccupation, either turn away from their children at important times or are there but not emotionally present. They give the example of a mother who could not hear what her child was saying unless the child forced the mother to look at him. They contrast this kind of dysfunction with the more usual parental functioning of uninterrupted investment as, for example, when a mother who is in the other room suddenly shouts, "What are you doing in there?" because it is unusually quiet.

This quality of intermittent decathexis by the parent has been striking in parents of both the narcissistic children and adults that I have seen. One adult patient described how at a very young age he would climb out the window of his home at night to be gone for hours playing with the neighborhood boys who were much older. His parents had no knowledge of this routine activity. This patient as a child was very precocious and grew up preoccupied with an elaborate fantasy of how he could survive alone in the world if it came to that. As an adult going on a camping trip he felt obliged to take every kind of imaginable provision for every possible occurrence, even if it was the shortest of trips.

One day Jane asked me what I thought of the dress she was wearing. I felt this direct question indicated an important change in our relationship. Carefully considering her question, I responded that the dress was quite nice but that I had liked the one she wore the other day even better. I had by this time been taught by her not to ask her why she was asking or to tell me more about her question. Jane said a heartfelt "Thank you!" and I asked her why she was thanking me. She replied that I had given her a truthful answer. And why was that so important to her, I inquired, secretly excited that we actually had a dialogue. She went on to describe an example of a common interaction with her mother. "If I was going to school that morning and was walking out of the house nude and I asked my mother what she thought of how I was dressed, my mother would say, 'That's nice dear.'" She went on to explain that her mother let her wear anything she wanted and always said it was wonderful. This was in fact true, since I had heard it from the mother. Furthermore, in the early part of the treatment Jane was always dressed in an odd way, all the while insisting that she was in the height of fashion. This changed during the course of her treatment.

I noted how puzzling that must be to Jane, since it appeared from what she was telling me that her mother was not paying attention, and that her comments that everything looked terrific must be experienced by Jane as insincere. I was then able to connect this to how demanding and clingy Jane would become with her mother as if this were the only way she could be sure of her mother's attention. Jane demonstrated that she had some understanding of her mother's failures. She told me that the maternal grandmother had been exceedingly intrusive with the mother, never giving her any choice in anything, so that Jane's mother was determined to let her own children make up their own minds and to be approving of them. Jane and I together were able to understand how her mother felt she was doing something that would be beneficial to her children, yet it had had the effect of making her feel that her mother did not really care. In addition, it had left Jane feeling very unsure of herself since, like all children her age, she needed a mother's opinion. Jane gradually was able to accept that many of her defenses were in the service of making herself feel more secure when in fact underneath she felt so very insecure. It was to this end that she often insisted that whatever she did was the right thing even when in reality it was not. I should add that Jane's mother was practically incapable of talking about any of her daughters without comparing them not only to one another but also to herself at that age. It was strikingly obvious that the mother could not see these children in their own right and consequently Jane's way of orienting herself in the world was primarily through imitation rather than through identification. Eventually, Jane came to feel more understanding and less critical of her mother and herself, which resulted in significant improvement in all areas of her life.

A case that appears to demonstrate some of these issues is Berta Bornstein's (1949) Frankie. It has justly become a teaching classic in the use of defense analysis with children. Furthermore, this case has an important place in the history of psychoanalysis because 17 years after its publication it was the focus for a discussion of obsessional neurosis at the International Congress (A. Freud, 1966). Ritvo (1966) analyzed Frankie as an adult and presented a report of this later analysis, offering a unique opportunity to correlate child and adult analyses. This case is of special interest because at that conference the issue of Frankie's diagnosis was still in question. The question then centered on whether his diagnosis changed from a phobic neurosis to an obsessional neurosis. More recently, Pine (1990) again took up this question and emphasized the defect in Frankie's capacity to bind anxiety.

Frankie was 5½ when he entered analysis. He suffered from a number of phobias, the primary being his inability to remain in school without his mother. His separation anxiety had existed for more than two years. In addition, he had severe insomnia, refused to use a bathroom outside the home, and retained urine for hours. While he could not move from his mother's side, he was at the same time rejecting of her. He was very jealous of his younger sister and treated both sister and mother in a very demanding and bossy manner. During the course of his analysis other fears emerged, including a fear of elevators and of imaginary wolves that stood guard under his bed at night. His compensatory fantasies and defenses took the form of grandiose and omnipotent behavior and thinking. His behavior in the latter part of his analysis was so out of control that the analyst finally resorted to threatening him with hospitalization.

Greenson, one of the discussants at the conference, noted that "if so skilful and experienced a therapist had to resort to so un-analytic a manoeuvre, we might well be dealing with a problem beyond the realm of neurosis" (1966, p. 149). Greenson as well as Winnicott emphasized the preoedipal pathology and in particular the pathology in the sphere of his object relations. Greenson stressed Frankie's desire for female identification as a way of being at one with his mother. Winnicott emphasized Frankie's experience of his mother as being held by "a split-off maternal function" (1966, p. 143).

To my mind Frankie shows many typical features of a child suffering from a narcissistic disorder. Although his phobias might be thought of as neurotic, symptoms alone are not reliable indicators of a diagnosis. His problems of severe separation anxiety and fears of abandonment seem to suggest a deeper disturbance. A disorder of narcissism may be inferred from his disturbed self-esteem regulation as evidenced by his need for admiration and attention, much like Jane's. He is obliged to devalue his mother and sister and at times inappropriately to idealize his nurse. His grandiosity and sense of omnipotence and uniqueness were expressed in his fantasies of being an all-knowing God and later in his King Boo-Boo fantasy. His play and his behavior had a provocative and controlling quality characterized by his insistence on being the boss and demanding that others do just as he wished. His object relations were predominantly dyadic in nature and strongly suggested a need for a self-object. The grandiose fantasies were an attempt to compensate for a shaky sense of self and feelings of vulnerability. Frankie's wish to be chased, caught, and lifted can be understood as an attempt to get close to his mother and to be touched and held by her in a nurturant way he had never fully experienced. The sadomasochistic quality of this behavior suggested the confusion between nurturance and sexuality typically seen in problems of unresolved separation-individuation. It is as if not having the security of nurturance and the consequent internalizations necessary to negotiate the tumultuous anal rapprochement crisis leads to an unclarity and confusion in each successive phase of psychosexual development.

Frankie did not respond to interpretations in the way we would expect of a neurotic child, even though the material suggests that these interpretations were accurate. Instead, the interpretations seemed to have a disorganizing effect. Berta Bornstein was working within a framework in which she viewed Frankie as neurotic and the core conflict as oedipal in nature. While Frankie was certainly also struggling with oedipal issues, what seems most prominent in retrospect were his narcissistic vulnerabilities.

DISCUSSION

Because the initial evaluation of a child very much influences the subsequent treatment approach, I will enumerate a set of characteristics potentially discernible at the evaluation stage that might alert us to the possibility of a narcissistic disorder. These characteristics include:

1. A disturbance in regulation of self-esteem. Overvaluation of the self may be observed behaviorally as a need for constant admiration, attention, and/or self-aggrandizement, or a need to devalue others. Grandiosity may be expressed in a sense of entitlement or uniqueness, or in other ways such as excessive daydreaming in which the child sees himself as a hero, or in play with others where he insists on being the leader and makes others do exactly as he wishes. Another typical overcompensation may be seen in pathological lying, used to maintain the child's grandiosity.

Undervaluation of the self may be observed in the tendency to feel easily injured and to experience mental pain through feelings of inferiority, worthlessness, and shame or guilt (Joffe and Sandler, 1967), or in a reactive need inappropriately to idealize others. It is not unusual for these children to have hypochondriacal preoccupations and extreme castration anxiety as evidenced by their fears of cuts and bruises, of hurting themselves at sports, or fears of death.

2. A compelling need for the self-object, that is, an object used in the service of the self in a very special way and experienced as part of the self. This may be observed in children who require a mirroring, exclusively dyadic relationship in order to maintain an ideal state of self. "In narcissistic disorders the object is frequently and primarily experienced (or felt) as part of the self; unlike Anna Freud's need satisfying object (1966) which is placed outside of the self, though it is used in the service of the self" (Bene, 1979, p. 210).

3. A lack of self-awareness which leads to both a lack of empathy for the needs and feelings of others and a lack of empathy and perspective on themselves. This lack of self-awareness may be most easily observed

in their problematic and precarious friendships. The capacity for successful peer relationships means that the child can indulge in teasing and sadistic behavior and accept it without feeling unduly injured or criticized. The narcissistic child does not have this flexibility. As a result, one often hears complaints from such children that they are being "teased," "picked on," or "talked about." Since the narcissistic child is still using the other largely as an extension of herself, she does not seem to have the capacity for more give-and-take in relationships. Thus, the peer relationships also replicate certain aspects of the transference.

4. Precocious ego development. This can be observed in the extreme unevenness of development, where certain capacities and functions may be highly matured or overdeveloped while others lag behind. This uneven development usually dovetails with the parents' inability to see the child as a whole in a developmentally appropriate way, and with their overemphasis on certain of the child's functions that fit in with their own narcissistic needs.

For example, the parents may give a good deal of praise and encouragement for independence, at the expense of emotional and physical closeness. Thus the child discovers that the parents will not accept his dependence, and learns early on to take care of himself. Or the parent may overvalue one particular ego function such as speech, so that speech becomes overvalued and used for defensive purposes rather than for communicative or thought-clarifying purposes (Newman et al., 1973). What happens to these children is that they tend to use intellectualization and become emotionally removed and aloof. Another outcome may be the child who functions emotionally and physically as a little parent in the family, i.e., when there is an extreme form of role reversal in the parent-child relationship (Buckholz and Haynes, 1983).

Observing and evaluating these characteristics in the child may help us in formulating a diagnosis and a treatment plan. Diagnosing a child as neurotic dictates an approach that will predominantly analyze transference and resistance and interpret the libidinal and aggressive conflicts. Utilizing this same approach with a narcissistic child may often lead to an impasse and be experienced as futile by the therapist. Here the major narcissistic determinants in such cases suggest a therapeutic orientation that would create more of a "holding environment" and focus on eventually establishing a mutuality in the object relationship. In such cases the child's low self-esteem, narcissistic vulnerability, and incapacity to view herself objectively must be addressed as an essential prerequisite before most interpretations of unconscious material, conflict, or transference become possible.

How a child relates to the therapist and how she experiences the treatment process as a whole are very important indicators of the child's personality and overall psychosocial development. Understanding that we are dealing with a narcissistic disorder should make a major difference in our expectations of how the case will unfold and also in our treatment technique. Finally, having this understanding may allow us to react in a more analytic way should we find ourselves constantly feeling frustrated or ineffectual when treating a child patient.

BIBLIOGRAPHY

ALPERT, A. (1957). A special therapeutic technique for certain developmental disorders in pre-latency children. *Amer. J. Orthopsychiat.*, 27:256–270.

BACH, S. (1985). *Narcissistic States and the Therapeutic Process.* New York: Aronson.

BENE, A. (1979). The question of narcissistic personality disorders. *Bull. Hampstead Clin.*, 2:209–218.

BERGER, M. & KENNEDY, H. (1975). Pseudobackwardness in children. *Psychoanal. Study Child*, 30:279–306.

BLEIBERG, E. (1984). The question of narcissistic personality disorders in children. *Bull. Menninger Clin.*, 48:501–518.

―――― (1988). Developmental pathogenesis of narcissistic disorders in children. *Bull. Menninger Clin.*, 52:3–15.

BORNSTEIN, B. (1948). Emotional barriers in the understanding and treatment of young children. *Amer. J. Orthopsychiat.*, 18:691–697.

―――― (1949). The analysis of a phobic child. *Psychoanal. Study Child*, 3/4:181–227.

BUCKHOLZ, E. & HAYNES, R. (1983). Sometimes I feel like a motherless child. In *Dynamic Psychotherapy.* New York: Bruner/Mazel, vol. 1, pp. 99–107.

EGAN, J. & KERNBERG, P. (1984). Pathological narcissism in childhood. *J. Amer. Psychoanal. Assn.*, 32:39–63.

FREUD, A. (1966). Obsessional neurosis. *Int. J. Psychoanal.*, 47:116–122.

―――― (1968). Indications and contraindications for child analysis. *Psychoanal. Study Child*, 23:37–46.

―――― (1976). Changes in psychoanalytic practice and experience. *Int. J. Psychoanal.*, 57:257–260.

FURMAN, R. A. & FURMAN, E. (1984). Intermittent decathexis. *Int. J. Psychoanal.*, 65:423–434.

GREENSON, R. R. (1966). Comment on Dr. Ritvo's paper. *Int. J. Psychoanal.*, 47:149–151.

JOFFE, W. G. & SANDLER, J. (1967). Some conceptual problems involved in the consideration of disorders of narcissism. *J. Child Psychother.*, 2:56–66.

KABCENELL, R. (1974). On countertransference. *Psychoanal. Study Child*, 29:27–35.

KAY, P. (1978). Gifts, gratifications, and frustration in child analysis. In *Child Analysis and Therapy*, ed. J. Glenn. New York: Aronson.

KERNBERG, O. F. (1967). Borderline personality organization. *J. Amer. Psychoanal. Assn.*, 15:641–685.

——— (1970). A psychoanalytic classification of character pathology. *J. Amer. Psychoanal. Assn.*, 18:800–822.

——— (1975). *Borderline Conditions and Pathological Narcissism.* New York: Aronson.

KOHUT, H. (1966). Forms and transformations of narcissism. *J. Amer. Psychoanal. Assn.*, 14:243–272.

——— (1968). The psychoanalytic treatment of narcissistic personality disorders. *Psychoanal. Study Child*, 23:86–113.

——— (1971). *The Analysis of the Self.* New York: Int. Univ. Press.

——— (1972). Thoughts on narcissim and narcissistic rage. *Psychoanal. Study Child*, 27:360–400.

MAHLER, M. S. & KAPLAN, L. (1977). Developmental aspects in the assessment of narcissistic and so-called borderline personalities. In *Borderline Personality Disorders*, ed. P. Hartocollis. New York: Int. Univ. Press.

——— PINE, F., & BERGMAN, A. (1975). *The Psychological Birth of the Human Infant.* New York: Basic Books.

MODELL, A. (1976). The holding environment and the therapeutic action of psychoanalysis. *J. Amer. Psychoanal. Assn.*, 24:285–307.

NEWMAN, C. J., DEMBER, C. F., & KRUG, O. (1973). "He can but he won't." *Psychoanal. Study Child*, 28:83–129.

PINE, F. (1990). *Drive, Ego, Object and Self.* New York: Basic Books.

REICH, A. (1953). Narcissistic object choice in women. *J. Amer. Psychoanal. Assn.*, 1:22–44.

RITVO, S. (1966). Correlation of a childhood and adult neurosis. *Int. J. Psychoanal.*, 47:130–131.

WEIL, A. (1973). Ego strengthening prior to analysis. *Psychoanal. Study Child*, 28:287–301.

WINNICOTT, D. W. (1966). Comment on obsessional neurosis and Frankie. *Int. J. Psychoanal.*, 47:143–144.

Rescue Fantasies and the Secret Benefactor

ROBERT D. GILLMAN, M.D.

The concept of rescue fantasies is traced from Freud's earliest idea of the rescue of the mother as the fallen woman to later ideas of ambivalent rescue of the father, siblings, and children. Clinical vignettes from work with children and adults illustrate these points as well as reparative rescue fantasies in response to trauma and narcissistic hurt. The contemporary family romance myth of the secret benefactor as rescuer is described. An analytic case presentation explores the narcissistic-masochistic and the positive and negative oedipal meanings of the secret benefactor rescue fantasy. Application to countertransference enactments in the analyst is suggested.

IN THE COURSE OF EVALUATING AN 8-YEAR-OLD BOY WHO WAS NOT COMpleting his schoolwork despite all the pedagogical tricks his experienced teacher had tried, I asked him how it was possible that a bright boy like him did not do his work. He replied that his mind wandered to other things. I then inquired, really not expecting an informative answer, what other things his mind wandered to. He said that there was a girl in the class whom he liked and he would sit there thinking that she was being kidnapped by two bad men and then, "I ride up on a white horse and rescue her."

Freud (1910) described the oedipal nature of such rescue fantasies: the defiance of the oedipal father, the wish to have the mother for oneself, and to give her a child. For some men, Freud said, rescue is a necessary condition for loving. The women who are rescued are de-

---

Supervising analyst and emeritus training analyst at the Baltimore-Washington Institute for Psychoanalysis.

Presented at the Annual Meeting of the Association for Child Psychoanalysis, Philadelphia, March 18, 1989, and at the Fall meeting of the American Psychoanalytic Association, Miami Beach, December 6, 1990.

based or sexually promiscuous, or prostitutes, representing the mother of puberty whom the child has discovered to be sexually active. The man rescues their virtue, convinced of their need of him. These women are overvalued, like the mother, and belong to another man. Jealousy is a component of this choice, and the men have a series of such relationships because none proves satisfactory.

Meyer (1984) described Gladstone, Mackenzie King, and other famous men who spent their lives rescuing a series of fallen, degraded women to redeem them from their lives of sex. Some, like George Gissing, fell in love and married two of them, both marriages ending in disaster. Meyer calls the split which forbids love of a suitable woman "neurotic exogamy," a defense against incest. Rescue bestows upon the beneficiary power and invulnerability—attributes of the phallic woman.

Meyer reasons that Pygmalion, written just after Shaw's mother had a stroke, was a rescue of his mother through a lowly woman, redeemed through perfection of speech. Higgins says to Eliza (Mrs. Shaw's middle name): "Five minutes ago you were a millstone around my neck. Now you're a tower of strength."

TYPES OF RESCUE FANTASIES

AMBIVALENT RESCUE

In contrast to the tender rescue of the mother and father is the defiant or ambivalent rescue of the father who has first been put in danger. Ten-year-old Sam, the son of a TV personality, a narcissistic character full of rage and revenge, repeatedly played out a rescue fantasy in which he was the police lieutenant on the beat reporting to me as the chief at headquarters. In his rounds he discovers a bank hold-up in which several well-known TV personalities (not including his father) have been taken hostage. Full of intense rage he takes the criminals prisoner and frees the hostages.

Esman (1987), reviewing rescue fantasies, writes that Stekel (1911) first noted the aggressive conflict in such rescue fantasies, the projection of the hostility and reaction formation against it. Abraham (1922) further elaborated the concept to include both the father and rival siblings as well as mother's rescue of an infant out of her fear of smothering it.

Lori, an 8-year-old girl, entered therapy for nightmares. She feared that a robber would kidnap her or her little sister. She said that, since the family was not rich, the children could not be held for ransom, so she reasoned that the kidnapper would be someone who had been unable to adopt a baby. In her puppet play, the baby prince wanders off. The Devil gives him the wrong directions to the Safeway store and kidnaps him. The older sisters search, find the Devil, and trick him, rescuing the prince. The Devil and all his disguises are then put in jail. In therapy Lori came to recognize the hostility behind her nightmares. She said, "When I learned that my mother was pregnant again, I was very upset. I was a princess for seven years and got used to it."

Sometimes the reaction formations are not so complete. A 35-year-old woman recalled that her mother sometimes left her alone with younger siblings from the time she was 6. She would pretend that the house caught fire, then put her brothers in a baby carriage, stuff it with toys, and rush them out of the house. There was more ambivalence after a sister was born. She rowed her to the middle of a lake, preoccupied with thoughts of rescuing her should they capsize; she wheeled her in her carriage past the Gypsies, but always went fast so her little sister would not be kidnapped. And in her fire-rescue play, as we uncovered in her analysis, she always managed to leave one sibling behind.

As she got older, this patient accepted a martyr role to rescue her little sister who had a marked physical deformity. The patient, in altruistic surrender, mothered her sister, protected her from critical remarks, gave her her own possessions, and viewed herself as the ugly one. The recovery of these rescue fantasies and enactments in her analysis led to the patient's first awareness that she had felt any ambivalence toward her siblings.

Sometimes there is even greater breakdown of the reactive rescue fantasy, with the hostile elements gaining more prominence. A 30-year-old doctor came for therapy after he had learned from his older sister that she had been sexually abused as a child by their father. He feared that he might abuse his infant daughter. Early dreams were filled with violence and intruders. One night he woke with the firm conviction that he heard noises in the house. He woke his wife and told her they would go quietly next door and call the police. As they prepared to leave, she asked, "What about Lisa?" He replied, "Oh, she'll be all right, she's sound asleep in her room."

Many times I have been rescued from coronary events and other misfortunes in the fantasies of patients I have kept waiting longer than usual.

Freud (1901) wrote of the fantasy of a man rescuing a king. The rescuer throws himself in front of the king's horse while it is out of control and puts the king in danger. The horse is stopped and the king steps out, saying, "I owe my life to you. What can I do for you." Freud had this fantasy when he was alone in Paris before he had found his patron, Charcot. This fantasy is like the Oedipus myth. There is a chance meeting between son and father. The son risks his life for the father, the censorship transforming the attack into a rescue. The son stops the movement of the horse, the primal scene out-of-control sexuality. The son controls the horse, the masculine potency. The murder is repressed and enacted in a reaction formation.

FURTHER RESCUE FANTASIES

Freud mentioned rescue fantasies in later papers. In 1920, he described in homosexual women the same fantasies that normally occur in men, the rescue of promiscuous women. In 1922, Freud examined a dream previously reported by Rank, a woman's dream of rescuing a man from water. He concluded that it signified the wish to be the man's mother or to have a baby.

In 1928, Freud referred to a story by Stefan Zweig. A 42-year-old woman tries to save a young man the same age as her son from compulsive gambling and suicide. This involves her having sex with him. The rescue attempt fails and he goes back to his compulsive play. Freud interprets this as a puberty wish of a boy that the mother rescue him from the vice of masturbation by initiating him into sex.

Frosch (1959) described family romance rescue fantasies in the transference. The patient hopes to be rescued by regaining the idealized omnipotent parent in the analyst. This is similar to the phenomenon seen in the analysis of adopted children who fantasize that in the analyst they have found their natural parent and thus have been rescued from adoption.

In two psychobiographies, the authors demonstrated how the lives of the protagonists were influenced by the fact that they survived their brothers. Niederland (1981) tells how Schliemann (the discoverer of Troy), a replacement child, grew up next to the church graveyard where his older brother of the same name was buried. The author ascribes Schliemann's interest in excavating lost cities to survivor guilt and rescue of the brother. Glenn (1986) tells how Thornton Wilder's survivor guilt over the death of his twin brother at birth led to unconscious fantasies of rescue in his literary works and in his life.

COUNTERTRANSFERENCE RESCUE

Rescue fantasies in the analyst were first described by Greenacre. Esman (1987) writes, "Greenacre (1966) identified the tendency to ascribe the origin of psychopathological conditions to hostile or 'unempathic' external forces, and to confer on analysts/therapists the capacity to redress the effects of these malign forces through their 'corrective' or 'transmuting' influence" (p. 269). In such instances the analyst rescues the patient from the early villain who caused the illness.

These rescue fantasies are a special problem in the treatment of children and adolescents. Glenn et al. (1978) show the source of difficulty when the child analyst sees the parents as neglectful or abusive and tries to replace the "bad" parent with an ideal parent. But sometimes the parents try to force these attitudes on the analyst when they see him as a rescuer of the child and of the whole family.

Palmer et al. (1983) described an "adoption process" in residential treatment where the members of the staff live out rescue fantasies by taking the role of surrogate parents in a countertransference response to the family romance of the children.

Brinich (1980) spoke about rescue fantasies of adoptive parents whose unresolved oedipus conflict and guilt over stealing a child led them to inappropriate parental behavior.

In all these countertransference reactions, the role of villain is relegated to parents, relatives, or to previous therapists from whom the patient will be rescued. There is overidentification with the patient and a failure adequately to consider internal sources of conflict.

REPARATIVE RESCUE FANTASIES

Child analysts see rescue fantasies daily in their work. Perhaps the most frequent is in the undoing of death: soldiers, animals, dolls, and puppets are killed and then miraculously brought back to life. Another class of these fantasies has to do with mastering trauma or restoring narcissistic equilibrium.

Matthew, an adopted boy, was 3 years old on a transatlantic ship with his parents. During a fire drill everyone went on deck and donned life jackets. When the drill was over, the father put Matthew's life jacket back on in order to take a picture of him because he looked so cute in it. Matthew panicked because he thought that he, the only one in a life jacket, was about to be thrown overboard. The frightening event was represented later in Matthew's analysis by pirate play in which he made his victims walk the plank. This was an overdetermined fantasy since by the time he was 3 his mother was feeling overwhelmed by his hyperactivity and wondered why she had ever adopted him. After the trauma at sea, Matthew became intrigued with matches and tried to light fires. At 5 he played out a rescue fantasy: he piled boxes and papers in the form of an archway in his basement, set fire to the pile, and darted through to rescue something on the other side. Far from mastering the trauma, he was severely burned and hospitalized for several weeks.

Sam, the 10-year-old boy who rescued TV personalities, was very unpopular in school, scorned and ostracized by his peers because he was so self-centered and unable to yield any ground. A fantasy he recounted to me pictured an attack on the school from outer space. He would then press a secret button known only to him, disclosing a spaceship buried on the school grounds. He took command of it, fought off the intruders, and became a school figure, just as famous as his father who was a public figure.

NARCISSISM, MASOCHISM, AND THE SECRET BENEFACTOR

Harold, a 32-year-old summa cum laude Rhodes scholar, came to analysis because he had lost four jobs in four years. In each case he had imagined his boss to have the extraordinary first-class mind he was looking to associate with. In each case he was disappointed to find his boss ordinary and superficial. He would react by withdrawing and sulking until he was asked to leave.

At 6 years of age Harold and his older brother were left in the care of an aunt and uncle at the start of World War II since both parents were in military service. The older brother became the companion of the uncle, while Harold withdrew and became the fantasied companion of the Lone Ranger. He and the Lone Ranger went on many escapades together. If one of them was captured, the other was immediately at hand to rescue him. They loved each other totally, and if one proclaimed his love, the other was proclaiming it simultaneously. Harold grew up a narcissistic personality with a problem of homosexuality, constantly searching for both women and men who fit his fantasy of complete mutuality and mirroring, whom he could rescue and be rescued by at moments of narcissistic impoverishment. This is the only case I know where the boy identified with a boy companion, a demeaned role to most children, rather than with the hero.

The Lone Ranger, like the cowboy in the classic Western, is a secret benefactor. His identity is unknown. The story has both an oedipal and a latency cast. The stranger comes to town, overthrows the evil man, and restores the town to the forces of good. A beautiful girl falls in love with him, but the hero rides off into the sunset, never claiming his love object.

Widzer (1977) shows that, like the cowboy, the comic book hero is a shared communal myth in which narcissism and omnipotence are restored in an idealized hero who acts out forbidden fantasies. Unlike the hero of antiquity who also takes revenge on the father and rescues the kingdom from wrongful rulers, these more current heroes are not accorded their birthright to the kingdom. Their identity remains secret. More modern stories again resemble the myths of the ancients. In the *Star Wars* trilogy Darth Vader is unmasked, and Luke eventually regains power in his own identity (Rojcewicz, 1987). In the original story, Superman is rescued in infancy when his scientist father places him in a space capsule before their planet Krypton explodes. He is adopted on earth by a humble couple and then, when he reaches maturity, uses his great strength to rescue people from calamity and evil. In the first strip he is defined as: "Superman, champion of the oppressed, the physical marvel who had sworn to devote his existence to helping those in need" (Feiffer, 1965). In *The Myth of the Birth of the Hero* (Rank, 1914), the natural mother is idealized, while an animal or a devalued woman of humble origin adopts and suckles the hero. In Superman's family romance, both sets of parents are disowned.

The secret identity shared by the Lone Ranger, Superman, Batman, the Scarlet Pimpernel (Orczy, 1898), Cyrano de Bergerac, and others is a significant aspect of these fantasies. The hero has to hide the power of his true identity. His narcissistic defenses protect him from oedipal conflict, and the secret identity means he can fight the evil powers and rescue the needy without jeopardizing his relationship to the family and without danger of punishment or castration.

Yet the secret identity contains both the wish for and fear of punishment. It represents a masochistic solution that can be understood in reference to beating fantasies (Freud, 1919; Ferber and Gray, 1966). For the boy, to be beaten is to be loved by the father. The conflict over passive feminine wishes results in sensitivity and irritability to anyone who represents the father. The feeling of being offended by the father figure brings back the imagined beating satisfaction. The repressed incestuous wish is satisfied regressively, whereas the castration threat is defended against or undone. The boy can maintain a fantasy of control or omnipotence in getting someone to mistreat him, but he cannot bring his competitiveness and achievement into the open. The danger is twofold: on the one hand, he will be punished by the authority he has tried to conquer; on the other hand, in projecting his hostility, he will be overthrown by the competitors he has surpassed and by the children he has fathered.

In his disguise as Clark Kent, the humble reporter, Superman is demeaned. He has to obey. He is threatened with rejection by his boss and is devalued and scorned by Lois Lane who sees him as impotent. He gets his revenge against the evil father, but sexuality is repressed. He may steal the father's phallic power, but he cannot openly use it.

The Scarlet Pimpernel is about a daring, impudent man who, in his various disguises, saves French nobility from the guillotine. The scarlet pimpernel is a humble, English, wayside flower whose petals close at the approach of bad weather. This is the manifest identity of Sir Percy Blakeney in real life: he appears as a lazy man with an inane laugh, sleepy, dull, and stupid. He is ridiculed by his wife and her noble guests, and he is too stupid even to notice.

CASE REPORT

I will present the case of a man who incorporates many aspects of the secret benefactor and rescuer. He was able to have a sexual relationship with the women he rescued, but he could not become a father. Mr. B. was of French origin, a tall divorced man in his 40s. At our first meeting he greeted me with a handshake with a grossly deformed right hand; then, as I stood in a corner, rushed past me, slapped his New York *Times* on my table, picked up my phone, and said, "I have to call my office. I left the safe open." It was only after several years that I saw the helpless passive man who wished to be treated in the hospital with sodium amytal. He complained of nervous tension, depression, spastic colon, a history of ulcers, a short temper on the job, and poor relations with "a woman who is no good for me." He had been hospitalized briefly with depression and crying spells 3 years earlier when his wife left him. After 12 years of shifting jobs as a newspaperman in Europe, he was now at a desk job where he felt stuck under his boss.

He was the second of four children in an immigrant family. His father was a flamboyant man, a house builder, who was both violent and paranoid. At various times he was either hospitalized or jailed. He beat his wife, and he beat his oldest son, the mother's favorite. The older brother wrestled, headlocked, scissors-gripped, cuffed, and tormented the patient. A younger brother who slept with the patient for 14 years, became paranoid schizophrenic with fears of homosexual assault.

The mother had grand hysterical seizures. The patient recalled his terror and helplessness when he was 5 and witnessed one of these seizures when he was alone with her. He was astonished how quickly a seizure stopped when his father unexpectedly arrived home. In later years he recognized the sexual symbolism in the seizures. The mother was a martyr who confided in the patient how much she was made to suffer at the father's hands, but she criticized him, controlled him, and provoked him to rage. Like the father, she was a perfectionist who drove the children to complete their chores.

A younger sister was the father's favorite. She was the only one who could go directly to him to ask for what she wanted rather than go through the mother as intermediary.

In this chaotic family, the patient was brilliant and creative. He helped his mother all day Saturday with chores, and he helped his father every afternoon and all summer. He acted as his father's secretary, composing and typing letters under his father's name. He became his father's building helper, feeling that only by doing the impossible could he get any recognition. He began to draw remodeling plans under his father's name. At the age of 12 he solved a difficult remodeling problem and by the age of 16 could plan and remodel an entire house by himself: the drawings, the carpentry, masonry, electrical work, the plumbing. By 17 he maintained and collected rents from 40 apartments. He was also a charming boy, a teacher's pet, a fine scholar, an accomplished violinist, and modeled in clay.

There were instances in which the superhuman accomplishments continued into his adult life. It was as if only by doing the impossible could he gain his father's admiration and his mother's love. At the age of 12 he had climbed a 3-story ladder with a hod of bricks in one hand. As an adult, after losing the fingers of his right hand, he climbed a 75-foot rope ladder to cover a newspaper story. Similarly, with one hand he built an outdoor brick barbeque for a friend in freezing weather. In his current job he spent almost the entire day writing or typing with his left hand rather than using dictating equipment.

He complained that his parents did not always give him credit for his work, but we discovered that much of what he did was done in secret with the hope that they would discover it and give him great praise. When I pointed out how much he had been the secret benefactor, how much he had been his father's ghost-writer and ghost-builder, he replied, "Of course, my favorite story was the Scarlet Pimpernel."

As a teenager, the patient had been instrumental in helping to get his violent father jailed and committed to a mental hospital. At 17 after a fight with his father he ran away from home to his uncle's house. When he struck his little cousin in a rage, his aunt said, "You should lose your hands for that." He took a job in a factory. With the conscious intent of pleasing his boss by cleaning his machine, he caught his right hand in the rollers where it was mangled and he lost his thumb and fingers.

After his hospitalization, skin grafts, and recovery, he went to an Ivy League college under a rehabilitation program (where he had an affair with the social worker who was helping him), then found a job as a newspaperman, writing under a pseudonym for fear that if his whereabouts were known, his father would extract revenge for their fights and for the time the patient helped to have him jailed for violence.

He moved to France after World War II and worked as a ghost-writer, benefiting others. When I first met him he was translating literary works into French under someone else's name. Twice he over-threw the president of a fraternal organization but disappeared when he was about to be elected president himself. In another instance he left his job just when he was about to be promoted to branch chief. In his current job as a writer he consistently gave co-workers ideas that they put forth as their own. As he became aware of his "force behind the throne but never the throne," he revealed that he had devised a traffic plan for Paris that was later published under someone else's name. Like Clark Kent, the Scarlet Pimpernel, Cyrano, and the masked rescuers, he hid his true identity.

While he hid his own contributions, his rescue of women was more open. He recalled at age 6 hearing his mother moaning and groaning. He ran into the bedroom to rescue her only to be greeted by her "What are you doing here? Get the hell out of here." Later he would rescue her by secretly doing chores she needed done, redoing chores assigned to his negligent brother, and by being her eager assistant in getting his father jailed or hospitalized.

His first marriage was to a women he rescued from war-torn France. She was abandoned by her husband, pregnant, penniless, and phys-ically sick. The eight years of marriage were stormy, marked by acri-mony and acts of revenge. Like his father, he struck his wife on occa-sion. He helped care for her illegitimate son. She had five abortions during the marriage, some of which took place when he did not even know she was pregnant, and some of which were the result of sexual affairs. He could never want a child of his own. He lost interest in her when she became successful in her own career and no longer needed rescuing.

The woman he was living with when I first met him became his second wife during the period of psychotherapy. She was also aban-doned by her first husband, physically ill, and penniless, the family fortune having been wiped out in the war. She had no chance of citizenship unless she married the patient, a marriage which would seriously jeopardize his career. Their brief marriage was marked by a stormy sadomasochistic relationship and her many affairs she freely told him about.

He married his third wife three years later during his analysis. He rescued her from a sadistic husband who unfortunately was a co-worker who successfully sued him for "criminal conversation and al-ienation of affection." While the first two wives represented the for-lorn, abandoned prostitute mother, this wife was the idealized mother.

Mr. B. entered therapy with an urgency to get things done and was chronically dissatisfied with his lack of progress, sometimes shouting at me for my poor performance. He externalized problems to his boss and his wife, constantly struggling to control anger with his boss and violence with his wife. He handled his guilt by becoming the slave-driving father and the perfectionist mother. From behind this fault finding, however, emerged a wish for reassurance and intense passive wishes for me to repeat the hospital sleep treatment he had previously experienced. But these wishes were in conflict: he recalled that at 10, hospitalized for infected tonsils, he thought he heard the doctors saying they would "have to cut it off."

If I was too silent he experienced me as about to kick him out—the calm before the storm. He secretly felt that he knew more than I and his boss, a feeling he handled by being too aggressive or too obsequious. He chronically feared abandonment and loneliness. A key memory was lying in bed sick at 2½, completely alone, rescued by an uncle who brought a bright red fire engine. But dependency feelings, feelings of caring or closeness were systematically defended against by indifference, denial, and identification with the aggressor. He recalled calmly sipping a martini when the telegram arrived announcing his father's death. It was many months before I learned that his father, too, had an injured right hand and depended on the patient's skills. The family lore was that the patient had injured his hand on the anniversary of the father's injury.

Much of the psychotherapy addressed his identification with the aggressor which warded off guilt and passive wishes, and his defenses against any warmth or caring. He became aware of the relief from tension he would feel if he could provoke punishment. I began to show him that tension occurred with thoughts of success. I had not considered psychoanalysis as a treatment for him because of his chaotic upbringing, his propensity for externalization which at times seemed to border on the paranoia from which his father and brother suffered, his two bouts with ulcers, and his decompensation after his first wife left him. After he broke up with his second wife in the fourth year of treatment he became intensely anxious. We increased the frequency of meetings from two to three times a week. He felt relief, but I began to notice a sense of sticky dependency: he began to look at me more and more closely, frequently studied me for reassurance, and sought clues to how interested I was in his productions and how much I approved or disapproved of what he was seeing.

THE ANALYSIS

In this setting of what I felt was a dependency unresolvable in our psychotherapy, I recommended analysis at four times a week. He readily complied but experienced the shift as a rejection of all he had done before. It confirmed his feelings of inadequacy, which he customarily abated by doing the impossible. Two events from the long psychotherapy were interferences in the beginning of analysis. First, I had given him some medication early in the psychotherapy, and this was a frequent request at the start of analysis. Second, during the therapy I had inquired about his role in the sadomasochistic relationship with his second wife. He had heard this as a criticism, and the focus on what took place outside the therapy made externalization easier for him.

The beginning of analysis was stormy and dramatic. His obsessional defenses, along with surface denial and indifference, were breached by onrushing transference feelings as he lay on the couch. He saw the analysis as an operating room, as a seduction: "What if I go to sleep? What if I become sexually excited?" He experienced free association as a pressure for performance in the father transference. In the second session he reported a dream: "I was in a room like a hotel and three men were beating me. I phoned you and you were very comforting, then you started to assault me sexually. I beat you with a stick, then I was with a woman and children and phoned you again at home." He added that in the dream I was charming and loving, and he thought, "He does have a bedside manner in his Sunday suit."

He wondered if his brother had ever tied and beaten him. His brother beat him in boxing, but the patient always came back for more. He remembered as a young child going to the store with his mother: when she said she ought to buy a whip, he found one for her. He recalled his wartime experience of seeing mutilated corpses. Suddenly he cried convulsively, thrashed around on the couch, knocking the pillow off, moaning. Although he had told me during psychotherapy about his hospital experience at 17 following his hand injury, he now relived it in its full fury and terror. He told how he woke to find his hand amputated. He recalled the skin grafts, his subsequent anger and tears, the phantom pain. He remembered his mother fainting, his brother's contempt, and the aunt who could not look at it. He continued the next day mourning the loss of his many skills—clay modeling, violin playing, caressing his mother, all his building skills. He told how people never appreciated his handicaps; he recounted many humiliating experiences. He had never told either wife the hospital details. And neither wife ever fully realized he could not open a Coke with a bottle opener. As he regained his composure, he said, "Now I realize what you meant, that I was keeping out my feelings. My feelings were amputated."

I was shaken by what analysis had unleashed, but Mr. B. soon re-established his defense of identification with the aggressor, by becoming the tyrant father who shouted at me for my poor performance, or the perfectionist mother who pointed out my failures. While he focused on his fear of attack in the transference, I focused on his fear of caring and tenderness. He said that many people had told him they were afraid of him because of his severe manner; they called him inhuman because of his indifference. Studied indifference, a goal he had tried to achieve since early childhood, protected against any hurt. He comforted himself further with what he called "secret revenge fantasies." He enacted the comforting thought, "I can get along without you," by doing the most difficult tasks with his left hand, constantly defying any sense that his body was damaged.

Within the first three months of analysis he impulsively began an affair with the woman who was to become his third wife at the end of the second year of analysis. The transference was split between me and the wife, the latter treated like the mother: he felt it was his task always to make her feel happy.

In the transference he felt that the timed analytic sessions held him prisoner like when he typed for his father and could not even go to the bathroom until he was dismissed. One day he came in excited. He had recalled memorizing Hamlet's soliloquy at 15. He now saw the oedipus complex, his own insight, with his new woman friend, L., as the mother and her children as his rivals. He found himself coming in second best again. In a dream I reached down and touched his shoulder. He turned around and I looked like L.'s husband. He screamed in terror and awoke. The triadic rivalry was sharpened further a few weeks later when he told me that L.'s husband was one of the co-workers who took the patient's secret ideas and got credit for the work. In his wish for and fear of closeness he turned me into a woman in a transference dream; he recalled a fleeting fantasy of kissing a colleague's penis. He associated closeness to the mutilating hospital experience and recalled how much easier it was for his sister to confront their father and win his admiration.

In the course of the work we discovered that the patient was a secret analyzer. He did a great deal of analysis at home, even tape recording his free associations, working hard as he did for his parents without sufficient recognition. Unknown to me for a long time, he was secretly competing with me, as he had done with his father, but because the work was kept secret, he constantly suffered narcissistic loss. He was the capable boy who could build an entire house by himself for his father. So long as he worked in secret his grandiose fantasies knew no bounds, but the solution was essentially masochistic: he never got credit in his own name. He had been embarrassed by his teacher's praise as a boy, thinking to himself, "I come from such a violent family, I don't deserve it."

His secret admiration for his father and the wish to be admired now entered the transference. For the first time he began to work on his fear of success. He recalled that he could never take credit for his own work lest his father retaliate. He knew too much: his mother had confided secrets of his father's violence to him, and he was constantly in fear of revealing the guilty knowledge. On his first job he wrote newspaper stories under a *nom de plume* and later he did translations under his wife's name. I noted that he never had become head of a family under his own name. He brought into the analysis his inhibition at work, his fear of writing creatively in relation to the father figures in the office. His fear of success and retaliation and his feeling that he did not deserve praise resulted in his giving his co-workers the fruits of his insights and not taking credit for his work. At first, Mr. B. kept his analysis secret from his wife. He associated to the conflict of allegiance in childhood: closeness to mother was a betrayal to father, but she interposed herself between them. He called himself a "guerilla fighter."

By the third year of analysis there were gains at work. He was no longer so anxious around his boss, and he was able to ask for what he needed rather than demand and apologize. He was writing more freely and using dictating equipment to make it easier. However, as his wife became the recipient of the tender mother transference and as Mr. B. planned for the first time in his life to buy a house of his own, he became impotent. He had a dream about an aggressive woman, who stood for the sadistic relationships characteristic of his first two marriages. He associated to the enemas his mother had given him. He was furious with the analyst who supposedly was working on fear of success, meanwhile providing a treatment that brought the worst failure of all. His potency returned as he worked on the mother transference to his wife and after a meeting at work in which there was full recognition of his contribution.

He settled into a more tender loving marriage than he had had before and became a mentor to his stepson. For the first time he had a home of his own. Even in childhood he had lived in a succession of houses under construction. For the first time I heard joy and enthusiasm, but he became depressed whenever his wife was unhappy. He recalled how hard he had worked for his mother to make her happy, but the work was mostly in secret because open praise was so embarrassing to him. He judged his accomplishments as nothing compared to his secret goals of restoring harmony in his family. He said, "I unpromote myself." Underneath was the grandiose fantasy, "I could have won my mother if I had done more." He recalled a long-standing rescue fantasy in which he saves a helpless woman who is afraid of attack. Because of her fears, he recognizes her impulses, and this advantage enables him to seduce her to have an affair.

I addressed the mother transference, how hard he worked for me in secret, and how he must have felt slighted when I failed to recognize what he had done. Associating to disappointment, his thoughts led to abandonment and loneliness in childhood. With two younger siblings coming in rapid succession he lost his mother and turned to his father. Now, as he trusted me more, he remembered that, in fact, his father had had great confidence in him: his father was not the enemy. He recalled for the first time how closely he had had to watch his father's eyes to catch his father's shifting moods. We now understood his dependent searching of my expression that had led to my recommending psychoanalysis.

In connection with loneliness and abandonment, he revealed character traits of delaying completion of projects: this extended not only to papers at work but to many aspects of his life, putting off as long as possible the completion of sex, eating, masturbation. In retrospect I felt these associations anticipated the ending of analysis.

Mr. B. was now showing his work to his boss who put him in charge of a crisis project, introducing him as "a man of many talents." He recalled both his father and older brother asking him, "Is that all you did today?" He finally recognized the teasing character of such remarks. He was excited by his new position and feared a heart attack or that the project would be taken from him. When I reminded him of the fears of retaliation by his older brother, he revealed for the first time his creative work in gardening and cabinet making, saying, in a brother transference, he always feared I would laugh at him if he told me.

He was now able to see his wife separately from his view of his mother. He dared to expose his vulnerabilities to her, even asking her not to go away on an optional trip because of his loneliness. He was finally able to integrate the two maternal pictures: the picture of the primal scene mother, beaten by father, suffering hysterical fits, versus the warm tender maternal relationship that he had avoided in his earlier marriages. He recalled, "I used to think that only a forlorn woman could care for me."

A significant turning point occurred when, through the transference, he was able to recapture tender, loving feelings of admiration for his father. With a lifting of repression he recalled his enthusiasm as a boy of 5, sexually excited as he climbed a pole, slipping and straining to see his father coming home from work. His mother had tried to restrain his enthusiasm, his brother laughed at him.

As the final summer vacation approached, he said, "You're like Linus's blanket, you're my mother and not my mother. I have trouble with separation. I didn't walk until I was 18 months old. Maybe I'll leave on vacation before you do." It was at this point that I suggested he had thoughts about ending the analysis.

A few days later he said, "I've worked it all out over the weekend, but I haven't told you yet." Tearfully he spoke of how much he had wished to be close to his father after turning from his mother. But closeness to father felt like a surrender: open praise felt feminine. He remembered at age 6 cutting off his curly forelock that had been so admired. He had the fantasy that when people discovered what he had done in secret, the admiration would be boundless. He recalled how proud he was for not spilling his food like the little ones, and for being able to hold his urine in school. He recalled how proud he had been of his father who had come to the United States an immigrant and then owned his own hardware store.

With further resolution of his negative oedipal conflicts he achieved a new, mutually cooperative relationship with his boss. He had now finished a paper under his own name and was getting full recognition for his contributions. Of one project his boss said, "I'm putting you in charge of this because you know more about it than anyone else." In the next session the patient said, "Being a boss and being in the open is like the Perils of Pauline." I reminded him that Pauline was the name of his cute little sister who openly approached their father and got his love.

After he returned from vacation, he worked on a paper entitled "Analytic Survey." He said the main work was completed. As we talked of termination, his self-analysis also came into the open. He felt depressed, saying, "I can do nothing." He saw his boss as human and frail and the analyst as less than omniscient. Then in recovery he said, "But I'm my own boss, I don't need that kind of approval anymore." He reviewed how he had turned to his father, but "feared his embrace." I said that he never let anyone know his wish, but it was gratified through arguments and punishment. He replied, "I can't be a great guy and a victim at the same time." As we reviewed his formerly secret wishes to admire and be admired, he said, "It would be found out that I was a woman. My second wife used to refer to you as my 'lover.' I never could admit I wanted to come here."

A date for ending was set three months hence. He recalled a dream from his early therapy of being strapped to a chair with his brother. He was aware of his conflicts over leaving: he had thoughts of ending precipitously, and thoughts of symptoms and problems that might extend the date. He reminded me that he had not given up smoking. He cried, "It can't be that the end of analysis means so much."

He and his wife had been trying unsuccessfully to have a baby. They were now discussing adoption. He had ideas for writing a novel. On the last day he had thoughts of not showing up but came "to sever the umbilical cord and have a Bar Mitzvah." He added, "I have worked for years with political and information analysts, but I have never experienced such careful analysis of details as this." Two years later I received a card that he was the father of twins.

DISCUSSION AND SUMMARY

I have presented an overview of rescue fantasies beginning with Freud's 1910 paper in which the rescued fallen woman represented the sexually active mother. Later papers and my own clinical vignettes from both adult and child cases demonstrate the ambivalence, the reaction formation against hostility, and guilt inherent in many rescues, especially the boy's rescue of the father. Lori's rescue of the baby prince and the woman who rescued her little brothers from an invented fire demonstrated the ambivalence characteristic of rescue fantasy of siblings. The doctor whose fear of harming his daughter led to dreams of intruders actually abandoned her while seeking help from a fantasied intruder.

The narcissistic reparative component of rescue play is seen commonly in work with children. This is enacted through identification with the aggressor in traumatized children as exemplified in the case of Matthew who played with fire. Narcissistic restoration was evident in Sam's Walter Mitty rescue of his school from the outer space invaders.

In our culture a special type of popular rescue fantasy is the story of the cowboy Western hero, interchangeable with the masked or incognito comic book hero. This is the story of the secret benefactor who is a stranger or whose identity is otherwise unknown or kept hidden. The omnipotent adventures of the hero are attempts to solve conflicts over dependence, phallic-oedipal conflicts, and conflicts of latency. Heroic phallic acts are performed to impress the mother, but the hero's identity must remain secret. He fears castration by the retaliatory father, but he must also defend against his wishes to be loved and admired by the father. After the heroic act he disappears: the cowboy rides off into the sunset, Superman becomes Clark Kent. This is essentially a mas-

ochistic solution through demeaning experiences, sadomasochistic relationships, and beating fantasies. The hero never gets credit for his
achievements.

The analysis of Mr. B. revealed many essentials of the character of
the secret benefactor. He combined Freud's oedipal object choice of
fallen promiscuous women with the need to keep his heroic acts secret.
He attempted to achieve narcissistic omnipotence through masochistic
solutions. His analysis revealed that his need to keep his remarkable
achievements secret represented both positive and negative oedipal
solutions, to ward off the fantasied revenge of his violent father on the
one hand, and to ward off the dangerous wish to be loved and admired
by his father on the other hand. Unresolved dependency wishes had
enhanced his attachment to his father after he had felt rejected by his
mother who, he believed, favored the older brother and produced two
younger siblings.

In his analysis he recalled the childhood fantasy, "I could have won
my mother if I had done more." Twice in his life he acted directly on his
oedipal fantasies. At age 6, hearing his mother cry for help, he rushed
into her bedroom to save her, only to be cruelly rebuffed. At 14 he
assisted in committing his father to a mental hospital. On his return
home he announced, "Now there are going to be some changes around
here." His mother rebuffed him again. After that his solutions were
typically masochistic. At 17 after a physical fight with his father he ran
away from home only to mangle his right hand in a factory machine a
few days later. His name and identity were systematically deleted from
his work from that time on. In his analysis he kept his extensive self-
analysis a secret.

Complementary to the understanding of Mr. B.'s rescue fantasies
was the understanding of the character traits that maintained his neurotic compromises. Although he was sexually active, he could not be
caring or intimate with women or men. He cultivated a haughty indifference and a severe countenance that put people off. His need to do
the impossible coupled with his fear of success left him working too
hard, victimized, and exploited. Frequently he could not complete his
work. He could not simply ask for anything for himself but became
demanding, argumentative, or obsequious.

His first two wives were fallen promiscuous women with whom he
had sadomasochistic relationships. Through analysis he was able to
love tenderly again and bring his achievements into the open. Pruett
(1985) quotes Dostoevsky: "Only when I became a father did I begin to
notice my own father's tender and intimate nurturing qualities" (p.
435). With Mr. B. it was the reverse: it was only after he was able to get

in touch with these qualities in his father and himself that he could become a father in his own right.

The work of an analyst in many ways resembles the life of the secret benefactor. Among them are the analyst's incognito, the fact that most of his work is done in secret and is never known outside the consulting room, and even when the work is reported, it is masked. Psychoanalysts must guard against countertransference attitudes and enactments that lead them to attempt to rescue patients, whether by replacing a bad parent with an ideal parent (Greenacre, 1966), or becoming a surrogate parent (Palmer et al., 1983), or rescuing patients from current parents (Glenn et al., 1978), spouses, lovers, and many varieties of enactments. The analysis of the secret benefactor alerts us not only to our manifold propensities for rescue, but also to the possibilities of defenses erected against such impulses. Countertransference attitudes derived from our patients' wish to be rescued and our own rescue fantasies can manifest themselves in inhibitions and reaction formations against the rescue attitudes as much as in the impulses themselves.

The impetus behind the popularity and ubiquity of the superhero rescue fantasy derives from its family romance quality (Freud, 1909), from "the devaluation of the mother and the revenge against and the eventual triumph over the father. Accordingly, every version of the family romance contains not only a symbolic oedipal victory, but also the symbolic presentation of defenses against the anxieties and fears that accompany and underlie this conflict. Every superhero demonstrates these qualities, manifested either in the manner in which the hero obtains his powers, or in the quality of his identity, his object relations, and his interaction with the environment" (Widzer, 1977, p. 572).

BIBLIOGRAPHY

ABRAHAM, K. (1922). The rescue and murder of the father in neurotic phantasy-formations. In *Clinical Papers and Essays in Psychoanalysis*. New York: Basic Books, 1955, pp. 68–75.

BRINICH, P. M. (1980). Some potential effects of adoption on self and object representations. *Psychoanal. Study Child*, 35:107–133.

ESMAN, A. H. (1987). Rescue fantasies. *Psychoanal. Q.*, 56:263—270.

FEIFFER, J. (1965). *The Great Comic Book Heroes*. New York: Dial Press.

FERBER, L. & GRAY, P. (1966). Beating fantasies. *Bull. Philadelphia Assn. Psychoanal.*, 16:186–206.

FREUD, S. (1901). The psychopathology of everyday life. *S.E.*, 6.

—— (1909). Family romances. *S.E.*, 9:235–241.

—— (1910). A special type of choice of object made by men. *S.E.*, 11:163–175.

—— (1919). 'A child is being beaten.' *S.E.*, 17:175–204.

—— (1920). The psychogenesis of a case of homosexuality in a woman. *S.E.*, 18:145–172.

—— (1922). Dreams and telepathy. *S.E.*, 18:195–220.

—— (1928). Dostoevsky and parricide. *S.E.*, 21:175–196.

FROSCH, J. (1959). Transference derivatives of the family romance. *J. Amer. Psychoanal. Assn.*, 7:503–522.

GLENN, J. (1986). Twinship themes and fantasies in the work of Thornton Wilder. *Psychoanal. Study Child*, 41:627–651.

—— SABOT, L. M., & BERNSTEIN, I. (1978). The role of the parents in child analysis. In *Child Analysis and Therapy*, ed. J. Glenn. New York: Aronson, pp. 393–426.

GREENACRE, P. (1966). Problems of overidealization of the analyst and of analysis. In *Emotional Growth*, vol. 2. New York: Int. Univ. Press, 1971, pp. 743–761.

MEYER, B. C. (1984). Some observations on the rescue of fallen women. *Psychoanal. Q.*, 53:208–239.

NIEDERLAND, W. G. (1981). An analytic inquiry into the life and work of Heinrich Schliemann. In *Lives, Events, and Other Players*, ed. J. T. Coltrera. New York: Aronson, pp. 175–202.

ORCZY, E. (1898). *The Scarlet Pimpernel*. New York: Airmont, 1963.

PALMER, A., HARPER, G., & RIVINUS, T. (1983). The "adoption process" in the inpatient treatment of children and adolescents. *J. Amer. Acad. Child Psychiat.*, 22:286–293.

PRUETT, K. D. (1985). Oedipal configurations in young father-raised children. *Psychoanal. Study Child*, 40:435–456.

RANK, O. (1914). *The Myth of the Birth of the Hero and Other Writings*. New York: Vintage Books, 1959.

ROJCEWICZ, S. (1987). Darth Vader. *J. Poetry Ther.*, 1:23–30.

STEKEL, W. (1911). Einige Bemerkungen zur Rettungsphantasie und die Analyse eines Rettungstraumes. *Zbl. Psychoanal. & Psychother.*, 1:591–593.

WIDZER, M. E. (1977). The comic-book superhero. *Psychoanal. Study Child*, 32:565–603.

The Boy from Outer Space

An Exploration of Psychotic Catastrophe

JANET MACDONALD

> A man's life-work is no more than a long journey to
> find again, by all the detours of art, the two or three
> powerful images on which his being opened for the
> first time.
>
> CAMUS 1937

*This is an account of the initial stages in the analysis of Morton, a
latency-age boy. Morton is an unusually interesting case for the exploration of fantasy, to which "we must look for the study of early mental
phenomena because phantasy is the* lingua franca *of that period"
(Grotstein, 1977, p. 412).*

MORTON WAS AN INTROVERTED CHILD, WHO WAS ABLE TO REFLECT DEEPLY
and was articulate in conveying his insights. I felt that he was struggling, in his own way, to reconstruct his shattered internal world. Because Morton was so eloquent and had so much to say about his own
condition, I have allowed considerable space for his voice to come
through.

The paper's theoretical background is derived from the tradition of
Freud, Melanie Klein, and W. R. Bion. More particularly, I have drawn
on the writings of James Grotstein, whose emphasis on primitive, preoedipal states seems particularly applicable to the treatment of borderline children; and I owe a debt of gratitude to Frances Tustin,

---

Tavistock-trained child psychotherapist, who worked for Brighton Health Authority,
East Sussex, England, and is now based in London. In preparing this paper, I acknowledge a debt to Mrs. Francis Tustin, with whom I discussed some of this case material,
and to Dr. James Grotstein for his comments. The views and opinions expressed are, of
course, entirely my own.

whose thinking about her work with autistic children has provided me with concepts which retrospectively illuminate the autosensual aspects of my patient's material.

Morton showed many characteristics of the borderline state, particularly the schizoid end of the spectrum. By borderline, I am referring to those patients whose development is arrested at a transitional phase between the formation of a body ego and that of a normal division between mind and body, where symbolic representation is possible. This transitional phase between autosensualism and symbiosis is a decisive one if development is to proceed normally.

Underlying my thinking is the hypothesis that psychic development is evolutionary, with one phase following through another. The success of later phases is determined, to some extent, by the quality of experience of earlier phases.

My present focus is on early psychotic catastrophe: the infantile psychotic state described by Bion (1962) which follows a state of organismic panic. Mine is, in a sense, an archaeological perspective, insofar as the schizophrenic personality develops out of the ruins of a catastrophe. I am trying to follow my patient's fantasies, which are active in the present, back into his earliest past in an attempt to reconstruct the causes and circumstances of his breakdown.

CLINICAL MATERIAL

Morton, the eldest of two children, was born to British parents in Borneo. Despite a difficult delivery, Morton settled well in the early months and apparently did not present any problems. His mother confessed to me that she had felt inexperienced in handling a baby; in retrospect, she wondered if she had had a close enough relationship with her son during his babyhood.

The family returned to Britain when Morton was ready to start infant school and about the time that their second son was born. Although Morton at first adapted happily to school, he later experienced times of being deeply disturbed and disoriented. It was difficult for him to fit in with other children, both in class and in the playground. He tended to be solitary.

At home, as Morton grew older, he became increasingly absorbed in his own world of computers and electronics, areas where he was precocious. As he approached the age of transfer to secondary school, there were doubts as to whether he would be able to cope without some additional educational support and, possibly, psychotherapy. With this background in mind, I agreed to meet Morton and to make an assessment.

THE ASSESSMENT SESSIONS

Morton presented as a rather special being: shy and sensitive, and graceful in his bearing. Ruffled brown hair framed his small face; his brown eyes, enlarged by glasses, dominated his appearance. His innocence reminded me of a young primate, and he evoked tender, protective feelings, like those a mother feels for her dependent young. In the countertransference, Morton evoked in me the qualities of a primal self-object—one which functioned as a protective presence in the background, organizing and synthesizing (Grotstein, 1984).

Morton was ready to tell me about his problems. He admitted that he found it difficult to do things that other children did, such as tying up his shoelaces, catching a bus, or finding the sticky tape when it got lost at home. He also demonstrated some of his problems as he settled to work. He kept touching the desk with both hands several times. Then he moved his elbows against his body three or four times as if to keep himself going. He often clicked his fingernails, and "had to do" it four times on each finger, or four beats with each foot. Another habit was making all his fingers touch the arms of the chair: clenching four times and touching four times. He explained that he felt threatened; if he did not do these things, then he was worried that something awful would happen. This was a way of keeping himself feeling safe inside.

These absurd habits, as Morton called them, were very prominent during the assessment sessions and seemed to be a necessary accompaniment to his work, whether he was talking, or drawing, or playing at the desk. They declined in intensity in the course of the assessment sessions; but during treatment, in the first part of each session, Morton continued to display more dilute and less worrying rituals. These, in contrast to the absurd habits, seemed to be an attempt to seek a boundary. Touching something—other than a part of his body—that left a firm impression on his skin surface gave Morton a sense of self-definition and a sense of safety.

In contrast to his ineptitude with everyday tasks, Morton impressed me with his sophisticated knowledge of space, electronics, computers, and the like—areas where his grasp of ideas was patently superior to my own. I felt inadequate to judge much of what he said. He narrated a saga about two races from outer space who were involved in a long-running conflict over a piece of land, taken by one race from the other. I felt quite burdened by the detail of his story. On a deeper level, too,

Morton was having a depressing effect on me and giving me a powerful experience of what it was like to feel trapped, mute, helpless, and above all increasingly subordinated.

In a later session, each tribe in the space saga produced a superhero. Between them, they saved the situation. At the end of the story the two tribes were sent to prison—a rather advanced sort of prison, as one might expect in Morton's view of outer space. Here they began to learn that they did not need to be at war all the time; it was better to arrive at an agreement by political means than by fighting. The moral of the story was that thinking together was better than fighting.

Another kind of superhero emerged during the assessment sessions. What follows is an account taken from my notes:

> First, after much thought, Morton ruled a rectangular frame—a bound-ary—and then after a pause quickly wrote, No. [for "number"]. One Super Heroes. After a while he began to draw, pausing to goad himself into action by bringing his elbows together against the sides of his body three or four times. He drew a large character with red eyes, with one hand and no legs, leaning into the frame, leaving the rest of its body cut off. Later he told me that the large person was the fealer [sic] . . . who had lots of bad feeling inside him and was a bit of a maniac and a bad person.
>
> Then Morton drew a little creature without ears but again with red eyes. Its right arm was extended into the picture. The little creature was a perfect sort of person [a "perfect baby"], but the maniac was the part that people knew about.
>
> Turning over the page, Morton ruled up more frames and wrote quickly, in a slightly feverish way, "Return of the Fealer; here I am locked in my thoughts." This third creature, he told me, was a "Force" that was in everyone and contained their thoughts. It was difficult to keep the Force in order and if it did get out of hand, then it could drive a person mad. These bad thoughts had to do with calling the fire brigade when there was no fire. Apparently this creature could be a practical joker and rather tricky. Morton was at pains to tell me that this was not an actual person; he was trying to draw an idea.
>
> The Force was not such a problem as it had been in the past. As Morton told me this, he found he had made a mistake. He had been carried away and had colored the Force's trousers the wrong color; he had meant them to be yellow.

Morton's reference to the Force was perhaps to a libidinous capacity, which he had been able, to some extent, to repress. He could, within limits, establish some order in his inner life. The following session Morton seemed to feel that he was in some kind of double lock or bind. He wrote:

When the good person's mind and someone else's mind locked me in my thoughts, the good person didn't believe hard enough that they had locked me in my thoughts. So if I concentrate very hard, I can unlock myself and be free.

In its active form, Morton felt the "abnormal personality" to be maniacal and dominating, whereas in its passive form (as we were to discover later in our work together) this personality was experienced passively as a lost part.

The Abnormal Twin

Bion (1957) has recorded his observations that two totally separate personalities—one psychotic, the other nonpsychotic—can exist side by side with their own separate entities; and Grotstein (1979) has suggested that the more immature of the personalities is often "felt to be a hostage" of the other.

In the notes and drawings I have just described, Morton was illustrating his damaged self-structure. The "perfect baby" represented the sane part of his personality, previously closed off by the "maniac" from experience which could lead to growth. The normal unborn personality—the "perfect baby"—had not developed because its feelings and the capacity to know them had been banished into space; into the realm of Bion's "beta elements" and "nameless dread." Morton was describing a return of these painful sensations and his anguish. The perfect baby wished to be rescued from the confinement of the unknown. As Morton said, "No one knows about the perfect baby." It could be known only by being sensed and felt and then thought about, since it was not initially open to verbal interpretations. The baby was almost silent, unlike its "maniac" twin.

It is likely that bonding with the mother, on an autosensual level, had been ruptured, leaving the baby vulnerable to states of "organismic panic." This would have a shattering and deforming effect on Morton's immature psychic structure; borne out perhaps by his mother's observation that her infant extended his arms as if "a charge of energy [was] going the wrong way."

The Stick Figure

In contrast to the foregoing drawn characters, Morton began physically creating a different kind of figure. He took a pipe cleaner, formed it into a circle, then took another and began to attach it to the circle. He tested the strength of the attachment and pulled the bits apart. Then for the next few minutes he worked hard connecting four pipe cleaners to the circle. For Morton this seemed to be a difficult undertaking, and he sighed from time to time and knocked the packet of pipe cleaners to the floor. When the figure was completed—significantly it had a hole in its head—he told me it was an ordinary person, not a superhero, just an ordinary hero. Morton made the figure attack him at face level.

It was nearly time to stop, and Morton was by now twirling the stick figure about. He said rather sadly that he felt he must be further away from other people; it seemed to be difficult for them to understand what he was saying. I wondered if he felt that way about me? "No," he said, "not only you, but everyone, but you less than other people." It sounded as if he felt that he did not speak the same language as other people. "I get sick of my own jokes—nobody seems to get them." After a bit, he said he wished he could come closer to other people. I felt his profound sense of aloneness, but most of all the poignancy of his communications.

Morton asked if he could take the stick figure home with him. I said that maybe he wanted the figure to keep him company—like a playful friend. Perhaps he wanted to keep in touch with this more ordinary part of himself, which he had found during the session; it was this part which could help him to feel closer to other people and less locked away in his own world.

It seemed to be a burden for Morton to have to be so special and to have to be a superhero. He now felt that if he wanted to be closer to other people, then he would have to change.

Summary

The material collected in the assessment sessions indicated to me that there had been a significant shift in Morton's internal world during these sessions. He had been able to relate to me, more consistently than he did later in treatment. He could bring his fantasies and feelings into play as he talked and modeled in plasticine and drew pictures to illustrate what he thought about. He could also make links and bring things together. Some themes which emerged at this stage carried over into therapy. These, and other elements of a positive nature in the material quoted, endorsed my feeling that, with his parents' agreement, Morton and I should proceed with psychotherapy three times a week.

THE THERAPY SESSIONS

The first stage of Morton's reintegration would be awareness of his body-self—going back to this "first act of mental life" (Grotstein, 1980a). During this phase of the therapy, Morton related to me predominantly on an autosensual level, which enabled me to make contact with a lost part of Morton, imprisoned by a perverse—in his words, "maniac"—part of his personality.

Shortly after Morton began treatment, I noticed that he seemed to need a time to experience *being*—first with this body-self. He seemed to be making a transition from "thinking with the body" to a more genuinely mental process, after which he would seat himself at the desk and begin to play and think and talk. He slipped into a kind of routine: always sitting in the same armchair at the beginning of the session. This made me wonder if he became fragmented between sessions, and whether during the first stage of each session, within the supportive framework of the treatment and my integrating presence, he was able to restore internal linkages which enabled him to relate to me.

The early part of the session had the quality of an infant observation about it, with me as participant observer. My training in how to watch and feel (which I drew on from infant observation) enabled me to observe Morton's overall behavior and aided the analytic reconstruction of his early development.

The "Armchair Position"

Over the course of the first few months of treatment Morton began to come to life, to wake up and reach out. He became increasingly aware of his immediate surroundings, their limits, and my place in relation to him. When he came into the room at the beginning of the session, he walked rather stiffly over to his armchair which sat beside the window. Sometimes he gave a forced smile in response to my greeting. Frequently he was in a state of deshabille, with his shirt hanging out and his shoelaces undone.

Flopped in his armchair, Morton sat quietly, as if getting his bearings. At times he reminded me of a young child making the transition from sleeping to waking, except that he often seemed fatigued. He reminded me then of a toy whose batteries had run down. The armchair was an important recharging point because it seemed to gather him up and support him physically, enabling him to get himself together; just as my interpretations seemed to support him on another level. Sometimes Morton expressed this internal change externally, by doing up his shoelaces and by gradually becoming more lively and talkative. In time he developed a close relationship with the armchair. He cuddled up into it and pressed his cheek against its back. Symbolically he was able to have that close relationship with the chair (and with me in the transference as a comforting object) which he had been seeking with his mother. In the countertransference, I found my self becoming very wrapped up in my patient, a feeling akin to that experienced by a mother who is engrossed in her new baby.

After getting himself more together, Morton usually began to reach out physically and touch something about him. He occupied himself by tapping his feet, or picking at the fabric of his jersey, or at his fingernails, or the zip on his trousers. Making contact with surfaces and different textures seemed to be a leading preoccupation; I was struck by his tactile sensitivity.

Frequently Morton reached out for his key which was secured to his pocket by a piece of cord. He played with key and cord, seeming to enjoy the hard feel of the key and the firmness of the cord against the softness of his skin. On occasion, he became engrossed by the play of light on the shaft of the key and by its reflection. He directed this onto the wall, creating a dancing image and perhaps a companion, for he did seem very solitary. Morton apparently needed to make contact with his body-self during the first part of nearly every session. It was as if, between sessions, the "I" had become alienated from awareness of self as object—from his needs, urges, and feelings.

On one occasion Morton seemed to be basking in the afternoon sun, like a lizard, looking over to me from time to time, for he was now more aware of me than he had been to begin with. He began playing with the key, dangling it between his legs, rubbing the cord and the key with his finger tips in a self-absorbed way, as if inducing a trance. I felt like an onlooker, viewing a private activity, of a sexual nature, a kind of intercourse. He stiffened up his arms and rocked back and forth for a bit. It was as if he was having some kind of spasm, or fit, which alarmed me. These feelings may once have been introjected by Morton in a situation to which he himself had been witness.

After he had emerged from this impenetrable state, Morton seemed to be drained, as though he had had an electric shock. I wondered with him about this afterward. He said, "When I'm rubbing the cord, I'm usually thinking . . . it helps me to think; it gives me the power to think, and it helps me to get in touch with a lost part, which, when I find it, helps me to think better." He agreed the cord was like a kind of "joiner" and a catalyst too, and that sometimes he found himself carried away by the power of his thoughts, perhaps to the extent of hallucinating at such times. What Morton confirmed is that until he could feel himself, he could not "be," and, until he could be, he was unable to think. In addition, he suggested that the relationship between "being" and "thinking" became possible because of the "joiner." I now wonder if Morton could only think thoughts by using his mind as a "muscular apparatus," when he was in this position in his session.

In time Morton became more aware of the inside of the room. His growing awareness of, and interest in, his surroundings were akin to familiarizing himself with the "habits" of the various objects within the room, almost as if they were living beings. He was beginning to project into the objects. This was a necessary phase before he could begin to introject.

Early in the sessions, after he sat down in the armchair, Morton often hooked the middle finger of his right hand through a cup hook placed in the window frame. Then he carried out a visual survey of points of interest, for example, the heater: he looked to see if it was going. Earlier, he had speculated where the little glow on the floor under the heater came from; he wondered if this came from a ray of sunlight which shone through the top of the heater.

Morton singled out certain features, particularly where there were two. The two locks on the door of the room puzzled him. "Why two?" he wondered. "Every other door that has that sort of lock is locked," he added. He had already checked these at the end of a session. He noted that one of the two was a cylinder type lock with the word UNION on it. Morton had read this upside down as NONIUN—perhaps a version of nonunion? He became interested in the relationship between pairs of things. For instance, he wondered whether the two telephones which sat on the floor could talk to each other. I thought this might reflect a change internally: that of a developing relationship between self and object, with both a state of fusion, as symbolized by the locks, and a state of reciprocity, as symbolized by the relationship between the telephones.

Now that his conception of relative space was developing, Morton was aware of a boundary—the walls of the room. At this point, he could conceive of "near" and "far" and "through," but probably not of inside and outside. Through the window, he observed a steeple of a church, topped by a symbol of a fish. It was, however, an old fort, standing on a little hill, which really captured his attention. It seemed a striking contrast to the buildings which, he told me, he had constructed (as a shelter against disaster) at the bottom of his garden. In the external world, Morton could not have chosen a more timeless object of contemplation. For 700 years the fort had been a focal point of the town and had served as a place of safekeeping in times of war and a haven in times of peace. Although weathered, the fort was fundamentally unchanged—a fact which fitted with Morton's fantasies, since a part of him was passionately opposed to change.

Morton happily recalled a visit to the fort which he had made with the school when he was younger. This memory brought about a feeling of warmth and closeness, as if we now had something in common—like the two telephones, with a line of communication. The fort came to stand for the developing transference relationship with me as the "background object of primary identification" (Grotstein, 1981). This initial shift probably enabled Morton to alter his focus and begin to search for what he could now experience having lost.

The Lost World

Morton appeared, in a sense, well aware of what had happened to him psychically. He came back to the idea of a "lost world" and to the part of himself which dwelled there. It seemed to me that only by rediscovering this lost internal world could he find a home for the absent "perfect baby."

Morton's concern to recover earlier memories was, therefore, an important feature of this phase of treatment. He told me that Borneo was home for him and was where he had lived his "first life." He felt that he had "lost" his memories of babyhood somewhere in Borneo. It was not clear to him why this had happened.

Morton was desperate to find these lost memories in feeling. But Borneo was far away, and it was difficult to keep in touch from such a distance. If he lost touch with Borneo, he could not do any work. As he told me about his life, he clutched the piece of cord to which the key was attached, as if it were a lifeline or an anchor. If he lost his grip on it, he might really drift off into space and lose contact with me, a reminder of the days when Morton, as he told me, feared he would lose contact with his parents if he were not tied to them with imaginary string: a physical image of bonding.

For Morton, these memories, or feelings, which constituted the lost ego, seemed to be experienced on a concrete level, embodied in the physical environment of his babyhood world in Borneo. In short, they had not undergone the transition from symbiotic objects to object representations, where a thought could stand for the object in its absence. "The only way of finding what's lost," Morton said, "is to go back there, and see it all again, just as it was during my first life, but that isn't enough. You have to do something with the bits." He told me that he had had a dream that if he did go back to Borneo, he would find it all changed. There would be tourists all over the beach and modern houses. He had dreamed that the old chief of the village he had known had died, and the house he had lived in had been blown down.

The only tangible thing Morton had left from those days in Asia was a ring. It had magical properties for Morton because it was a way of getting in touch with baby feelings lost in Borneo, feelings "that nobody knows about." Thinking about Borneo, Morton said, was like having a pain, and being "surrounded by five robots who are going to kill you, or being imprisoned for ten years"—the length of his life so far. It was not, he explained, that he was being punished, but, if nobody understood, then "they" might try to get rid of him: "they" being people who had minds like robots, and who would take over the world. Borneo would be the only place where there would be human beings.

When Morton referred to his "first life" (Grotstein, 1982–83), he may have been in touch with a sense of his first internal world; one which existed before the processes of repression led to the creation of a second world, at about the time of the oedipus complex. The association with the memories is one of paradise lost. Morton felt that he had been expelled from some secure and sunlit place. The "first life" could also be a reference to the internal object container, the "object world" of the foetus. This level of consciousness became more apparent later on in treatment, when depths came increasingly to the surface.

Bion (1970) has suggested that a feeling of depression is "the place where a breast or some other lost object was," and is a "space where depression or some other emotion would be." For Morton, this depression came to be experienced on an internal level as the loss of an organ, like the heart; or—in a future session, on a mental level—was expressed symbolically in the disappearance of a film from his camera. He seemed to think that his missing part could provide a photo-memory of the lost experience, without which he felt incomplete and doomed to a half-life.

In the next phase of treatment (in what I have called the "deskchair position" of each session) Morton began an imaginative re-creation of what was, in both senses of the word, a genesis myth. Morton's difficulty at this stage was an inability to re-create internally this lost paradise. It was a transition he had not yet made.

In general, transitions seemed difficult for Morton. To take one example, he had an odd and awkward way of making the transition from the armchair, in which he started each session, to his later position at the desk. Seated in the armchair, Morton would hook his middle right-hand finger around a cup hook in the window frame, and then rock back and forth, building up enough momentum to lever himself out of the armchair. He then used the desk chair as a kind of crutch, as if he did not have a backbone strong enough to support him. This crawling across was reminiscent of a very old man—or of a young baby, able to pull himself up and move about using furniture as a support, but not ready to stand and walk unassisted.

The "Desk-chair Position"

Once in his desk chair, Morton again approached his toy box in a typical way. He drew it toward him with both hands and turned it on its side, extending all of the flaps, so he faced a large open mouth through which the contents of the toy box spilled out. Sometimes his head seemed almost to disappear into the box as he raked around among the contents. These were useful as vehicles for the expression of fantasies which related to the lost paradise. Among these fantasies was Morton's idea of the creation and its creatures. The first of them was the Superjoy, who resembled a prehistoric creature.

In practice, the theme of creativity was evident in Morton's material from the outset of our work together, and originality was its hallmark. But originality does not necessarily lead to creativity, and the potential for creativity can be limited by infantile omnipotence. In this case, it could be that a preoccupation with creativity was an expression of too little genuine creativity.

After the assessment, there had been a break of several months. When Morton came for his first psychotherapy session, he commented, as he took hold of his toy box, that it felt a bit different: "heavier maybe than it had done before." As he surveyed the contents through the opening of the box, he was able to recall many items of the contents. In the transference, Morton may have thought that I too was different; getting heavier may have been associated with pregnancy: an identification with his mother's pregnancy when he was 4 years old. On another level, Morton may have been preparing for a rebirth of a part of himself, a part which had been split off in the trauma of his birth.

The subsequent material which evolved over a number of sessions related on a primitive level to Morton's omnipotent fantasy of his conception. This had happened parthenogenetically: ostensibly without parents. Because of a mutation, a part of Morton became the first creature of his kind, and therefore unique. He seemed to be absorbed in re-creating a lost infantile self, that subjective me-ness which he felt he had to find.

The Superjoy

The notion of birth without parents ran through Morton's fantasies at this stage of treatment, though later he moved to an acknowledgment of at least one parent's role in his creation. The following material is quoted directly from my notes.

> To begin with Morton took up the cup into which he had thrust several unused different-colored strands of plasticine at the end of the assess-

ment sessions. He gave these a deft twist, so that the strands of color broke; then he joined them up again so that the colors were aligned differently, as if there had been a mutation.

He thought they looked more original. When I wondered what he meant by "original," he said that it was "either the first thing of its kind or something very different." He wanted to make something original that would please people—but how could you please people when everybody was so different? How could you know what they would think?

Morton fashioned a creature with four legs; with a hand and a sort of trunk sticking out of its mouth. He told me that it was as if the creature had one of its four fingers sticking into its mouth, while the other hand held on to the first hand. It was feeding itself. A small horn was added to the top of its head. This was a receiver for cosmic power. Its eyes were powerful, too, in that they could see a long way. When I asked about the creature, Morton thought for a bit. He then said maybe it was a unicorn, but he was not sure if they really existed, or were just imaginary creatures in Greek mythology. . . . At times too, Morton may have doubted the reality of his own sense of self.

With only a few minutes to go until the end of the session, Morton set to work; having got a red ballpoint going, he drew a copy of the unicorn creature; but his drawing went wrong and he put a cross through it. He said he had to bring his camera to get a picture; it was too difficult to draw. It was difficult for him to reproduce an image of what he perceived externally and also to re-create this image internally and keep it clearly in mind.

Morton remembered to bring along his Uniko box camera to his next session, but when he came to take a photograph, he found that the roll of film was missing from inside. He was puzzled by this and thought that somebody had removed it without telling him. As he talked, he continued to turn the camera over in his hands, examining the back opening where the roll of film was inserted; and then, more particularly, the lens, the cyclopean eye of the camera. Perhaps this stood for his mind's eye, that missing capacity which would allow him to visualize an object in its absence externally.

Morton's difficulty in keeping a picture in mind was expressed symbolically by the loss of the film from inside the camera. The film seemed to stand for the loss of his capacity to internalize and process images and to record these in memory. He probably needed my help in recovering this capacity, because I found myself functioning, in the countertransference, as a recorder and retainer of images.

Gradually Morton and I built up a picture together, over many sessions, of the unicorn creature; of its physical evolution and the characteristics with which it was endowed internally. And in time the unicorn was joined by the green man, "the sort of character you get in comics—not ordinary." At one moment the green man and the unicorn were joined together by the green man's nose and the unicorn's horn. They both looked dead from the outside, but inside they were hollow and teeming with life.

The unicorn evolved into a Superjoy, apparently by accident. It happened when Morton put the plasticine into his cup. Nonetheless some of the characteristics of the unicorn were inherited by the Superjoy, for example, the horn which could receive cosmic power, and the eyes which could see a long way. The Superjoy was both man and woman, but more woman. She was, Morton thought, a good character with feelings, but not human. She had stopped being grown up and had become young again.

In time the Superjoy had two babies, a boy and a girl. It was able to reproduce without a mate, suggesting a state of parthenogenesis or hermaphrodism; but in a later session, Morton thought that babies came into being from the remains of the green man.

There was an idea of splitting, of fission, in Morton's account of the Superjoy's genesis. For example, each baby had only one eye, and their eyes differed in color. In time the blue-eyed Superjoy (the perfect baby) remained unchanged, as a reminder or prototype of how Superjoys began. However, the green-eyed Superjoy baby grew four legs, like the mother, and eventually changed into the green man, "who was underneath all the time."

It is interesting to note the Siamese-twin paradigm (Grotstein, 1980b) in the foregoing material, in that the green man and the unicorn were joined together face-to-face by the green man's nose and the unicorn's horn, while the rest of their bodies were physically separate. This material portrays the evolution of our relationship in the transference, which was one of symbiosis; we were felt to be joined in some respects and separate in others. It also illuminates the evolution of internal objects in space, as they progress through a symbiotic stage to become transitional objects. Eventually they reach symbolic representation, through the processes of splitting, projection, and subsequent reworking during internalization. At this stage of the therapy, Morton was describing the gradual coming to life of his inner world, from the viewpoint of infantile omnipotence. That is to say, it was a preoedipal view.

Later, Morton composed a rhyme about the now male Superjoy, "who had been happy in space/ before the earthmen had come with their rain./ He pretended he was dead,/ so the earthmen decided they had lost head/ and they returned to the good old earth,/ having decided they had no service with a smirff. . . . The smirff creature came back to life again;/ he only pretended he was dead."

On a subsequent occasion, Morton gave another account of the Superjoy story, which was a variation on the same theme. The Superjoy was happy until men from earth came to hurt him, as if he were an elephant. Maybe they were wanting his horn for its cosmic power. The Superjoy pretended he was dead, saying, "Oh dear, oh dear," and the men from earth thought they must be out of their minds, so they returned to earth, leaving Superjoy to his happy life.

The Infantile Psychosis

This pretense of death seemed to be an echo of infantile psychosis. A part of Morton massively denied experience, and when, perhaps, he died mentally, he lost the capacity to experience. Now, in therapy, the question was, did he dare to exist again?

In the Superjoy story, and more particularly in the rhyme, Morton was describing this traumatic situation when he had sensed that his very existence was under threat. Primal omnipotence could not protect him; and having not developed an internal protective structure, he experienced a state of overwhelming panic. Unable to escape physically, he avoided the experience on a mental level—by massive projection into the external world of a part of his infantile consciousness. Behind a psychically dead front—a kind of shell or refuge, similar to that of the "green man"—Morton withdrew into his body-sensation-self the remaining part of his infantile awareness. This part was omnipotent and magical in character.

Such massive projection occurs, as Melanie Klein (1952) discovered, when the infant feels overwhelmed by persecutory anxiety. This anxiety takes the form of the predator-prey fantasies. Bowlby (1969) writes about these primeval fantasies which are released by the experience of birth and fill the void psychically until the infant experiences safekeeping within the primal relationship and is then able to surmount them.

What had happened to Morton in infancy? What had constituted such a trauma? My hypothesis is that the following story provides a screen memory for an event which occurred during his "first life." This is one of a number of such screen memories.

The story of Drago and Tharg was set in Borneo, in 3,000 A.D. As Morton narrated this story, he shredded a paper tissue between the fingers of one hand and crumbled a bit of plasticine in the other.

Morton was Tharg, the editor of a comic book. He was in his office on a Thursday afternoon (or perhaps it was nighttime) when he heard the red alert going off. It was offstage to begin with. He could hear screams of something terrible happening. At this point Morton seemed to withdraw, and I felt that he was either not strong enough to tell me more about what was happening because it was too painful, or that he wanted to add something. He placed pages 1 and 2 of the comic book that he was making between us, seeming to indicate that I should read about what was happening. In the meantime, Morton turned away to add something to page 3.

In the story, Drago, a giant octopus with black shoes, had come up on the screen in Tharg's room at the same time as the red alert, which went off four times. This seemed to be a visual briefing for Tharg. He took off as Super Tharg, flying in an aura of light. Together we could see his large diamond-shaped bottom facing toward us. As we turned the page, we could see the front view of Tharg. The sequences which followed were censored, meaning that we could read the words but could not see the pictures. We could have only half of the story, because all of it would be too painful.

Tharg commanded Drago to stop attacking him and tried to throw Drago over his back. Then Drago threatened Tharg, saying that he had better watch out. The fight was on. Drago disappeared from view several times as they fought together. Tharg wanted Drago's telepathic power which was in his tentacles [feelers?], a power which allowed him to see a long way off. His tentacles were very strong and they could go a long way off into space, into other people's minds. In the end, Tharg defeated Drago and minced him up, putting the messy bits of Drago into a space capsule which was shipped off into space for 100 years. Tharg, in destroying Drago, also destroyed his own power of feeling and his capacity to identify with others. The lost capacity for insight was still another facet of the power of self, which he felt he had lost.

I wondered, with Morton, if this story was a screen memory for something dreadful that had happened a long time ago, something which he had shipped off into space and which was now returning. This coincided with the end of the session. As Morton got slowly to his feet, I noticed that he was holding in his hand a little octopus made from the crumbs of plasticine.

Infantile Omnipotence

Schizophrenics, Grotstein (1977) has said, have a disastrous relationship to omnipotence. When parents fail to protect and communicate, the baby develops and entrenches its own protective omnipotence, which occludes the development of infantile sexuality.

The evolution of the Superjoy illustrates Morton's archaic, omnipotent fantasy of his own conception. In his world—the world of the first dimension—he was self-created. Perhaps he saw himself as having been part of the breast, as symbolized by the plasticine-filled cup from which he created the Superjoy. His use of omnipotence enabled him to deny dependence on his parents for his own creation and probably survival on every level.

In the story of Drago and Tharg, Morton used his omnipotent fantasies as a way of defeating persecutors. Perhaps he needed to practice defending himself in his inner world in fantasy, as a way of reducing persecutory anxiety, until he had a stronger sense of inner self. His need to employ omnipotent fantasy reflected a feeling of powerlessness over himself in his environment, rather than the reverse. In short, he suffered from a deficiency of omnipotence.

Birth

As we approached a break in treatment, drumming began to occupy a central position in the sessions. Morton would take different combinations of things in the room to drum on and would bring together different patterns of sounds. For example, he took the large roll of sticky tape and an empty plastic shampoo bottle and played with these, or he drummed on an upturned drawer or a chair. This sound of drumming, he said, reminded him of the Far East.

When I asked why people drummed in Borneo, Morton said that sometimes it was to drive away evil spirits, or to get in touch with dead ancestors, or to dance and sing. Morton told me, once again, that he had been conceived in Borneo, and that would have been when he first heard drumming.

On reflection, I have wondered if Morton was replicating different patterns of sounds which he had experienced in the womb. The drumming may have constituted a rhythmic and constant mode of communication, which signaled his being in touch with mother's world from inside, one that he later had difficulty in finding inside himself.

In a subsequent session, Morton began drumming again, but this time with more force. He substituted a glue bottle for the shampoo bottle. As the end of the session approached, he worked up a very intense rhythmic pitch. When it was time to stop, he said, "Oh," as if disappointed, because he had not had enough time to reach a climax. Perhaps the drumming signaled his view of his conception in which he felt he had played a part. However, it also signaled the quality of organismic panic of birth, one in which the rhythmic unity—that continuing sense of "at-one-ment" between mother and foetus—had been disrupted by what Morton may have experienced as a catastrophe.

This was borne out by his mother's earlier observation, "If he felt the way I did after the birth, it must have been terrible for him."

CONCLUSION

In contrast to an earlier essay (Macdonald, 1988) in which I sought to chart the course of a long analysis and to describe the restoration of my patient's self-structure, this is not primarily a "treatment paper." Instead, I have used material from the initial stages of an analysis in an attempt to reconstruct on an imaginative level an event which had shattered my patient's integrity and damaged his self-structure. This is a study of early fantasies, whose "evolution, transformations and pathological alterations should . . . be an invaluable guide to the study of schizophrenic psychosis" (Grotstein, 1977).

During the period of treatment, the analysis progressed in the present and also moved backward, to the time of Morton's birth, which had in reality been difficult. From one point of view, Morton's material appeared to reflect a trauma at birth, in which his sense of psychobiological oneness had been shattered. The intrauterine bonding may not have been strong enough to carry the couple through the trauma of birth, and to assure the baby of a sense of safety amid the chaos of physical change. He seems to have felt that he had lost a part of himself in that process. It left him with a sense of incompleteness, at a time before he could deal with this emotionally. The same loss a few months later may have meant the loss of the object without the added loss of part of the subject.

As is evident, the causes of the trauma were also complex. In addition, it may have been difficult to rectify the developmental consequences of such a trauma postnatally by the development of a maternal relationship which would heal the breach. This left Morton dependent on his physical surroundings and thus vulnerable to external change. So long as his outer circumstances did not alter too massively, he could maintain some inner stability.

In the assessment sessions, Morton portrayed the split in his personality, and described the lost and traumatized infant. During the first stage of each session, in the transference, he became wholly identified with this regressed part of his personality. At such times, his use of autistic objects (Tustin, 1981), such as the key, provided a feeling of safety and helped to fill "holes" through which threatening things might enter. Sensations generated by autistic shapes (Tustin, 1986) such as the plasticine generated a soothing, tranquilizing effect. By this means Morton was able to regulate his fundamental anxiety, his fear of failure of "going on being" (Winnicott, 1960). My feelings of empathic attunement bridged the gap between us and assisted the beginning of attachment and bonding with the lost part. This could occur only in a relationship where Morton felt safe.

The work during this phase of each session was primarily on a non-verbal level. The countertransference (or, more precisely, counteridentification) was the medium of communication for primitive sensations and feelings. It was as if Morton and I could feel together, as one; much as the mother feels for her baby before birth and during the weeks immediately thereafter. Only by making good, on a nonverbal level, the rift in that primary at-one-ment could the alienated infant-self experience a return to a welcoming, safekeeping relationship.

Through the medium of this relationship, Morton explored fantasies of a primitive nature, in which sometimes chaotic states of being were transformed into states of mind. These imaginative excursions constituted a healing experience and enabled him to begin to rework "unexperienced experiences" of loss which he had not been able to work through in infancy and which had handicapped his subsequent development. The lost-world material exemplifies this process. Until Morton had mourned what he had lost, his capacity to feel and think was handicapped. In the transference, unconsciously, he was beginning to make good his loss through his relationship with me.

During the second part of most sessions, Morton explored similar themes but in a more objective way, creating examples of the figures of his fantasies. The shift in position during the session seemed to be associated with the recovery of an additional dimension, which enabled him "to work better." I would suggest that this shift could be accounted for by the "dual-track conception," described by Grotstein (1977), where the infant experiences two simultaneous and continuing sides of experience: separateness and nonseparateness, a dual consciousness from the beginning of life; a realistically experienced external world and a fantasied inner world. In Morton's case, I am suggesting that at the outset of postnatal life, he had suffered a trauma, which resulted in the loss of one part of this dual consciousness.

I want to stress that I am not suggesting Morton dwelled entirely in the domain of the first world; rather, the parts of his personality which had been split off had remained in this domain. When they made their way back into inner space, these split-off parts were very retarded developmentally and essentially preoedipal. Of course, there was a more mature aspect of Morton with which I was able to form a relationship. It was this part which enabled us to work together for the sake of the deprived parts.

POSTSCRIPT

It is some years since I worked with Morton, and during this time there have been significant findings in early mental evolution from the field of child development. They have implications for clinical work in the field of child psychoanalysis and psychotherapy.

> Now that earliest infancy has been given a psychology, one that is populated by phantasied objects which are inherent residues and precursors to the awarenesses of external objects (pre-object objects, if you will), the importance of the developmental point of view can at last be harvested, especially in terms of psychoanalytic technique and understanding. The course of mythic personality progression would ontogenetically dictate that each successive stage of development unfolds as an assimilation of the previous stages and is directly and indirectly modified by them. Thus the order of priority in psychoanalytic technique would be directed to the deeper and earlier stages of development. Analysing an Oedipus complex initially would run the hazard of disallowing the optional evolution of a more nearly-complete Oedipus complex as a result of the therapeutic analysing of the adhesion which impeded and altered its evolution initially [Grotstein, 1977, p. 422].

In my work at this time, I tended to interpret the more obvious oedipal elements of the material, despite feeling uncomfortable with that emphasis. It conflicted not only with the strong feelings which were often manifest in the countertransference, but also with my patient's reaction to some interpretations. While I felt these interpretations might be narrowly "correct" (in that they addressed the oedipal part of Morton's personality), I can see with hindsight that they were not relevant to the more primitive part. Not surprisingly, they became a source of irritation.

It could be argued that I had added insult to injury, or compounded the damage and neglect which this part of the personality had suffered. Despite the foregoing, there is evidence, from the way the material began to develop, that Morton sensed my feeling of empathy with, and understanding of him, which led to bonding. At the time of treatment I had not consciously realized that the Kleinian approach relates much more to primitive infantile neurosis than to abnormal infantile psychosis, and that I had to get in touch with the primitive, schizophrenic personality, rather than concentrate on verbal interpretations (Grotstein, 1983).

To follow this path necessitates a shift in emphasis from weaning interpretations, which are appropriate to the neurotic part of the personality, to increased emphasis on bonding interpretations, which would facilitate the psychotic transference and a relationship with the psychotic part of the personality. When I refer to bonding interpretations, I am describing those empathic observations of the patient's state of being, but more particularly a recognition of his feelings of loss of a part, or something which he felt needed to be restored. In short, there would be more focus on the defective or damaged bond or attachment, whether it be primary or secondary.

Such a shift in technique emphasizes the development of a sense of boundaries and a sense of safety in the patient, rather than simply analyzing the patient's fantasies. These, however, from a different point of view, offer us a field for exploration of early mental phenomena and inevitably of schizophrenic psychosis.

With increased focus on the primitive part of the personality, the patient is given a second chance to work over unmetabolized experience relating to the infantile psychotic episode, experience which has led to a distorted pattern of development. Contact with these lost parts, and subsequent bonding and nurturing, lead to increased development and psychic integration.

BIBLIOGRAPHY

BION, W. R. (1957). Differentiation of the psychotic from the non-psychotic personalities. In *Second Thoughts*. New York: Aronson, pp. 43–64.

———— (1962). *Learning from Experience*. London: Heinemann.

———— (1970). *Attention and Interpretation*. London: Tavistock Publications.

BOWLBY, J. (1969). *Attachment and Loss*, vol. 1. New York: Basic Books, 1982.

CAMUS, A. (1937). *L'Envers et l'endroit*. Paris: Gallimard, 1958.

GROTSTEIN, J. S. (1977). The psychoanalytic concept of schizophrenia. *Int. J. Psychoanal.*, 58:403–425.

———— (1979). Demoniacal possession, splitting, and the torment of hope. *Contemp. Psychoanal.*, 15:407–445.

———— (1980a). The significance of Kleinian contributions to psychoanalysis: II. *Int. J. Psychoanal. Psychother.*, 8:393–428.

———— (1980b). A proposed revision of the psychoanalytic concept of primitive mental states. *Contemp. Psychoanal.*, 16:479–546.

———— (1981). *Splitting and Projective Identification*. New York: Aronson.

———— (1982–83). The significance of Kleinian contributions to psychoanalysis: III. *Int. J. Psychoanal. Psychother.*, 9:487–510.

———— (1983). Deciphering the schizophrenic experience. *Psychoanal. Inq.*, 3:37–69.

———— (1984). A proposed revision of the psychoanalytic concept of primitive mental states. *Contemp. Psychoanal.*, 20:77–119.

KLEIN, M. (1952). Notes on some schizoid mechanisms. In *The Writings of Melanie Klein*, 3:1–24. London: Hogarth Press.

MACDONALD, J. (1988). Odd one out. Unpublished paper.

TUSTIN, F. (1981). *Autistic States in Children*. London: Routledge & Kegan Paul.

—— (1986). *Autistic Barriers in Neurotic Patients*. London: Karnac Books.

WINNICOTT, D. W. (1960). Ego distortion in terms of true and false self. In *The Maturational Processes and the Facilitating Environment*. New York: Int. Univ. Press, 1965, pp. 140–152.

The Function of Humor in a Four-year-old

EUGENE J. MAHON, M.D.

A child's attempt at humor in the midst of a psychoanalytic session is examined. A joke is told that began as a dream which the 4-year-old analysand attempted to modify. The joke is not entirely successful from a formal standpoint. This "failure" is examined from the point of view of the anxiety that may have derailed the joke and the developmental immaturity that may have compromised it. A developmental line of the symbolic process is suggested, double meanings and multiple meanings becoming more complex as development proceeds.

A 4-YEAR-OLD, IN THE FULL THROES OF OEDIPAL ROMANCE, LEAVES HIS mother in the waiting room and dashes into the analyst's office and sits on the analyst's chair. This is a new game which is a tribute to the several months of analytic process that have preceded it. The 4-year-old who began the analytic journey with tentative footsteps is now comfortable enough to steal the analyst's chair and even "free associate" somewhat to the theft. He beams when the analyst suggests that he is pretending to take over the whole world and be big like his doctor and maybe even order people around, especially fathers and doctors. In this "humorous" mood he asks the analyst if he would like to hear a joke and then proceeds to tell what he thinks is a joke but might not qualify as such to adult ears.

Q: "Why did the chicken steal the bagpipes?"

A: "Because he wanted to have a perfect house."

Since this did not sound like a joke, I tried to get more information about its origins and developmental function for the child. It turns out

---

Faculty (child analysis and adult analysis) at Columbia University Psychoanalytic Center for Training and Research; assistant clinical professor of psychiatry, College of Physicians and Surgeons, Columbia University, New York.

that this joke began its psychological life as a dream that subsequently became a joke as the dreamer tried to "play" with it in a waking state. I was not sure if my young patient fully understood what bagpipes were. But as clay was manipulated into the shape of the primitive musical instrument producing an object decidedly like a scrotum with an erect penis, it became clear that he not only knew what bagpipes were but also sensed their symbolic phallic possibilities. This became clear as "phallus" got chopped from "scrotum" in repetitive attacks on the clay instrument. There was further corroborative associative evidence in drawings in which father's initials were erased and the patient's own initials preserved. A variation on this oedipal theme in script showed father's name erased with the word *no* after it, and his own name preserved with the word *yes* after it. At moments such as these he would leave the office to check on his mother in the waiting room. He readily agreed with the interpretation that he wanted to be sure she could still love him even if he played out murderous wishes against her husband. He even gave me "a star" for this interpretation.

Returning to the function of the joke, it is interesting to note that even if this attempt to turn dream into a joke did not work, the capacity for understanding of comic mechanisms was present, as the following joke he told in the same analytic hour makes clear.

Q: "Why was there a fight in the bakery?"

A: "Because two loaves were fresh!"

In a subsequent session, the child "steals" my chair gleefully and the game of theft begins again. At one point he returns the chair to me, saying, "I don't want your chair. I want your job." When I wonder what I will do without a job, he reassures me that I will get his father's job. The link between stealing father's job and my job seems obvious. The theme returns to the chicken stealing the bagpipes, the joke he had made up out of a dream. Does he make jokes up all by himself? Yes, and he demonstrates: "I'll steal your chair. I'll take your job." This mock-serious threat is presented as a joke. At this stage of development, is pretense synonymous with the comic?

When I "enter into" this joke, saying, "Oh, what will I do without my job and my chair?" he says reassuringly, "Oh, it's only a joke." For a moment he must have felt that I was seriously pleading for the return of my property and status. The line between illusion and reality seems precarious in this animistic world of beliefs and make-believe. The "scene" shifts to the construction and destruction of an elephant out of clay. After making body, trunk, limbs, tail, the whole construction is torn apart limb from limb. Going behind my chair, he "knocks" on my head. "Oh, you've become a head knocker. A new job, eh?" I ask playfully. Next minute he is fixing my shoes and saying he has many jobs—destroyer, fixer, head knocker. The wish to castrate and the wish to undo the castration seem obvious. This is all playful, even comic. At one point he makes spells, writing scribble on paper and chanting gibberish that will make doors open and close magically. "The spells are like jokes or different?" I ask. "They are the same," he says, "but spells don't have any words." I muse, "Jokes and spells are wonderful. What would children do without them?" The child responds, "If the parents took all the jokes away and hid them in a closet, they could get them back by being good." It is fascinating to watch him go from action to play to spell to joke as he struggles with oedipal conflict. An adult analysand could probably contain all these components of oedipal conflict in one sequence of verbal associations, a tribute to the adult ego's facility with language, frustration tolerance, renunciation of instinct, sublimatory channels, etc. A child's ego, on the other hand, relatively new to language, new to joking, represents the conflict partly in action, partly in language as it tries to put a comic face on issues that are not necessarily funny.

Discussion

The relationship between humor and the unconscious has been brilliantly exposed by Freud (1905). The developmental aspects of humor have been well documented by Wolfenstein (1954). What I would like to focus on is the 4-year-old's impulse to make a joke and to examine its components even when the joke is unsuccessful and might not qualify as a joke in the strictest sense of the definition.

The relationship between joke and dream became clear to Freud very early in his psychoanalytic explorations. Strachey (1905) suggests that when Fliess brought the similarity between dreams and jokes to Freud's attention in 1899, it came as no surprise to Freud since the subject already had been on his mind for a few years. If a joke can be defined as a device that uses primary processes to sneak forbidden impulses past the censor, thereby making a laughing stock of instinctual taboos for a brief period, its similarity to the dream is obvious. The similarities end of course when the primary processes of the sleeping state bend the semiotics of dream out of all recognizable shape, the disguise being completely victorious over communication, as is often the case. Unlike the dream, the joke has to obey some of the rules of waking life. Primary process cannot totally disguise all meaning: communication is essential.

Let us consider the 4-year-old's joke again.

Q: "Why did the chicken steal the bagpipes?"
A: "So that he could have a perfect house."

We can assume that this dream turned joke disguises the oedipal wish to steal father's penis and make off with a possession that would give the anatomically underdeveloped robber the perfect body he feels so lacking in. The dream-joke disguises the infantile oedipal intent with a few displacements (child becomes chicken, penis becomes bagpipes, body becomes house). The fact that this joke does not meet the criteria envisioned by older jokesters should not diminish an appreciation of the 4-year-old's impulse to put a comic mask on a dream that may have revealed too much of its dark intent to the little boy on first waking. The secondary revision may have needed a little assistance from what Arieti (1967) has called "the tertiary processes" of creativity to displace the meaning a little further from its oedipal core.

From a formal point of view, it is interesting to evaluate the joke and define what it lacks and what additional revisions would help it to qualify as a "real" joke. If the joke is modified so that the question, "Why did the chicken steal the bagpipes?" is answered, "Because he wanted to be a rooster-booster," the joke would bear more semblance to the usual adult counterpart. This is not a very good joke, to be sure, but the clang association "rooster-booster" might qualify it as a joke. The disguised oedipal theme of the chicken stealing the bagpipes so that he can crow like a rooster with the assistance of his stolen musical instrument and thereby "boost" his father's great sounds with some of his own would add weight to the joke and provide a few extra chuckles. If the joke were modified even further so that the question, "Why did the chicken steal the barbecue?" was answered, "So that he could be a rooster-roaster," the oedipal theme would be more obvious and the joke a little funnier perhaps. The point here is not to construct funny jokes (which I am obviously incapable of doing) but to identify what is lacking from the 4-year-old's joking repertoire. It is clear that he understands certain elements of the joke vocabulary even if the example under scrutiny shows less than a full grasp of the whole joking process. Clearly, he knows how to appreciate the joke about the bakery and the double *entendre* of the loaves being "fresh." In his own joke one final displacement, one double *entendre* such as the use of "fresh" in the bakery joke or "rooster-roaster" in the amended version of his own effort would add the necessary finishing touches and qualify it as a recognizable joke.

It is unusual perhaps to be able to witness a joke so embedded in the therapeutic process. Before, during, and after the joke the stealing of my chair looms as preamble and postscript to the comedy in action and word as it unfolds. The "theft" enacted in play is at once day residue and association to a joke that never quite makes it, given the amount of anxiety it is attempting to deal with and the developmental equipment of the comedian. One can only marvel at the developmental courage of the 4-year-old who plots the overthrow of his father with one side of his mouth and makes a joke out of it with the other. It is clear that the parents have the power not only to steal his bagpipes but steal his jokes as well and lock them in the closet. Even infantile omnipotence in the forms of "spells" may not work against such formidable opponents. In latency when the oedipus complex has been repressed and the child's ego comes into contact more and more with the nonincestuous group life of that developmental phase and all its heritage of riddles and games and jokes, it may be easier to joke about the return of the repressed with classmates than the crime and the act of repression itself with your father or analyst.

I have argued (Mahon, 1991) that the dissolution of the oedipus complex which is accomplished mainly through the psychological mechanisms of identification and repression gets crucial assistance from cognitive processes as preoperational intelligence is superseded by "the operations" of latency. The reversible operations of latency, e.g., $3 + 3 = 6$; $6 - 3 = 3$, require a full grasp of "the abstraction of numbers." In prelatency six baseball bats may appear larger (even numerically) than six toothpicks to a child who is "perceptually bound." To fully grasp the abstraction of numbers such perceptually bound errors have to be repressed, so to speak, and a more mature confederacy of cognitive conventions have to be embraced, *identified* with. I believe it is clear in this very brief and highly compressed rendition of complex Piagetian and Freudian ideas that the psychological and the cognitive assist each other as the oedipus complex succumbs to infantile amnesia at the beginning of latency.

Humor may require similar developmental fruitions before it can fully establish itself. If the "chicken" is in danger of being caught in the act of stealing the bagpipes not figuratively but literally, it is difficult for him to joke about it at a time when repression is no match for instinct and magical thinking makes no clear distinction between wish and *fait accompli*. There is no question that humor can appear as early as age 2 (Chukovsky, 1925). But it seems clear that until infantile amnesia separates the age of magic from the age of reason with distinct cognitive and psychological demarcation, the comic may be too close to the tragic for jokes to be really funny at least to a 4-year-old.

If anxiety does not derail the would-be comic achievements of the 4-year-old, developmental immaturity may play a part. If one were to draw a developmental line from the first acquisition of symbol and word at 12 to 18 months to the full appreciation and manipulation of language not only as straight talk but also as transmitter of ambiguity, humor, and irony, the line would stretch across prelatency, latency, and adolescence into adulthood. Even in adulthood the developmental process would be subject to progressive and regressive movements. With this imaginary line as a guide, one can trace the evolution of double *entendre* from its origins in very rudimentary symbolic play and pretense to the more sophisticated use of metaphor in jokes and artistic achievements of a very complex nature. Symbol seems to need action to get it off the ground (Mahon, 1989, 1991), but as development proceeds the sensorimotor actions that inspired the symbols in the first place are largely theoretical and impossible to trace. (The tendency to describe a spiral staircase by making spiral motions with a finger to assist words shows the contiguity between the sensorimotor and the symbolic even in adulthood.)

There is a progression from stealing the chair in play to stealing bagpipes symbolically in a joke. The 4-year-old seems to need to do some of both to *represent* his conflicts. Adults require less action to represent their conflicts in transference or in language, but the concept of acting out suggests that adults too "take action" when they are unable to confine all the elements of transference to the consulting room. In children the issue is even more palpable given the child's intimate relationship with action and play. Consider these three examples: A 4-year-old may need to "steal" the analyst's chair to represent his oedipal desires. A 7-year-old analysand playing chess with the analyst wondered why a pawn could not change into a king in the middle of the game. A 5-year-old who longed to be as big as his analyst, not to mention his father who would not let him share the parental bed at nighttime, looked out the window of the consulting room and commented, "Flowers grow so fast, children take a while." (There is some resignation in the comment as well as oedipal longing, an example of a 5-year-old being philosophical rather than action-oriented in the face of frustration.) The only point being stressed in these brief oedipal vignettes is that children have a variety of ways of representing their oedipal dilemmas depending on their developmental equipment and maturity.

The tendency for adult sublimation to sever its connections with its instinctual, sensorimotor past is the very essence of defense after all. The "sublime" nature of language and creativity makes a human being feel *almost* superior to the infantile sexuality of his "ridiculous" past. Rooster-roaster, for instance, produces a laugh that in one breath celebrates a *tour de force* of linguistic cleverness even as it expresses the forbidden oedipal murder of the father. Indeed, one could argue that rooster-roaster seduces the superego for a moment with wordplay so that the chicken is not caught red-handed in his oedipal crime. When a child, in latency perhaps, is able to tell rooster-roaster jokes, he has achieved sufficient mastery of humor to cover one-track oedipal instincts with clever double *entendres*. The exploitation of double meanings in language and humor sends a signal to the adult community that the child has won a relative victory over instinct and is ready and able to transform desire into compromises that repress and express all at once in the double *entendres* of defense. The 4-year-old who has not fully mastered this process receives our sympathy and even recognition since every analysand in the regressive sensitivities of the transference neurosis may lose his capacity to view experience as a mosaic of multiple meanings when the single-mindedness of infantile desire becomes an obsession at the height of regressive sensations. It was such considerations, after all, that lead Kubie (1969) to remark upon the destructive potential of humor in psychotherapy. When an analyst laughs or jests in the psychoanalytic situation, it is important to be aware whether the analysand feels he is being laughed at or laughed with. At the height of transference regression in the midst of a transference neurosis is every adult not 4 years old emotionally and unable to laugh about the preposterous nature of infantile wishes given the compelling conviction of transference and illusion? It is this capacity for regressive empathy that links the sensitive grownup with the humor of 4-year-olds even when their acts of sublimation fail and their jokes are not really funny.

Summary

A 4-year-old's joke which was told in a psychoanalytic session is examined from the point of view of content and formal properties. Sessions before and after the joke provide a context of associations that make interpretation possible. The joke does not work as a joke. The reasons for the failure are examined. Certain minimal elements are added to the joke to get it to work, and then the reasons for their absence in the child's product is inferred. It is argued that both anxiety and developmental immaturity played a role in undermining the attempted sublimation.

BIBLIOGRAPHY

ARIETI, S. (1967). *The Intrapsychic Self.* New York: Basic Books.
CHUKOVSKY, K. I. (1925). *From Two to Five*, ed. & tr. M. Morton. Berkeley: Univ. Calif. Press.

FREUD, S. (1905). Jokes and their relation to the unconscious. *S.E.*, 8.

KUBIE, L. S. (1969). The destructive potential of humor in psychotherapy. Grand Rounds, St. Lukes-Roosevelt Hospital, New York.

MAHON, E. J. (1989). Play, pleasure and reality. In *Pleasure Beyond the Pleasure Principle*, ed. R. A. Glick & S. Bone. New Haven: Yale Univ. Press, pp. 26–37.

—— (1991). The "dissolution" of the oedipus complex. *Psychoanal. Q.*, 60:628–636.

STRACHEY, J. (1905). Editor's preface. *S.E.*, 8:3–8.

WOLFENSTEIN, M. (1954). *Children's Humor*. Bloomington: Indiana Univ. Press.

Transformations of
Transference

ROBERT S. WHITE, M.D.

Transference can be understood to have complementary aspects: the experience in the here-and-now of the relationship with the analyst and the repetition of old relationships. The concept of an enactment is proposed to describe the vivid reexperience of childhood relationships in the here-and-now of the analytic relationship. Countertransference contributions to the enactment are discussed. Transference transformation results from the juxtaposition of the regressive transference enactment and transference experiences that are new and novel to the patient. The analyst can promote such changes by his interpretation of resistances both to the reexperience of the transference repetition and to awareness of the new and novel elements that spontaneously appear in the relationship with the analyst.

PSYCHOANALYSIS, AS A THERAPEUTIC PROCESS, HAS BEEN DEFINED AS "THE development of a regressive transference neurosis and the ultimate resolution of this neurosis by techniques of interpretation alone" (Gill, 1954, p. 775). This emphasizes the emergence of transference in the analytic setting and its interpretation as the central therapeutic instrument. However, the idea of resolution of transference is misleading if we mean that transference is quantitatively decreased or destroyed. Rather, the transference neurosis is modified and transformed into a more mature object relationship with the analyst in which there is a combination of cognitive insight, recovery of memory, and experience of new emotions. Follow-up studies have shown that the transference neurosis is attenuated but does not disappear (McLaughlin, 1981).

Assistant clinical professor of psychiatry, Yale University. At the time that the paper was written, I was a candidate at the Western New England Institute for Psychoanalysis. Earlier versions of this paper were read at the Hospital of St. Raphael psychiatric clinic and the Western New England Psychoanalytic Society.

329

Internalization and structuralization of the transformed relationship then allow for subsequent object relationships in which transference is less an unconscious repetition, but more an informant of mature expressivity and object choice.

Freud discovered the importance of transference in the Dora case (1905) and realized its power, both to disrupt treatment and to promote the healing process. Freud (1912) called the manifest loving aspects of transference the "positive transference" (p. 105), which he further subdivided into friendly or affectionate feelings and unconscious erotic feelings. The transference of aggressive feelings was called the "negative transference." The affectionate, unobjectionable feelings were thought to contribute significantly to the therapeutic relationship with the analyst, providing the cohesion in the treatment during periods of resistance. The unconscious erotic feelings form the basis of transference repetition and resistance. After the formulation of the structural theory, Freud suggested that aggression could also serve as a basis for repetition and resistance. Given these two broad strands of loving in the transference, it is not surprising, as Schafer (1977) points out, that Freud spoke of transference love sometimes as a repetition and sometimes as fresh and genuine in the new relationship with the analyst.

The repetitive side of transference has its origin in the past history of childhood relationships and its tendency to seek out and repeat these old relationships with new partners, including the analyst. Freud (1912) stated, "This produces what might be described as a stereotype plate (or several such), which is constantly repeated—constantly reprinted afresh—in the course of a person's life" (p. 99f.). In speaking of repressed childhood conflict, he said, "the patient does not *remember* anything of what he has forgotten and repressed, but *acts* it out. He reproduces it not as a memory but as an action; he *repeats* it, without, of course, knowing that he is repeating it" (1914, p. 150). This is the essence of transference as repetition. The repeated impulses and their associated intrapsychic defensive structures are reexperienced as a reengagement in the transference. The repressed memories of childhood's painful losses and disappointments return in symbolic actions and fantasies, and the defenses become manifest in the interpersonal relationship with the analyst as resistance.

Yet there is another side to transference. In his first discussion of transference, in the Dora case, Freud (1905) spoke of transference as "new impressions" or "revised editions" (p. 116). Later (1912), he said, "The patient regards the products of the awakening of his unconscious impulses as contemporaneous and real" (p. 108). And in 1914: "The transference thus creates an intermediate region between illness and real life through which the transition from the one to the other is made. . . . It is a piece of real experience" (p. 154).

Here then is the complementary thread of the transference, not experienced as resistance, but as the more direct manifestation of libidinal and aggressive impulses, available to seek more vital, creative, and satisfying relationships in the present. Schafer (1977) sums it up well: "On the one hand, transference love is sheerly repetitive, merely a new edition of the old, artificial and regressive . . . and to be dealt with chiefly by translating it back into its infantile terms. . . . On the other hand, transference is a piece of real life that is adapted to the analytic purpose, a transitional state of a provisional character that is a means to a rational end and as genuine as normal love" (p. 340). Clearly these two threads of transference remain intertwined throughout life. At the beginning of an analysis, the thread of genuineness and vitality is often only potentially present, but may emerge during the treatment in a new and creative experience with the analyst.

James Strachey (1934), in his concept of the mutative interpretation, discussed and contrasted these two threads of transference. Using the language of his day, he described the analyst as being initially internalized as an "auxiliary ego"; that is, the analyst is experienced as an object that is felt as "real and contemporary," separate and distinct from the rest of the patient's internalized objects. On the other hand, there is a constant pressure to experience the analyst as a repetitive transference object. The patient identifies with the analyst both as a real object and as a fantasy object determined by the transference projections. The most powerful tool of the analyst is the mutative interpretation, in which the repetitive side of transference, as experienced in the analytic relationship, is articulated and simultaneously contrasted with the real relationship with the analyst. "The analyst gives permission for a certain small quantity of the patient's id energy . . . to become conscious . . . the quantity of these impulses . . . will become consciously directed toward the analyst. This is the critical point. If all goes well, the patient's ego will become aware of the contrast between the . . . character of his feelings and the real nature of the analyst. . . . [The patient] will become aware of a distinction between his archaic phantasy object and the real external object" (p. 142f.).

The first phase of the interpretation aims at making the transference fully conscious as a direct interpersonal experience, what Gill (1982) calls the interpretation of resistance to awareness of transference. Strachey noted that this phase often takes place in "an immense number of minute steps" (p. 144). He emphasized that the id impulses

must be at a "point of urgency" (p. 150), that the patient must experience the repetitive aspect of transference as an immediate and real
force. The second phase of the interpretation is the patient's "sense of
reality," developing the insight that the transference is a projected
fantasy, and that a different relationship is possible.

While Strachey has correctly identified these two vital therapeutic
forces, he leaves a number of questions unanswered. It is not clear how
the patient retains "the sense of reality" to see the analyst as a new and
distinct object when he or she is under the full sway of the repetitive
transference, nor is it clear what the analyst can do to promote the
awareness of this reality, other than maintain his neutrality. Gill (1982)
calls this phase the interpretation of resistance to the resolution of
transference; the patient learns through interpretation that his
thoughts and fantasies about the analyst contain determinants that are
outside the current analytic situation. Interpretation can be focused on
the distortions in the here-and-now of the analytic situation or on the
past emotional determinants. Gill (as does Strachey) believes that
the interpretation of the here-and-now aspect of transference is often
the most powerful step which can then lead to the recognition of the
past and its distortion of the present. Gill also believes that emphasis on
the here-and-now experience leads to a new interpersonal experience
that the patient recognizes as more beneficial than transference distortions.

Loewald (1960, 1971) emphasizes the interpersonal aspects of the
analytic situation, through his concept of the development of a new
object relationship between patient and analyst. The goal of psychoanalytic treatment is the resumption of ego development, which has
been frozen by neurotic processes, toward higher levels of structural
differentiation and integration. These processes of growth are started
and made possible by the relationship with the analyst, who, through
empathic listening, clarification, and interpretation, is available as a
new object. The possibility of a new object relationship is one meaning
of the positive transference. It is this hope that makes possible the
initial attachment of the patient in the analysis and carries the patient
through the anxiety and pain of facing and working through various
resistances. Interactions between the patient and the analyst throughout the work can lead either to more primitive interactions (ego disin-
tegration) or more advanced interactions (ego integration). The patient at the beginning always has the tendency to make this new
relationship into an old one (repetition). Interpretation during these
stages attempts to induce ego disorganization, to transform the repetitions into a true regression in which the "ghosts" (unconscious com-

plexes) are allowed to taste "blood" (the passions) and awake to life (become fully conscious).

This touches on another meaning of transference for Loewald, the vital and ongoing interplay between the buried passions of the past and the preconscious fantasies of the present. The analyst's functions are twofold: progressively to remove transference barriers to a new object relationship, while at the same time holding for the patient the image of this new relationship and his "emerging core." There is a gradual movement from possibility to actuality of new and novel interaction with the analyst. These new interactions—this new object relationship with the analyst—are internalized and result in structural change and higher levels of ego integration. Loewald (1971), speaking of the transference neurosis, stated, "We may regard it as denoting the retransformation of a psychic illness which originated in pathogenic interactions with the important persons in the child's environment, into an interactional process with a new person, the analyst, in which the pathological infantile interactions and their intrapsychic consequences may become transparent and accessible to change by virtue of the analyst's objectivity and of the emergence of novel interaction possibilities" (p. 309).

Winnicott (1954), writing about regression, came to much the same conclusions, using his own peculiar language. He, too, understood development as a process of growth embedded in the matrix of relationships. Neurotic processes are called "a freezing of the failure situation . . . [a defense against] environmental failure" (p. 281). This captures rather well the original childhood trauma, in which the needs of the child are not adequately met, and the repetition of that trauma through subsequent development and relationships. There are two major types of regression: that which seeks to return to the early failure situation and its associated defenses (transference repetition) and that which seeks to return to early success situations involving memories of dependency. This implies that the child has experienced both good and bad environmental adaptation to his ego needs. I believe that here Winnicott is making explicit what Loewald only implies. In order for the patient to hold the hope and possibility of a new object relationship with the analyst, there must have been "early success situations" which the patient can refind via the true regression. The return to dependence forms the starting point for a new object relationship and resumption of developmental growth. Winnicott postulated a sequence that describes microscopic movement in an analytic hour, as well as macroscopic shifts through longer phases of an analysis. The analytic setting gives the patient the confidence and safety to regress. Regression involves a simultaneous seeking of the early dependence and an acting out, a transference repetition. Through the analyst's statement of what happened in the acting out of the transference, the patient develops an understanding of what happened in the original failure situation. In favorable cases, an unfreezing of the failure situation takes place, leading to anger related to the early environmental failure, felt and expressed in the transference, and a new sense of self, based on true dependence. Out of this develops a genuine vitality and vigor of current needs and wishes.

What I am interested in examining clinically in this paper are the processes involved in the movement in the analysis between these two poles, past and present, repetition and creativity. The neurotic complex results in the repetition of old patterns of love and hate; it causes an arrest of growth somewhere between a "true regression," where the passions of the past are fully relived, and the novel interactional possibilities of the present. Clinically, in analyzing and interpreting the elements of transference repetition as consistently and fully as possible, one should then see the emergence of oscillating and reciprocal shifts toward a truer understanding and reliving of the past, and a corresponding freshness and vitality in the current relationship between patient and analyst. As we witness the intensification of the transference resistance, these two poles emerge most clearly. By a truer understanding of the past, I have in mind the release of repressed childhood anxieties and affects, the filling in of details about important childhood traumas, and the recasting of a personal myth (Kris, 1956). By novel interactions in the present, I have in mind a newfound freedom to love and hate the analyst in the inevitable deprivations and intimacy of the psychoanalytic situation.

CASE REPORT

The patient was a middle-aged man who entered psychoanalysis through the psychoanalytic clinic for an obsessional character disorder. Due to issues of confidentiality, I will not touch upon his history or his course in the analysis, except as it is referred to in the themes of the hour to be discussed. It was the last hour before the August break in the sixth year of the analysis. A synopsis of the process of the hour is laid out in sequence, with each section numbered for later reference.

I. I asked him if he had any further thoughts about the proposed fee increase. He stated that he felt it was reasonable. We then finalized the amount and date to start the fee increase.

II. He stated that he had a planned agenda, but was suddenly aware of spontaneous feelings. He then talked about my ending for vacation. He should feel something.

III. I asked, "Is that being compliant?"

IV. He responded, "Yes, but there's more . . . feeling sad." He talked about the upcoming job interview in another city.

V. I said, "This may be a potential ending for good."

VI. He said, "There's something different, your tone [begins to get tearful], you're not trying to hold onto me, you're not angry with me, not controlling [openly and uncontrollably crying]. I never felt that way before."

VII. I ventured, "Your parents were and are controlling. It is sad that you may leave and miss the potential benefits of the analysis."

VIII. He replied, "The first is true. Now I understand that I've felt the same way about you. Second, I appreciate your feelings, but I don't feel you're trying to impose them."

IX. I reminded him that, "Last year at this time, you also thought about leaving."

X. He said, "I forgot about that. You must feel I give you a hard time."

XI. He thought of an example at work where he tried to take control of a case from someone he supervised. He felt this was not good.

DISCUSSION

This hour is an example of a "mutative interpretation" or a "true regression" and the emergence of a new transference configuration. However, the interpretations offered are scant and brief and could not in themselves account for the dramatic shifts in affect within the hour. The mutative interpretation often takes place over a long block of time. The transference resistance, analyzed repeatedly in small bits, may dramatically come to a quick and unexpected resolution. Of course, this resolution itself may be unstable and require a period of working through before it reaches the level of a stable insight. I would like to sketch some of the factors that I believe coalesce to bring this hour to a "point of urgency" and that might be applicable to the larger question of the therapeutic action of psychoanalysis.

In an ordinarily successful analysis, various transference themes will arise that are unique to the interpersonal relationship between patient and analyst. These themes are metaphors, words, symbolic actions, and fantasies that are a product both of the patient's transference and of the analyst's particular style and countertransference. As the themes directly express transference meaning, they preexist and are independent of the analysis, yet their particular shape and direction may well be pulled by forces coming from the analyst. As the analysis proceeds, these themes will come to express aspects and elaborations of a core transference repetition (the transference neurosis) and, in fact, their sum will carry the meaning of the core transference. The themes tend to come and go during the day-to-day work, are gradually added to and altered, and can be transformed into new and unexpected meanings. These themes may have a life of only a few days or may continue through the entire analysis. In this particular hour, one can identify five such transference themes of varying lengths and degrees of elaboration. I will list the five themes and give a brief history of their life in the analysis.

1. CONFLICT ABOUT THE FEE

This theme was introduced into the hour at the very beginning (section I), through the finalization of a fee increase which had been proposed by me about a month before and had been discussed during the last month. The patient had been quite agreeable to the idea, raising no objections, although I had felt he wanted to avoid any extended discussion of his feelings about the matter. The history of conflict about the fee goes back to the beginning of the analysis when he had wanted a free analysis. When I did not accept this wish, he felt a fleeting resentment, worried that I was angry with him, and then agreed to the fee I proposed. This set a pattern that was repeated throughout the analysis, in which action on his part and reaction on my part took predominance over reflection and analysis. During the first three years of the analysis, he periodically did not pay the monthly bill, gradually accumulating a large debt. The patient had had serious monetary difficulties all of his adult life, and the transference acting out merely repeated these difficulties with me. However, certain conditions and difficulties on my part (this being a clinic analysis, my not setting clear boundaries about payment of the fee early in the analysis) certainly shaped how the conflict unfolded. Repeated attempts to analyze this only resulted in protestations that he could not pay me for various external reasons out of his control. This shifted any responsibility away from himself and allowed him not to see any internal conflict. He thought of it as wanting "unconditional love" from his father, feeling entitled to my giving him something without any obligations in return. Interpretations would be followed by brief intellectual compliance, but no lasting change in his behavior. Only after I set a limit, telling him the analysis would end immediately if he did not pay his monthly bill on time, did he begin to pay regularly, and gradually we could analyze the emotional determinants. In retrospect, he and I could never really extricate ourselves from a series of enactments in which both of us were caught up in.

Interpretation had been primarily directed toward the resistance to awareness of transference. In particular, he became more aware of his resentment toward me and his fear of provoking my anger. More recently, his view of me gradually changed from someone who was passive to someone who was clear and decisive; correspondingly, he developed pride in meeting his obligations and feeling less subservient to and more "equal" with me. However, these views remained intellectualized and unstable. This whole process, then, represented a gradual elaboration of the paternal transference described above, with the twin dynamic themes of longing and resentment.

2. CONFLICT ABOUT ENDING FOR VACATIONS

This being the last hour before our month-long interruption, he spontaneously mentioned my vacation (section II). In the past, he had consistently denied any reactions to my absences. This also had been analyzed as a resistance to awareness of transference. While he would intellectually agree that it was unusual not to be affected by my absence, he was never aware of feeling anything before or while I was gone. This was the first time he had ever brought up my vacation or other interruptions without my prompting. This denial of absence represented the prevailing transference in which he was the stoical, passive son who never complained, and I was the absent father. The theme had remained static and frozen, with the transference largely unconscious.

3. THE JOB IN ANOTHER CITY

He mentioned an upcoming job interview in a distant city (section IV). It represented a more recent turn in the analysis. Three months prior to this hour, he had brought up plans to look for a job in that city and move there. He had raised this idea for several years, but had made no earnest efforts to look until now. Over the last three months, I had attempted to analyze his searching for a job as a flight from the transference. He saw it only as external pressures and did not want to see any transference meaning, but several points did emerge gradually. He thought I was too rigid and authoritarian and did not give him enough support. He was aware of wanting to rebel against me. He did not want to depend upon me and guarded against "feeling boyish" or being a "crybaby." While he was aware of these feelings, they remained isolated and not consciously connected to his wish to leave the analysis. The strong resistance against seeing his wish to leave the analysis as a transference remained in effect.

4. SHOES ON THE COUCH

This was not mentioned in this hour, but a major shift in this theme was closely linked to his looking for a job, helping to illuminate the meaning of his flight from the analysis. From the first hour, he had taken off his shoes to lie on the couch. When asked about this, he had felt deferential to me and did not want to "dirty" my couch. In an hour adjacent to bringing up the job search, he spontaneously and without comment had started to leave his shoes on. Later, when asked about this, he said that he liked leaving them on, which suggested to me that he felt less subservient, more equal and aggressive toward me (similar to theme one). However, he never acknowledged any transference meaning to the change, although he did feel critical and rebellious when he discussed looking for a job (see theme 3).

5. WANTING TO SEDUCE ME INTO LIKING HIM

In three adjoining hours, three months prior to the reported hour, he had brought up the search for a job, started wearing his shoes on the couch, and spontaneously told me of a new fantasy configuration about me. He was aware of wanting "to seduce me into liking him," and revealed that he liked looking at me. This was a completely new creation in the analysis. Over the next several months, we touched briefly on a number of points related to this fantasy. He became aware of needing to flirt with both sexes: telling sexual jokes to men, and acting seductively with women. He wondered several times if he had homosexual feelings about me. He had a brief but urgent wish to hold me in a session. He talked for the first time about an underlying feminine identification, weak, passive, and dependent, which he hid behind his stoical masculine image. He very clearly did not want to depend upon me in any way, that being too feminine. While this theme, too, was not directly mentioned in the hour under consideration, the meanings that started to emerge from the transference fantasy were a major influence on his flight from the analysis (see theme 3). His fear of being "boyish" or "a crybaby," linked to a fantasy of being a girl, was a reason for his fear of depending upon me. Out of this developed some insight that his aloofness and lack of emotional response to me was an avoidance of dependency, but that he wanted to be dependent at the same time. He could see, for example, that his lack of response to my vacations was odd (see theme 2). These insights remained intellectual and isolated, yet they represented a completely new turn in the transference, a revealing of the other side of his paternal transference. These five themes are either mentioned or alluded to (through linkage to a related theme) at the beginning of the hour under discussion. In their elaborated meanings, they carry the current transference resistance.

Transference, as a here-and-now experience, often becomes a true enactment. One definition of the word enact is "to represent . . . as on a stage, to personate (a character) dramatically, play (a part)" (*Oxford English Dictionary*). Previous psychoanalytic writers (see Jacobs, 1991) have emphasized the aspect of performance, seeing enactments as a behavioral expression of unconscious wish fulfillment and a need to involve the analyst as witness and gratifier of the wish. I use the term enactment in a broader sense, to mean the vivid reexperience of a childhood role played out on the stage of the analyst's consulting room. The analyst is assigned a part and is expected to join the play. Both parties lose their sense of distance and get swept up into the verbal and nonverbal interactions; both contribute intrapsychic dynamics to the shape of the interaction. The patient attempts to actualize the transference and evokes in the analyst an emotional reaction, rather than a reasoned analytic response (McLaughlin, 1991; Chused, 1991). The enactment captures the dual aspect of transference, as a compelling experience in itself yet an unreal and artificial creation; that is, it's just a play. In this view, enactments become a frequent transference experience. The patient's participation in the enactment consists of unconscious transference displacements and conscious aspects of the therapeutic alliance and the real relationship with the analyst. The real relationship includes a reaction to the analyst's personality and style and to the analyst's countertransference. The patient's unconscious transference contributes the primary dynamics to the content of most enactments.

If the transference is to be enacted in the here-and-now, the reciprocal question of how the analyst participates in the enactment is raised. The analyst's emotional response is a mixture of his own transference to the patient and an empathic response to the pressure of the patient's transference (McLaughlin, 1981; Loewald, 1986). There is a range of countertransference responses, from a quiet signal function for the analyst, to a minor lapse in his technique in which the patient then distorts or projects, to a more organized and sustained participation in the patient's transference. The analyst usually participates silently in this process. He observes his own reactions, emotions, fantasies, and memories, measuring them against his knowledge of his own customary and usual reactions. This allows him to separate his transference to the patient from his reaction to the patient's expectation of his response (the patient's transference) (Chused, 1991). Loewald (1986) points out that both analyst and patient have transferences to each other, as well as countertransferences, reactions to the transferred mental contents from the other person. What is generally called countertransference on the analyst's side would consist of a mixture of the analyst's transference and of his counterreaction to the patient's transference. The resulting knowledge about the patient, integrated with previous analytic work and the prevailing transference themes, may lead to a verbal interpretation by the analyst. Intrusion of the analyst's countertransference into the actual enactment of the transference is spontaneous and inevitable, a circumstance that must be distinguished from a prescriptive approach, in which a particular attitude or feeling of the analyst toward a patient is postulated as desirable or helpful.

There are two ways in which the analyst may participate in the enactment. The patient may pick out aspects of the analyst's personality or minor slips as evidence for his neurotic expectations, or the analyst may be pulled by the patient to experience himself as the patient neurotically expects him to be. The countertransference usually occurs in subtle ways, through tone of voice, silences, inattention, choice of words, and would be a regular part of every analysis. In most analyses, there also is an occasional more gross intrusion into the process by the analyst. Each analyst has his own blind spots which lead to countertransference difficulties with certain transference configurations. Increased anxiety, tiredness, or physical illness in the analyst all result in a greater tendency to act out countertransference pressure. During the period of heightened transference neurosis, there is a more sustained pull into the enactments. (For a detailed discussion of some of these issues, see Gill, 1983.)

Several months prior to the hour detailed above, I had become aware of feeling angry with the patient and realized that my "pushing" a transference interpretation contained an angry, controlling, and critical tone. For example, about a month prior to the hour under discussion, he had brought up his search for a job, which I attempted to shift to a discussion of his wish to leave the analysis. He replied that he felt he had accomplished all he needed to. Significant material, quite relevant to the transference concerning issues of dependency and his seductive feelings toward me (theme 5) then emerged. However, I was finding his shift away from the question of termination frustrating, echoing my view of his prevalent use of denial throughout the analysis, and the added urgency I felt that he would prematurely terminate the analysis. As he characteristically resisted my attempts to interpret his denial that there was significant unanalyzed material, I found myself becoming more insistent. After a period of silence, we had the following interchange. I said, "We've been discussing how you keep yourself distant and aloof. It's a question of whether you want to dig into this, or do you want to leave?" He replied that it was not he who wanted to leave, there were outside factors. I then said that we needed to examine his need to keep things how they were, which felt safer. He replied that he had already made big progress. He did not agree with me when I kept bringing up termination, because it could be months or years away.

It is not hard to see my angry countertransference. I abruptly shifted away from promising material, criticized him for being aloof, and demanded he "dig into this or leave." After he responded in his characteristic way, I again made a demanding critical statement, which he responded to with more visible anger and denial. Soon after this hour, I became more aware of my anger and need to be controlling, and silently made an effort to correct it. I thought of my personal tendency to become quietly angry and subtly controlling when faced with a loss. As a candidate, I felt some internal pressure to complete a successful case, adding to my anger. In the hour being analyzed, I believe he alluded to a perception both of that countertransference and of my correction of that countertransference. In section VI, when he spoke of my "tone," he was referring to his experience of my trying to hold onto him and control him and the later experience of my not trying to hold onto him. These were accurate perceptions of my countertransference and its correction. Later in that hour, my angry countertransference crept back in when he was discussing his feeling that I was not trying to impose upon him (section VIII) and I abruptly shifted to his "leaving" (section IX), certainly a shift away from promising new material. He responded by a guilty reaction to my angry statement, "You must feel I give you a hard time" (section X).

It appeared to be crucial that the analyst was able to modify his countertransference and withdraw from the enactment, although there was evidence in the hour that this transference/countertransference interplay continued in a subtle way. The patient was able to experience the analyst both as the transference figure he expected and as a figure who responded to his pressure in a new and novel way. This perception of something different (section VI), the patient's contrasting experiences of the analyst's countertransference, facilitated the emergence of affect and the transference transformation. The analyst's responses to the patient were organized and sustained over several months.

Could we not call this a countertransference neurosis? Can the transference be a real and vivid repetition in the here-and-now without the participation and involvement of the analyst? As Bird (1972) puts it, "the patient must be enabled to include the analyst in his neurosis . . . to share his neurosis with the analyst" (p. 279). For Loewald (1986), the transference/countertransference matrix, in its unconscious rapport between patient and analyst, is a necessary condition for any deeper understanding of the patient's unconscious conflicts. He states, "The resonance between the patient's and the analyst's unconscious underlies any genuine psychoanalytic understanding and forms the point of departure for eventually arriving at verbal interpretations of the material heard or otherwise perceived" (p. 283), and "the capacity for countertransference is a measure of the analyst's ability to analyze. Countertransference, in this general sense, is a technical term for the analyst's responsiveness to the patient's love-hate for the analyst" (p. 286).

Whether the analyst's countertransference participation in the transference enactment has been silent or overt, what is crucial is his ability to disentangle himself from the enactment, organize his understanding of the mutual experience, and communicate his understanding to the patient through interpretation. Does this not suggest that the analyst's neutrality is not a static phenomenon, but a dynamic interplay between pressures from the patient's transference and from his own unconscious conflicts? Jacobs (1986) describes neutrality as having an outer aspect orientated toward the patient and an inner aspect oriented toward himself. In subtle (and not so subtle) ways, the analyst is constantly pulled into and pulls away from transference enactments. The analyst participates in and experiences both disintegrative and integrative interactions with the patient. He differs from the patient only in having better control and insight over his own transference. Both Bird (1972) and Jacobs (1986) point out how difficult it is for the analyst to sustain this level of involvement with the patient, and the various unconscious ways the analyst can avoid or dampen transference. Loewald (1986) suggests that the analyst often attempts to rationalize and screen out his own unsettling transference/countertransference responses, thus colluding with the patient's defensive tendencies.

From the patient's point of view, the analyst is always experienced as a participant in the enactment, even if the analyst is a "blank screen." However, the experience of the analyst as remote, unemotional, and uninvolved is likely to promote heightened transference resistance rather than a regressive enactment. It may be that the inevitable countertransference of the analyst, by intensifying the transference enactment, propels the analysis forward by promoting a true regression, as long as the analyst can pull back and interpret the enactment. I have found, for example, that a countertransference slip on my part has occasionally triggered an intense transference enactment in the patient's mind, opening up previously unacknowledged material for exploration. Likewise, any action, verbal or otherwise, on the analyst's part, may be misinterpreted by the patient and serve as such a trigger. The analyst may then be able to reflect upon his own involvement in the enactment, enabling him to see more clearly the patient's transference. It is this contrast between action and reflection that makes possible an interpretation of resistance to resolution of the transference in the here-and-now.

Gray (1987, 1990), on the other hand, points out a major danger to this type of transference work. It is the analyst's use of "suggestion" (often using countertransference awareness to intuit unconscious motivations in the patient) to locate and interpret the drive derivatives that are represented in the transference, bypassing the defensive operations of the ego. This is a constant temptation for the analyst, for it often evokes a countertransference of seduction or power, which can be highly gratifying to the analyst. This naming of drive derivatives can be quite effective in promoting transference enactments, yet will lead to a type of ego passivity, which results in a tendency to depend on the transference and a lack of structural change in the ego. Gray (1990) recommends that interpretation be directed toward "the ego's surface-near manifestations of resistance" (p. 1095), but might also include "a thin slice of drive derivative" (personal communication). He rightly points out that the effective analysis of resistances "will *of itself* allow gradual, analytically sufficient ego assimilation of the warded-off mental elements as they are able to move less fearfully into consciousness" (p. 1095).

The transformation of the transference started in section II when the patient became aware of spontaneous feelings, an unusual event for him, and of sadness (section IV), a breakthrough of repressed affect. Then in section VI, laid out and fully felt for the first time, was a further elaboration of the transference repetition and a new experience of me. What he had felt rebellious about was a view of me as needing to hold onto him, forcing him to stay, and being angry that he might not stay. I had been aware that his father had such a need of him, but this was the first time it had emerged so clearly in the transference. I, too, had participated in the enactment for a period of time as an angry, controlling agent. Indeed, this analysis had been dominated by action and a series of unrecognized enactments. This point represented a first departure from that mutual repetition. As the transference repetition was fully felt by both of us, there was the simultaneous emergence of new affects (tears and sadness), and a perception of himself and me in a new way. He saw that I was neither controlling nor seducing, yet remained available to him. I could tolerate both his aggression and his love. For himself, he was aware of his prior aloofness, of losing me, and of his deeply felt love and dependency. In section VII, there was a further elaboration of the transference. He acknowledged that he felt I had been controlling, no longer was, and he now felt freer to hold a divergent view without the need to fight or hurt me. At the end of the hour (section XI), there was a further comment on the established transference/countertransference through a parallel example in his current life, in which he was the controlling and seducing father figure. He developed spontaneous insight into his role which paralleled the insight in the transference. This hour opened up the possibility for further analytic work on the transference themes. However, as the enactment described was not rooted in an ongoing genuine psychoanalytic process and the patient was actively considering termination, it was not clear if that possibility could be realized.

Gray (1987, 1990) emphasizes the experience of the ego's resistance in the here-and-now of the analytic setting and the subsequent mutual observation of these defensive operations. He believes that the insight gained by repeated experiences and understanding through interpretation of characteristic defensive patterns strengthens the ego and leads to a gradually increased consciousness of drive derivatives. I am emphasizing the here-and-now of the analytic setting, but beyond that an aspect of transference enactment, and its subsequent mutual examination by analyst and patient. This type of analytic work belongs in the phases of the analysis during the height of the transference neurosis, when both the resistance and drive derivatives are near the surface.

In all of the transference themes in this clinical example, the work has been almost exclusively in the here-and-now, with the interpretive effort toward resistance to awareness of transference. The aim was to bring transference into conscious awareness to be relived as an interpersonal experience. Interpretation of resistance to the awareness of transference could be seen more broadly as the effort of the analyst to help the patient enter into the enactment of the transference in the here and now. There had certainly been a concurrent focus on the patient's direct relationship with his father, both in the present and in the past, but I made no attempt to link that to transference themes in this particular analysis. I would suggest that the here-and-now enactment of transference repetition should be the *leading edge,* coming before the patient can fully accept the past as a determinant of present conflicts. Interpretations linking the past to the current transference should then be part of the working through, following awareness in the here-and-now. There is a synergism in which the released affects in the transference energize and fill in the past, which, in turn, illuminates the origins of the transference. As the transference repetition is enacted as an interpersonal experience, the analyst, too, is drawn into and participates in the enactment (silently or not so silently). The skill of the analyst is in being able to participate in the enactment, and then in being able to draw back, observing his own participation and interpreting to the patient the nature of the enactment. It is this enactment, brought to the "point of urgency," that leads to transference transformations.

Transformations may come from a variety of analytic efforts. In this paper, I am presenting a type of transformation that produces a flash of insight. This is experienced as a mutual sense of transcendence. For the patient, a sense of new vistas suddenly opens up and invites exploration. The analyst, too, can empathize with the patient's excitement as well as relook at his own conflicts and memories. Slow and patient interpretation of details of transference themes producing a gradual transformation may be more common. There are two parts to the transformation, a vivid experience of the transference repetition, the "true regression," and the simultaneous experience of a "new and novel" relationship with the analyst. The patient must have experiences of transference repetition and experiences that do not conform to transference expectations. Both types of experience must be present to allow for the possibility of a transformation. Then, as the transference enactment is brought to a true regression, repression of affects connected with the repetition and with deeper layers of resistance is loosened. Memories and affects of earlier traumatic experiences, along with contrasting memories and affects of safety and satisfaction (Winnicott's early success situation) are also called forth. This emergence of a mixture of memories and affects of both disintegrative and integrative experiences, in the here-and-now of the transference and from the past, allows for the transformation to something new and novel with the analyst. On the other hand, this possibility of a new relationship gives the patient courage to feel what he has heretofore avoided.

In general, it is easier to understand entering into a transference enactment; it is the result of the traditional work of analysis of transference resistance. Resistance to resolution of the transference might more broadly be seen as the mutual effort of patient and analyst to work out of the transference enactment; that is, the resolution of the transference repetition and the recognition of new interpersonal aspects in the relationship with the analyst. How the patient can work out of the enactment is more mysterious. The aim of the resistance at this point is to maintain the repetition and the enactment. The patient is under the full sway of the transference repetition and yet must grasp that it is a distortion of what is possible and available in the current analytic relationship. The concept of the enactment suggests a way out of this dilemma. The patient as protagonist and director assigns a role to the analyst and *expects* a certain response. When the analyst reacts differently than expected, the patient is *surprised*. It is the analyst's ability to step out of the play and call attention to the various roles being played out, gradually teaching the patient to develop a similar ability (the split between the observing and experiencing ego). It is often this element of surprise that starts the process of the patient pulling away from his role. Interpretation of resistance would be aimed at demonstrating the nature of the repetition, through memories of prior integrative experiences with the analyst, examination of spontaneous new experiences with the analyst, and memories of similar emotional configurations in earlier developmental periods. Even though the development of insight can be sudden and dramatic (as in this hour), it must result from the accumulation of repeated disintegrative and integrative experiences with the analyst, along with interpretation of those experiences over a long period of time, another aspect of the working-through process.

These transformations are part of the effort toward resolution of the transference, but at this stage of the analysis, the transformed transference is experienced by the patient as a new or long-ignored aspect of the core transference. The newly transformed transference then becomes a transference resistance to further transformations. Here, the patient's self-experience of rebellion hid the deeper layer of homosexually tinged dependency which is not fully conscious. Working through, at this stage, is the constant and tedious reworking in the here-and-now of the details of the transference themes, with regressive movement back into the transference repetition and progressive movement forward into the transformed themes. This would lead toward both an increase in complexity and the gradual transformation of these themes, producing a more complete view of the core transference. As the core transference becomes more fully realized and accepted, a shift starts toward other core transferences. In this example, there is the beginning of a movement from the oedipal paternal transference to the oedipal and preoedipal maternal transference. The working through also gradually rounds out the transformation of the perception of the analyst as someone different from transference expectations, where a new and more mature relationship is possible. This sequence of transference transformations leading to shifts in the core transferences is not a linear process, but a shifting mosaic in the actual analytic work, as different transferences may appear and disappear according to the multiple internal and external pressures felt by both patient and analyst.

Psychoanalytic technique should not be rigidly applied. It will vary depending on the patient, the stage of the analysis, and the particular dynamic themes. Blum (1983), in a review of extratransference interpretations, points out that not all conflicts and compromise formations appear within the transference. The "point of urgency" may be focused on an extratransference relationship, current reality, or past memory. Rangell (1991) proposes that transference is more revealing of conflicts and anxieties concerning separation than intrapsychic conflicts and anxieties concerning bodily harm and castration. He suggests that castration anxieties often lie behind separation anxieties and are less accessible in a transference approach. Dream interpretation and reconstruction often provide a more direct experience of castration anxieties.

I have highlighted the role of experience, both the reexperience of old configurations and the new experience of possible configurations, as a crucial force in the therapeutic action of psychoanalysis. The relationship between experience and insight is complex. I have suggested that experience of transference in the here-and-now of the analytic setting leads to one avenue of insight. What I have not explored in this paper and needs further elucidation is the step from recognition of the experience by the analyst to the gaining of insight by the patient. What can we say and how can we say it that will help the patient gain some distance from his or her repetitive tendencies? Along with Gill (1983), I believe that insight into present and past interpersonal relationships, while at the same time the patient experiences a new interpersonal relationship, provides optimal conditions for personal change in psychoanalysis.

BIBLIOGRAPHY

BIRD, B. (1972). Notes on transference. *J. Amer. Psychoanal. Assn.*, 20:267–301.
BLUM, H. P. (1983). The position and value of extratransference interpretation. *J. Amer. Psychoanal. Assn.*, 31:587–617.
CHUSED, J. F. (1991). The evocative power of enactments. *J. Amer. Psychoanal. Assn.*, 39:615–639.

FREUD, S. (1905). Fragment of an analysis of a case of hysteria. *S.E.*, 7:7–122.
——— (1912). The dynamics of transference. *S.E.*, 12:99–108.
——— (1914). Remembering, repeating and working-through. *S.E.*, 12:147–156.
GILL, M. M. (1954). Psychoanalysis and exploratory psychotherapy. *J. Amer. Psychoanal. Assn.*, 2:771–797.
——— (1982). *Analysis of Transference*, vol. 1. New York: Int. Univ. Press.
——— (1983). The interpersonal paradigm and the degree of the therapist's involvement. *Contemp. Psychoanal.*, 19:200–237.
GRAY, P. (1987). On the technique of analysis of the superego. *Psychoanal. Q.*, 56:130–154.
——— (1990). The nature of therapeutic action in psychoanalysis. *J. Amer. Psychoanal. Assn.*, 38:1083–1097.
JACOBS, T. (1986). On countertransference enactments. *J. Amer. Psychoanal. Assn.*, 34:289–307.
———(1991). The interplay of enactments. In *The Use of the Self*. Madison, Ct.: Int. Univ. Press.
KRIS, E. (1956). The personal myth. In *The Selected Papers of Ernst Kris*. New Haven: Yale Univ. Press, 1975, pp. 272–300.
LOEWALD, H. W. (1960). On the therapeutic action of psychoanalysis. In *Papers on Psychoanalysis*. New Haven: Yale Univ. Press, 1980, pp. 221–256.
——— (1971). The transference neurosis. Ibid., pp. 302–314.
——— (1986). Transference-countertransference. *J. Amer. Psychoanal. Assn.*, 34:275–287.
McLAUGHLIN, J. (1981). Transference, psychic reality and countertransference. *Psychoanal. Q.*, 50:639–664.
——— (1991). Clinical and theoretical aspects of enactment. *J. Amer. Psychoanal. Assn.*, 39:596–614.
SCHAFER, R. (1977). The interpretation of transference and the conditions for loving. *J. Amer. Psychoanal. Assn.*, 25:335–362.
RANGELL, L. (1991). Castration. *J. Amer. Psychoanal. Assn.*, 39:3–23.
STRACHEY, J. (1934). The nature of the therapeutic action of psychoanalysis. *Int. J. Psychoanal.*, 15:127–159.
WINNICOTT, D. W. (1954). Metapsychological and clinical aspects of regression within the psycho-analytical set-up. In *Through Paediatrics to Psycho-analysis*. New York: Basic Books, 1975, pp. 278–294.

APPLIED
PSYCHOANALYSIS

The Moment of Recognition

Rabbinic Discourse, Infancy, and Psychoanalysis

ALAN J. FLASHMAN, M.D.

Professionals and educated laymen agree that the past 30 years have brought about a revolution in our understanding of infant development during the very first months of life. The inchoate "blooming buzzing confusion" once felt to characterize the neonate has given way to a well-documented realm of finely tuned perceptions and highly complex interactions. These shifts in our thinking are generally assumed to imply that periods chronologically more remote from our own are conceptually more remote from our modern achievements. But in fact, they are not. I here examine ancient and medieval rabbinic texts and find these "modern" issues discussed. The formulations of these texts, I suggest, sharpen the psychoanalytic focus on the role of the integrative function in very early development.

RABBINIC DISCOURSE

THE TALMUDIC TEXT

THE MISHNAH KETUBOT 5:5 (3RD CENTURY C.E.) LISTS AMONG THE WIFE'S duties that of "nursing her son." The *Babylonian Talmud, Ketubot* 59b

Adjunct faculty, Paul Baerwald School of Social Work, Hebrew University, Jerusalem. A more extensive Hebrew version of this paper appeared in *Alon Uziel Memorial Volume*, ed. D. Boyarin, Jerusalem, 1990. I am grateful to Prof. D. Boyarin for his encouragement and wish to thank Albert J. Solnit for his steadfast support of the English version. Ms. Rosanna Lake and Ms. Sherry O'Neil were extremely patient and helpful in preparing this manuscript.

(5th-6th century) points out that this clause in the *Mishnah* accords with the opinion of the school of Hillel. The opposing view of the School of Shammai is cited, namely, that nursing is not among the wife's financial obligations. The source for this view is the *Tosefta Ketubot* 5:5, which reads as follows:

> If [the wife] vowed not to nurse her son, the School of Shammai says she takes her nipple right out of his mouth, and the School of Hillel says [the husband] can force her to continue nursing. If she is divorced, she cannot be forced to nurse. *If her son has already come to know her,* she receives compensation and must continue to nurse, *because of the danger* [to the infant from interrupting the nursing] [Lieberman, 1967, p. 73].

In short, a divorcee is not required to nurse her son according to both schools. The exception to this rule is in the case where the infant knows or recognizes his mother. In this circumstance, she is obliged to the child, not to her ex-husband, lest interruption of the nursing endanger the child.

The *Babylonian Talmud Ketubot* 59b–60a proceeds to discuss this enigmatic, vague phrase, "if he knows her."

> Up to what point [does the baby know his mother]? Rava said in the name of R. Jeremiah bar Abba who said in the name of Rav: three months. Samuel[1] said: thirty days. R. Isaac said in the name of R. Yohanan: fifty days. R. Simi bar Ashi said: The law is according to [the opinion of] R. Isaac in the name of R. Yohanan.

The Talmud has trouble accepting the formula of 30 days quoted in the name of Samuel.

> We can easily comprehend the opinions of Rav and R. Yohanan, as each infant will develop according to his individual quickness. But with regards to Samuel's opinion, is such [precocious] development a common finding? When Rami bar Ezekiel came [from Palestine to Israel] [Albeck, 1969, p. 208] he said: pay no attention to such formulae composed by my brother Judah in the name of Samuel. What Samuel really said was: At any time that he [a given baby] knows her [his mother].

Could Samuel mean that the average baby knows his mother at 30 days and that therefore cessation of nursing after 30 days would be a dangerous practice sufficient to *require* the reluctant divorcee to continue nursing? Surely 50 days or 3 months would be within the spec-

---

1. I present the primary texts in what I believe to be their most acceptable form. For discussion of the textual variants the interested reader is referred to the Hebrew version of this paper (1990).

trum of usual development, but 30 days? Rami bar Ezekiel answers this question by reinterpreting Samuel's statement. Samuel never cited an age at all, but rather held that each infant would be judged according to his own development. Rami's brother, Judah bar Ezekiel, illustrious founder of the Pumbedita academy in Babylonia, redacted Samuel's statement, which should be taken to mean, "Even as early as, say, thirty days."[2]

> A [divorced] woman came before Samuel [wishing permission to stop nursing]. He [Samuel] said to R. Dimi b. Joseph, "Go check her." He went and seated her in a row of women. He took her baby and brought him round to the women. When he came to her [the mother], he [the baby] lifted his eyes toward her. She [the mother] forced her eyes away from him. He said to her: Lift your eyes up. Get up and take your son.

A practical example is brought from the court of Samuel. A mother-infant dyad is examined according to the baby's capacity to form a discernibly different visual contact with his mother. The mother attempts to avert her gaze, but Samuel (or his associate R. Dimi) cannot be fooled. The baby is deemed to recognize his mother, and she is required to continue to nurse him.

Another important question, apparently related to the case in Samuel's court, is raised: if one examines recognition visually, how could one examine a blind child? The answer is offered by R. Ashi (5th century) of the last generation of Amoraim in Babylon: he can be tested by recognition of the smell and taste of his mother's body or milk.

MAIMONIDES

The greatest medieval codifier, Maimonides (12th century), formulates the law as follows (*Mishneh Torah,* Hilkhot Ishut 21:16):

> A divorced woman cannot be coerced to nurse. Rather, should she so desire, he [the father] pays her a fee and she nurses the baby, and should she not so desire, she gives him [the father] his son for him to take care of. All this pertains in the circumstance that she has not nursed him to the point that he [the baby] knows her. But, if he knows her, even if he is blind, he is not to be taken away from his mother, due to danger to the baby. Rather, she is to be coerced to nurse him, for a wage, until he is twenty-four months of age.

---

2. A possible explanation of this redaction would be to facilitate memorization. The dates cited correspond exactly to dates that a Rabbinic student of Talmudic days would have known from memory in the *Mishnah Bechorot* 4:1, on a different matter. See Mikliszanski (1982), who emphasizes the mnemotechnic factor in Talmudic redaction.

What is patent in Maimonides' formulation is the lack of any spec-ified age. His text adheres closely to the general formulation of the *Tosefta,* "if he knows her," and to Samuel's opinion according to Rami bar Ezekiel, "at any time that he knows her." Two matters are left ambiguous. "Even if he is blind" could refer to the ability of even the blind baby to know his mother or to our ability to ascertain such recog-nition even in the case of a blind baby. Nor is "danger to the baby" articulated. As nursing is the matter at hand, one might assume that the danger has to do generally with a failure in nutritional intake. This could refer to nursing from another woman at an early age or refusal to take other foods at ages closer to 24 months. Here the infant's recognition of his mother is used as a *sign* that cessation of nursing *could* endanger the baby.

RASHI

The greatest medieval Talmudic commentator, R. Solomon b. Isaac ("Rashi") (11th century), takes an entirely different tack:

> "If he knows her" = that he doesn't want to nurse from another woman.
> "up to what point" = At how many months are we to say that he knows to recognize her rather than to nurse from another?

He interprets the *Tosefta* as relating to the *direct* endangerment of the infant due to his recognition of his mother. Recognition here is not a sign of a potential danger. The recognition itself, by which is meant the ability to distinguish between mother and another nursemaid and thus to refuse the latter, is the *source* of the danger. When Rashi interprets Samuel's opinion, he deletes the matter of refusal to nurse.

For Rashi, the general gist of the text and the question "until when" refer to the baby's refusal to nurse from another woman as a sign of recognition and as a direct source of danger. However, the opinion of Samuel, at least according to Rami bar Ezekiel and to the story told of Samuel's court, is that there is some other, apparently visual, form of recognition that is to be checked. Since Rashi interprets the original *Tosefta* source in a manner inconsistent with Samuel, we would be justified in concluding that Rashi would not decide the law according to Samuel. We would then assume that he would adopt the opinion of R. Yohanan, i.e., 50 days, as normative, and consider the rest of the discussion to be of academic interest.

Indeed, later medieval sources corroborate that Rashi holds R. Yohanan's opinion to be the lawful one, but they disagree on Samuel's opinion and the normative milestone of R. Yohanan. Some commentators try to harmonize these sections by interpreting R. Yohanan's 50 days as the age at which a baby is considered capable of recognition and therefore requiring examination. Prior to 50 days examination is unnecessary, but if it is clear even without formal examination that recognition is present, the mother must nurse in all cases in deference to possible danger. A more creative harmonization is suggested by HaMeiri (13 century). Samuel's case involved a divorcee whose baby, prior to the age of 50 days, refused to nurse from another woman. The visual recognition test was employed to corroborate the meaning of the baby's refusal to nurse from another woman prior to the age at which recognition would be assumed to account for such a refusal (Sofer, 1968, p. 251). A third opinion has Samuel examine a child older than 50 days who has already refused to nurse from another woman. The examination is valid only *after this age,* to confirm that refusal to nurse is a sign of recognition. Prior to 50 days the refusal to nurse from another woman is presumed to be of no ultimate importance. Thus, at any age a child who will transfer nursemaids need cause no alarm and his mother may stop her nursing.

JERUSALEM TALMUD

In the parallel discussion of the *Tosefta* in the *Jerusalem Talmud* (4th century), R. Jeremiah's opinion, quoting Rav, of 3 months is cited. From this point the text differs significantly from that of the *Babylonian Talmud:*

> R. Zeira gazed at him [R. Jeremiah]. He said, "What are you looking at me like that for? I could go even further in Samuel's opinion, and say three days." But then Samuel had his particular view here. Samuel, after all, used to say, "I can remember [or recognize?] the midwives who delivered me." R. Joshua b. Levi said, "I can remember the man who circumcized me." R. Yohanan said, "I can remember the women who stayed with mother through her labour [with me]" [5:6, 36b].

The conversation takes place between R. Zeira and his student R. Jeremiah (Albeck, 1969, p. 235). The text emphasizes the visual nature of recognition, the broad, even extreme range of ages in the development of the capacity for visual recognition, but it says nothing about refusal to nurse. It is easy to appreciate the logic behind the conclusion of some sages that this text accepts Samuel's opinion.[3]

3. This section is *not* cited in Maimonides' own abridgement of this chapter of the Jerusalem Talmud (Lieberman, 1947, p. 55). However, see a review of this work by Mikliszanski (1976).

On the literary level, one is struck by the dominance of the visual mode. When R. Zeira hears R. Jeremiah's statement, he *stares* at him, apparently in amazement, perhaps with questionable recognition? R. Jeremiah understood this stare as a question. In other words, teacher and pupil engaged in effective, nonverbal, visual communication!

ISAIAH DI TRANI

A different approach to the text is offered by the 13th-century scholar Isaiah Di Trani (The Elder):

> Our teacher [Rashi] interprets recognition to mean refusal to nurse from another woman. I can't accept this, for if that's the case, why ask "Until what age" and where is there room for sages to disagree about which age? When we see such a refusal, we will force her [to continue nursing]. What's more, that woman who was placed in a lineup of women, who needs such an examination!? Just try and see if he will nurse from another woman! Therefore, it seems to me that even though the baby will accept a different nursemaid, if he recognizes his mother, she is required [to continue nursing] *because since he knows her, if she gives him up, separation from him will be very hard on him and lead him into danger.* For this reason the question "until when" is asked, to wit, by what age is the infant capable of knowing his mother *such that he will be endangered by separation from her.* Even this test that is reported, checking if he recognizes all those women, according to [Rashi's] solution if he refused to nurse, why tell us he lifted up his face. Quite the contrary, he nursed from other women, but nonetheless because he recognized his mother she was forced [to continue nursing him]. The terms themselves bespeak this by stating "if he recognized her" and not "if he refused to nurse from another woman."

DEVELOPMENTAL RESEARCH

METHODOLOGICAL CONSIDERATIONS

In turning to a comparison of these ancient texts with modern research, I must first list some caveats:

1. In the ancient world and up until the not so distant past, mortality, in the first two years, and especially in the first few months, was exceedingly high. Any infectious illness was cause for alarm, potentially lethal, and entirely untreatable. Any nutritional disturbance would be felt to predispose a baby to potentially grave risks (Holt and Howland, 1920, pp. 43ff., 127f.). Thus the "danger" in the text might refer to any disturbance that raises the global risk of danger, not necessarily a risk of direct demise due to malnutrition.

2. The question of the *Talmud* is pragmatic and hermeneutic. The *Tosefta* tells us a practical legal outcome of the baby's recognition of his mother: that she can be coerced to continue nursing due to danger. The question of the *Talmud,* "at what age," refers to the *Tosefta:* at what age would the *Tosefta* mean to coerce the mother. On the other hand, modern research would ask a theoretical question in order to interpret reality, not to legislate it. Research could only demonstrate the presence or absence of behaviors taken to indicate an abstract construct, "recognition." So the recognitions spring from different contexts, answer different questions, and employ different methods. One would hardly ask modern science, under the circumstances, to validate or invalidate the legal pragmatic conclusion (Lewis, 1973; Stern, 1985).

3. The text can tolerate a range of interpretations. At one end of the spectrum, giving greater emphasis to the rights of the mother, the question could be taken to mean: at what age could we assume that most babies know their mothers to the extent that cessation of nursing would endanger them? At the other extreme, if we give priority to avoidance of danger, the question could mean: at what age are there even the smallest signs of recognition in at least some babies? Intermediate positions are obviously possible. The different opinions offered could refer to a difference of opinion about the facts of development. They could also be a sign of disagreement not about fact but about the very meaning of the question, that is, with which developmental fact is the law concerned? Developmental research may assist us in mapping developmental facts with greater accuracy, but it could hardly be expected to determine the legal relevance of these facts.

VISUAL PERCEPTION

In the discussions regarding Samuel's opinion, there is silent consensus that a baby is capable of visually perceiving his mother's face at or before 50 days, at 30 days, even at 3 days. This consensus would have met with "scientific" ridicule 50 or even 30 years ago. The young infant was "known" to perceive only shadows and movement. It was only in the late 1960s, with the convincing work of Fantz (1963, 1965), that developmental researchers came to accept the newborn's ability to perceive visually with astonishing accuracy. What accounts for this modern "rediscovery"? First, the newborn's visual accuracy can be demonstrated scientifically only by comparing minute but quantifiable behavioral and physiological differences between his response to visual stimuli that are novel and his responses to familiar stimuli. Our ability to quantify these response differences depended upon technological advances in recording and especially the video camera with its potential for microanalysis of split-second changes. Second, and of greater interest, is the finding that the newborn is capable of visual accuracy at a fixed distance. The capacity for accommodation, that is, to focus alternately on objects at different distances, develops only later. Thus, it was only after researchers examined the newborn's capacities within the context of this limitation that these capacities could be proven (Cohen et al., 1979; Aslin, 1987). The newborn perceives with clarity in a plane at a distance of 18 cm. from his eyes. It turns out that this plane is ideally suited for perception of his mother's face during nursing and other intimate interactions. Indeed, the sensitive lay person commonly places his face at about this distance when cooing with a newborn. This developmental discovery may help us to understand Samuel's procedure of *bringing* the baby into close face-to-face contact with each woman in the row, or perhaps seating the child in each woman's lap and inspecting his visual response.

VISUAL INTERACTION

In Samuel's test, the mother notes a visual interaction initiated by her baby and attempts to interrupt this sequence by gaze aversion. Visual interactive sequences have been well documented in recent studies. Researchers have convincingly demonstrated the infant's distress when a mother presents an unresponsive blank face. The infant begins to manifest this response from age 2 to 3 weeks and by 7 weeks his distress is striking and unmistakable (Bennett, 1980; Robson, 1968; Stern, 1974, 1977). Thus we have confirmation of a form of test which would be valid earlier than R. Yohanan's 50 days, and even at or before the age of 4 weeks.

INDIVIDUAL DIFFERENCES

The Talmudic text is satisfied to explain the discrepancy between R. Yohanan and Rav based upon individual differences in developmental achievements. Are there indeed individual differences in a matter so basic as recognition of mother and the capacities involved in this recognition? The classic work of Sybil Escalona (1968) gives a clear affirmative reply. She studied the paths of development of 32 infants, focusing on inborn differences in level of activity, which was found to vary greatly from infant to infant. The activity level, in turn, greatly influenced each infant's ability to organize perceptually the outside world. In analyzing the behavior of babies 4 to 12 weeks of age, Escalona found that the less active babies developed a greater ability to concentrate and attend to a face presented to them and had an increased capacity for visual perception (pp. 101ff.). For Maimonides and those who interpret recognition as visual recognition, the Talmudic dictum, "Each according to his individual quickness," gains laboratory credibility.

THE BLIND CHILD

What is known of the development of attachment and recognition between a blind baby and his mother? Selma Fraiberg (1977) devoted many years of patient and sensitive study to blind children. From a cohort of 10 blind infants she concluded that the blind babies developed attachment and recognition at the same chronological ages as their sighted peers. The babies learned best to distinguish mother from others via auditory perception. It was especially the nuances of and interactions with mother's voice that mediated attachment and recognition (see also Burlingham, 1975; Nagera and Colonna, 1965). What then of R. Ashi's answer: taste and smell? According to one interpretation R. Ashi's statement answers the question, "How can we *examine* the blind baby?" One could well assume that a method of examination would need to be free of mother's intentional interferences. Her voice would hardly do, whereas smell and taste (of mother or of her milk or both) would fit the bill. Infant olfactory and auditory discrimination of mother from others is a well-documented result of modern research (Lozoff et al., 1977).

THE MOMENT OF RECOGNITION

What does modern infant psychiatry research contribute to "scientific" determination of the infant's recognition of his mother? What observable phenomena related to such recognition have been elicited?

1. The earliest signs are demonstrable in the first weeks and even days of life. Brazelton et al. (1974, 1979) were able to characterize a difference in the form of organization of the infant's behavior, for example, attention span and coordination of behaviors, in the presence of mother versus other women. These differences can be noted at 2 or 3 weeks of age and are clearly present at 4 weeks. By that age, the reciprocal interactional pattern has become a special "dance" which is reserved for a special partner. The earliest signs of discrimination between mother and others can be regularly observed when attention is given to interactional patterns rather than "capacities" present in the infant. That is, the laboratory came to investigate an *in vivo* situation more closely resembling the interactional home *in vivo*, and began to discover evidence of discrimination at earlier ages (see also Carpenter, quoted in Anders and Zeanah, 1984).

2. The most readily observed sign of a socially significant discrimination between mother and others is the "selective smile" which the baby presents to mother only. Developmentalists generally cite the presence of a nonspecific "social smile" between 1 and 2 months, with passage to the selective smile between 2 and 3 months of age. Often an unstated assumption accompanies this finding, that is, that the failure of the infant to inhibit a smile to strangers constitutes proof of lack of recognition of mother. Obviously, this gross milestone dates from the period prior to careful observation of interactional proximity. I would restate this milestone in a different manner: all agree that recognition of mother announces itself beyond possible mistake in the form of a selective smile at about 3 months (Solnit et al., 1986, p. 10).

3. What about a transfer of maternal figure? One way to read the Talmudic text would be that the question involves not just changing of nursemaids but wholesale transfer of parental figures. The most moderate form of such a reading would describe the situation as follows: The baby has had continuous contact with both mother and father, moves from mother's to father's home where nursing is transferred to a hired nursemaid, and some continuity of contact is maintained with mother. The most extreme reading would propose the following: The baby has been attended solely by mother. All contact with mother is interrupted, the baby is transferred to the exclusive care of a heretofore unknown father and nursemaid.

It is with regard to the more extreme situation that the work of Yarrow and Goodwin (1973) is of some relevance. These researchers documented the responses of infants placed at birth in foster care and subsequently transferred to an entirely new adoptive home. Of the 70 infants studied, 9 were in the age group 1 to 3 months at the time of the transfer, 10 were from 3 to 4 months, 18 were 4 to 5 months. In the youngest group not a single baby suffered from a disturbance of eating. Of course, none were breast-fed. Nor were there any "social" disturbances. One suffered sleep disruption, another an "emotional" disorder, and 2 developmental regression. In the older groups the percentages of gross disturbances rose appreciably. It is of interest that in all age cohorts the incidence of eating disturbance was less than the incidence of other disturbances. These workers summarize their conclusions as follows:

> Before three months of age, few infants show any clear reaction to the change in environment. Of the nine children who were under three months at the time of placement, two show definite disturbances and three show behavior interpreted as indicating a very mild reaction. . . . In the four to five months group 36 percent of the cases show disturbed

behavior. By five months, 50 percent of the infants give evidence of disruption; in the six months placement group, 86 percent manifest behavior suggesting that the separation was a disturbing experience. All the infants separated from foster mothers between 7 and 16 months showed clear-cut evidence of disturbance. . . . Under three months, 55 percent of the children show no reaction; 45 percent give a very mild reaction. . . . By four months there is a clear change: 72 percent of the infants show moderately severe to very severe reactions. . . . Our data also indicate that there is no point in early infancy at which infants are completely insensitive to the changes in environment associated with a change from a foster to an adoptive home. It seems unlikely, however, that the reactions of the youngest infants represent responses to the loss of a mother figure. It seems more parsimonious at this point to interpret the reactions in terms of response to a general environmental change [p. 1037].

These workers cite their own previous work, dating from 1967, in which they found "a significant number of infants are giving highly discriminating responses to their mothers and other adults" only at 4 to 5 months of age (p. 1038; compare Bowlby, 1973, pp. 52ff.).

One might wonder if the "objective" finding of some reaction in 45 percent of babies under 3 months of age would be interpreted as more significant in the light of later interactional studies. In addition, there is no breakdown of ages in the group of 1 to 3 months, so that we have no clue whether the incidence of mild reactions is related to age.

In summary, it is possible to demonstrate subtle, but consistent signs of discrimination between mother and others within the first few weeks of life. This discrimination becomes much more obvious between 2 and 3 months. Beyond 3 to 4 months most infants manifest striking disturbances upon separation from mother. The general range of this developmental spectrum coincides roughly with the range in the Talmudic text.

TRANSFER OF NURSEMAID

The Talmudic text deals with a case that would hardly occur in modern times and is therefore impossible to study directly. However, a particularly modern quandary sheds light from a different angle. A woman gives birth to a baby whom she has decided in advance to give up for adoption after a few weeks. Ought she nurse the baby? After noting the impossibility of achieving a certain answer, Winnicott (1987) devoted the following thoughts to this question:

Therefore it may be better, when arranging an adoption, to be contented with the poorer start of a reliable bottle-feeding technique, which, by the very fact that it does not so intimately introduce the mother herself, makes it easier for the infant to feel that there is consistent management in spite of the fact that several people are engaged in the feeding process. It seems quite likely that the baby who is bottle fed from the beginning, although poorer for the experience, or perhaps *because* of being poorer for the experience, is able to be fed by a series of minders without too much muddle, simply because at least the bottle and the feed remain constant. Something must be reliable for the infant at the beginning [pp. 56–57].

Here the emphasis is placed upon the *difference* between mother and other, rather than on separation per se. That Winnicott assumes the infant's ability to discriminate mother's breast feeding from another's bottle feeding is clear.

ANACLITIC DEPRESSION

"He will be endangered by separation from her" is the watchword of the thirteenth–century rabbi, R. Isaiah Di Trani. What danger may ensue from separation from mother? In their well-known, pioneering work Spitz and Wolf (1946) studied 123 infants placed in institutions. They described a new syndrome in 19 of these infants. The babies cried excessively, refused direct eye contact with caretakers, and decreased in their degree of activity. Some lost weight, some slept poorly. All developed increased susceptibility to infection. There was a general developmental regression. All suffered from prolonged separation from mother. All were between 6 and 12 months of age. Spitz coined a new diagnostic category, "anaclitic depression." Despite subsequent controversy regarding the source of depression-separation from mother versus poor physical and human conditions in the institution, it is generally accepted that prolonged separation from mother in the second half of the first year could endanger the infant. The full syndrome, however, has not been documented in the first few months of life (Bennett, 1980).

PSYCHOANALYTIC CONSIDERATIONS

Anna Freud characterized infant observation as watching "the procedures by which the small body of the infant creates for itself the beginning of a mind" (1953, p. 12). I want to expand on two parts of this elegant and precise remark. First, in the early preverbal period, there are no reliable psychoanalytic data based on clinical reconstruction. The more we approach the "beginning of a mind," the more we rely on the far reaches of more speculative analytic theory. We can at best hope for a "meaningful interpenetration" (Hartmann, 1950, p. 9) between analytic *theory* and observational *data*. Second, I want to stress the active role of the infant in his own development. This activity involves at first "procedures," rather than mental contents. I believe that what characterizes these procedures which create a mind is the increasingly central place of the integrative function in them. The infant's recognition of mother, I propose, plays a very important role in the consolidation of this integrative function.

Even in the rarefied atmosphere of drive theory, the recognition of mother enhances the baby's development. Jacobson (1964) proposed the existence of a primal, undifferentiated drive which in the course of early infancy becomes differentiated into the libidinal and aggressive drives. She suggests hunger as an example of this primordial drive that still needs to be differentiated. According to Rashi's school of thought, the baby would rather tolerate hunger than nurse from another woman. I see this achievement as the *process of differentiation* of the drives *in statu nascendi*. I have in mind a separating out of aggressive from libidinal aspects of the inchoate "drive" when the baby is in a state of frustration, hungry but refusing to relieve his hunger because of his "recognition" of mother. I would further conjecture that these aspects of drive energy preserve their newly differentiated quality, but become fused when the baby is in a state of gratification, relieving simultaneously his hunger and his attachment to his newly "recognized" mother.

This "procedure" of drive differentiation and integration is inseparable from the beginnings of the early ego. In this area the synthetic function plays a crucial role in advancing the development of the ego itself (Freud, 1920, 1923, 1926, 1933). I want to examine Maimonides' interpretation of recognition in this light. According to him, the baby's recognition of mother is demonstrated by the presence of a distinct, observable, visual interaction between baby and mother. In ascribing to this interaction the complex, integrated function of recognition, Maimonides implicitly enters into the modern discourse regarding the interpretation of laboratory demonstrations of the very young infant's specific interaction with mother (Brazelton et al., 1974, 1979). The distinction is between *discrimination,* a purely behavioral event, and *recognition,* a complex, mediated, and regulated event. I propose that it is the degree of activity of the synthetic function of the ego that distinguishes discrimination from recognition. In the creation of this integrated recognition, the baby expresses the synthetic function itself. This utilization enhances the synthetic function and thereby contributes to the preliminary structuralization of the location of this function, the beginning of the ego (Hoffer, 1950, p. 21).

As to the procedure for detecting this integrative recognition, I suggest that the procedure of Samuel's court relates to this synthetic ego function. This procedure assumes that "recognition" is an event intuitively recognizable to the adult. Only a complex, synthetic method of observation such as intuition is to be trusted in attributing complex and synthesized function to the baby's observable behaviors (Kohut, 1977; Pine, 1990).

The integrative function expresses the baby's *agency* in his actions and gives the baby authorship of these actions (Kegan, 1982). Rashi's interpretation of recognition can be further examined from this perspective of agency. As I pointed out earlier, HaMeiri harmonizes Rashi's view with the test of Samuel's court. He defines the case before Samuel's court as one in which a baby younger than 50 days has refused to nurse from his mother. Beyond 50 days, the baby should be considered the author of his refusal. This is the meaning of R. Yohanan's milestone. If a baby less than 50 days refuses to nurse from another woman, HaMeiri explicitly raises the very modern question of the meaning of this refusal (Lewis, 1973). Here, Samuel's case demonstrates the manner in which the meaning of the baby's refusal to nurse is determined by the presence of another behavior felt to demonstrate recognition. Thus, at least at an early age, refusal to nurse from another woman could conceivably be an isolated, nonsynthetic, and thus nonauthored event. However, if recognition is demonstrable through visual interaction, then the refusal to nurse from another woman can be understood to be a synthetic, authored event.

The integrative function plays a central part in the realm of object relations as well. I would argue that current research demonstrates the presence in the infant of an earlier and greater awareness of the outside as distinct from himself than had previously been postulated (Mahler et al., 1975). Aspects of mother are experienced as external from the start. These aspects are not, at first, integrated by the infant into recognition of a mothering figure. At a particular juncture, "the moment of recognition," the baby synthesizes a primitive external part object out of these external traces. From the moment of recognition, the baby enters into a period characterized by *wishes and attempts to treat aspects of the primitive external part object as part of the self*. These attempts are motivated, they are not entirely successful, and they are only very slowly relinquished. The "moment of recognition" would then be characterized as a synthetic event, the *creation of mother out of previously loosely collected memory traces* (see Pine, 1985, 1990). The transition *into* the "symbiotic" phase would be marked by a recognition of the mother as *external*, which now allows the symbiotic *activity* to proceed. The ages under discussion fall precisely within the early to latest spectrum for commencement of symbiosis. The presence of special eye-to-eye interaction would be well suited as evidence of a pulling together of memory traces into an interactive part object partner. The sequence would be complex enough to require integration of various aspects of mother into a recognizable, synthesized, *external* other. Refusal to nurse from another might express a somewhat more *advanced,* and as such *more symbiotic* striving, where, as mother's breast is experienced or wished for as part of oneself, another woman's breast would be rejected on the basis of its being foreign, even at the cost of increasing frustration and decreasing homeostasis. A willingness to tolerate hunger while rejecting a breast offered by another woman is at least evocative of a situation where mother and her breast are experienced or wished for as part of a *milieu interieur* (Mahler et al., 1975, pp. 43ff.).

To the extent that a complex construct such as self may be applied to the earliest months (Kohut, 1971, p. 29; Stern, 1985), I would suggest that the rudiments of the sense of self are related to these synthesizing functions involved in recognition of mother. I would argue that recognition of the mother is not just one among many integrative activities, but rather the leading, organizing, perhaps motivating synthesis—an activating and promoting activity (Winnicott, 1965, p. 5). An analogy from later development is helpful. In Selma Fraiberg's (1969) work on object permanence, she found that in the presence of adequate mothering, the mother gained cognitive permanence prior to inanimate objects. By analogy, I would suggest that mother may be the first leading object of the synthetic activity of recognition. This integrating, synthetic activity itself can be considered the kernel of the rudimentary sense of self. The self thus finds its first roots in its first accomplishment, the recognition of mother.

Pine (1990, pp. 104ff.) extends his prior observations regarding the significance of "background experiences" (1985) into a notion of "moments" in the infant's development. He suggests that given experiences are particularly relevant as "moments" within the infant's various spheres of existence. Competing conceptual models emphasize different sets of "moments" in which phenomena relevant to each model are prominent. Pine then addresses the question of how the different strands become integrated. He introduces the notion of "personal hierarchies" to embody the form that an individual gives to the relations between the various developmental strands.

I have used the term "moment" in a complementary manner.

Throughout this discussion the "moment of recognition" could be conceptualized as a moment of synthesizing activity, a moment when the integration of the various developmental strands is simultaneously created and demonstrated. I would refer to such a moment as a "meta-moment," a moment by definition common to all the strands (see Waelder, 1930); a moment when by force of the unavoidable synthesis, the *form* of that synthesis is forged, the shape of the "personal hierarchy" is fashioned. The moment of recognition, moreover, recommends itself as the first such metamoment (compare Spitz, 1965).

In summarizing this section, I would emphasize what is well known to students of Rabbinic discourse: serious discussion begins with a serious question. We have seen that the seemingly naïve, simple question, "When does an infant know his mother?" opens areas for investigation and discussion in all forms of psychoanalytic consideration and in all aspects of the personality. And like all great questions, it bears no simple, no final answer. Questions such as this can and must be asked over and over again.

CONCLUSIONS

I propose three general lines of conclusion:

1. From the perspective of infant psychiatry, the most modern observations have innovated a method for *demonstrating* the nature of the newborn's recognition of his mother. The ancient and medieval texts suggest that the kind of *observations* appearing in scientific studies have long been available to nonscientific human experience. Such earlier observations, it would seem, were motivated by practical legal issues, and were *applied* in this sphere as long as the observations were felt to be reasonable.

2. From the perspective of psychoanalytic theory, the seductively simple question of the Talmud leads us into a thicket rich in theoretical fruits and thorns. The first few months of life are an area of speculation and controversy in nearly all areas of analytic inquiry. I have attempted to place the question within the context of theories of drive, ego, self, and object development. I have stressed that the baby's active, integrating function is central in each of these areas.

3. From the perspective of the history of science, I would question the "linear" direction of scientific discourse. Periods more remote from our own chronologically are not necessarily further removed from our modern observations and conclusions. The infant who was assumed neither to see nor to interact is clearly not the dark product of *all* earlier human ignorance. In this rift the question opens up: when

and in what manner was such an infant created? Between the ancient and medieval infant and the modern infant, Western society *created* the blank infant. I leave inquiry into the motivations, methods, and uses of this creation to further research (see Richards, 1984; Foucault, 1973, 1982).

BIBLIOGRAPHY

ALBECK, C. (1969). *Introduction to the Talmud.* Tel-Aviv: Dvir.

ANDERS, T. & ZEANAH, C. (1984). Early infant development from a biological point of view. In *Frontiers of Infant Psychiatry,* ed. J. D. Call, E. Galenson, & R. Tyson. New York: Basic Books, vol. 2, pp. 55–69.

ASLIN, R. N. (1987). Visual and auditory development in infancy. In *Handbook of Infant Development,* 2nd ed., ed. J. Osofsky. New York: Wiley, pp. 5–57.

BENNETT, S. (1980). Infancy. In *Child Development in Normality and Psychopathology,* ed. J. Bemporad. New York: Brunner-Mazel.

BOWLBY, J. (1973). *Separation.* New York: Basic Books.

———— (1982). *Attachment,* 2nd ed. New York: Basic Books.

BRAZELTON, T. B. & ALS, H. (1979). Four early stages in the development of the mother-infant interaction. *Psychoanal. Study Child,* 34:349–369.

————, KOSLOWSKI, B., & MAIN, M. (1974). Origins of reciprocity. In *Effects of the Infant on Its Caregiver,* ed. M. Lewis & L. Rosenblum. New York: Wiley.

BURLINGHAM, D. (1975). Special problems of blind infants. *Psychoanal. Study Child,* 30:3–13.

COHEN, L. B., DELOACHE, J. S., & STRAUSS, M. S. (1979). Infant visual perception. In *Handbook of Infant Development,* ed. J. D. Osofsky. New York: Wiley, pp. 395–438.

ESCALONA, S. (1968). *The Roots of Individuality.* Chicago: Aldine.

FANTZ, R. L. (1963). Patterned vision in newborn infants. In Stone et al. (1973), pp. 314–319.

———— (1965). Visual perception from birth as shown by pattern selectivity. In Stone et al. (1973), pp. 622–630.

FLASHMAN, A. J. (1990). When does an infant recognize his mother? In *Alon Uziel Memorial Volume,* ed. D. Boyarin, Jerusalem.

FOUCAULT, M. (1973). *The Order of Things.* New York: Vintage.

———— (1982). *The Archaeology of Knowledge.* New York: Pantheon.

FRAIBERG, S. (1969). Libidinal object constancy and mental representation. *Psychoanal. Study Child,* 24:9–47.

———— (1977). *Insights from the Blind.* New York: Meridian.

FREUD, A. (1953). Some remarks on infant observation. *Psychoanal. Study Child,* 8:9–19.

FREUD, S. (1920). Beyond the pleasure principle. *S.E.,* 18:3–64.

———— (1923). The ego and the id. *S.E.,* 19:3–66.

———— (1926). Inhibitions, symptoms and anxiety. *S.E.,* 20:77–175.

———— (1933). New introductory lectures in psycho-analysis. *S.E.*, 22:3–182.

HARTMANN, H. (1950). Psychoanalysis and developmental psychology. *Psychoanal. Study Child*, 5:7–17.

HOFFER, W. (1950). Development of the body ego. *Psychoanal. Study Child*, 5:18–23.

HOLT, L. E. & HOWLAND, J. (1920). *The Diseases of Infancy and Childhood*. New York: Appleton.

JACOBSON, E. (1964). *The Self and the Object World*. New York: Int. Univ. Press.

KEGAN, R. (1982). *The Evolving Self*. Cambridge, Mass: Harvard Univ. Press.

KOHUT, H. (1971). *The Analysis of the Self*. New York: Int. Univ. Press.

———— (1977). *The Restoration of the Self*. New York: Int. Univ. Press.

LEWIS, M. (1973). The meaning of a response. In *The Competent Infant*, ed. L. Stone, H. Smith, & L. Murphy. New York: Basic Books.

LIEBERMAN, S., ed. (1947). *The Laws of the Yerushalmi of Rabbi Moses ben Maimon*. New York: Jewish Theological Seminary of America.

———— ed. (1967). *The Tosefta*. New York: Jewish Theological Seminary of America.

LOZOFF, B. ET AL. (1977). The mother-newborn relationship. *J. Ped.*, 91:1–12.

MAHLER, M. S., PINE, F., & BERGMAN, A. (1975). *The Psychological Birth of the Human Infant*. New York: Basic Books.

MIKLISZANSKI, J. K. (1976). *Values and Evaluations*. Jerusalem: Neuman.

———— (1982). On quoting one's sources by name. Posthumous MS.

NAGERA, H. & COLONNA, A. B. (1965). Aspects of the contribution of sight to ego and drive development. *Psychoanal. Study Child*, 20:267–287.

PINE, F. (1985). *Developmental Theory and Clinical Process*. New Haven: Yale Univ. Press.

———— (1990). *Drive, Ego, Object & Self*. New York: Basic Books.

RICHARDS, B., ed. (1984). *Capitalism and Infancy*. London: Free Association Books.

ROBSON, K. (1968). The role of eye-to-eye contact in maternal-infant attachment. In *Annual Progress in Child Psychiatry and Child Development*, ed. S. Chess & A. Thomas. New York: Brunner-Mazel.

SOFER, A., ed. (1968). *Beit HaBehirah, Tractate Ketubot*. Jerusalem.

SOLNIT, A. J., COHEN, D. J. & SCHOWALTER, J. E. (1986). *Child Psychiatry*. Philadelphia: Lippincott.

SPITZ, R. A. (1965). *The First Year of Life*. New York: Int. Univ. Press.

———— & WOLF, K. M. (1946). Anaclitic depression. *Psychoanal. Study Child*, 2:313–324.

STERN, D. N. (1974). Mother and infant at play. In *Effects of the Infant on Its Caregiver*, ed. M. Lewis & L. Rosenblum. New York: Wiley.

———— (1977). *The First Relationship*. Cambridge, Mass: Harvard Univ. Press.

———— (1985). *The Interpersonal World of the Infant*. New York: Basic Books.

STONE, L., SMITH, H., & MURPHY, L., eds. (1973). *The Competent Infant*. New York: Basic Books.

WAELDER, R. (1930). The principle of multiple function. *Psychoanal. Q.,* 5:45–62, 1936.

WINNICOTT, D. W. (1965). *The Family and Individual Development.* London: Tavistock.

————— (1987). *The Child, the Family and the Outside World.* Reading: Addisson-Wesley.

YARROW, L. & GOODWIN, M. (1973). The immediate impact of separation. In L. Stone et al. (1973), pp. 1032–1040.

Some Psychoanalytic Implications of Chinese Philosophy and Child-Rearing Practices

NADINE M. TANG, M.S.W.

An examination of Chinese philosophy serves to highlight the differences between Chinese and Western Europeans with regard to beliefs about the nature of man, the ideal man, and general world view. These guide child rearing practices which in turn encourage specific personality traits and values. This paper deals with some implications that these differences have for psychoanalytic theory.

IN RECENT YEARS THERE HAS BEEN A GROWING RECOGNITION OF THE existence of cultural differences, some of which may require modifications in clinical understanding and therapeutic technique. Though much has been written about the applicability of psychoanalytic psychotherapy techniques to Chinese patients (Sue and Morishima, 1982; Ng, 1985), few attempts have been made to reconcile psychoanalytic theory with the development of a Chinese child. If there are, in fact, meaningful differences between Chinese and Westerners, to what can these be attributed? An examination of the guiding philosophical values as they pertain to a vision of an ideal person, the nature of man, and so to child-rearing beliefs and practices may be of some value in understanding these. In this paper, I will review the major philosophies influencing the Chinese. I should note that in speaking of philosophies, I do not refer to the erudite thoughts of the intellectual elite. Chinese philosophies are what guides everyday life and can be viewed as the "habits of the heart" of the Chinese people (de Tocqueville, as

Social worker in private practice in Berkeley, California.

quoted in Bellah et al., 1985, p. vii). This will be followed by descriptions of assumptions about the basic nature of man, the values for an ideal man, and how these influence child-rearing practices.

These values for an ideal man are of particular importance in understanding a culture. One might even postulate that much of cultural differences can be found in the varying contents of ego ideals and in the superego. Freud (1914) noted that "The ego ideal opens up an important avenue for the understanding of group psychology. In addition to its individual side, this ideal has a social side; it is also the common ideal of a family, a class or a nation" (p. 101). The term ego ideal here is used to describe that agency which combines both "narcissism (idealisation of the ego) and identification with the parents, with their substitutes or with their collective ideals. As a distinct agency, the ego-ideal constitutes a model to which the subject attempts to conform" (Laplanche and Pontalis, 1973, p. 144). I will also include some examples of parent-child interactions that are illustrative of Chinese child-rearing practices and will theorize how these might lead to differences in the process of separation and individuation, in views of the self, and in defensive structure. As will become obvious, the Chinese culture will have a differential impact on male and female development. Though a subject of tremendous importance, it will not be addressed here. It is also true that many of these practices vary according to geographical location, social and economic class, and whether the family is urban or rural. This paper addresses the more general issues and not those specific to these regional or socioeconomic areas.

Philosophical Influences

The earliest, most important, and best-known of the Chinese philosophers was Kung Tzu, commonly latinized as Confucius, who lived from 551–478 BC. His was a social philosophy in which man was seen as a relational being with a specific role to which duties and responsibilities were attached. In the feudal society in which he lived, he saw the way to peace and prosperity as residing in harmonious relations within the family. He believed that with clear lines of authority, respect for the status of others, and the subordination of self to the good of the family, peace and riches would accrue. This was extended to the society at large so that each person was due the respect of his rank. Thus, "Let the prince be a prince, the minister a minister, the father a father, and the son a son" (*Analects* XII, 11).

The *Analects* assume that the central unit of society is the family, not the individual. It is the connections and assistance that one can expect from others in the family's name that makes one's surname so important. In such a family state, the authority is autocratic and hierarchical since the father is the natural superior to the son. Confucius stressed five cardinal relationships: between Emperor and subject, father and son, husband and wife, brother and brother, and friend and friend. There is a contractual quality implied in each of these since both had responsibilities and duties to perform for the other.

Obviously the family and its members' relationships to each other were of great importance. To overcome one's own autonomy and desires is considered a highly desirable trait and is the essence of "Keqi." This encompasses various qualities such as generosity, politeness, courtesy, and, above all, consideration only for the other's wishes and needs. For this reason, emotional expressions are discouraged because they are not only an individual's utterance, but also an infringement on others. Being at the mercy of one's feelings is seen to promote poor judgment. A disciple asked how he would characterize one who might fitly be called an educated gentleman. The master replied, "He who can properly be so called will have in him a seriousness of purpose, a habit of controlling himself, and an agreeableness of manner" (Baskin, 1972, p. 20). In the interests of maintaining harmony, "The nobler-minded man will be agreeable even when he disagrees" (p. 19), thus also preserving the dignity of the other out of loyalty. Assertiveness is thus discouraged; rather it is considered an achievement to agree publicly with something with which one privately disagrees.

Both Confucianism and Taoism postulated an inevitable order in the universe. For Confucius, this was expressed in the concept of "Ming" which can be translated as fate or destiny. One should do one's duty regardless of success or failure so as to be free of anxiety. In recognizing that Ming is beyond control, one can simply fulfill one's duties and never fail. This leads to happiness. Thus, "The wise are free from doubts; the virtuous from anxiety; the brave from fear" (Fung, 1948, p. 45). Certainly this might lead one to conclude that such a philosophy encouraged total passivity and conformity. However, there is room for disagreement and revolt should the ruler not conform to his legitimate role and become tyrannical or negligent in his duties.

Second only to Confucianism in importance in Chinese philosophy is Taoism. Lao Tzu, which simply means "old master," who recorded the basic beliefs of Taoism, lived from about 480–390 BC. Very simply, one must live according to the Tao or way by the practice of virtue and inaction, having no ambitions and simply accepting fate. One basic law is that "when a thing reaches one extreme, it reverts from it" (Chinese saying). Therefore, "It is upon calamity that blessing leans, upon blessing that calamity rests" (Fung, 1948, p. 97). This fundamental law is evident in a certain apparent modesty among Chinese about their accomplishments or those of their relatives, or the subdued affect over joyful events. To act otherwise would encourage a reversal of fortune. In the same way, severe hardship can be tolerated since it would inevitably be followed by good fortune. It is also deemed essential to one's behavior that to achieve anything, one must start with its opposite. In describing a sage, Lao Tzu stated, "He does not show himself; therefore he is seen everywhere. He does not define himself; therefore he is distinct. He does not assert himself; therefore he succeeds. He does not boast of his work; therefore he endures. He does not control, and for that very reason no one in the world can contend with him" (Fung, p. 99). This is illustrative of Lao Tzu's solution to how one can preserve life and avoid harm.

Chuang Tzu (c. 369–286 BC) also preached a rationalist approach to emotions. The more a man understands, the more he can reduce his emotions and avoid the associated mental torture. The idea is to use reason to disperse emotion. With complete understanding of the nature of things, the sage has no emotions. Hence for different reasons, for the Taoists because it is painful and contradicts the Tao, for the Confucianists because it causes irrational acts and disharmony within the family, emotional expressions are undesirable traits.

The final major philosophical influence that I shall mention briefly is Buddhism, which was most likely introduced to China in the first half of the first century AD. Indian Buddhism interpreted with Taoist ideas formed the synthesis which became Chinese Buddhism. This was called the "Ch'an" sect or Zen in Japan. Not surprisingly, much of Taoist thought on nonaction is incorporated. One should simply perform one's tasks, nothing more. Thus one will have no craving for or possessiveness of objects. If one is truly enlightened, there is no room for emotions. More importantly, Confucianist ethics and traditions already dominated Chinese society at the time of the introduction of Buddhism. Both Confucianism and Taoism were essentially tolerant of other philosophies so that all coexisted in peace. Both Taoist and Buddhist religions are polytheistic, and there is no demand for absolute fidelity to one supreme being. The major contributions of Buddhist philosophy were in stressing the ideas of compassion and social conscience (Wright, 1959). In Buddhism, the welfare of all beings was important. This also provided a further explanation for the notion of divine retribution which had been but vaguely understood before. Here, divine retribution for the individual became divine retribution on a family basis and worked through a "chain of lives" (L-s. Yang, 1957, p. 299).

THE IDEAL MAN

Given these major influences of Chinese culture, what kind of person would one wish to raise? Certainly, one important common thread is the attitude toward affects. The noble man is one who has control of his feelings so that they are not hurtful to himself and do not infringe upon others. Chuang Tzu would have seen feelings as appropriate only when they mirrored an external event. As with a mirror, the reflection disappears as soon as the event is over. The enlightened person is one who has no attachment to his emotions—true understanding of events obviates them.

From Taoism comes the injunction against pride or self-family aggrandizement since this is inexorably followed by loss or failure. One does not talk about one's accomplishments, either as an individual or as a family. Self-restraint in all things is highly encouraged. Equally important is the manner in which one carries out the responsibilities inherent in one's particular role. As one is an integral part of the family unit, the expression of individual needs and desires is considered selfish. As part of the contract between family members, it is assumed that those in authority, that is, the older men, will know best what is necessary to maintain the harmony and prosperity of the unit. It is these needs that take precedence over one's own. It would be unthinkable to try to assert one's own feelings or opinions, especially if they are not in agreement with the authority's or are unfilial. A case in point was a 30-year-old Chinese man whose mother came to live with him on the death of his father. Though he found the situation very trying, he would not consider having her move elsewhere. If a man truly believes his superiors to be in error, then he can raise this only with great deference. An illustration of this was a young woman who dealt with her parent's objections to a man she liked by increasing her acts of filial piety. She attended to their every need, bought sweets and delicacies for them until they were forced to give up their objections because she had proved herself to be such a good daughter (J. Hsu, 1985).

Socially, a true gentleman behaves with courtesy, kindness, and consideration for others. There are customary regulations which govern social relations so that siblings are expected to show respect and behave properly toward each other. This is true for all relationships—the parents fulfill their responsibilities toward their children and therefore should have respectful and dutiful children. As a teacher, Confucius stressed education and the search for knowledge as means of character development. It was also, in those times, the only way of advancement in a feudal society. Scholars maintained the highest status throughout the millennia. Their status was determined by their performance on exams established during the Han dynasty (c. 200 BC) and really continues in some form even now.

In sum, an ideal person is one who shows self-restraint, is in control of his emotions, places his family's needs above his own, recognizes and fulfills the duties of his role within the family, and pursues knowledge to the best of his ability with the goal of developing his character.

THE NATURE OF MAN

All three philosophies agree that man's nature is basically good. There is an assumption that children want to be taught the correct ways to behave so that they too can contribute to the harmony and betterment of the family. Lao Tzu taught that man's essence is "calm and pure in its original state, and only becomes clouded and restless through contact with the objects that cause desires and emotions. In its purity the essence of man is one with DAO" (*Tao Te Ching*, p. 108). The way to allow this basic goodness to operate is simply to follow one's inner voice since this goodness is innate and requires no action or effort. It is selfish desires and emotions that lead people astray. Rather than being seen as autonomous beings from the start, children are born with a set of responsibilities to their families. Nothing makes this clearer than the *Hsiao Ching* or *Book of Filial Duty* which dates back to 400 BC and *The Twenty-four Examples of Filial Duty,* dating from the Ming period (1368–1644). These provide numerous examples of dutiful sons, including one who is willing to kill his own 3-year-old son to provide more food for his aged mother. The rationale was that one only has one mother, whereas one can always have more children. Children are seen as fitting into a fixed hierarchy, and are taught early on their proper hierarchical relationships to everyone in the family. These are based on age, sex, and kin. Chinese culture discourages egalitarian relationships. Age has its privileges, and it is of interest to note that the Chinese term for "sir" or "mister" is "first born" or *hsien sheng*. It is through strict adherence to the fulfillment of one's duties to family and in respectful dealings with seniors and juniors that one shows strength of character. The highest achievement one can attain, the true mark of maturity, is the ability to conform to one's duties. It is important to note the lack of any notion of the unconscious as part of the makeup of man. One's actions and not one's motives are at issue.

Thus, the Chinese vary in some important ways from Western Europeans and Americans in what they consider to be the qualities of an ideal man, the basic nature of man, and the general world view. These differences are undoubtedly reflected in what the Chinese deem to be developmental tasks. I would suggest that both the form and the timetable of development are affected by these.

IMPLICATIONS FOR CHILD-REARING PRACTICES

Confucian teachings suggest a contractual nature to the relationships of child to family. It is in the proper fulfillment of one's role that love is expressed. There is a great deal of indulgence of children up to the age of 4 or 6 (Ho, 1986; Wolf, 1978), at which point the child is assumed to be more reasonable. This indulgence means that not only are physical needs anticipated and catered to, but children are also given a great deal of freedom as to when they eat and sleep. They are included in family events, meals and banquets, and eat "at any other time when and if they can get hold of some food" (F. Hsu, 1948). The exceptions to this are in the areas of physical aggression, masturbation, and body exploration. In one study comparing Chinese-American and Caucasian mothers, 74 percent of the Chinese mothers made no demands for aggression even in appropriate situations. This compared to a majority of American mothers who not only expected aggression but also to 15 percent who stated that they would punish children who ran home for help (Sollenberger, 1968). Evidently, Chinese mothers relied much more heavily on the values of sharing, noncompetitiveness, and setting good examples for younger siblings. Part of the implied contract is the complete physical care of the child. It is not unusual for the child to sleep with the parents so that his or her physical needs may be met immediately. The idea of privacy is one that refers to the family, and not an individual.

There is evidence that this attitude of indulgence continues until the child is 4 or 5 years of age, and for boys until they are 6, at which time the focus changes to the child being taught filial duties toward parents. Simultaneously, a great deal is also expected from children. It is not unusual for a mother sternly to instruct her 18-month-old toddler to interrupt an activity so as to properly address an older female acquaintance as "auntie" or "grandma." They are to be neat and clean, perform their assigned chores, and, most importantly, learn how to behave toward others. Discipline is usually in the form of scolding, spanking, or shaming. With young children, it is not uncommon to hear mothers tell their "disobedient" child that he will be taken away by a policeman or some equivalent authority figure if he does not behave. Threats to abandon the child are also used effectively. It is considered appropriate for older relatives to correct the child. The central focus is on teaching children impulse control, proper behavior toward siblings, parents, and relatives, and there is less interest in the child's expression of opinions, creativity, and independence. Chinese parents want a child who will "become a strong healthy adult who is obedient, respectful, and capable of supporting them in their old age." This son should also "not embarrass or impoverish them by his excesses, . . . maintain if not increase their standing in the community" (Wolf, p. 224).

In spite of the shift in focus, it is my impression that in the area of physical needs, the attitude of indulgence persists. There is less attention paid to expressions of feelings and of individual needs. This is true of almost all of the Chinese patients I have seen, who report that when they tried to talk about their feelings, they were accused of being too sensitive, or exhorted to be strong and not to let their feelings affect them. Furthermore, in a study of San Francisco Chinese by Lum (1979), a clear belief emerged that mental illness was a result of character weakness, a lack of will power, and dwelling on morbid thoughts. Wolf also notes that both mothers and fathers whom she studied in a village in Taiwan agreed that to let a child know that you loved him was to risk losing control of him, thereby making it impossible to maintain his obedience and respect. A certain amount of social and affective distance seems to be in order at this age, at least between parents and children. There is evidence that this is not the case with grandparents who can be open in their expression of affection.

It is not considered good for an infant to be allowed to cry so that he or she is quickly picked up and comforted. In a study done of Chinese mothers in New Guinea (Wu, 1985), most of the mothers reported picking up their infants when they began to cry. The exceptions were those mothers who were born in New Guinea and who sought Western medical care, which encouraged them to let the babies cry. In agreeing to do so, they explained that it was good for the baby's lungs to let them cry. In their departure from traditional practice, the explanation was still one that fit the cultural demands, that is, it was for the infant's physical well-being.

Perhaps it is the very attention paid to the physical needs of the child that encourages the somatic presentation of problems. The very language of affect is in somatic terms. Depression or sadness is "pressure on the heart," psychosexual difficulty is "weak kidney," and rage is "fire in the liver" (Cheung, 1985). Given the importance of rationalism over emotion in Chinese philosophy, a child is more likely to be coddled if he complains of a stomachache rather than fear of the dark. Indeed, I have observed mothers deny a child's subjective feeling in the interest of peace and harmony. In one case, two Chinese mothers in their mid-20s, one American-born and the other from the Far East, were present when the 18-month-old son of the American-born mother fell and began to cry. Both mothers told the child, "Don't cry" several times, then said, "It doesn't hurt" when the child continued to cry.

The degree to which rationalism is valued over emotions is well demonstrated in Kleinman's work (1986) in China in which he noted the large numbers of patients who were suffering from depressive, dysphoric symptoms, none of whom received a diagnosis of depression. Instead, they were diagnosed as neurasthenic. Apparently this diagnosis was more acceptable because it implied some physical condition. He observed that these patients were taken care of by their spouses, often given reduced work loads, or were transferred to better jobs. Many of the cases cited were dealing with some sense of personal failure, for example, not being able to pass a school entrance exam or being in a low-status or demeaning job. Somatization provides one way of coping with the loss of face.

With the family and not the individual as the basic unit of society, the individual's actions are not his own and are in fact considered to be representative of the family, past, present, and future. One way seriously to criticize someone is to say, "There is a lack of virtue in your past eight generations of ancestors" (J. Hsu, 1985). There is a great deal of tolerance for an individual who acts in the best interests of his family, even if it means doing something illegal and to the detriment of others. Confucius purportedly berated a son who turned his father in for stealing a sheep. The connectedness of the individual to his family is aptly expressed by F. Hsu (1981) when he notes that "since the remotest times, the Chinese have said that their individual successes derived from the shadow of their ancestors and that their individual successes, in turn, shone upon their ancestors" (p. 249). Obviously, if this is the case, an individual gains no credit for his own triumphs and therefore deserves no praise.

The lack of stature reserved for the individual is the result not only of a family orientation but also a philosophical one in which man is seen as just a part of nature and his role is to live in harmony. A comparison between Asian and European art is illustrative of this. From early Greece on, there have been the heroic figures of men and women, portraits in oils and marble. Chinese painting after the tenth century usually shows scenes of nature; if there are any humans at all, they are very small in próportion and certainly not the focus of the work. The film *Ran* by Akiro Kurosawa is an interesting example of the way emotions are expressed in this kind of culture. It is relevant to note that Western film critics found it to be an unemotional and cerebral version of King Lear. This is both a misunderstanding and a misreading of the film. There is a tremendous amount of emotion in the film, but little dialogue about feelings. What is suggested is far more important than what is made explicit. The characters are rarely shown in close-up, but more often are juxtaposed against the grandeur of nature—clouds, mountains, etc.

Since concern with shame or loss of face comes up so often in the descriptions of Chinese, it merits some discussion. It is shame that parents and elders use in helping the child to conform to his role requirements once he attains the age of 5 or 6. The shame then is not that which is associated with toilet training and the control of one's eliminative functions. It is not the shame that often leads to doubt and obsessiveness (Erikson, 1950). In fact, there is some evidence that in the area of toilet training, Chinese mothers are extremely patient and tolerant (F. Hsu, 1948; Wolfenstein, 1950; Wolf, 1978). They may begin to hold an infant over a toilet from a month or so on but with no expectation that the child will actually be trained. Toilet training is certainly much less emphasized as a developmental milestone than it is in Western cultures. It is clearly shame that is functioning when parents make allusions to other people's children who are doing so well. While they enhance their family's honor, the implication is that you bring shame to yours. More extreme examples are given in *Fifth Chinese Daughter* by Jade Snow Wong (1950), who describes taking a piece of fabric from an old peddler when she was 5. Upon discovery, her father makes her sit out on the stairs in front of their house, holding the piece of cloth and awaiting the peddler's return. Should anyone ask what she was doing, she was to tell them she had stolen the cloth. She describes knowing that she had to learn to be upright and well-mannered, yet never was clear on what that entailed. Another example occurs when she runs to her mother after the son of a neighbor has spit on her. Her mother beats her before other women since she must have done something to make him spit on her. Given how tremendously important families are felt to be in an unsafe world, it is before the eyes of the family that one must behave and be punished. Wong's disturbance of her mother's peace was inexcusable since she added to her mother's burden.

In certain aspects of Chinese moral development, shame has a far greater role than guilt. In a society where other people are always affected by one's actions, it is before them that one must answer. Sanc-- tions and prohibitions are an interpersonal matter. So too is the re- quirement for self-cultivation which can only occur in interaction with others (Tu, 1985). Shame and guilt are associated with actions which demean the family, but not necessarily with thoughts and desires. In fact, there is no requirement in Chinese upbringing that there be any consistency between one's actions and one's inner convictions. This is in direct contrast to much of Western thought which condemns the wish as much as the action. In this respect, the Chinese would seem to have less guilt associated with their thoughts. Possibly from the Taoist idea of opposites and the belief that speaking of success is to court disaster, there is an aura of humility and downright denial about the accomplishments of oneself or one's family. In some respects, to do well is simply to fulfill one's duty and therefore is not worthy of com- ment.

A number of Asian American patients report feeling belittled, not only by the lack of recognition, but also by the constant references made to other people's children, and how successful they are. The combination left them feeling that they were not good enough. This is not expressed to children complete with the rationale, but rather comes in the form of criticism or lack of comment. There seems to be an important, almost ritualistic denial when a child is praised by friends of the family. A 19-year-old Chinese American described how de- graded she felt by her father. On social occasions, someone might comment on how pretty she was. Her father would say, "No, she's not pretty but your daughter is really beautiful." She rather plaintively queried, "Why couldn't he just have said thank you for once?" This occurs not only between families but also within the family itself. Max- ine Hong Kingston (1976) describes this process in *The Woman Warrior*. Raised in the United States, as an adolescent she flares up in anger at her mother,

"And it doesn't matter if a person is ugly; she can still do schoolwork."
"I didn't say you were ugly."
"You say that all the time."
"That's what we're supposed to say. That's what Chinese say. We like to say the opposite" [p. 203].

Given the Confucian and historical emphasis on education, it is not surprising that higher education is highly stressed in Chinese families. While this used to be a pursuit reserved for men, more women are experiencing the same pressure to perform and achieve in academics. In a study by Ho and Kang (1984) in Hong Kong, the most frequently named characteristics expected by parents related to competence and achievement, moral character, and controlled temperament. It appears that the expectation of academic pursuits holds true even in the United States if one is to believe the popular press reports of Asian "whiz kids."

There appears to be a specific set of methods and attitudes in Chinese child-rearing practices. These include tremendous indulgence as well as high expectations early on, instillment of the notion of duty to family and reciprocal responsibilities, the denial of affective experiences, and the lack of praise. These methods would seem to lend themselves to the raising of the ideal person according to the philosophical values mentioned.

IMPLICATIONS FOR PSYCHOLOGICAL THEORY

One of the difficulties in understanding this attitude to child rearing and the kind of ideal man so highly praised in Chinese culture is that so much of it conflicts with the theories of what constitutes health and of the ideal man as seen in an American society. Even the very terms that can be used to describe Chinese character traits carry with them negative or pathological connotations. The Chinese hero might be one who has a strong sense of family, is self-contained but mindful of his duties. Many popular Chinese movies involve plots of revenge for the wrong done to an individual's family. A great deal of attention is paid to the entire family history. This contrasts with the highly individualistic heroes of American poetry and television. Henry David Thoreau exalted this when he wrote: "If a man does not keep pace with his companions, perhaps it is because he hears a different drummer. Let him step to the music which he hears, however measured or far away." This kind of behavior would be considered most peculiar in a Confucian-based society. There are inherent difficulties in trying to describe in Western psychological terms the development of a Chinese individual. While Americans value independence, autonomy, assertiveness, and openness of expression of feelings and opinions, the Chinese value interdependence on the family, restraint in emotions and personal views, and conformity to the rules of good behavior.

There are two main areas in the development of the individual that I think are different from those raised and nurtured in Confucian-based cultures. These are in the separation-individuation process as expounded by Mahler et al. (1975) and in the individual's sense of self. I have found Balint's paper, "Friendly Expanses—Horrid Empty Spaces" (1955) particularly useful in providing a framework for viewing these differences. Balint proposes two defensive reactions to the trauma of recognizing that one is separate. One reaction is to see oneself as "alone, relying on his own resources." This involves a world view of "friendly expanses dotted more or less densely with dangerous and unpredictable objects" (p. 227f.). To survive in this world, one must develop the necessary skills to conquer such dangers as might appear. One must also have confidence in the efficacy of these skills. This is the direction in which I would place most Western psychological theory in its emphasis on independence and self-determinism. The other reaction to the recognition of separateness is to cling desperately to objects. In this view, the "world consists of objects, separated by horrid empty spaces" (p. 228). This world relies more for safety on physical proximity and seems to be more characteristic of the Chinese. Indeed, C. K. Yang (1959) describes the traditional Chinese family as providing a "relatively warm atmosphere in which the individual found not merely economic security but also the satisfaction of most of his social needs. Beyond this warm atmosphere lay what the traditional individual considered the cold and harsh world wherein his treatment and fate became unpredictable" (p. 11). Although these are obviously extreme positions, they are useful in describing two different world views and defensive postures, one that relies on the skill of the individual, the other on objects.

For the Chinese, the view of the individual is togetherness. For Westerners, it is an essential aloneness. Mahler et al. (1975) and others see the task of the infant to become separate and to individuate. This is true for the healthy development of any individual. It is my impression, however, that both the form and timetable may be different for the Chinese child. If one presumes a symbiotic phase, then the only way in which to grow is away from the mother. Independent and autonomous functioning become the hallmarks of healthy, normal development. This is communicated particularly during the rapprochement subphase in which Mahler et al. say of the mother that "her emotional willingness to let go of the toddler—to give him, as the mother bird does, a gentle push, an encouragement toward independence—is enormously helpful. It may even be a sine qua non of normal (healthy) individuation" (p. 79). It would appear that the physical separateness is emphasized here. The Confucian mother, on the other hand, does not encourage this move away at this time. The whole idea of physical separation may be considered less important until the child is 5 or 6.

Why then are Chinese not borderline as one might expect given a "failure" in the rapprochement phase? I would suggest that the Chinese mother neither encourages nor discourages such a move away. Since independence and autonomy are not values to which she aspires for herself or her child, any physical behavior symbolic of this, such as attempts to feed himself, is unlikely to receive the acclaim accorded it by Western mothers. A distinction needs to be made between the importance of physical versus emotional separateness in the healthy separation of an infant. There is less concern in the Chinese culture about the child being able to develop the skill to function independently and to be physically alone. What becomes important at the point where language develops, however, is the ability to be emotionally separate. Especially after the infant has "hatched," Western mothers are encouraged to interpret feelings to the infant. They tell the baby that he is silly, angry, or proud when he grasps and throws an object, for example. Chinese mothers, who place little value on the expression of feelings, are not likely to be interpreting feeling states to the child. These are experiences not to be shared or discussed. Even before the child has a sense of a verbal self, he is already left alone with his feelings.

Obviously, a Chinese mother who is concerned about the physical well-being of the child would be unlikely to encourage physical exploration and daring exploits. Furthermore, if a child does hurt himself, it is often seen as irresponsible behavior to have caused the parent concern. This relates to the Confucian notion that it is unfilial to injure oneself because "The body with its hair and skin is received from parents; do not cause it harm" (*Hsiao Ching*, p. 16). The observation that Chinese mothers are more likely to discourage active exploration is supported in the study carried out by Kagan et al. (1978). In this comparison of Caucasian and Chinese mothers and their infants and toddlers, Chinese mothers tended to describe their children as staying close to mother and being afraid of the dark. Caucasian mothers chose talkativeness, laughing, and activity to characterize their children.

This leads me to the second point, the kind of sense of self that a traditionally reared Chinese child is likely to have. In a way, the whole idea of a sense of self is anathema since the primary identity of a child so reared is that of a "family part," as it were, and not an individual. Thus, the sense of self is going to be dependent on how one's family is regarded or on one's own role in society. Winnicott (1960) describes the true self and the development of a false self out of the need to comply with maternal wishes. This refers to very early interactions between mother and child where the mother's "failure" to respond appropriately to the infant's needs results in the hiding of the true self. However, in health, "the False Self is represented by the whole organization of the polite and mannered social attitude, a 'not wearing the heart on the sleeve', as might be said" (p. 143). There is an assumption that the true self is the preferred one. It seems to connote a certain spontaneity, freedom of thought, and expression of feelings, an openness or frankness in discussions, in short, to be oneself. The ideal person in Chinese culture could, in fact, be described as a good false self.

Does this mean that the true self for a traditionally raised Chinese is completely lost? I think not. The mother's tremendous investment in the child's physical well-being and the extended period of indulgence and leniency until the age of 4 or 5 should be sufficient for the formation of a true self. This presumes that the mother is mostly normal. It is on this true self that the healthy false self is constructed. It is probably true that much more value is placed on the formation and maintenance of a good false self in a Confucian culture. The development of the self in later years is very much geared toward appropriate ritual responses and not to the exploration of inner feelings. What a true gentleman strives toward is the development of his character which comes only with age and experience. Winnicott (1960) captures this idea of a healthy false self when he says, "In the healthy individual who has a compliant aspect of the self but who exists and who is a creative and spontaneous being, there is at the same time a capacity for the use of symbols. In other words health here is closely bound up with the capacity of the individual to live in an area that is intermediate between the dream and the reality, that which is called the cultural life" (p. 150).

The Confucian idea of the natural state of man is radically different from that put forth by Freud. Where Freud proposed the existence of basic drives, the Confucian view is that "In its true and original state the heart did not experience pleasure, anger, grief or delight. But once a man begins to pursue his own private ends, harassed by rage and desire, he ceases to be in any proper sense a man" (*Analects*, p. 35). Thus the drives are seen to arise from a deviation from the Tao. The way to overcome one's personal self is through the practice of ritual. It is not surprising then that the false self assumes such great importance in a Chinese society. It is the mark of a cultivated person not to acknowledge his or her feelings, especially to others, no matter how close. The idea of a private self is different for a traditionally raised Chinese. It is likely to encompass a larger "space," if you will, than it does for most Westerners. Statements of opinions and feelings are considered best kept to oneself.

Given the role of shame in Chinese upbringing, it is important to understand its impact on the individual's intrapsychic development. As a working definition from which to clarify the difference between shame and guilt, I have drawn upon the distinctions made by Piers and Singer (1953). Shame is the result of conflict between the ego and the ego ideal, whereas guilt is the result of conflict between the ego and superego. Another important difference is that the anxiety related to shame is the threat of abandonment and not castration. Freud (1914) postulated that the formation of the ego ideal was in response to the infant's recognition of separateness and helplessness. The child attempts to regain that sense of omnipotence by substituting this ideal. It is made up of "the critical influence of his parents (conveyed to him by the medium of the voice), to whom were added, as time went on, those who trained and taught him and the innumerable and indefinable host of all the other people in his environment—his fellow-men—and public opinion" (p. 96). In a culture which has remained relatively unchanged for several millennia, the ego ideal has proved to be remarkably consistent through the generations. Given that the Chinese view of the world is that it is a treacherous place, and that safety lies within the bonds of one's family and relations, it is not surprising that shame is such a powerful force in shaping behavior because one could not possibly survive the experience of being abandoned.

Since it is the degree to which the ego measures up to the ego ideal that determines how one measures one's self-esteem (Chasseguet-Smirgel, 1975), the failure to measure up leads to feelings of shame, loss of face, and the loss of self-esteem. This results in depression which is often dealt with by somatization, as Kleinman (1986) demonstrated. Shame coupled with the paucity of parental praise leads to doubts about one's self-worth.

Given the demands to conform to prescribed role requirements, the fact that even if one's parents are mean and murderous, one must still be filial, and the prohibition of expressions of affect, particularly aggression, it is not surprising that the dominant defense is that of reaction formation. The superego strictly forbids actions in one's family that might be disloyal, unfilial, or angry. There is also much to be gained in delaying gratification and in not acting out since so many benefits await one as we grow older. There is the reverence and care due to the elderly and the permission to become an autocrat when one has established his own family. One way in which anger can be worked out is to become a model son. To do otherwise is to risk abandonment, social sanction, and being cast out into an unpredictable and scary world. Displacement is another possible solution where one can beat one's wife or children, or act aggressively with people to whom one has no obligation or connection. Another way in which anger can be expressed is along socially or institutionally sanctioned avenues such as the father who can beat his child, or the members of Chairman Mao's Red Guards who unleashed a reign of terror and murder that lasted for a decade. It is my belief that a great deal of aggression is sublimated and manifests itself in fierce academic or mercantile competition. It is what lies behind the demand for face-enhancing, extravagant, expensive weddings, funerals, and ancestral halls.

CONCLUSION

Chinese philosophy clearly defines the characteristics of an ideal man and the basic nature of man. It also implies a view of the world which is unfriendly and unpredictable. With the emphasis placed on harmonious relations, rules for proper conduct are quite clear. An examination of these can provide a useful frame of reference to highlight cultural differences. Obviously, what one sees as ideal in a person, what one presumes about the child's nature, and how one experiences the world will determine the methods of child rearing and the way one conceives of developmental tasks. Insofar as these are at odds with Western beliefs, there are likely to be disparate views on proper developmental tasks and ideal character traits for the individual. Unlike the American culture in which dependent feelings are deprecated or viewed as practically sinful, the Chinese individual is provided with a tremendous sense of security as a result of his dependence upon and obedience to his family. There is no reinforcement for an individual's sense of self, yet he is cared for, fed, clothed, and provided for in return for the fulfillment of his obligations. These different views will doubtless affect the way in which children are taught personal values and appropriate ways of behaving. In such a socially oriented culture, I have described how important the use of shame is in such teaching.

BIBLIOGRAPHY

Analects of Confucius, tr. A. Waley. New York: Vintage, 1938.
BALINT, M. (1955). Friendly expanses—horrid empty spaces. *Int. J. Psychoanal.,* 36:225–241.
BASKIN, W., ed. (1972). *Classics in Chinese Philosophy.* Totowa, N.J.: Rowman & Allanheld, 1984.
BELLAH, R., MADSEN, R., SULLIVAN, W., SWIDLER, A., & TIPTON, S. (1985). *Habits of the Heart.* New York: Harper & Row.
CHASSEGUET-SMIRGEL, J. (1975). *The Ego Ideal,* tr. P. Barrows. New York: Norton, 1985.
CHEUNG, F. M. (1985). An overview of psychopathology in Hong Kong with

special reference to somatic presentation. In *Chinese Culture and Mental Health,* ed. W-S. Tseng & D. Wu. New York: Academic Press, pp. 287–304.

ERIKSON, E. H. (1950). *Childhood and Society.* New York: Norton, 1963.

FREUD, S. (1914). On narcissism. *S. E.,* 14:73–102.

FUNG, Y-L. (1948). *A Short History of Chinese Philosophy.* New York: Free Press.

HO, D. Y. (1986). Chinese patterns of socialization. In *The Psychology of the Chinese People,* ed. M. H. Bond. London: Oxford Univ. Press, pp. 1–37.

——— & KANG, T. K. (1984). Intergenerational comparisons of child-rearing attitudes and practices in Hong Kong. *Develpm. Psychol.,* 20:1004–1016.

HSIAO CHING, tr. I. Chen. London: John Murray, 1908.

HSU, F. (1948). *Under the Ancestors' Shadow.* Stanford: Stanford Univ. Press, 1967.

——— (1981). *Americans and Chinese: Passage to Differences.* Honolulu: Univ. Hawaii Press.

HSU, J. (1985). The Chinese family. In *Chinese Culture and Mental Health,* ed. W-S. Tseng & D. Wu. New York: Academic Press, pp. 95–113.

KAGAN, J., KEARSLEY, R., & ZELAZO, P. (1978). *Infancy.* Cambridge: Harvard Univ. Press.

KINGSTON, M. H. (1976). *The Woman Warrior.* New York: Knopf.

KLEINMAN, A. (1986). *Social Origins of Distress and Disease.* New Haven: Yale Univ. Press.

LAPLANCHE, J. & PONTALIS, J.-B. (1967). *The Language of Psychoanalysis,* tr. D. Nicholson-Smith. New York: Norton, 1973.

LUM, R. (1979). Impact of mental illness in Chinese families. Unpublished doctoral dissertation.

MAHLER, M. S., PINE, F., & BERGMAN, A. (1975). *The Psychological Birth of the Human Infant.* New York: Basic Books.

NG, M. L. (1985). Psychoanalysis for the Chinese. *Int. Rev. Psychoanal.,* 12:449–460.

PIERS, G. & SINGER, M. (1953). *Shame and Guilt.* Springfield, Ill.: Charles C. Thomas.

SOLLENBERGER, R. (1968). Chinese-American child-rearing practices and juvenile delinquency. *J. Soc. Psychol.,* 74:13–23.

SUE, S. & MORISHIMA, J. (1982). *The Mental Health of Asian Americans.* Palo Alto, Ca.: Jossey-Bass.

Tao Te Ching, tr. R. Wilhelm. London: Arkana, 1978.

TU, W.-M. (1985). Selfhood and otherness in Confucian thought. In *Culture and Self,* ed. A. J. Marsella, G. DeVos, & F. Hsu. London: Tavistock Publications, pp. 231–252.

WINNICOTT, D. W. (1960). Ego distortion in terms of true and false self. In *The Maturational Processes and the Facilitating Environment.* New York: Int. Univ. Press, 1965, pp. 140–152.

WOLF, M. (1978). Child training and the Chinese family. In *Studies in Chinese Society,* ed. A. Wolf. Stanford: Stanford Univ. Press, 1978, pp. 221–246.

WOLFENSTEIN, M. (1950). Some variants in moral training of children. In *Child-*

hood in Contemporary Cultures, ed. M. Mead & M. Wolfenstein. Chicago: Univ. Chicago Press, 1955, pp. 349–369.

WONG, J. S. (1950). *Fifth Chinese Daughter.* New York: Harper.

WRIGHT, A. F. (1959). *Buddhism in Chinese History.* Stanford: Stanford Univ. Press, 1971.

WU, D. (1985). Child training in Chinese culture. In *Chinese Culture and Mental Health,* ed. W-S. Tseng & D. Wu. New York: Academic Press, pp. 349–369.

YANG, C. K. (1959). *Chinese Communist Society.* Cambridge: M.I.T. Press, (1972).

YANG, L-s. (1957). The concept of "Pao" as a basis for social relations in China. In *Chinese Thought and Institutions,* ed. J. K. Fairbank. Chicago: Univ. Chicago Press, pp. 291–310.

Hilda Doolittle and Creativity

Freud's Gift

ARLENE KRAMER RICHARDS, Ed.D.

The problem of work inhibition in a woman is addressed in terms of a specific case. The paper investigates the patient's view of how such an inhibition was cured in a brief analytic treatment of the American poet Hilda Doolittle conducted by Freud in 1933–34.

FREUD MAY WELL HAVE WONDERED WHAT IT IS THAT WOMEN WANT, BUT IN the case of one woman who went into analysis with him and went on to tell the tale, it was clear that he gave a woman what she wanted. That woman was Hilda Doolittle (1886–1961), an American poet with a purported writing block, a work inhibition. Applegarth (1977) observed work inhibitions among women in our times. If Freud managed to help Doolittle with it, there may be inferences to be drawn for current versions of this problem in women.

Doolittle had written some wonderfully terse imagist poems, a minor play, and letters to her friends before her analysis with Freud. She was 27 when her first poem was published in *Poetry* magazine. Four years later a slim volume of her poetry was published. The quality of her early work excited other poets so much that Pound considered her to be the founder of a whole new poetic aesthetic, a school which became known as Imagism. The only way to convey what that early work was

---

Training and supervising analyst at the New York Freudian Society and at the Institute for Psychoanalytic Training and Research in New York.

Thanks are due to the Beinecke Rare Book and Manuscript Library, Yale University for their hospitality and cooperation in the research for this paper. Mr. Louis H. Silverstein was particularly helpful. The letters quoted are all from their collection. Unusual spellings, grammatical peculiarities, pet names, and code words may make reading them difficult. I chose not to alter them in order to preserve immediacy even at the expense of correctness.

like is with a sample. This is the first poem in *Sea Garden,* her first book of poetry, published in 1916:

SEA ROSE

Rose, harsh rose,
marred and with stint of petals,
meager flower, thin,
sparse of leaf,

more precious than a wet rose
single on a stem—
you are caught in the drift.

Stunted, with a small leaf,
you are flung on the sand,
you are lifted
in the crisp sand
that drives in the wind.

Can the spice-rose
drip such acrid fragrance
hardened in a leaf?

This poem is on the small scale typical of women's poetry, but brings this scale down to the exquisitely tiny, making the moment in time and the few square inches of space occupied by the rose itself fill the entire poem. The rose is unsentimental, absolutely opposite to the lush, sweet, round, full-scented flower of prior poets. It is not given by a lover to his lady, it conveys no sentiment. What is important is the image, the thing itself. And the image is a tough one. Consider the words used to describe the rose: "harsh," "marred," "meager," "thin," "sparse," "stunted," "flung," "acrid," and "hardened." The action of the poem is what happens to the passive rose. She is "caught," "flung," "lifted." Doolittle's inventive use of language is as new as today; the sand is "crisp." Surely this is the contradiction of everything the rose had been in Western culture. Yet the image of this rose is sweeter, the poet asserts, than the overblown fullness we have been accustomed to admiring. And the image convinces.

Although there was no break in Doolittle's productivity, the quality and originality of her work had diminished by the time she sought analysis (Duplessis, 1986). She wrote three unpublished and undistinguished novels in the 1920s. A play of no great interest had been completed when she entered treatment with Freud in 1933 at age 47. Freud had requested copies of her work prior to her analysis, in order to become acquainted with her personality through her work. Once he took her on as a patient, he was clear in his intent to enable her to create and equally clear in his recall of this goal afterwards. He wrote to Hilda Doolittle on October 27, 1933: "I am deeply satisfied to hear that you are writing, creating, that is why we delved into the depths of your unconscious mind I remember." After her analysis she wrote and published epic poetry of a scope rarely attempted in our century and even more rarely in any age attempted by a woman. Her epics are remarkable for their quality and coherence. In 1960 she was the first woman to receive the American Academy of Arts and Sciences medal. She also published several distinguished works of prose in the 25 years of her life after her brief analysis. What, one may wonder, was it that Freud gave Hilda Doolittle?

Fortunately, she left much evidence in her published works about what she thought he gave her. Moreover, inferences may be drawn from the letters she wrote to her friends and those she received from Freud and others. From March 1 to June 12, 1933, she visited Freud six days a week for her treatment. She resumed treatment for five weeks from the end of October through December 2, 1934. By modern standards, this would be far too short a period of treatment to qualify as a complete psychoanalysis, but by any standards, the therapeutic effect would have to be considered spectacular. Whatever it was that Freud gave her, it was clear that she lived on it for the rest of her life. She described it most directly in *Tribute to Freud* (1956), her memoir of that analysis. Her most important novels, *Bid Me to Live* and *The Gift,* bear the imprint of her experience with Freud. In addition, her major poems, "Trilogy," *Helen in Egypt,* and "The Master" all deal with her analytic experience, reworked through several metaphors: as a war, as an island idyll, as a rebirth, and a journey. It provided not only material to be worked over for the next quarter of a century, but also the freedom and inner wholeness to do the work even without immediate access to publication.

Doolittle's life was a sexually ambiguous one. Her position in the world of letters was established early by a man, her then former fiancé Ezra Pound. Her career, her daughter, her analysis, and her life were supported by her wealthy female lover Bryher (born Winifred Ellerman). Doolittle had married once and had become pregnant twice before her liaison with Bryher. She also had several male lovers even during the time she was living with Ellerman. Thus her sexuality was complex, with male and female partners both important to her. Furthermore, there is general agreement (Duplessis, 1986; Friedman, 1981; Robinson, 1982) that Doolittle retained intimate friendships with former lovers for decades after their passions had cooled.

Yet her work prior to analysis was not androgynous, but entirely in the female tradition. She wrote lyric poems, short and full of intense private emotion, like that of other major women poets. But after her analysis she wrote epic poems, in which adventure themes like those explored in the Oddessy and the Iliad were dominant. Thus, not only the fact of her work but the form of it was what had previously been thought of as exclusively masculine. In addition, she was able to use the epic form to express content no poet had ever used before to express it. She developed a way to explore the classical themes of war and its aftermath which combined travel, exploration, and adventure with specifically female concerns of maternity and nurturance.

The puzzle is how she was able to achieve this creativity. Her letters to Bryher, written daily, and even several times some days, attest to her sense of the importance of what she was doing, her awe of Freud, and her determination to make the analysis work for her. Her letter to Bryher of February 28, 1933 relates the awestruck attitude she encountered in the manager of her hotel before the actual beginning of her treatment: "The manager is terribly impressed, we of Vienna did not know that Doctor Freud took any but the most learned professors, does he now take—ah, er, patients? I said I was working with him through a friend also a lieber Gott Herr Professor of London or words to that effect."

The fact of the letters and their frequency support the idea that she was eager to keep in touch with her family through the analysis, and to reassure them that she was not forgetting them. The family at that time was a complicated one, including Bryher, Doolittle's daughter, and Kenneth MacPherson. MacPherson had been Doolittle's lover. Bryher had married him, supposedly to stabilize the relationship. Although he subsequently became homosexual, the three adults lived together as a family and raised Doolittle's child. If every family has trepidations about what the change in the family members in analytic treatment will mean for the others, this particular, highly irregular family would have had even more to worry about than most. Would Doolittle become heterosexual? Would she lose interest in Bryher? Would Freud try to "cure" her of homosexuality? The reassurance she attempted to provide in her letters surely colors her presentation of Freud himself and the process of her work with him. But it is worth sifting through her correspondence for evidence of what the effective therapeutic action of her analysis consisted of in her own opinion as well as for clues to what may have affected her without her awareness.

On March 1, 1933 she writes: "I stuck to the coat, was ushered into the waiting room and before I could adjust before joyless street mirror, a little white ghost appeared at my elbow and I nearly fainted, it said 'Enter fair madame' and I did." Doolittle presents Freud as both little and a ghost. She refers to this ghost as "it," a presence rather than a person. She may be minimizing the power of this ghost by calling it "little," or she may be emphasizing his spiritual power by contrast with his lack of physical strength. She goes on in this first account of her first visit with Freud: "We talked of race and the war, he said I was English from America and that was not difficult. 'What am I' [asked Freud] I said 'Well, a Jew.' He seemed to want me to make the statement—then went on to say that that too was a religious bond as the Jew was the only member of antiquity that still lived in the world." Here Doolittle describes the opening phase of the treatment in which Freud encouraged transferential statements, especially of a negative kind, since to be a Jew in that time and place was to be hated and persecuted. Freud would have had to know of Doolittle's preoccupation with the ancient world from her poetry which used images of the classical Greek world as its universe of discourse. Therefore, by describing himself as a member of an antique people, Freud fostered her identification with him. To describe himself as a member of an antique race was also to say that he was allied to the source of her poetry.

By March 2, she described him in quite different terms: "He got off his desk, an Ivory Vishnu that the Calcutta psychs sent him, and dug out a Pallas, about six inches high that he said was his favorite. O lovely, lovely little old papa." On March 10 she already saw what the outcome of her treatment was to be: "And note all papas remarks, which may be ammunition against the world, for all time." This intense positive transference was the vehicle for her exploration of her past. On March 23 she described their work together as follows:

> F. says mine is the absolutely FIRST layer. I got stuck at the earliest pre-OE stage and 'back to the womb' seems to be my only solution.
> My triangle is mother-brother-self. That is, early phallic-mother, baby brother or smaller brother and self. I have worked in and around that, I have HAD the baby with my mother and been the phallic baby, hence Moses in the bulrushes. I have HAD the baby with the brother hence Cruikshank, Cecil Grey, Kenneth, etc. I have HAD the 'illumination' or back to the womb WITH the brother hence you and me in Corfu (island=mother) with Rodeck always as phallic mother . . .[1] well, well, well I could go on and on and on but once you get the first idea, all the later diverse looking manifestations fit in somehow. Savvy? Its all too queer and at first I felt life had been wasted in all this repetition etc., but

---

1. Doolittle's ellipsis.

somehow F. seems to find it amusing, sometimes and apparently I am of a good 'life' vibration as I went on and on repeating, wanting to give life and save life, never in that sense to destroy life (except self-rat to get back to the womb phase, all most natural).

This view of her life and the repetitions of situations of her earliest days seem to have been an acceptable story to tell her lover and patron, to reassure her that the analytic work was not a danger to the relationship and that she was getting her money's worth.

But all was not so simple. No letters from Doolittle survive to tell of the negative transference, but two letters to her from Kenneth MacPherson, undated, but probably from 1933, imply that it not only existed, but was communicated to Bryher as well. Bryher is referred to by her pet name "Fido." "Chaddie" is Doolittle's first analyst, an Englishwoman who seems to have also treated MacPherson. Kenwin is the name of the country house they shared in England. The first letter says:

I understand from Fido that your hour with Papa is now becoming the hour of the dog-fights. That must be too Kenwin to be pleasing! Certainly it wouldn't induce a smooth flow of inner consciousness.

The second letter enlarges on this theme:

You! You and your old man of the mountains. It must be a peculiar state of affairs. I wonder if you like it as much as you thought you would? More? Less? Certainly its an unique experience, if that's any consolation. That playwright female who committed suicide got tangled up with p.sa. I expect she went to some sort of Chaddie. No, someone worse, for it must be said for Chaddie, awful as she is, she DOES put one on one's mettle, till one feels to hell with the old baggage, who is SHE anyway! . . .[2] Anyhow I expect you to yowl gloriously on Papa's couch. Power to you.

MacPherson encouraged her not to be too much in awe of Freud's power or prestige, to keep her sense of humor and her sense of self intact, thus implying that he believed her to be frightened or discouraged by her anger toward Freud. Her fears that psychoanalysis might precipitate suicide were addressed, but MacPherson tried to reassure rather than alarm her.

By May 3, Doolittle had a completely new understanding of her difficulties which she communicated to Bryher this way:

Papa has a complete new theory but he says he does not dare write it, because he does not want to make enemies of women. Apparently we

2. MacPherson's ellipsis.

have all stirred him up frightfully. His idea is that *all* **women are deeply rooted in penis-envy, not only the bi-sexual or homosexual woman. The advanced or intellectual woman is more frank about it. That is all.** But that the whole cult and development of normal womanhood is based on the same fact; the envy of woman for the penis. Now this strikes me as being a clue to everything. The reason women are FAITHFUL when men are not, the reason a Dorothy R. or a Cole will stick like grim death to some freak like Alan or Gerald, the reason mama or my mother went insane at the oddest things, the reason for this, the reason for that. I was awake all last night and up this morning just after 7 . . .[3] as this seemed to convince me more than anything. What got me was his saying the *homosexual woman is simply frank and truthful,* but that **the whole of domestic womanhood,** *is exactly the same,* but has built up its cult on deception. **Well he did not say deception.** He just flung out the idea. *I screamed at him 'but the supreme compliment to* **women** *would be to trust women with this great secret.'* I said Br.,[4] the princess and myself would appreciate it and keep it going. Or something like that. Any how, do you see what I mean??? We have evidently done some fish tail stirring, and if Papa bursts out like the Phoenix with his greatest contribution NOW, I feel you and I will be in some way responsible. This is a thing, for instance that Chaddie fought against, and tried to make out that the monthly is interesting and that men envy women. Well men do. But the whole thing must be 'built on a rock' anyhow, and I feel S.F. is that rock and that perhaps you and I (as I did say half in joke) ARE **to be instrumental in some way in feeding the light.** Now you see all this in the ucn may also be assisted by our liking the little-dog, as I think we certainly do, . . .[5]

This letter is partly written in red ink, indicated here by the bold lettering. It contains much underlining and some words in all capital letters. It is the only place in all the correspondence with anything like such emphasis. Doolittle was clearly excited as she wrote it, excited by the idea, and perhaps excited by the notion that Freud himself was afraid to say it aloud lest women become too angry with him. More than 50 years later, feminists still find penis envy the most provocative of Freud's ideas. It is considered insulting to women, destructive to the development of young girls, and to be understood, if at all, only as a metaphor. For Doolittle the idea was not a metaphor. Her reference to the "little-dog," a coy pet name for the clitoris, shows that she is thinking of the actual penis, not an equivalent or metaphor. Doolittle's excitement suggests that she considered it the crux of her analysis. It was an idea Freud had been elaborating since he first proposed it in his

3. Doolittle's ellipsis.
4. Bryher.
5. Doolittle's ellipsis.

"Three Essays" (1905). What may have seemed new was the notion that all women, homosexual and heterosexual, shared this dynamic.

The idea of the actual thing, rather than the metaphor, became a theme in the analysis. On May 15, H.D. wrote to Bryher:

> But the cure will be, I fear me, writing that damn vol straight, as history, no frills as in Narthex, Palimp and so on. I keep dreaming of literary men, Shaw, Cunningham, Grahame, now Noel Coward and Lawrence himself, over and over. It is important as book means *penis* evidently and as a 'writer' only am I equal in ucn in the right way with men. Most odd. However we will work it all out, only I am sick of myself at this moment. I do, do, do wish you were here.

Doolittle seems to have had a need to feel equal to these literary men in her circle. She could achieve the equality she longed for only by writing, not by the relationship with Bryher. By May 18, Doolittle was regretting having communicated this idea that she could be cured only by writing of her experiences from the time of her marriage in 1913, through pregnancies and the establishment of her relationship with Ellerman in 1919. Their habitual use of initials, nicknames, and pseudonyms, the searching for metaphors in ancient cultures, all the ways that reality had been falsified and evaded must be given up, at least temporarily. Doolittle knew that this would not be easy for Bryher to accept. She wrote:

> This is a bone to you, I realize, but Papa seems to believe explicitly that it would be best for me to make this vol. of mine about 1913–1920 explicit. I am merely collecting data, from the outside, not working with the dream or "stream of consciousness" at all. Papa says that my dreams show that a bridge in the uc-n has been made somehow and that the whole ps-a is more or less 'over' in the primitive sense, but it will need a lot of guts (my word) my end, to get the thing done in a stern manner and not leap goat-like on the top of things in a dope-y stream of consciousness like Narthex.

This part of her analysis was complete. Doolittle went alone to Switzerland to write of her analysis and what she had learned. The manuscript she produced that summer remained in Switzerland during World War II. In London in 1944 she wrote *Tribute to Freud* (1956). On her return to Switzerland after the war, she wrote a gloss on *Tribute*, using her personal notebooks. It was published as "Advent," the coda to *Tribute*. Many of the details in the letters are reproduced in "Advent": the Vishnu, the Athene, the discussion of Freud's Jewishness, the triangles, the literary friends, and the concern about what is real, what is dream, and what is fantasy. "Advent" skips over the events of

April and May, but in June Athene is mentioned again and connected with earlier goddesses. The final note reads: "Some of us, a group of six or eight, now seated on a mountain slope, ask, are we dead?" (p. 187).

The theme of death was to be prophetic. When Doolittle returned to Freud in the autumn of 1934 for more analysis, it was to deal with questions relating to the fear of death. Her manifest impetus was the death of another of Freud's patients, the young man who had had the hour before hers during her first treatment. He had died in an airplane accident. Doolittle feared Freud's death, both because he was an old man and because of her understanding of the Nazi intentions toward all Jews. This had revived her fears of her father's death when he had a severe head injury with much bleeding when she was a child. On November 14, 1934, she wrote to Bryher: "The whole now of the psa is about death, not so very cheerful, but I suppose the boil in the uc-n has bust." This theme was no doubt very important to Doolittle. She had grown up in a family in which death was all too present. Her father's first wife and their daughter had died; her two older brothers had survived their mother's death. Her own mother's eldest child, a girl, had also died. The family often visited their graves when Doolittle was a little girl. Her earliest experiences thus included the idea that females were especially vulnerable to death. When she was a young woman, she experienced the death of her first child as well as the deaths of her parents, grandparents, and siblings. Shortly following Doolittle's first treatment with Freud, Bryher's father had died. He was so significant a figure to Doolittle that she had written to Bryher on September 22, "THE FATHER is the great mind, the sweep of sea and sky, my own father, yours and our dear old 'papa'. . . . Those three men are the three wise men to me." Of them, only Freud was now left alive.

But death was not the only theme of the second phase of Doolittle's treatment. The issue of sexuality reappears as the decisive issue in her letter to Bryher of November 24, 1934.

It appears that I am that all-but extinct phenomina [sic], the perfect bi-.

I can keep up being a 'woman', even a 'nice woman' for about two hours, then I get a terror of claustrophobia, this is no joke—and have to get to an intellectual retreat, book or pages—to prove I am a man. Then I prove back again. The only thing I want is the cloak of invisibility. That is why it is so hard to be at Audley for more than a few hours. I can act perfectly, the part, for a few hours, then I feel I shall go mad. This makes me, as a 'genius', if I may use the word, but breaks me, as a

person. I know you will make allowances and try to understand. It has
meant everything to have this connection with Freud.

The understanding achieved was that creative work, not social or
sexual gratification, was Doolittle's satisfaction in life. The bisexuality
was a resolution that allowed Doolittle to bow gracefully out of the
lesbian activity without rejecting Bryher, and thus without biting the
hand which had so generously fed her. The resolution was strengthened by a consideration of the role of identification in forming the
perfectly bisexual personality. On November 27, Doolittle wrote to
Bryher:

> Also, usually a child decides for or against one or other parent, or
> identifies himself with one. But to me it was simply the loss of both
> parents and a sort of perfect bi-sexual attitude arises, loss and indepen-
> dence. I have tried to be man or woman, but I have to be both. But it will
> work out papa says and I said now, in writing. Masturbation with me
> only breaks down the perfection, I have to be perfect (in bo bo mica?) I
> may get that in writing and will become more abstract toward the writing
> in life, now that I know WHAT I am. O, I am so grateful and happy, Fido

At this juncture Doolittle had found a way out of her dilemma. By
seeing herself as *perfectly* bisexual, by finding childhood roots for her
choice, and receiving the permission from Freud to consider herself
perfect, she was able to give up trying to make what was for her an
impossible choice; now she was free to pursue writing as her main
source of pleasure and satisfaction. As it turned out, she wrote for
several hours a day, seven days a week for the next two decades and
produced poetry and prose of great quality. Some of these works were
produced during the time she lived with Bryher in very tight quarters
in London during the blitz.

It was especially amazing that World War II with its hardships and
terror did not interfere with her ability to write. She had terrible experiences in World War I; the cold, starvation, loss of her baby, the deaths
of her younger brother and her father, and the break-up of her marriage had all happened in that war and its aftermath. World War II
evoked memories of all of that. She had always required peace, solitude, and freshly sharpened pencils on her desk in order to work. In
the blitz nothing was orderly, solitude was impossible, and quiet did not
exist. Her newfound capacity to write what she thought undisguised
allowed her to write even under these trying conditions.

Among the things she produced in London during the blitz was an
account of what she recalled of her experience with Freud. And the
central interpretation as described in this book consisted of a moment

when Freud handed her a small bronze statue of Pallas Athene, "'She is perfect,' he said, 'only she has lost her spear'" (p. 69). Such an interpretation would hardly seem likely to empower a woman writer. But for this particular woman writer, the remark had resonances other than the universal one of penis as organ of power and woman as castrated person without power. Freud had asked for and read her published works. In 1927 she had written a play called *Hippolytus Temporizes* which contains the line: "let tall Athene have the broken spear" (p. 31). The tall Doolittle may well have seen Athene as one aspect of herself. The spear is, in fact, not part of Athene, it is only her weapon. If she loses it, she has lost her tool, not her capacity. Similarly for Doolittle, if she does not have a penis, she is perfect anyway. She still has her capacity to create. All she needs is the pencil, the paper, and the will.

"The Master," a poem written in homage to Freud, expresses the same idea:

> I was angry with the old man
> with his talk of the man-strength.
> I was angry with his mystery, his mysteries,
>
> I argued until day-break;
>
> O, it was late,
> and God will forgive me my anger,
> but I could not accept it.
>
> I could not accept from wisdom
> what love taught,
> woman is perfect [1983, p. 455].

The alternative to accepting the idea that a woman could be perfect without a penis was, for Doolittle, to hallucinate. The play deals with this possibility. In the play Hippolytus tries to attain love and passion by entering the woods of Artemis, the huntress, and rejecting the rational world of his father Theseus, king of Athens. By choosing the woods over the city, and Artemis in place of Athene, Hippolytus winds up in the bed of his stepmother Phaedra, loses his moral judgment, his sanity, and ultimately his life.

Freud's understanding of the play as well as his recall of the line must have been condensed into the interpretation. His meaning is not that the woman is castrated, but that she is subject to the laws of reason, and that reason is preferable to madness, restraint to lawlessness, and human interaction to the life of the outlaw. Athena is the lawgiver, the goddess who delivered the Greeks from the horrors of talion law, and the passing down of feuds and sins from generation to generation in the House of Atreus. To accept the perfection of Athena is to accept reason, balance, the possible rather than the perfect. It is better to live with the world one is given than to run away into madness.

For Doolittle, madness had been preferable to the acceptance of her woman's body. She had actually courted the hallucinations she experienced years earlier on a trip to the Greek Islands with Bryher. Freud seems to have convinced her that her hallucinations were symptoms, not illuminations, and had helped to reconcile her to her femininity and her bisexuality. After the analysis, Doolittle understood her bisexuality to entail elaboration of the fantasy through her work. She came to understand as well the need for activities that shored up her feminine identity to alternate with the more masculine activity of writing. The fantasy (or theory) of bisexuality replaced her earlier fantasy of damaged femininity. The hallucinations had been a maladaptive compromise. The poetry was a supremely adaptive one (Brenner, 1982). Freud had not only helped her to become more creative, but had also helped her to accept herself as a person. He bade her not only to write, but to live.

Discussion

Would a modern analyst have attempted to analyze this woman? The hallucinations are diagnostic of psychosis, or, as Freud called it, narcissistic neurosis. The unorthodox household arrangements, Doolittle's age at the time of seeking treatment with him, her failure to benefit from previous analytic treatments, all were factors suggesting that analysis could not help this woman. Modern analysts inclined to diagnostic categories different from the ones Freud used would certainly consider her to have a "borderline personality." Based on these diagnostic possibilities, an inference of early narcissistic trauma would be made. Early narcissistic trauma would be expected to make analysis long, difficult, miserably painful, and likely to precipitate a psychotic episode or end in a stalemate. The particular interpretation of penis envy would not be used even if she was treated with an analytic therapy. Such an interpretation would be thought to be likely to be misunderstood because such a patient would be unable to hear it as a metaphor (Grossman and Stewart, 1977).

These ideas make it very difficult to accept what happened in this particular treatment. One way of understanding it is to say that the treatment was not, after all, an analysis. Freud was old by then, worn down by his continual bout with cancer, his endless pain, and his precarious situation as a Jew in the increasingly anti-Semitic political climate of Germany and Austria as well as the rest of Europe. One could say that he was merely assuaging her pain as he faced his own, that he taught her to bear her troubles as he bore his.

Theories about what Freud gave Hilda Doolittle have been put forth by Holland (1969), Riddel (1969), Friedman (1981, 1986), and Jeffrey (1992). While Riddel focuses on the interpretation of her penis envy, Holland considers all psychosexual stages. Jeffrey emphasizes object relations, i.e., Doolittle's idealization of Freud and her identification with him. Friedman (1986) concludes that Doolittle attributed to her treatment with Freud the "explosion of her creativity in the last twenty-five years of her life" (p. 329). In Friedman's view, Hilda Doolittle came to Freud with a readiness to oppose him and gained from him the permission to do that. Friedman specifically discounts any possibility of a therapeutic benefit from interpretation based on Freud's theories of female sexuality. She understands that theory thus: "He argued that in reaction to the traumatic revelation of their 'castration,' girls either became 'normal' feminine women, passive in their relation to men; or masculine women who sublimate their desire for a penis into their competition with men; or neurotic women, blocked in love and work." It is Friedman's conclusion that this theory cannot serve as "a source of empowerment for women's creativity" (p. 329).

Friedman therefore attributes the therapeutic effect of their work together to the complexity of Freud's character. She believes that Freud's maternal aspects and his delight in independence encouraged Doolittle to oppose what Friedman considers his destructive ideas. She argues that Freud succeeded with Doolittle by breaking his own rules, by using intuition (a code word for feminine style intellectual functioning), and by reciprocity rather than hierarchy. Friedman concludes that Freud and Doolittle had a sort of symbolic intercourse which enabled her to continue producing their mutual gifts to posterity for the rest of her life.

Friedman's ideas seem to me to have some serious contradictions. If what enabled Freud to help Doolittle was his feminine way of receiving opposition passively and thinking intuitively, how can he have helped her by fertilizing her? The image of impregnation is surely the quintessential image of male functioning, the one thing anyone must understand to be the good masculine act. To attribute this impregnation to Freud's feminine side results in a muddle of feminine and masculine traits rather than a blend or interaction of them. There must be more to it than this. While I am not satisfied with her conclusions, I believe that Friedman is on exactly the right track to finding the answer to the

puzzle of what happened in the brief treatment that allowed Doolittle
to leave with such a brilliant result. The issue of sexual ambiguity is the
crucial one.

Brenner (1982) would see the therapeutic action of the interpretation to have been a revision of the compromise formation. While
Doolittle had been androgynous in her sexuality and feminine in her
poetry before the analytic work, she became essentially feminine in her
love life and capable of encompassing both feminine and masculine
themes in her poetry after the analysis. This view describes the situation elegantly, but I believe that it can be supplemented by a consideration of the narcissistic features of sexual ambiguity.

One could hypothesize that Freud considered Doolittle to be a possible disciple, taught her some principles of psychic functioning and
some ideas about development, and thereby gave her narcissistic gratification which helped heal the early narcissistic wound. This point of
view would rest on ideas about the etiology of narcissism advanced by
several theorists (Kohut, 1971; Kernberg, 1975). These ideas are, to
my mind, best adumbrated by Bach (1985):

> Similarly narcissistic "phantoms" such as transitional objects, imaginary
> companions, doubles, vampires, ghosts, muses and the creative product
> itself may be regarded as readaptation phenomena to correct distortions
> in the sense of mental and physical well being, particularly when these
> distortions have occurred before the establishment of a firm sense of self
> [p. 15].

The idea that the "phantoms" are in principle interchangeable suggests that the principle of treatment for these narcissistic phenomena is
interchange. For Bach, the therapeutic action of psychoanalysis derives from the capacity of the patient to see multiple perspectives. If
she can only tolerate a world in which everyone is concerned with her,
she is hurt every time other people fail to respond to her needs. If she
fails to see herself as the center of her world, she experiences a catastrophic loss of self-esteem. Either experience can precipitate psychic
disaster. If the patient can see that she is simultaneously the center of
her own world and a peripheral person in someone else's world, she is
not vulnerable to narcissistic wounding. Psychoanalysis allows the person to see both sides of the truth at the same time. If this idea is applied
to Doolittle's analysis, by seeing herself as not having a penis but being
perfect, and by seeing this as a wonderful secret of which she and a few
trusted others are the keepers, Doolittle changes from a patient to an
acolyte. By seeing herself as perfect and bisexual, she changes from a
sexual outlaw or freak into the perfect artist, the genius. As she re-
makes her view of herself, she turns symptom into adaptation.

I believe that the capacity to understand fantasy as unreal while at the same time treating it and experiencing it as real is crucial. The idea of alternating between being a man in fantasy and feeling like a woman, which Doolittle so poignantly describes as her bisexuality, is so important because it provides the prototype of the fantasy experience of being and not being, having and not having, doing and not doing. It also seems to me that this view takes account of the adaptive value of fantasy formations as well as the potentially maladaptive consequences (Arlow, 1969a, 1969b). In this view, psychic change may consist of the development of multiple points of view, multiple fantasies, and relatively easy transition from one fantasy to another, rather than replacing fantasy with reality or accepting the inevitable.

SUMMARY

Hilda Doolittle's successful analytic treatment for work inhibition, a writing block, was conducted by Freud in a way which impressed the patient as especially helpful because he made two important interpretations. The first was a reconstruction of her early wish to be a phallic partner in a relationship with her mother and little brother. This was encoded in her book about her analysis in the statement that Pallas Athene was perfect, only "she has lost her spear." "She is perfect" was the idea which enabled Doolittle to accept her capacity to create while acknowledging her femininity. Second, the idea of bisexuality as "perfect" was implied in the later interpretation of her identification with both parents at once as having resulted from her infantile belief that she was suffering loss of both parents at the same time. The resolution she achieved was to tolerate alternating views of herself as masculine in her work and feminine in other aspects of her life, especially her love life and social relations.

BIBLIOGRAPHY

APPLEGARTH, A. (1977). Some observations on work inhibitions in women. In *Female Psychology*, ed. H. P. Blum. New York: Int. Univ. Press, pp. 251–268.
ARLOW, J. A. (1969a). Unconscious fantasy and disturbances of conscious experience. *Psychoanal. O.*, 38:1–17.
——— (1969b). Fantasy, memory and reality testing. *Psychoanal. O.*, 38:28–51.
BACH, S. (1985). *Narcissistic States and the Therapeutic Process*. New York: Aronson.
BRENNER, C. (1982). *The Mind in Conflict*. New York: Int. Univ. Press.

DOOLITTLE, H. (1916). *Sea Garden*. Boston: Houghton Mifflin.
——— (1927). *Hippolytus Temporizes*. Redding Ridge, Ct.: Black Swan, 1985.
——— (1956). *Tribute to Freud*. New York: McGraw-Hill, 1975.
——— (1960). *Bid Me to Live*. New York: Grove.
——— (1961). *Helen in Egypt*. New York: New Directions.
——— (1969). *The Gift*. New York: New Directions.
——— (1983). *H.D. Collected Poems*. New York: New Directions.
DUPLESSIS, R. (1986). *H. D.: The Career of that Struggle*. Bloomington: Indiana Univ. Press.
FRIEDMAN, S. (1981). *Psyche Reborn*. Bloomington: Indiana Univ. Press.
——— (1986). A most luscious *vers libre* relationship. *Annu. Psychoanal.*, 14:319–343.
FREUD, S. (1905). Three essays on the theory of sexuality. *S.E.*, 7:3–122.
——— (1937). Analysis terminable and interminable. *S.E.*, 23:209–254.
GROSSMAN, W. & STEWART, W. (1977). Penis envy. In *Female Psychology*, ed. H. P. Blum. New York: Int. Univ. Press, pp. 193–212.
HOLLAND, N. (1969). H. D. and the "Blameless Physician." *Contemp. Lit.*, 10:474–506.
JEFFREY, W. (1992). Lazarus stand forth. *Int. J. Psychoanal.* (in press).
KERNBERG, O. F. (1975). *Borderline Conditions and Pathological Narcissism*. New York: Aronson.
KOHUT, H. (1971). *The Analysis of the Self*. New York: Int. Univ. Press.
RIDDEL, J. (1969). H. D. and the poetics of "spiritual realism." *Contemp. Lit.*, 10:447–473.
ROBINSON, J. (1982). *H. D.: The Life and Work of an American Poet*. Boston: Houghton Mifflin.

Index